Visual Basic .NET Solutions Toolkit

Rockford Lhotka, Editor

Written by

Thomas Abraham
Scott Wylie
Matt Miller
Maria Petit
Jeff Ferguson
Rockford Lhotka
Jeff McIntosh
James Hart
Jeff Cowan

® Wrox Press Ltd.

Visual Basic .NET Solutions Toolkit

First published July 2002

wrox

Published by Wrox Press Ltd,
Arden House, 1102 Warwick Road, Acocks Green,
Birmingham, B27 6BH
United Kingdom
Printed in the United States
ISBN 1-86100-739-6

Trademark Acknowledgments

Wrox has endeavored to provide trademark information about all the companies and products mentioned in this book by the appropriate use of capitals. However, Wrox cannot guarantee the accuracy of this information.

Credits

Authors
Thomas Abraham
Scott Wylie
Matt Miller
Maria Pettit
Jeff Ferguson
Rockford Lhotka
Jeff McIntosh
James Hart
Jeff Cowan

Technical Reviewers
Phil Powers-DeGeorge
Mark Horner
Jeff McIntosh
Anthony Naylor
Andy Olsen
David Schultz
Erick Sgarbi
Imar Spaanjaars

Technical Editors
James Hart
Benjamin Hickman
Nick Manning
Andrew Polshaw

Commissioning Editor
James Hart

Managing Editor
Jan Kolasinski

Project Manager
Beckie Stones

Index
Michael Brinkman
Andrew Criddle
Bill Johncocks

Production & Layout
Abbie Forletta
Sarah Hall

Proof Reader
Chris Smith

Cover
Natalie O'Donnell

Special thanks goes to Joseph Ackerman, Peter Gratzinger, Fred Johnson, and Ben Runchey for providing us with ideas for classes to be included in this book.

About the Authors

Thomas Abraham

Thomas Abraham has over eleven years experience in software development, primarily with Microsoft technologies. Currently, he is a Senior Consultant with Magenic Technologies in Minneapolis, MN. Thomas has extensive experience with high-performance, enterprise applications using technologies such as Visual C++, MFC, ATL, COM/COM+ and MSMQ, and has worked on high-profile software development projects for many clients including Nasdaq and Microsoft Great Plains Business Solutions. His broad background also includes many years of experience in networking and systems administration. Thomas holds a bachelors degree in computer science from the University of Minnesota's Institute of Technology, Twin Cities.

Thanks to my parents for helping out here and there while I spent all my free time working on this book. Also, thanks to my co-authors for all of their hard work, particularly Scott and Matt. We made it after all!

Thomas Abraham contributed Chapters 5, 6, 10, 15, 16, 22, 27, 28, and 29.

Scott Wylie

Scott Wylie is a Microsoft Certified Solution Developer and currently working as a senior consultant for Magenic Technologies (http://www.magenic.com) in Oakland, California (although his home will always be Vancouver, British Columbia, Canada). He began his true professional career as a developer with the release of Visual Basic 3.0 and has continued working with VB with each subsequent release. When he is not working he spends almost all his free time living and breathing auto racing (Gilles Villeneuve is a god!). Scott's greatest personal accomplishment to date is graduating from Skip Barber Racing School at Laguna Seca Raceway in California.

I would like to thank a number of people who have helped me in my development career and who unknowingly assisted in writing this book through their experience and friendship: Carol S., Sandy M., Steve S., Bart S., John S., Rosemary S., Dean O., Rob P., Darcy S., Dalia H. and Larry L. Thanks for giving me a chance in the beginning and being some of the best developers who I have ever worked with.

Also I would like to thank Victoria for putting up with me during the many hours spent on this book, but most of all I would like to dedicate this book to my late grandmother who taught me to try everything and to just be myself.... I miss her very much!

Scott Wylie contributed Chapters 2, 7, 8, 9, and contributed towards Chapters 14 and 18.

Matt Miller

Matt Miller is the president and founder of the Yovaly Fan Club. He has a wonderful wife named Yovaly who manages to remain married to him despite the amount of time he spends sitting in front of a computer. Matt has been programming since 1996, working for many large (and not so large) clients including Microsoft Great Plains, Syngenta Seeds, Academic Press, and Stanford University. He would enjoy getting a university degree at some point in his life, but would trade that in for some Green Bay Packers season tickets if he had the chance.

Matt Miller contributed Chapters 20, 21, 23, 24, and 25.

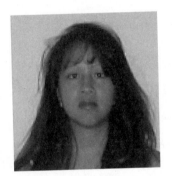

Maria Pettit

Maria Pettit is a Microsoft Certified Solution Developer and currently working as a consultant for Magenic Technologies (http://www.magenic.com) in Oakland, California. She grew up in Walnut Creek, California and now lives less than two miles from her old neighborhood. She graduated from the University of California at Santa Cruz in 1994 and started her professional career as a video game programmer. When she relaxes at home, she loves cooking elaborate meals for her husband, gardening, and building sculptures (with Play Doh) with her toddler son.

I would like to give special thanks to the two people that have shaped my career into what it is today. Thank you to Christian Madsen, for always pushing me to be the best, and thank you to Glenn Walton for always taking the time to teach me everything about Microsoft. Most of all, I would like to thank my husband, Joe Pettit, for trying so desperately to stay awake while I was up working late, only to end up snoring on the couch.

Maria Petit contributed Chapters 3, 19, and 30.

Jeff Ferguson

Jeff Ferguson is a senior consultant with Magenic Technologies, a software consulting company dedicated to solving business problems exclusively using Microsoft tools and technologies. He has been a professional software developer since 1989 and has developed software using C, C++, and C# for Unix, DOS, and Windows systems. Send e-mail to Jeff at JeffF@magenic.com (remember to include all three 'F's in the name portion of the address).

For Jody.

Jeff Ferguson contributed Chapters 11, 17, and contributed towards Chapter 18.

Rockford Lhotka

Rockford Lhotka is the Principal Technology Evangelist for Magenic Technologies, a company focused on delivering business value through applied technology and one of the nation's premiere Microsoft Gold Certified Partners. Rockford is an author for several Wrox Press titles, including Fast Track Visual Basic .NET, Professional Visual Basic Interoperability - COM and VB6 to .NET and Visual Basic 6 Distributed Objects and is a columnist for MSDN Online and contributing author for Visual Studio Magazine. He regularly presents at major conferences around the world - including Microsoft PDC, Tech Ed, VS Live!, and VS Connections. He has over 15 years experience in software development and has worked on many projects in various roles, including software architecture, design and development, network administration and project management.

This book is dedicated to the great team of people at both Magenic and Wrox that made this project come together – thank you all!

Rockford Lhotka contributed Chapters 4, 13, and contributed towards Chapter 14.

James Hart

James is an author, programmer, and technical communicator at Wrox in Birmingham, UK. As a member of the editorial team he has been helping others to teach programming concepts for the last three years. Originally a Java developer, he is now applying his hard-earned knowledge to the .NET Framework, transposing his experience with that language's object-oriented concepts to the new platform.

Thanks to everybody on the Rapid team at Wrox, and the writing team at Magenic, for all their hard work on this book. And as always, thanks to Chris for putting up with the late nights slaving over a Visual Studio project.

James Hart contributed Chapter 26.

Jeff Cowen

Jeff Cowan is a Sr. Consultant with Magenic Technologies. Jeff has spent over seven years creating software solutions with Microsoft technologies. He has done this in several roles including architect, project manager, and software engineer. Jeff, more than anything on this planet, enjoys spending time with his two children.

Jeff Cowen contributed Chapter 12.

Jeff McIntosh

Jeff McIntosh is a Senior Consultant with Magenic
Technologies. He has over 14 years of software
development experience, specializing in enterprise
business applications built with Visual Basic, COM,
and SQL Server. He has worked as a developer,
tester, designer, architect, and project manager. Jeff is
continually on the lookout for ideas and techniques
to improve the software development process. He is
deeply interested in design and architecture.

Jeff McIntosh contributed Chapter 1.

VB.NET Solutions Toolkit

Table of Contents

Table of Contents

Application Components

This section contains classes that can be used to assist in your application development, including features that can be used across most applications.

1: Splash Screen   13

This class provides a splash screen to show during your application's start-up. In this chapter, you will learn about event handling, threading, and the `System.Threading.Timer` object.

2: Product Licensing   25

The three classes shown in the chapter create a license for an application and verify that it is correct. You will learn about using public/private key cryptography via the `System.Security.Cryptography` namespace, and how to strongly name your assemblies.

3: Application Settings Writer   39

This class allows you to easily create and update a `.config` file for your application. You learn about using the `XmlNode` and `XmlDocument` classes of the `System.Xml` namespace to update a text file, as well as how to use reflection to discover the name of your application and so the name of the relevant configuration file.

11: ListView Sorter

This is a class that allows you to specify sorting rules on the items and columns of a ListView control. It makes use of the IComparer interface to specify the sorting rules, and reflection to retrieve the data types so they are sorted appropriately.

12: Text Image Generator

This class would be best used with ASP.NET. It uses the System.Drawing namespace to create an image that contains the text specified, formatted in a certain way with embellishments. This makes use of the System.Drawing.Graphics class to manipulate an image, and the System.Drawing.Bitmap class to actually create the image and output it to a stream.

Network and File System

This section deals with IO and other issues relating to network and file system management.

13: Stream Helper

This is a collection of shared helper methods for dealing with streams that can be used directly when the relevant assembly is referenced and namespace imported. It makes use of the System.IO namespace, and of System.Drawing for output of a stream to an image.

14: Smart Socket

This is a pair of classes to allow easy management of the transmission of object data across raw streams, like TcpClient. It makes use of the System.Threading, System.IO, and System.Net.Sockets namespaces and teaches how to make use of the ThreadPool class, serialization, and various events to control the sending and receiving of data.

15: Memory Mapped File Stream

This class provides a way of directing a stream to a location in memory, so that you can manipulate its contents entirely within memory space before directing it towards a file, network, or other stream. For this to work you need to access the Win32 API layer using P/Invoke.

16: MP3 ID3v1.1 Tag Editor

This class allows you to read and edit the ID3 tags on MP3 files. It uses a number of file system classes to search and manipulate these files, and shows how to output Unicode as used by the .NET Framework into ASCII, as used by ID3 tags.

This class provides authentication and authorization using the Windows Logon scheme. It interoperates with the operating system layer using P/Invoke.

This class provides authentication and authorization using an XML file, and will encrypt any password passed to it to match against an encrypted password in the XML file. This class uses the System.IO, System.Xml, System.Text, and System.Security.Cryptography namespaces to achieve this.

Patterns and Algorithms

This section contains a number of common patterns and algorithms that are not implemented in the .NET Framework class library.

This makes use of the Singleton design pattern and provides a template to use with your own classes that you wish to be instantiated only once. The template used provides thread safety and is still guaranteed to contain only one instance if the object were deserialized and serialized.

Simple doubly linked lists are not provided in the .NET Framework class library, although they are the bases for many other different lists and collections. This class implements the IList interface to provide such a simple list.

A binary search tree is a pattern that allows for easy sorting of data. This class makes use of any objects that implements IComparable, to provide a tree that is sorted according to certain rules and can be added to, or taken away from, easily. It implements the ICollection interface.

A CRC-32 is a 32-bit checksum that is calculated using a CRC algorithm, which is ubiquitous in computing and is used, for instance, in file systems. It makes use of System.IO to allow validation of a file and makes use of bitwise calculations to implement the algorithm.

Huffman encoding is a popular algorithm used for compressing files used, for example, by WinZip. This provides the code for compressing and decompressing data from within your .NET code and uses the System.Collections and System.IO namespaces to achieve this.

Foreword by Wrox Press

Some ideas have a tendency to develop a mind of their own so that the final result is sometimes quite different from what was originally intended. This book is the result of just such an idea.

The brainchild of a conversation over a cup of coffee, the idea was to develop a book that would give Visual Basic developers a set of "tools" in the form of classes. Paramount in our minds was the practicality of the classes that would be dissected: rather than obscure coding antics illustrating the virtuosity of a few authors, the Toolkit, as it was later named, should comprise recipes that we were sure would be used on a regular basis. Our driving principal was to enable the programmer to save time, and typically money. We also did not want to do all the work, but rather provide a set of basic templates that could easily be extended to work across a large number of circumstances.

As the project evolved, however, and thanks solely to the quality and professionalism of both the writing and editorial teams, we realized that the scope of what we were trying to achieve had considerably changed. As the code coming in was a lot more complete than we expected, the template idea was partially abandoned, although, in most instances, extensions to the original class were provided. A template is usually perceived as a "fill in the gaps" tool; these classes have very few gaps. Rather, they form a sound basis for robust object-oriented development (and in some cases, just great functionality). I believe that the project has not lost any of its usefulness in the process.

For most of us, this project has been a great learning experience. Several programmers I spoke to have mentioned that developing with .NET implies a short-term loss in productivity that is later reversed as confidence grows. We have certainly experienced this. As we endeavored to find the best possible way to write a particular class, code was revisited over and over as new areas of the Framework were brought into the equation. I think in the process, our respect for what Redmond has achieved has grown. As a result, this book is not only a compilation of useful code, but also a journey into .NET.

Jan Kolasinski
Managing Editor

Foreword by Magenic

The idea of a tool kit or toolbox of useful code has been evolving for some time. I hope this book represents the next step in this process. I've had conversations with people at Microsoft, other authors, and other conference speakers and everyone agrees that it would be a great idea. At the same time, everyone struggles with the mechanics of building a professional quality toolkit.

There have been attempts – various web repositories and even a rich client code database back in the VB 3.0 days. While many of these have some excellent code and are very useful, they aren't really 'professional' quality. There's little to no prose discussing the whys and wherefores of the code, and typically the code is not reviewed through any formal process.

So when Wrox approached its authors with the idea of a 'template' or 'toolkit' book for Visual Basic .NET, I was pretty excited. Here was a chance to at least start the process of creating a professional quality toolkit for developers. With this approach, the code is surrounded by prose discussing why the code is important, the concepts behind it, how it works, and how you can use or adapt it to meet your needs. The material in the book has been reviewed, revised, and edited through a formal process.

A toolkit should draw from many people to get different perspectives and expertise. The resulting toolkit will then include diverse code and ideas coming from a group of experts.

When I mentioned the possibility of writing this book, the management and consultants at Magenic were very interested. Greg Frankenfield, the CEO of Magenic took a personal interest in the idea and has been very supportive of the effort. A number of consultants stepped forward as well, eager to share their experience and ideas about .NET.

I am often asked why I work at Magenic – and this is the answer. Magenic employs consultants who not only have a high degree of technical expertise, but also have the drive to share it through their consulting as well as through mentoring, writing, speaking, and other activities. I love working with a group of people that constantly challenge each other and me with new and different ideas, concepts and approaches. This book represents the hard work, code, and ideas from a number of Magenic consultants.

This book is a great collection of very useful code that either solves problems you'll face, or illustrates techniques and concepts that you can modify and apply to suit your needs. Is this book a complete toolkit that handles everything you'll ever need to do? Absolutely not. To collect all the great ideas, code snippets and techniques out there would take many volumes. Hopefully this book represents a workable concept around which our industry can rally to create ever more professional quality toolkit materials. I, and many other people, would dearly love to find a workable mechanism by which this type of material can be made available industry-wide, and perhaps this is it.

I hope you enjoy reading and using the material in this book, and I hope that it saves you sweat and toil in your development efforts.

Code well, have fun!

Rockford Lhotka

VB.NET

Solutions

Toolkit

Introduction

Introduction

The concepts that underlie object-oriented programming are ultimately aimed at increasing a programmer's productivity through the idea of code reuse. In fact over the past few years, a number of companies have specialized in the development and commercialization of components: little pieces of specific functionality, streamlined and ready to fit any and all programming scenarios. Ultimately these are classes, historically mainly coded in Visual C++ in order to make them theoretically more efficient.

The release of .NET means that a lot of these components will need to be re-engineered and re-coded; and so will a number of classes or class libraries that development teams have painstakingly developed and compiled over the years. Chances are that even the simplest of snippets developed in older versions of Visual Basic will not only need updating but could be completely re-architected so as to take full advantage of the new features of the Framework. This process will not only require an understanding of the changes in the language's constructs but also a thorough investigation of the capabilities provided by .NET's base classes.

Who Is This Book For?

This book assumes that you are already familiar with Visual Basic .NET, the language's syntax, and some of the concepts introduced by the .NET Framework, such as reflection, remoting, threading, etc. As this book is a compilation of solutions, it will rarely fall into theoretical discussions of the key concepts often used to develop some of the classes within.

As the book provides a number of ready-made solutions for you to use with minor adjustment in your programs, the value to you should be first and foremost in the time it will save you. However, as each decision taken during the development of each recipe has been thoroughly explained, this book is also a learning companion, using practical applications to illustrate sometimes-complex concepts.

What Will You Learn?

The book is a collection of 30 classes, logically grouped according to their relevant functionality into five parts:

❑ **Part 1 – Application Components**

The classes in this part of the book are a collection of utilities for deployment, application start-up, or shut down. Typically, they can be used as they are and plugged directly into your application. They include a Splash Screen and a Product License Class, a class to deploy applications remotely to a large number of machines, a class to manage process initialization remotely or locally, a class to persist application settings, and a class to parse application arguments.

❑ **Part 2 – GUI and Graphics**

In the second part of the book, we examine classes that provide user interaction functionality, or generate graphical interfaces. They include a number of validation Textboxes for both Windows and Web forms applications, highly extendable so that you can add your own masking rules, a Windows Required Field Validator class, a class to sort items within a ListView control, and a web image generator.

❑ **Part 3 – Network and File System**

As applications are often deployed across networks, this part concentrates on classes that are useful in such an environment. They include a Smart Socket class acting as both a client and a server, a Stream Helper class to manage streams of data across a network, a class to map files in memory, an MP3 ID3 Tag Reader, a class to browse folder contents, a Namespace Locator, and an active directory searching class.

❑ **Part 4 – Security**

Part four is a compilation of classes that will allow you to add security features to your applications. They include an encryption class, a class to sign and verify your XML documents, a class to manage your file security settings, and three versions of a logon class.

❑ **Part 5 – Patterns and Algorithms**

The classes in part five can form the basis of many applications through their features and functionalities. These classes illustrate a Singleton pattern, inked list and binary tree structures, a class to calculate CRC32 sums, and a file compression class.

Additionally each class is presented along the following structure:

❑ **Introduction**

Presents the class and the reasons for its inclusion in the book.

❑ **Scenario**

The scenario section explains when you would use this class. It describes the general purpose of the class, and provides example cases where the class is deemed invaluable.

❑ **Technology**

The technology section explains any fundamental technical concepts crucial to the operation of the class, and exposes any particular technical obstacles that need to be overcome.

❑ **Design**

This section describes why the particular approach taken by this class has been followed, explains how the particular implementation fulfils the scenarios described in the earlier version, and how it overcomes the technical obstacles explained before.

❑ **Implementation**

This section contains the actual code implementation of the class.

❑ **Demonstration**

This section shows how the class, once implemented, can be used to solve a particular problem.

❑ **Limitations**

The limitations section explains in what ways the class as implemented is limited.

❑ **Extensions**

The extensions section contains suggestions for how the class might be altered to offer slightly different functionality.

All the code included in this book is available for download from the Wrox website at http://www.wrox.com/.

What Do You Need?

To make use of this book, you need to be able to compile and execute code written in Visual Basic .NET. This means you will require either:

❑ The .NET Framework SDK obtainable from Microsoft's MSDN site (http://msdn.microsoft.com), in the Software Development Kits category. The download page at time of publication could be reached via the following URL:

http://msdn.microsoft.com/downloads/sample.asp? url=/msdn-files/027/000/976/
msdncompositedoc.xml

❏ A version of Visual Studio .NET which incorporates Visual Basic .NET. The 2002 edition of the Visual Basic .NET IDE is included with the following Microsoft products:

- Microsoft Visual Basic .NET Standard

- Microsoft Visual Studio .NET Enterprise Architect

- Microsoft Visual Studio .NET Enterprise Developer

- Microsoft Visual Studio .NET Professional

The product homepage can be found at http://msdn.microsoft.com/vstudio/.

There are several .NET implementations for other platforms underway, but at the time of publication, none supported VB.NET compilation.

VB.NET

Solutions

Toolkit

Application
Components

Splash Screen

It is very common for a Windows application to display a splash screen when the application first begins. This gives the writers of the application an opportunity to display important information about a program, like the name and version, a logo, or some other form of brand/product identification. It reassures the user that the application has started, and also serves to keep the user from getting impatient as the program starts up and performs its initialization tasks.

Splash screens are nothing new. Even with VB4 you could create a form, display it, and make an API call to ensure that it appeared on top of all other windows. The screen would sit there as the program went about its startup logic. The program would complete its initialization and unload the splash screen. A splash screen of this type, though, is very static.

.NET, with its free threading model, makes it much easier to build a more dynamic splash screen. A threaded splash screen can run its own activities without blocking the execution of the main program. Such a splash screen can interact with the user. It can monitor the startup process and inform the user of what activities are taking place. If your application has a lengthy startup process, a dynamic splash screen can allow the user to dismiss it, so that the user can easily work in other applications which otherwise would have been obscured by the splash screen.

Here, we will present a splash screen that utilizes the power of free threading, so that it can perform activities that are not blocked by the initialization activities of the rest of the program.

Scenario

If an application takes a long time to complete its initialization and startup routines, we'll often require a splash screen that will display during the startup process. We might want the screen to be able to display to the user the progress that is being made in loading the application. It is also important that the user should be able to dismiss the screen if they want the application to load in the background while they get on with some other task.

Technology

The Windows operating system is an event-driven system. Events are manifested as messages sent by the operating system whenever the user performs an action. Each of these user-action messages is posted into a message queue for the application for which the operating system believes it was intended (depending on where the user clicked the mouse, or which window has the keyboard focus). An application typically gets messages one at a time from its message queue, and then sends each message to the appropriate window in the application. This is usually where our code comes in (although obviously the standard window controls do a lot of the event handling work for us). Our code ultimately either handles the message or ignores it. The application generally continually loops, retrieving events from its message queue, until a quit message is received. The cycle of retrieving and dispatching events in an application is called a message loop pump.

Why do we care about message queues and message loops? We need to understand this because we're going beyond single threading and diving into multithreading. In a single-threaded application, the message loop pump runs on a single main application thread. This thread sequentially retrieves a user event message, works out which window it is intended for, runs any instructions in the appropriate event handlers, then loops round and retrieves another message, and so on. Our entire application has one message queue, and events coming into our application are processed in sequence, one at a time. Many applications only need one thread. However, if an application does have more than one thread, each thread will have its own message queue. Each thread can create windows and have a separate message loop. Messages for windows running on different threads will be placed into different message queues. The computer's processor divides its processing time between all the running threads on the system, so when it is executing one of the threads, events for that thread's window will be retrieved and passed on to event handling code; when it is executing the other thread, events for the other thread's window will be retrieved and handled.

.NET Windows Forms windows and controls must always process messages on the same thread that created them. .NET controls implement the `ISynchronizeInvoke` interface to make it easier to deal with the threading and thread message queue issues. We can basically use its `Invoke()` method to ask a control to call a method of our choosing, on its thread, when it gets a chance.

If this seems complicated, don't worry too much. .NET and the operating system take care of most of this for us. What little remains will be simply presented in the code below, and you'll be able to use this code just by calling a method on an object.

Design

The most important component we need to develop is a basic splash screen form. This form will have the physical attributes of a splash screen (no control box, no title bar, centered in screen, and so on). It will have code to provide three ways to dismiss the splash screen:

❑ When the user clicks it

❑ After a set amount of time passes

❑ When told to disappear by code outside of the splash screen

To add a splash screen to an application, you will create a form that inherits from this base form, and add your application-specific appearance and functionality to the form. Your splash screen will inherit all of these capabilities.

To make the splash screen able to do all these things and not block code that wants to run in the program's startup routines, the splash screen will need to run on a worker thread, separate from the main thread that the runs the code in the rest of the application. A form can create a thread, but the form cannot run on a thread it creates. In order to get a form to run on a thread, the thread needs to be created first, and then the form can be instantiated on the thread. We will create a SplashScreenController class to house the code to do this.

SplashScreenController is the logical center of this chapter. It will wrap the SplashScreen form and encapsulate all the thread creation and manipulation logic. For our purposes, it will expose only a Show() method and a Hide() method. These will be simple method calls, so they will be easy for the developer to work with. Show() will create the worker thread and make the splash screen run on that thread. Hide() will make a call to the SplashScreen that will run on the worker thread to hide the form and end the thread. If the developer had more methods to add to the splash screen, they should also be wrapped and exposed as methods in the SplashScreenController class.

There is no need to display multiple splash screens at the same time. We'll prevent that by making the SplashScreenController non-instantiable, by providing a private constructor, and making the Show() and Hide() methods Shared methods. We can then include code to prevent it from creating another worker thread if it has already created a worker thread.

Implementation

Since this is a visual class, we'll explain how to develop it in Visual Studio .NET.

In a new solution, create a class library project, called SplashScreen, and as usual, remove the default namespace. Our project will have two components: a Windows Form class to provide the base splashscreen, and a non-visual class, SplashScreenController, to provide the threading support. We'll develop the splash screen form first.

Add a Windows Form to your project called SplashScreen. Add a timer from the Windows Forms toolbox to the form, and change its name to Timer. Set the following properties:

❏   SplashScreen.ControlBox = False

❏   SplashScreen.FormBorderStyle = None

❏   SplashScreen.StartPostion = CenterScreen

❏   SplashScreen.TopMost = True

❏   Timer.Modifiers = Protected

These settings give the form a splash screen appearance by removing the borders, title bar, close box, and minimize/maximize buttons. Setting StartPosition to CenterScreen ensures that the form is loaded and displayed in the center of the screen. Making TopMost True ensures that the splash form is not overlaid by other forms or applications. Setting the Timer's Modifiers to Protected allows forms inherited from this form to manipulate the Timer control.

Now it is time to add some code to the form. Switch to the code window for the form and add the following.

```
Namespace Wrox.Toolkit.UI

    Public Class SplashScreen
        Inherits System.Windows.Forms.Form

        Private cycleCount As Integer = 1
        Private maxDisplayTime as Integer = 0
```

This is where the form-designer's code goes.

HideSplashScreen() is designed to be invoked by the SplashScreenController class that we'll create in a little bit. Its purpose is to dismiss the splash screen. It accomplishes this by closing the form.

```
    Public Sub HideSplashScreen()
        Close()
    End Sub
```

The following event handler will provide the first way to dismiss the splash screen – it closes the screen when the form is clicked.

```
Private Sub SplashScreen_Click(ByVal sender As System.Object, _
                    ByVal e As System.EventArgs) _
                    Handles MyBase.Click
    HideSplashScreen()
End Sub
```

The next property and event handler implement a timeout on the form, providing a mechanism for the form to keep track of how long it has been open, and when a set time has elapsed, dismissing it.

```
Public WriteOnly Property MaximumDisplayTime() As Integer
    Set(ByVal Value As Integer)
        maxDisplayTime = Value
        Timer.Interval = 1000
        If Value > 0 Then Timer.Start()
    End Set
End Property

Private Sub Timer_Tick(ByVal sender As System.Object, _
        ByVal e As System.EventArgs) Handles Timer.Tick
    cycleCount += 1
    If cycleCount > maxDisplayTime Then
        HideSplashScreen()
    End If
End Sub
End Class

End Namespace
```

The timer is configured to raise the `Tick` event once per second. The code in `Timer_Tick()` keeps track of how many times it has executed (since the timer is set to tick once per second, this is the same as how many seconds the splash screen has been displayed). When the time that the splash screen has been displayed exceeds the maximum allowed time, it calls `HideSplashScreen()`.

That's it for our basic splash screen class. On its own, it doesn't do much, but we can create subclasses, which inherit all the behavior, but can add a specific appearance.

Now, add a new class file to the project called `SplashScreenController.vb` and replace the code with the following:

```
Imports System
Imports System.Threading

Namespace Wrox.Toolkit.UI

    Public Delegate Sub HideMethod()
```

This delegate type is used when we invoke the `Hide()` method on our splash screen from a different thread.

The `SplashScreenController` class is the heart of this example. Private shared variables are declared for the worker thread and for the splash screen form. These variables are `Private` so that only the code in this class can use them. They are `Shared` so that they can be referenced without the class being instantiated. Remember that in the design section we said that this class would effectively be non-instantiable. These `Private Shared` variables and the `Public Shared` methods that follow allow the class to be non-instantiable.

```
Public Class SplashScreenController
    Private Shared splashThread As Thread
    Private Shared mySplashScreen As SplashScreen
    Private Shared maxDisplayTime As Integer
```

Our next step is to add the code that will display the splash screen.

```
Private Shared Sub ShowForm()
    mySplashScreen.MaximumDisplayTime = maxDisplayTime
    mySplashScreen.ShowDialog()
End Sub
```

This is a pretty simple method. It simply sets the splash screen timeout, if any, and then it displays the form. The form is displayed as a dialog so that the form stays on the screen until it is closed. If you use `mySplashScreen.Show()`, the screen will flash briefly and then disappear. When displayed as a dialog the form gets focus and blocks execution of code in the `ShowForm` method until the form is no longer displayed.

The importance of using `ShowDialog()` to display the splash screen must not be underestimated, nor dismissed lightly. By showing the form modally, execution of the code in `ShowForm` is blocked until the form is dismissed. That gives the form the opportunity to run its own code (the `Timer_Tick`, for example), and for the main thread to make calls to public methods of the form via `mySplashScreen.Invoke()`. If the splash screen wasn't shown modally, the `ShowForm` method would be complete in a moment and the splash screen would be of no value to anyone.

This method needs to be executed on the worker thread, so that the splash screen starts up on the worker thread. Before starting the worker thread, our code will need to ensure that there is a splash screen ready to be displayed in the `mySplashScreen` variable, and the appropriate timeout value has been stored in `maxDisplayTime`.

The public method that sets up the worker thread is `Show()`. It takes two arguments: an instance of a form that inherits from `SplashScreen`, and an integer value specifying the form's timeout.

```
Public Shared Sub Show( _
        ByRef aSplashScreen As SplashScreen, _
        ByVal MaxSecondsToDisplaySplash As Integer)
```

First, it checks that a worker thread hasn't already been started. If it has, then we throw an exception.

```
If Not splashThread Is Nothing Then
    Throw New InvalidOperationException("Splash screen " _
        + "already showing")
End If
```

Next, we set up a thread that, when started, will execute the ShowForm() method. We give it a name to ease debugging, and set it to run as a background thread. Foreground threads keep a process from terminating; background threads do not. If background threads still exist when all the foreground threads are terminated, the background threads are aborted. For us, this means that the splash screen will disappear if the main thread crashes or is terminated during the startup process.

```
splashThread = New Thread(AddressOf ShowForm)
splashThread.Name = "SplashScreenWorker"
splashThread.IsBackground = True
```

The values of the method's two parameters are stored in the class's shared variables, so they will be accessible to the worker thread. We don't want to set mySplashScreen.MaximumDisplayTime here, because this code is executing on the main thread; the value we'd set would not available to the worker thread. This has a major impact on how the form runs on the worker thread.

It is important to be aware of this relationship between forms and threads, not only in this example, but anytime you're working with forms and threads. If you're not aware of this relationship you may someday find yourself faced with unexpected behavior that can be very difficult to diagnose and correct.

```
mySplashScreen = aSplashScreen
maxDisplayTime = MaxSecondsToDisplaySplash
```

Finally, we start the thread. It is placed in a running state, and when it is scheduled for execution, it will begin by running the ShowForm() method.

```
splashThread.Start()

End Sub
```

There's one more significant part of the SplashScreenController class that we need to implement. That is the Hide() method, which will allow us to call from the main thread to execute code that will run on the worker thread – in this case, the instruction that the splash screen should disappear. The Form's Invoke() method is the key to making this happen.

```
Public Shared Sub Hide()
    Dim hideSplashScreen As New HideMethod(AddressOf _
                        mySplashScreen.HideSplashScreen)
    Try
        mySplashScreen.Invoke(hideSplashScreen)
    Catch
        ' do nothing - the form is already gone
```

```
      End Try
        mySplashScreen = Nothing
      End Sub
```

`HideMethod` has been declared as a delegate. Here we allocate and instantiate a variable to contain a `HideMethod` delegate, and give it the location of the code it is to execute – the `HideSplashScreen()` method of the `mySplashScreen` object. Then we make a call to `mySplashScreen.Invoke()`, passing the variable holding the `HideMethod` delegate. `Invoke()` executes a delegate on the thread that owns the control's underlying window handle. For us, that means that `HideSplashScreen()` will execute on `mySplashScreen`'s thread.

We have now provided our third method for the splash screen to be dismissed; it can be told to go away by code running on the main thread, through a call to this `Hide()` method.

There's just one more small piece to add to the `SplashScreenController` class. We need to make the class's constructor private and have it do nothing, so that the class can't be instantiated. Add the following code to the class:

```
      Private Sub New()
        ' prevents instantiation
      End Sub

    End Class

End Namespace
```

That completes the splash screen implementation.

Demonstration

To show the splash screen in action, we'll create a simple Windows Form application. It will have a code module to display the splash screen, perform the startup tasks, dismiss the splash screen, and display the application's main form.

In Visual Studio, add a new Windows Application project to your solution. Name this project `SplashDemo`. Make this project the startup project for the solution. Add a reference to the `SplashScreen` project. Change the properties of the project so that the startup object is `Sub Main` rather than `Form1`.

The project will have a form, `Form1`, by default. We will use this as the application's main form. Place a `TextBox` control on the form. The text box is there to make it obvious when the form has focus. Since we're not really going to add functionality to this form, it doesn't matter what the form or its controls are called. We do need to make sure that this form appears as the frontmost window when it is launched, so we need to modify the form designer-generated code a little. Go into the code view of the form and add the highlighted lines:

```
#Region " Windows Form Designer generated code "

    Public Sub New()
      MyBase.New()

      'This call is required by the Windows Form Designer.
      InitializeComponent()

      'Add any initialization after the InitializeComponent() call

        Me.Visible = True     'needed so .Activate will run
        Me.TopMost = True     'forces the screen to the foreground
        Me.Activate()         'gives the screen focus
        Me.TopMost = False    'allows other windows to go in front

    End Sub

    . . .
```

We also, obviously, need to create a splash screen for our application. Add a new
inherited form, called DemoSplashScreen.vb, to your project, and tell it to inherit
from Wrox.Toolkit.UI.SplashScreen. You can now add any user-interface
features you choose to the splash screen, such as images, icons, about buttons, credits
listings, and so on. For this demo, we'll settle with a low-key label, with its text set to
Application Starting, and another label, with its name set to ProgressLabel,
and its text property set to blank.

Below the form, you should see the inherited timer control. Double-click it to add an
event handler for the timer Tick event to this form. Add the highlighted code below:

```
Public Class DemoSplashScreen
    Inherits Wrox.Toolkit.UI.SplashScreen

' Windows Form Designer generated code goes here

    Private progress As Integer

    Public Sub Timer_Tick(ByVal o As Object, ByVal e As EventArgs) _
        Handles Timer.Tick

        progress += 1
        ProgressLabel.Text = String.Format("{0} seconds", progress)

    End Sub

End Class
```

This adds another event handler to the timer's Tick event, which will fire every second
while the form is visible. We simply keep track of how many seconds we've been
displaying for, and show the user via the ProgressLabel label control.

Now, we need to tie the splash screen and main form together into an application. Add
a code module to this project, and name it MainModule. Add the following code to
the code module:

```
Imports Wrox.Toolkit.UI

Public Module MainModule
  Public Sub Main()
    System.Threading.Thread.CurrentThread.Name = "SplashMainThread"

    Dim baseSplash As SplashScreen
    baseSplash = New DemoSplashScreen()

    Try
      SplashScreenController.Show(baseSplash, 12)
    Catch e As Exception
      MsgBox(e.Message)
    End Try

    'Mimic doing Initialization work
    System.Threading.Thread.CurrentThread.Sleep(15000)

    SplashScreenController.Hide()
    Application.Run(New Form1())
    Application.Exit()
  End Sub

End Module
```

This is the entry point for the program. As we stated before, naming the thread makes debugging easier, but it's not compulsory. We create an instance of our application's specialized splash screen, DemoSplashScreen, and put it into a local variable. The call to the Shared method SplashScreenController.Show() is where things really start to happen. The call is wrapped in a Try ... Catch construct because Show() can throw an exception. SplashScreenController.Show() has all the code to create a new thread and display the splash screen on that thread. We pass in our splash screen, and the timeout value: 12 seconds, in this case.

Once the new thread has been started, the main thread can go about the business of performing all the startup/initialization tasks that are needed before displaying the application's UI. For demonstration purposes we've just put the main thread to sleep for 15 seconds, to mimic a lengthy startup. During this time, the worker thread displaying the splash screen remains active, and can provide a dynamic experience, complete with user interaction. We'll see this with the Timer_Tick handler we've added. Because we've told the SplashScreenController class to display the splash screen for a maximum of 12 seconds, the timer on the splash screen will be started, and the splash screen will update the label once per second.

Once the initialization is complete, the call to the shared SplashScreenController.Hide() method takes care of dismissing the splash screen and terminating the worker thread, if the screen hasn't already disappeared (which, in this case, it will have done, three seconds earlier).

Finally, it is time to display the application's main form, Form1(). The Application.Run() command displays Form1, and transfers control of the main thread to Form1 until it is closed. The main part of the application is represented here by Form1. For our purposes, it is uninteresting, which is why it is nothing more than a form definition in this example. Once it is up and visible, your users are able to start using your application, and the multithreaded splash screen options are all complete. Once Form1 is closed, control transfers back to our Sub Main() and the Application.Exit() method is executed, fully closing the application.

Now, you should be able to build the project and execute it. All being well, the splash screen will appear, and count up the seconds until it disappears after 12. Then, a few seconds later, the main form will appear.

To demonstrate the splash screen responding to user input, simply start the application and click on the splash screen any time it is visible. It will immediately disappear. The main form will still appear 15 seconds after the application started. Try changing the values of the amount of time the main thread sleeps, and the splash screen's timeout value, to see the application automatically dismiss the splash screen when it has finished starting up.

Limitations

While the base splash screen can be extended to produce any number of different splash screen variants, to keep the class simple, we've not given the deriving class much control over the basic behavior of the splash screen. So, all splash screens derived from this class will be able to be dismissed with a mouse click, and so on. This may not always be desirable. In such circumstances, it is necessary to create a customized version of the splash screen form, rather than simply deriving a new one from it.

Extensions

The functionality that can be added to a dynamic splash screen derived from this class is almost limitless. With a resource file and the timer, you could rotate through a series of images stored in the resource file. With text in a resource file, you could load a "tip of the day", and display that in the startup form. Add Back and Next buttons, and you'd have a way for the user to walk through the daily tips, images, or even a multimedia presentation. By reading and writing to the application's configuration file, the application can remember which resources have been viewed, and which ones should be displayed the next time the application starts.

By including more public methods in SplashForm, and providing a wrapper method in SplashScreenController that uses SplashForm.Invoke() (as was shown here with HideSplashScreen()), you could create a mechanism for the main thread to have the splash screen show progress, to take on a different appearance, or otherwise respond to call from the main thread.

A useful extension to the splash screen would be to add a set of generic progress reporting methods, that would enable the main thread to simply call reporting methods on the `SplashScreenController`, and have these translated into method calls on the splash screen that can be used to update a status line, or progress bar, to indicate how application startup is progressing.

Product Licensing

If you are a developer who has written a shareware or retail type application, the possibility of someone not paying for your work is a real worry. There are many different ways of licensing or registering a product to help keep track of legitimate users. This class will provide you with a technique to license your product as well as introduce you to the .NET Cryptography namespace and some of its features.

Scenario

After you have developed and before you have shipped your first application, you need to think about protecting your intellectual property. The more unauthorized users of your software, the less money you make.

There are many different kinds of registration, product license, and copy protection schemes. All of them have their appropriate uses and can be good at stopping, to a certain degree, illegal usage. This class will look at one particular type of product license algorithm for protecting your software. This class forces the user to register your application with you, the developer, and is then returned an encrypted file that is the product license for that user to use your application on that particular machine. How this is implemented in your application, or how product licenses are obtained isn't important here. The infrastructure will be in place, for you to generate your own licensing mechanism that is difficult for a pirate to crack.

Technology

The main technical aspect of this class is encrypting and decrypting the product license information in an industry-standard format that can't easily be broken. Nothing is unbreakable, but by using industry-respected secure algorithms, we can make it safe against even an above average pirate.

A few cryptographic primitives make up the basis for all cryptographic schemes. Symmetric cryptography (private key encryption) uses a single key (normally inputted as a password) that is shared between both parties for encrypting and decrypting information. Asymmetric cryptography (public key encryption) uses a public key for encrypting the data and a private key for decrypting the data. If you have one key, it is virtually impossible to deduce what the other is using some calculation, and it is impossible to use the same key for encryption and decryption. Cryptographic signing uses a digital signature to ensure that the received data has originated from the correct specific party. Public key encryption means encrypting some data with the public key such that only the private key can decrypt it, whereas digital signing means encrypting some data (usually a checksum) with the private key so that only the public key can decrypt it. As the algorithms are one way, if a public key decrypts the message, then you know it must have been encrypted using the private key, and vice versa. Cryptographic hashes take any type of data and convert it to unique fixed length byte sequence.

Design

The design of the Product License classes means the user can send registration information to the developer, that file will be sent back to the user, and during application startup the product license will be read to confirm if it is valid, before continuing to execute the application. There are three main classes: `GenerateKeys`, `CreateLicense`, and `VerifyLicense`, with each containing one method for generating the public and private keys, encrypting the license, and decrypting (verifying) the license, respectively.

This class uses an asymmetric cryptographic algorithm. This means that the license and the public key can be made available to the application, and the public key can decrypt the license and discover if the value contained within is what is expected (the name of the person who registered the application). As the license will be encrypted using the private key, only the holder of the public key (the developer) could have supplied the license. This allows the application to know that the license is valid and so know that the product is licensed.

The application must have a copy of the public key, and this should be hard coded into the application itself, and passed to the relevant method of the `VerifyLicense` class as a `String`, so that a hacker cannot just change the public key to another – it doesn't matter if someone discovers what the public key is. This class will give you a glimpse into the .NET Cryptography namespace. The .NET Cryptography namespace is the most extensive security library that Microsoft has created to date and contains several different types of encryption techniques, as well as many different types of standard encryption algorithms for each technique.

To create a license file that will be used to authenticate the product, you will need some specific information from the user. Generally, this is the user's name, address, and other similar information. This would then be encrypted and a value would be created. Upon execution of the application, the encrypted value would be checked against this entered information and if it matches, then the application would execute. In this implementation, when the user clicks the Registration button in the application (this will depend on your own application of how to get the user information to you the developer for encryption) it will send the registration information to the encryption application (perhaps using a web service in an actual application).

Once the user has submitted their information, you as the developer will use different classes (in an administration type program) to generate the license file. This file will contain an encrypted version of the registration information. This file will then be sent back to the user (if you have an install program it can be automatically generated during the registration process).

Once the user has received the new license file, it will attempt to verify the license file when they execute the associated program. The application will use the same class, compiled in to it, to decrypt the license file to see if the application directory create date and machine name are the same as they are on the actual machine. If these are the same then the program will continue. If they do not match, the application will shut down (first informing the user), or in the case of a shareware type application perhaps revert to a demo mode.

This design will help prevent illegal use of your application and be more secure than a simple registration number match.

Implementation

These classes will be incorporated into any application that needs a product license. Only the validation classes needs to be distributed with the application itself.

Create a class library project and call it ProductLicense. The class will import the following namespaces: System.Security.Cryptography for the actual encryption and decryption, System.IO for saving the encrypted information to a file, and System.Text for converting strings to byte arrays.

```
Imports System.Security.Cryptography
Imports System.IO
Imports System.Text

Namespace Wrox.Toolkit.Util
    Public NotInheritable Class VerifyLicense
        Private Sub New()
        End Sub
```

This class is declared `NotInheritable` as we need to keep the validation routines as private and unchangeable as possible. The class is also declared as shared by giving it a private constructor, as both methods used will be shared. We next define the important routine, the one that actually validates the license based on the public key:

```
Private Shared Function ValidateLicense(publicXMLKey As String, _
                                        userInfo() As Byte) _
                                        license() As Byte, _
                                        As Boolean
    If publicXMLKey Is Nothing Or userInfo is Nothing Or _
        license Is Nothing Then
        Throw New ArgumentNullException
    ElseIf publicXMLKey = String.Empty Or userInfo.Length = 0 _
            Or license.Length = 0 Then
        Throw New ArgumentException("Parameters must not be empty")
    End If
    Dim rsad As New RSACryptoServiceProvider()
```

The function is given `Private` accessibility as correct validation depends on the correct public key being used. The assembly that this class will be compiled into should contain all the validation code and so the public methods supplied to the application should be as restricted as possible to help prevent malicious crackers from changing the validation routines by changing some of the IL. The `publicXMLKey` parameter contains the XML string containing the RSA public key `userInfo` contains a byte array, which holds the various user registration details used to create the license. The `license` variable contains a byte array representing the encrypted user information.

The `rsad` variable will be used to create the RSA object that can be used to validate the license file.

```
    rsad.FromXmlString(publicXMLKey)
    Return rsad.VerifyData(userInfo, New _
        SHA1CryptoServiceProvider(), license)
End Function
```

The above lines first read in the `publicXMLKey` string, generating a new RSA Crypto object with the passed in public key. It then attempts to verify that the encrypted data in `license` matches the data in `userInfo`. It uses a `SHA1CryptoServiceProvider` object to provide the hash value for this validation. If they match, it returns `True`; if not it returns `False`.

Access to this method will be strictly limited to a public parameter-less function, which is detailed below. A different implementation can be provided here depending on the needs of your application.

```
Public Shared Function Verify() As Boolean
    Const LICENSEFILE As String = "license.lic"
    Const USERINFOFILE As String = "userinfo.txt"
    Const PUBLICXMLKEY As String = _
        . . .
```

This function is a proxy for the `VerifyLicense()` method described above. We hard code the values into constants before passing them to the `VerifyLicense()` method. The `PUBLICXMLKEY` string is a long string, an example is shown below, and it will be used to store the XML representation of the public key. It is hard coded, as it would be trivial to change an external file.

```
<RSAKeyValue><Modulus>09Yty1WF5tOoeGSOmOa0Tw/3CXGdMPVJvMErPjBUf3rdy66k
Srlndlbr2bpGB7HiyV3OGphnEa6TFvOy4dJLVyuD5Z8MdxMeQE7v7dFd286fHrrGSoSBBM
XwMb7YAvOgiY7+CfzgI9HkgcTZ1W8bKQf31PkIRxxYHJnqPeWIpqk=</Modulus><Expon
ent>AQAB</Exponent></RSAKeyValue>
```

The license and user-specific information is stored in external files with the application.

```
        Dim sr As StreamReader

        sr = File.OpenText(LICENSEFILE)
        Dim license() As Byte = _
          Convert.FromBase64String(sr.ReadLine)
        sr.Close()

        sr = File.OpenText(USERINFOFILE)
        Dim userInfo () As Byte = _
          Encoding.Unicode.GetBytes(sr.ReadLine)
        sr.Close()
```

Above, a new `StreamReader` object is declared before going on to use it. The `File.OpenText()` method returns a stream object from a text file. We then convert the Base64 encoding used in the license file into a `Byte` array and store it, before calling the `Close()` method on the stream object. The same happens with the user information file, only as this is stored as Unicode, the `GetBytes()` method is used to retrieve a `Byte` array.

```
        Return ValidateLicense(PUBLICXMLKEY, userInfo, license)
      End Function
    End Class
End Namespace
```

The result of the `ValidateLicense()` method is returned here. Because we are passing `Byte` arrays into another method, we could have a synchronization problem if any individual element of this array was changed on another thread. However, as none of this code updates the elements in these arrays, we won't have a problem here.

We can now compile this assembly and distribute it with our application. However, there is still a major flaw in this; the public key is accessible to any hacker, and so it could be changed by any malicious person. This would allow someone to generate their own public/private key pair, enter their own user registration information, generate the license from their private key, and stick the public key into the assembly. This can be worked around by using **strongly named** assemblies.

Strong Naming Assemblies

A strongly named assembly is one that has been versioned and digitally signed. When it is digitally signed, then if any of the code in the assembly has changed since signing, the CLR will refuse to run the code in that assembly. This means that the public key for the signature is also embedded in the assembly, and a checksum is generated and encrypted using the private key. If when the checksum is decrypted it matches the checksum regenerated by the CLR, then the assembly is valid. In addition, when you add a strong named assembly to a project in Visual Studio .NET, it recognizes that it is strongly named and so in the assembly metadata for your code, it will demand that the particular version of this strongly named assembly is required.

The public key of the strong named assemblies should be digitally signed by Verisign or another trusted third party so that the Windows machine of the user can confirm that the code was indeed generated by the relevant party. If this did not happen, then a hacker could quite easily change the metadata information in the application and referenced assembly. This would destroy all the security put in place so far. At least with this in place, there are fewer weak points. A determined hacker could still extract all the content from the assemblies and place it in their own assemblies, with their own metadata, but that would be extremely hard work. In addition, they wouldn't be digitally signed by the correct third party, which wouldn't matter for most users, but the CLR can be set to only execute digitally trusted assemblies, even from the local drive.

You can make this assembly strongly named by following the following steps. First, you need to create a public-private key pair using the following command in a Command Prompt window:

```
> sn /k C:\Documents and Settings\Andy\My Documents\
  Visual Studio Projects\TestRegistration\MyKey.snk
```

You will need to change the path name slightly, but this generates a public-private key pair in the MyKey.snk file. You can then pass this to a trusted third party, such as Verisign, to sign. Now, in the AssemblyInfo.vb file in Visual Studio, add the following to the bottom of it:

```
<Assembly: AssemblyVersiion("1.0.0")>
<Assembly: AssemblyKeyFile("C:\Documents and Settings\Andy\My
Documents\Visual Studio Projects\TestRegistration\MyKey.snk")>
```

When compiled, this will now contain a signature encrypted using the private key, and will also embed the public key. When you reference this assembly in another project, it will reference it by strong name. The signature is included in the project that references this assembly as well, so if the two signatures and the checksum of the assembly don't match, then it will not use this assembly.

License Generation

You now need to add another class library, called `GenLicense`, to the project, so that we can add the methods needed to generate the public and the private keys, and to generate the license file. The way this program works demands that the license is generated by code at the software house and so both of these methods can be located in the same assembly.

```
Imports System.Text
Imports System.IO
Imports System.Security.Cryptography

Namespace Wrox.Toolkit.Util
    Public Class LicenseCreator
        Private PrivateKeyFile As String
        Private LicenseFile As String

        Public Sub New()
            Me.New("privatepublickey.xml", "license.lic")
        End Sub

        Public Sub New(privateKeyFile As String, licenseFile As String)
            If privateKeyFile Is Nothing Or _
                licenseFile Is Nothing Then
                Throw New ArgumentNullException()
            ElseIf privateKeyFile = String.Empty Or _
                licenseFile = String.Empty Then
                Throw New ArgumentException()
            ElseIf Not File.Exists(PrivateKeyFile)
                Throw New Exception(PrivateKeyFile & " does not exist")
            Else
                Me.PrivateKeyFile = privateKeyFile
                Me.LicenseFile = licenseFile
            End If
        End Sub
```

We can use the same library for both classes, but we'll cover the `LicenseCreator` class first. There are two class-level fields, `PrivateKeyFile` and `LicenseFile`, and two constructors. The default constructor just uses default values for these fields, whereas the parameterized constructor allows you to specify different filenames. Much error checking occurs here to ensure the values passed into the constructor are valid and that `PrivateKeyFile` does exist.

```
Public Function Create(ByVal encryptText As String) As String
    If encryptText Is Nothing Or encryptText = String.Empty Then
        Throw New ArgumentException()
    End If
    Try
        Dim sr As StreamReader
        Dim sw As StreamWriter
        Dim RSA As RSACryptoServiceProvider = New _
            RSACryptoServiceProvider()
```

For the `Create()` method, we retrieve the value to be encrypted using the private key saved in the license file, by passing in a string object as a parameter. This allows the registration information to be as complicated as you like, perhaps based on machine-specific information. The `StreamReader`, `StreamWriter`, and `RSACryptoServiceProvider` objects will be used throughout this method.

```
sr = File.OpenText(PrivateKeyFile)
        RSA.FromXmlString(sr.ReadLine)
        sr.Close()
```

The above code reads in the private key from the file specified and passes it to the
FromXmlString() method of the RSACryptoServiceProvider object to
reconstruct a new RSA object that can be used to generate the license file.

```
Dim licenseBytes() As Byte = _
    Encoding.Unicode.GetBytes(encryptText)
Dim encryptBytes() As Byte = _
    RSA.SignData(licenseBytes, New SHA1CryptoServiceProvider())
```

The next thing we do is to convert the Unicode string passed as an argument to this
method into a Byte array. We then digitally sign the bytes in this array (using the
private key) and pass it to a new Byte array, encryptBytes.

```
Dim signedLicense As String = _
    Convert.ToBase64String(encryptBytes)
```

We then convert the byte array into a Base64 encoded string, signedLicense. This is
necessary as the data isn't stored as mere text, but as binary data – hence why the data
is output into a Byte array.

```
sw = File.CreateText(LicenseFile)
sw.WriteLine(signedLicense)
sw.Close()

Return signedLicense
Catch ex As Exception
    MsgBox("An error occurred in the Create() method: " & _
        ControlChars.NewLine & ex.Message)
    Return String.Empty
End Try
    End Function
End Class
```

Finally, we open the license file and put the contents of signedLicense into it,
before returning the contents of signedLicense to the calling method.

Public/Private Key Generation

This class contains the code necessary for generating the public and private key pair.
Remember this is part of the same assembly and so goes directly under the current
class declaration:

```
Public NotInheritable Class KeysGenerator
    Private PrivateKeyFile As String
    Private PublicKeyFile As String

    Public Sub New()
        Me.New("publicprivatekey.xml", "publickey.xml")
    End Sub
```

```
Public Sub New(privateKeyFile As String, publicKeyFile As String)
    If privateKeyFile Is Nothing Or publicKeyFile Is Nothing Then
        Throw New ArgumentNullException()
    ElseIf privateKeyFile = String.Empty Or _
            publicKeyFile = String.Empty Then
        Throw New ArgumentException()
    Else
        Me.PrivateKeyFile = privateKeyFile
        Me.PublicKeyFile = publicKeyFile
    End If
End Sub
```

Like `LicenseCreator`, `KeysGenerator` has a constructor to initialize the private fields that contain the locations of the relevant files.

```
Public Function Generate() As Boolean
    Dim RSA As New RSACryptoServiceProvider()
    Dim sw As StreamWriter
    Dim publicKey As String
    Dim privatePublicKey As String
```

`Generate()` returns a Boolean to indicate success or failure, while declaring the variables used in this method. `RSA` generates a public and private key pair on construction, and it can be used immediately afterwards.

```
Try
    privatePublicKey = RSA.ToXmlString(True)
    publicKey = RSA.ToXmlString(False)
```

The `ToXmlString()` method will output the public and private keys as an XML file. The XML files will contain different elements depending on whether the private key is returned or not. If `False` is passed, then just the public key is output, whereas if `True` is passed, then both are output. The `privateKey` variable will contain the text representation of the `RSAKeyValue` element containing `Modulus` and `Exponent` elements as immediate children. Their contents are long streams of `UTF-8` Unicode characters, that represent a very large number. In one invocation, 172 characters were generated. The contents of the `Exponent` element represent an exponent for this number. This very large number is used in the algorithm to encrypt or decrypt data.

The `privateKey` variable will contain the text representation of the `RSAKeyValue` element containing `Modulus`, `Exponent`, `P`, `Q`, `DP`, `DQ`, `InverseQ`, and `D` elements as immediate children. The `Modulus` and `Exponent` elements are the same as those for the public key. The others represent the private key that can be used with the RSA Algorithm to decrypt data encrypted by the public key, or encrypt data to be decrypted by the public key.

```
sw = File.CreateText(PrivateKeyFile)
sw.WriteLine(privatePublicKey)
sw.Close()

sw = File.CreateText(PublicKeyFile)
sw.WriteLine(publicKey)
sw.Close()
```

The above code outputs the text in the `privatePublicKey` and `publicKey` variables into the files specified during construction. The `File.CreateText()` shared method creates a new `StreamWriter` object using the filename passed as an argument.

```
        MsgBox("This is the private key: " & _
            privatePublicKey)
        Return True
    Catch ex As Exception
        MsgBox("The Generate method returned the following error: " _
            & ex.Message)
        Return False
    End Try
  End Sub
 End Class
End Namespace
```

Finally, we output the private and public key pairs to a message box, and then return `True` to indicate success. If any exceptions were thrown, it informs you of this, outputting the text of the exception in a message box, before returning `False`.

This the entire of the classes used to manage basic license generation. Compile these into two assemblies.

Demonstration

To demonstrate how this code works, create a new solution in Visual Studio .NET. Add a Windows Forms project to the solution; this will be your application to which you are going to add a product license. In the solution, reference both assemblies compiled in the previous section and build a form that looks like the following:

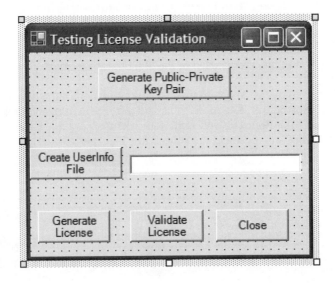

The controls on this page are as follows:

Control Type	Name
Form	TestRegistration
Command Button	cmdKeyGenerate
Label	lblUserInfo
Command Button	cmdCreateUserInfo
Textbox	txtUserInfo
Command Button	cmdGenerateLicense
Command Button	cmdValidate
Command Button	cmdClose

We will now add the code behind these controls. First, we need to code the form's load event and it should look as follows:

```
Private Sub TestRegistration_Load(ByVal sender As System.Object, _
                          ByVal e As System.EventArgs) _
                          Handles MyBase.Load
    If Not File.Exists("publickey.xml") Then
      lblUserInfo.Text = "Public-Private Key not generated"
    End If
    If Not File.Exists("userInfo.txt") Then
      lblUserInfo.Text &= " and no user info file created"
    End If
End Sub
```

This merely confirms the existence of the public key and user information files. We are using the defaults and so can hard code them in here. If any of the files don't exist, it says so in the label.

```
Private Sub cmdKeyGenerate_Click(ByVal sender As System.Object, _
                          ByVal e As System.EventArgs) _
                          Handles cmdKeyGenerate.Click
    Dim KG As New KeysGenerator()
    If Not KG.Generate() Then
      MsgBox("Public-Private key pair not generated")
    End If
End Sub
```

When you click the cmdKeyGenerate button, it creates a new KeysGenerator object, using the default constructor, and then tests to see if the Generate() was successful. If not, then it informs you of this.

```
Private Sub cmdCreateUserInfo_Click(ByVal sender As System.Object, _
                          ByVal e As System.EventArgs) _
                          Handles cmdCreateUserInfo.Click
    If Not txtUserInfo.Text = String.Empty Then
```

```
Dim sw As StreamWriter

    sw = File.CreateText("userInfo.txt")
    sw.WriteLine(txtUserInfo.Text)
    sw.Close()

    lblUserInfo.Text = String.Empty
    If Not File.Exists("privatepublickey.xml") Then
      lblUserInfo.Text = "The public private key hasn't been "& _
                         "created" & ControlChars.NewLine
    End If
    lblUserInfo.Text &= "User Info file created"
  End If
End Sub
```

Upon filling in some text (perhaps your name) in the txtUserInfo textbox, clicking the cmdCreateUserInfo button cause the application output the text to a file. We then clear the label and if the private key still hasn't been generated, then add a message to indicate this. Then we inform the user that the user info file has been created.

```
Private Sub cmdGenerateLicense_Click( _
            ByVal sender As System.Object, _
            ByVal e As System.EventArgs) _
            Handles cmdGenerateLicense.Click
  Dim KG As New LicenseCreator()
  Dim sr As StreamReader
  sr = File.OpenText("userInfo.txt")
  Dim license As String = KG.Create(sr.ReadLine)
  If Not license = String.Empty Then
    MsgBox("The license looks like: " & license)
  Else
    MsgBox("License not generated")
  End If
End Sub
```

This method handles license generation. It creates a new LicenseCreator object with the default constructor. We read in the userInfo.txt file, and pass the contents of this file as a string to the Create() method. The license generated is stored in the license.lic file, and returned as a string from the method. If an empty string is returned, then the operation failed and we display a relevant message. If not, then we display the contents of the license file.

```
Private Sub cmdValidate_Click(ByVal sender As System.Object, _
                      ByVal e As System.EventArgs) _
                      Handles cmdValidate.Click
  Try
    If VerifyLicense.Verify() Then
      MsgBox("License Matches!")
    Else
      MsgBox("License doesn't match.")
    End If
  Catch ex As Exception
    MsgBox("An error was returned" & _
          ControlChars.NewLine & ex.Message)
  End Try
End Sub
```

The above method merely calls the public Verify() method and displays a message indicating success if it returns True, and one indicating failure if it returns False. We catch all exceptions and return them in a message box.

```
Private Sub cmdClose_Click(ByVal sender As System.Object, _
                          ByVal e As System.EventArgs) _
                          Handles cmdClose.Click
    MyBase.Close()
End Sub
```

Finally, the above event handler just closes the form.

Remember that the public key is hard coded into the application, so once the public key has been generated, open up the file in notepad and copy all the contents into the PUBLICXMLKEY constant of the VerifyLicense.Verify() method. This is a little ugly, but essential.

Limitations

As with nearly any type of copy protection product license scheme, it is not foolproof. With a standard type registration number scheme, you generally can use that registration number on any computer with the application and it will work. The demonstration application just uses any entered text, but machine specific attributes could be used that almost require that only one license file will work per machine.

Another limitation is .NET itself. Since applications are compiled to IL and then upon execution JIT compiled to specific machine code, IL code can be disassembled and with enough patience and work, the assemblies could be recreated to use the hacker's public-private key pair, or the validation code could be not used at all. If the string used for the product license is found, the unlicensed user can change their system so that the license file will be accepted.

Extensions

To help prevent your .NET code from being disassembled, the use of an obfuscator will make it more difficult for the person attempting to read your code to figure out your product license string. Obfuscator's only make it more difficult to read the code (by using non descriptive variables etc.) they do not change the code so it can't be disassembled.

If you make the product license string contain unique information, the more difficult it will be for someone to duplicate it on an unregistered computer. One very unique identifier on most machines is the network card unique ID. All network cards have a unique ID throughout the world so using this in the product license string make it nearly impossible for someone to use a license file on another machine. This value however is not available in standard .NET namespaces so you will have to use P/Invoke to call a Win32 API method to find it.

In the .NET System.Security.Cryptography namespace, a number of different methods of symmetric encryption techniques can be used (RC2, DES, TripleDES and Rijndael – all of which are described in the VB.NET help files). You can also use a different size key to increase the complexity of the encryption.

Because the important private Validate() method accepts its parameters as strings and byte arrays, you can obtain the data you need from different sources in the public version. You could store the license in the Windows registry, and the user registration in an XML file. The data just needs to be converted to a byte array before being passed to the private method.

Application Settings Writer

.NET provides a simple mechanism for applications to store configuration information – the settings can be written in a specially formatted XML file in a particular location. The .NET `System.Configuration` namespace provides mechanisms for reading the data in this file. In particular, the `System.Configuration.AppSettingsReader` class can read the value from the file that is associated with a particular key. This enables us to configure certain aspects of the application's behavior by editing its configuration file.

Visual Basic .NET makes use of these configuration files to provide an easy way to make forms and controls configurable. If you look at the properties panel for any form or control in Visual Studio .NET, you'll see one of the options is labeled (Dynamic Properties). Click on the (Advanced) tab and you're presented with a dialog which allows you to request that certain properties be initialized with values taken from the configuration file. Visual Studio .NET inserts initialization code into the form that uses the `System.Configuration.AppSettingsReader` to initialize the appropriate properties from the configuration file.

Unfortunately, there is no class that provides the ability to amend the configuration file. Changes can only be written to the file manually. Additionally, through the Visual Studio .NET form editor, only a few dynamic properties are exposed such as `MaximizeBox`, `MinimizeBox`, and `ShowInTaskbar` (although it is possible to expose others). Other useful properties such as `Size` or `Location` are not exposed. If only we had another class to complement the `AppSettingsReader` class. This other class could write the value of any property, not just the few exposed dynamic properties, to the configuration file. The addition of this new class will allow us to easily persist properties, so that subsequent launches of the application would load everything the way we had it before. In this chapter, we are going to build the `AppSettingsWriter` class that will write out the values of application properties so that they can be loaded upon the next launch of the application.

Scenario

Most application users find it very convenient when an application saves the settings used during a session. For example, if I arrange windows in an MDI application just the way I like them, I do not want to have to set these windows again tomorrow when I run the application again. I want them to load exactly the way I adjusted them. With the `AppSettingsWriter`, we will be able to save and reload those settings.

Technology

The schema for application configuration files is described in the .NET SDK documentation, along with the details of how the file for a particular application is located. For a particular .NET application, `foo.exe`, the configuration details will be stored in a file in the same directory called `foo.exe.config`.

Here is a simple example of an application configuration file:

```
<?xml version="1.0" encoding="Windows-1252"?>
<configuration>
  <appSettings>
    <add key="ApplicationName" value="My Configurable Application" />
  </appSettings>
</configuration>
```

In this example, the application has a setting called `ApplicationName`, and we have specified its value as `My Configurable Application`.

As application configuration files are XML documents, the `AppSettingsWriter` class will use an `XmlDocument` object to do most of the work. The `XmlDocument` object loads the application configuration file, parses it, and then writes it back out again after updates are made. To obtain the node for a particular setting, we use an XPath query.

Because the application configuration file's name is based on the name of the application, we use reflection, which allows us to obtain information about loaded assemblies at run time, to obtain the name of the application, and thus the name of the configuration file.

Design

`AppSettingsWriter` is very compact and only needs two methods and a `Default` `WriteOnly` property:

❑ `New()` – this constructor method creates and loads the application configuration file

❑ `SaveFile()` – stores the updated settings in the application configuration file

❑ `Value` – a property used to create or update a key-value pair

Implementation

The following is the complete code with an explanation for each important section. For this exercise, we will be addressing a single form purely for ease of demonstration and understanding. Building a sample that uses an MDI application can be left as an exercise to the reader.

Open Visual Studio .NET and create a Windows Application project naming it AppSettingsSample. Next, go to the Form1 properties and change the Name property from Form1 to AppSettingsSampleForm. Rename Form1.vb to AppSettingsSampleForm.vb. Then right-click on the project in the solution explorer and select Properties. Change the startup object from Form1 to AppSettingsSampleForm. Next, expand the DynamicProperties item. Select Advanced then the ellipsis... that appears to open the Advanced property page. Scroll down the list and select Text. Accept the default key mapping (AppSettingsSampleForm.Text). After you close the property page, an app.config file will be added to the project.

The Windows Form Designer adds this subroutine to your derived form:

```
<System.Diagnostics.DebuggerStepThrough()> _
    Private Sub InitializeComponent()

   Dim configurationAppSettings As _
       System.Configuration.AppSettingsReader = _
       New System.Configuration.AppSettingsReader()
    '
    'AppSettingsSampleForm
    '
    Me.AutoScaleBaseSize = New System.Drawing.Size(6, 15)
    Me.ClientSize = New System.Drawing.Size(292, 268)
    Me.Name = "AppSettingsSampleForm"
    Me.Text = CType( _
       configurationAppSettings.GetValue("AppSettingsSampleForm.Text", _
       GetType(System.String)), String)

   End Sub
```

Notice that an AppSettingsReader is created and there is code that gets the value from the AppSettingsReader and places the value in the correct form property.

Open the app.config file by double-clicking the item in the solution explorer. Look at the line:

```
<add key="AppSettingsSampleForm.Text" value="Form1" />
```

Change it to:

```
<add key="AppSettingsSampleForm.Text" value="My Form" />
```

Save the file and build the project. Navigate to the project's bin directory to launch
AppSettingsSample.exe. Make sure that you do not run the application from the
debugger for the rest of this exercise; otherwise, the sample will not work correctly since
the class is meant to operate during run time. Notice that the form loaded has a caption that
says My Form. The built-in features of dynamic properties have just been demonstrated.

This is great for loading settings, but what about writing them out? Now we are going
to create the AppSettingsWriter class.

AppSettingsWriter Class

Add a new class file to the project and rename it from Class1.vb to
AppSettingsWriter.vb and then replace the Class1 code with the following:

```
Imports System.Xml

Public Class AppSettingsWriter

    Private configFileName As String
    Private document As XmlDocument
```

For now, the class simply has two private variables – the name of a configuration file,
and an XMLDocument object. Now let's add the New() (constructor) method after
the variables:

```
Public Sub New()

    Dim asmy As System.Reflection.Assembly
    Dim tempName As String

    asmy = System.Reflection.Assembly.GetEntryAssembly()
    tempName = asmy.Location

    configFileName = tempName & ".config"

    document = New XmlDocument()
    document.Load(configFileName)

End Sub
```

Upon class creation, the configuration file is found using reflection. The assembly name
is found and .config is simply appended to it. The configuration file that is used by
the application during run time is not the app.config file that is listed in the solution
explorer. When the solution is built, it is copied to
AppSettingsSample.exe.config. Then this file is loaded.

Now let's add a property Set() method to create or update the key-value pairs:

```
Default Public WriteOnly Property Value(ByVal key As String) _
    As String

    Set(ByVal Value As String)
        Dim Query As String
```

```
Dim Node As XmlNode
Dim Root As XmlNode
Dim Attribute1 As XmlNode
Dim Attribute2 As XmlNode

Query = "/configuration/appSettings/add[@key=" & _
    Chr(34) & key & Chr(34) & "]"
Node = document.DocumentElement.SelectSingleNode(Query)

If Not Node Is Nothing Then
  Node.Attributes.GetNamedItem("value").Value = Value
Else
  Node = document.CreateNode(XmlNodeType.Element, "add", "")

  Attribute1 = document.CreateNode(XmlNodeType.Attribute, _
    "key", "")
  Attribute1.Value = key
  Node.Attributes.SetNamedItem(Attribute1)

  Attribute2 = document.CreateNode(XmlNodeType.Attribute, _
    "value", "")
  Attribute2.Value = Value
  Node.Attributes.SetNamedItem(Attribute2)

  Query = "/configuration/appSettings"
  Root = document.DocumentElement.SelectSingleNode(Query)

  If Not Root Is Nothing Then
    Root.AppendChild(Node)
  Else
    Throw New InvalidOperationException( _
        "Could not add node to config file")
  End If
 End If
 End Set
End Property
```

All of the properties saved to the configuration file are represented as nodes named "add". This method looks for a node named "add" that contains the supplied key in the attributes collection. If found, it replaces the old value with a new one. If the node can't be found, a new one is created with the specified attributes and appended to the appropriate parent. Next, we'll need to add a method to save the file:

```
Public Sub SaveFile()
  document.Save(configFileName)
 End Sub
End Class
```

Demonstration

Now we are going to show how to use the AppSettingsWriter class to save properties. Open the app.config file and add the following lines:

```
<add key="AppSettingsSampleForm.size.width" value="500" />
<add key="AppSettingsSampleForm.size.height" value="500" />
<add key="AppSettingsSampleForm.x" value="25" />
<add key="AppSettingsSampleForm.y" value="25" />
```

Add these lines to the top of AppSettingsSampleForm:

```
Imports System.Configuration
Imports Wrox.Toolkit.Util

Public Class AppSettingsSampleForm
  Inherits System.Windows.Forms.Form
```

Double-click on AppSettingsSampleForm to add a Load event and insert the following code:

```
Private Sub AppSettingsSampleForm_Load(ByVal sender As Object, _
  ByVal e As System.EventArgs) Handles MyBase.Load

  Dim configurationAppSettings As AppSettingsReader
  Dim width As Int32
  Dim height As Int32
  Dim x As Int32
  Dim y As Int32

  Try
    configurationAppSettings = New AppSettingsReader()

    width = CType(configurationAppSettings.GetValue( _
      "AppSettingsSampleForm.size.width", _
      GetType(System.Int32)), Int32)

    height = CType(configurationAppSettings.GetValue( _
      "AppSettingsSampleForm.size.height", _
      GetType(System.Int32)), Int32)

    x = CType(configurationAppSettings.GetValue( _
      "AppSettingsSampleForm.x", GetType(System.Int32)), Int32)

    y = CType(configurationAppSettings.GetValue( _
      "AppSettingsSampleForm.y", GetType(System.Int32)), Int32)

    Me.ClientSize = New System.Drawing.Size(width, height)
    Me.DesktopLocation = New System.Drawing.Point(x, y)

  Catch ex As Exception
    MsgBox ex.ToString
  End Try
End Sub
```

We want the code to reside in the Load event as opposed to the OnLoad event override. The Load event fires before the form is actually loaded. This is where you want to put all the form initialization steps. The OnLoad event is the mechanism that raises the Load event.

After you build the project and run the executable, the form will be sized at 500 x 500 and start in position (25, 25).

Now add a `Closing` event to `AppSettingsSampleForm` with the following code:

```
    Private Sub AppSettingsSampleForm_Closing(ByVal sender As Object, _
        ByVal e As System.ComponentModel.CancelEventArgs) _
        Handles MyBase.Closing

        Try
          Dim Writer As New AppSettings()

          Writer("AppSettingsSampleForm.size.width") = _
              CStr(Me.ClientSize.Width)
          Writer("AppSettingsSampleForm.size.height") = _
              CStr(Me.ClientSize.Height)
          Writer("AppSettingsSampleForm.x") = CStr(Me.DesktopLocation.X)
          Writer("AppSettingsSampleForm.y") = CStr(Me.DesktopLocation.Y)

          Writer.SaveFile()

        Catch ex As Exception
          MsgBox(ex.ToString)
        End Try
      End Sub
    End Class
```

XML files are case-sensitive, so make sure that your code reads and writes items that are spelled exactly the same.

Build the project and run it by locating the `AppSettingSample.exe` file in the project's `bin` directory, then resize and reposition the form. If you close the form and restart it you should see that the settings on closing have been retained. If you look in the `AppSettingSample.exe.config` file you should see the new settings stored.

Limitations

Application configuration files are XML files and as such are case-sensitive. This could cause confusion if a person were to think of configuration files as synonymous with INI files or the windows registry, both of which are not case-sensitive.

Extensions

Using this class, a developer could save any number of properties. Other properties that might be useful to save would be color preferences, language settings, or font settings. Although the example focuses mainly on Windows applications, the same general technique can be used for Web applications. Additionally, the `AppSettingsWriter` can be used to save any type of setting not limited to form properties. For example, an application can use the `AppSettingsWriter` and the `AppSettingsReader` to remember options that the user typed in on the previous session such as file names and sorting options. The possibilities are unlimited.

AutoDeploy

One of the most important features of .NET is the ease by which applications can be deployed. Microsoft makes use of **XCOPY** deployment, but even that requires handling the client machines. The example developed here loads and executes code from both DLLs and EXEs on a client machine *without* having to manually copy files.

Note that this only works with .NET DLLs and EXEs. If the application also includes COM components, they will need to be deployed and registered using traditional deployment methods.

Scenario

When deploying a networked Windows Forms application the biggest challenge is getting the application out to the client workstations. In VB6/COM DLL versioning issues, the Windows Registry, and so forth, complicated this. The .NET platform solves these issues, allowing us to deploy applications by simply copying files to the client machine.

However, copying files to hundreds or thousands of client machines is still a big issue. It would be great to have true *zero touch* installation of applications, so they auto-deploy to the client workstations as needed? With minimal code, .NET provides this functionality virtually out of the box. All that's required is that the client machines have the .NET Runtime installed.

Technology

The technology required to auto-deploy assemblies to a client is built into the .NET Framework via reflection. Reflection allows us to write code that examines and interacts with .NET assemblies, types, and objects. We can use reflection to dynamically load an assembly into memory from a URL (or the hard drive). Once the assembly is in memory, reflection allows us to interact with it.

We can place .NET assemblies in a virtual directory on a web server, and .NET can download the files to each client machine automatically. On the server this requires nothing special, just a virtual directory or other directory that can be accessed via URL from the client. Into that directory we can place all the EXE and DLL files required by our application. The web directory does not need to be browsable, nor does it need any aspx, asmx, or other web-related files.

Once the files are accessible via URL, the client workstation can use them. In fact, it is possible to simply create a web page with a link to the remote executable. When the user clicks on that link .NET will automatically download the EXE and run it on the client. If the EXE depends on any DLLs, they will also be automatically downloaded as needed.

These automatically downloaded files are placed into a user-specific client-side cache. On subsequent attempts to run the application, the cached version is checked against the server version and any updates are downloaded automatically. If updates are not required, the cached version is run.

There are three problems with the standard implementation:

1. If we create a desktop shortcut or attempt to use Start | Run to launch an application via URL, the browser will appear, then disappear and the program will launch. This is because any use of a URL invokes the browser, which then detects that it isn't needed and so it goes away.

2. There is a bug in .NET that prevents auto-downloaded code from using the SoapFormatter or BinaryFormatter to deserialize objects. This can be a serious limitation in application design since it precludes the use of distributed objects.

3. If the web server has .NET installed, the application will be unable to read its configuration file. All files with a .config extension are unavailable for download after ASP.NET is installed on a server. This precludes the use of normal application configuration files for auto-downloaded code, and that is a serious problem in many cases.

Fortunately, with a small amount of code wrapped into a reusable library, we can overcome all three limitations. We will be able to auto-download applications from a URL using a desktop shortcut or from Start | Run without the annoying browser flicker. The auto-downloaded application will be able to deserialize objects and can employ distributed object technology, and we'll have a partial, but good, solution to the configuration file issue.

If the assembly is an EXE available via a URL, we'll be able to launch the program from the client, causing .NET to auto-deploy a .NET program from a URL to our client workstation and then run it. This allows us to run virtually any .NET program on our client workstation, with the only deployment effort being to put the program's files into a virtual root on the web server.

If the assembly is a DLL available via a URL, we'll be able to create objects by using the classes defined in the DLL. The DLL will be automatically downloaded to the client and loaded into our client process. Once that's done we can create instances of objects from the DLL and use them within our application. This allows client-side applications to dynamically access DLLs from a web server as needed.

In either case, any other DLLs that our auto-deployed EXE or DLL require will be auto-deployed to the client on demand, with no extra work on our part at all. .NET automatically detects when an EXE or DLL requires another DLL, and it automatically goes back to the directory or URL where the original file came from to look for any of these required files. If the file is not available, then the application will fail. This can happen because the file doesn't exist at the URL, or because the network has become unavailable.

For instance, say we run an EXE from a URL. If that EXE requires a DLL, .NET will automatically detect this and will automatically look at that same URL to find the DLL. If the DLL is there, it will be automatically downloaded to the client. If it is not there, the application will fail because the DLL is unavailable. This is no different from putting a program into a local directory on the client hard drive. We are effectively using a remote URL as if it were a local directory.

Design

Though not a lot of code is required to implement the auto-deployment functionality, it is very powerful code.

Remember that this code will all be running on the client machine. On the server the only requirement is that we set up a virtual directory or other web directory accessible via URL into which our application files (EXEs and DLLs) will be placed.

We need to understand how this works at a high level. On the client, we need to manually deploy both the .NET Runtime (if it isn't already there) and a bit of custom code to start from. Typically this custom code will be in the form of a program that the user launches, and then this program will use auto-deploy to invoke any other assemblies that are required. We can think of this program as a client-side launcher or shell application.

Preventing Browser-flicker

By having a client-side launcher, we are able to prevent the **browser flicker** effect that occurs when an application is run from a URL via a desktop shortcut, or the Start | Run command. The client-side launcher causes .NET to download and run the application, bypassing the need to invoke the browser at all.

Of course this client-side launcher or shell application must be deployed to the client first. This is typically done by creating a standard setup program to install the launcher, or by using XCOPY to get it to the client workstation. As we'll see, the launcher can be totally generic and so this is typically a one-time effort, after which we can auto-download all of our applications as needed.

The class we'll create here can be used to create a variety of launcher applications ranging from a generic launcher that can run any .NET program from an URL to a cohesive MDI menuing application that dynamically creates its menus, and loads its components, using auto-deployment.

As stated earlier, there are two caveats we need to address in this launcher class. First, auto-deployed code is treated a bit differently than code from a local source and so we need to catch an event from the AppDomain to ensure that deep deserialization (deserialization using the SoapFormatter or BinaryFormatter) works properly for auto-downloaded code. Second, an auto-deployed EXE can't read its own configuration file. Instead, it will use the one from the EXE we originally ran on the client.

Solving the Deserialization Issue

In the auto-deployment class itself we'll include code that catches the event that occurs when deserialization fails and we'll fix the issue. This will allow our auto-deployed code to use all the features of .NET.

The problem with deserialization is this. Auto-downloaded assemblies are loaded into our client AppDomain just fine, but within the AppDomain there are two separate lists of assemblies. One list contains assemblies loaded locally; the other list contains auto-downloaded assemblies. Almost all code in .NET treats these two lists the same, but the SoapFormatter and BinaryFormatter only look at the local list when deserializing objects, and so they fail to find the assembly containing the appropriate code. When this happens, the AppDomain raises an event indicating that there was a failure to locate the assembly. We can handle this event, providing a reference to the 'missing' assembly by merely scanning the complete list of assemblies loaded in the AppDomain to find the one it needs.

Supporting Application Configuration Files

As we noted earlier, files ending in a .config extension are not available for download from a web server when ASP.NET has been installed. Therefore, our application configuration files will become unavailable when provided through IIS. The ability to have a configuration file with an <appSettings> block is very powerful and is a feature you wouldn't want to lose just because your clients are auto-downloading the code.

Before we get too far into this, remember that an auto-downloaded program is not written in any special way. A .NET EXE run from a local installation can be auto-deployed simply by placing it into a virtual directory and then launching it from the client. The caveat is that it then loses access to its configuration file.

What we really want is a way for a program to automatically detect whether it is auto-downloaded so it can read the local configuration file if running directly from the hard drive, or a remote configuration file if it was auto-deployed.

To solve this issue, we'll create a class that is a drop-in replacement for `System.Configuration.ConfigurationSettings`, providing transparent access to either the local application configuration file or a remote configuration file, depending on whether the EXE was launched via auto-deployment or directly.

Any application using our new `ConfigurationSettings` class will run as normal when run locally from a hard drive, and will also run just fine when run via auto-deployment.

The final issue is one of security. All auto-deployed code runs in a sandbox and thus will have restricted security clearance. In fact, .NET SP1 precludes running remote code entirely by default. When the .NET Runtime is installed on a client workstation, the installation includes the tools necessary to change security settings for a specific URL, so that we can grant the appropriate level of trust to our remote code and so run safely on the client workstations. Alternatively, you could strongly name your executables and assemblies so that the local client code will specifically allow signed assemblies to execute with enough permissions from that location, This means we don't need to alter the security settings on every client machine. However, strong-naming assemblies is out of scope for this book (for a discussion of strong naming assemblies you might want to refer to VB .NET Class Design Handbook, ISBN 1861007086).

Implementation

The following is the complete code with an explanation for each important section.

Create a new file called `AutoDeploy.vb`, and we'll create two classes in this project – one to launch or load EXE and DLL files via URL, and one to take care of remote application configuration files. Ensure the root namespace has been removed in Visual Studio .NET by inspecting the property pages.

Launcher Class

The `Launcher` class will dynamically create an object from a DLL that is accessible via a URL. It will also include functionality to run an EXE that is accessible via a URL, and will contain the code to work around the bug with deserialization, as mentioned earlier.

As you'll see later, this class can be used to create a generic launcher application, or a shell program, to dynamically run code on the client. The Launcher class itself will run on the client and it auto-downloads any required DLL or EXE files as required. The System.Xml and System.Collections.Specialized namespaces have been imported for use in the next class, but they are shown here:

```
Imports System.Reflection
Imports System.Xml
Imports System.Collections.Specialized

Namespace Wrox.Toolkit.Util
  Public Class Launcher
    Private Sub New()
      ' Prevent instantiation of the class
    End Sub

    Shared Sub New()
      Dim CurrentDomain As AppDomain = AppDomain.CurrentDomain

      AddHandler CurrentDomain.AssemblyResolve, _
        AddressOf MyResolveEventHandler
    End Sub
```

This defines a class that cannot be instantiated; we want this behavior because the methods we'll be adding are shared and so there is no need to create an instance of the Launcher class.

We've also defined a shared constructor. The shared constructor method will be automatically called before any other method on the class is invoked, so we can use it to initialize any members of this class. We'll be defining a handler method later and this attaches the method to the AssemblyResolve event.

Now let's add a shared method to create an object from an auto-deployed DLL. Add this method to the class:

```
Public Shared Function GetObject(ByVal AssemblyURL As String, _
                                 ByVal TypeName As String) _
        As Object

  Dim RemoteAssembly As [Assembly]

  RemoteAssembly = [Assembly].LoadFrom(AssemblyURL)
  Return RemoteAssembly.CreateInstance(TypeName)
End Function
```

This method uses the LoadFrom() method of the Assembly class to load an assembly from a URL. The result of this method call is that the client-side cached assembly version is compared to the version on the URL, and the assembly is automatically downloaded from the server to the client if it isn't present locally, or if the client version is out of date. It is placed in a local cache for the current user. To see what is in the current user's cache we can use the gacutil command-line utility:

```
> gacutil -ldl
```

This will list all the assemblies in the current user's download cache.

Once the assembly has been downloaded, it is also loaded into memory in the current process. This makes all its types available for our use. The final line of code in the method creates an instance of the requested type and returns it as a result.

A similar thing happens when downloading an EXE from a URL. Add the following method to the class:

```
Public Shared Sub RunApplication(ByVal AssemblyURL As String)
    Dim RemoteAssembly As [Assembly]

    RemoteAssembly = [Assembly].LoadFrom(AssemblyURL)
    AppDomain.CurrentDomain.SetData("RemoteEXE", AssemblyURL)
    RemoteAssembly.EntryPoint.Invoke(RemoteAssembly.EntryPoint, _
                                Nothing)
End Sub
```

Again, we are using the `LoadFrom()` method on the `Assembly` class to download the assembly to the client's cache and to load the assembly into memory.

However instead of creating an instance of a specific class, in this case we are launching an application. All .NET applications have a specific method called an **entry point**. The entry point is the method that the .NET runtime calls to launch the application, and the compiler creates it automatically when we build any application. The assembly object dynamically loaded has an `EntryPoint()` method, which returns a reference to this special method. In addition, we have set some data in the current domain to indicate that a remote assembly has been called. This will add further functionality to the application, as we shall see later.

Any DLLs required by this EXE will be automatically downloaded from the same URL by .NET. No extra work or special coding is required for this to happen – it's automatic. Using the `EntryPoint` property, we can call its `Invoke()` method to run that method – effectively launching the application just as if we were the CLR itself. The result is that the application begins running as it would normally.

As we mentioned earlier, auto-deployed code is loaded differently from locally loaded code, and because of a bug in the Soap and Binary formatter objects we are unable to deserialize objects in auto-deployed code without raising an error. Fortunately we can avoid this error by trapping an event on the `AppDomain` object.

Let's add the event handler to the class:

```
Private Shared Function MyResolveEventHandler( _
                    ByVal sender As Object, _
                    ByVal args As ResolveEventArgs) _
                    As [Assembly]
    ' Get a list of all the assemblies loaded in our appdomain
    Dim Assemblies() As [Assembly] = _
        AppDomain.CurrentDomain.GetAssemblies()
```

```
' Search the list to find the assembly that was not found
' and return the assembly from the list
Dim asm As [Assembly]
For Each asm In Assemblies
    If asm.FullName = args.Name Then
        Return asm
    End If
Next
End Function
End Class
```

The problem is that, even though the auto-deployed assembly is loaded into memory, the deserialization code only scans through the list of *locally* loaded assemblies. Thus it is unable to find our dynamically loaded assembly when it tries to do the deserialization.

To overcome this, all we need to do is loop through the list of assemblies loaded in our AppDomain (which *does* include the dynamically loaded ones) and return a reference to the assembly.

When .NET fails to find an assembly, the AppDomain object raises an AssemblyResolve event, allowing us to dynamically resolve the assembly on its behalf. All we have to do is handle this event with the code we just wrote, and that happens in the shared constructor, as shown earlier.

Since the shared constructor is always called before the GetObject() and RunApplication() methods, we can be certain that the class is initialized and the event handler registered before any assemblies are dynamically loaded.

That's the end of this class, but we now need to add another class, ConfigurationSettings, to this namespace.

ConfigurationSettings Class

At this point, we have everything we need to create objects from dynamically loaded and auto-deployed DLLs. We also have everything we need to launch any .NET executable from a URL as long as that program doesn't use an application configuration file.

The thing to consider with configuration files is that they are loaded automatically, and the configuration file is always loaded for the currently running program. This will always be our shell or launcher program, rather than the dynamically loaded EXE.

As mentioned earlier, we're typically auto-deploying our EXE from a web server, and if that web server has ASP.NET installed, then we cannot access any files ending in a .config extension. This file extension is protected so that no one can read a web.config file, for instance. While this is a very good security feature in most cases, it does get in the way when we want to use the configuration file in auto-downloaded code.

What we'll do to overcome these issues is to create a clone of the
ConfigurationSettings class from the .NET Framework, which understands auto-
deployment. If the program has been auto-deployed, this new
ConfigurationSettings class will read a .remoteconfig file from the URL,
instead of trying to read the .config file.

The .remoteconfig file might be created by simply copying an existing .config
file. As implemented here, our code will read the <appSettings> element from the
.remoteconfig file assuming the same syntax as if it were in a regular .config file.

This is the one change that needs to be made to the dynamically launched EXE for it to
work correctly with the launcher code: it will need to use
Wrox.Toolkit.Util.ConfigurationSettings instead of
System.Configuration.ConfigurationSettings. Other than this one small
compromise, we'll have created an infrastructure where any .NET EXE can be launched
via a URL.

Create a new class in this namespace:

```
Imports System.Xml
Imports System.Collections.Specialized
...
    Public Class ConfigurationSettings

    Private Shared LocalCache As NameValueCollection

    Private Sub New()
        ' Prevent instantiation of the class
    End Sub
```

Since the only method on this class will be shared, we're preventing an object from
being created from external code by implementing a private New() method.

We're declaring a shared variable named _Cache as well. The configuration file should
only be read once, since it requires us to go back to the server to get the file. After
we've loaded it the first time, we'll cache the results in this variable.

The only part of the configuration file that we'll support in this case is the
<appSettings> element. Since this is simple XML, we'll just load the remote
configuration file into an XmlDocument and read through it.

Of course we only want to use the remote configuration file in the case that we're
being launched via auto-deployment. Remember that there is no reason the application
can't be run from a local hard drive instead of from a URL, other than this .config file
issue. To make sure it works as expected when run directly from a hard drive, it
should read from a regular .config file. However, when run via auto-download from
a URL, it should read from a .remoteconfig file. This way we not only support both
scenarios, but we have an easy way to have some different application configuration
settings for auto-downloaded code from locally deployed code.

All we need to do now is check to see if the application is being run locally or remotely. Remember that we had a line in the RunApplication() method as follows:

```
AppDomain.CurrentDomain.SetData("RemoteEXE", AssemblyURL)
```

This line of code puts the URL of the remote EXE into the application domain's shared memory space as a name-value pair. The value is now available to any code running in the AppDomain; including the ConfigurationSettings class.

It's time to add some more code to the ConfigurationSettings class. Since we're only dealing with the <appSettings> element, a typical .remoteconfig file might look like this:

```
<?xml version="1.0" encoding="utf-8" ?>
<configuration>
  <appSettings>
    <add key="MyValue" value="Remote" />
  </appSettings>
</configuration>
```

This is no different from what we'd put in a standard .config file, which is good news, since we're trying to keep as much parity as possible between code run locally and code run via a URL.

First, we'll write a method that reads a configuration file's <appSettings> element into a NameValueCollection. The NameValueCollection is the type returned by the usual AppSettings property.

```
Private Shared Function LoadSettings(ByVal config As String) _
                        As NameValueCollection
    Dim col As New NameValueCollection()

    Dim xml As New XmlDocument()
    xml.Load(config)
    Dim root As XmlElement = _
        xml.GetElementsByTagName("configuration").Item(0)
    Dim settings As XmlElement = _
        root.GetElementsByTagName("appSettings").Item(0)

    Dim cmd As XmlElement
    For Each cmd In settings.ChildNodes
        Select Case cmd.Name
            Case "add"
                col.Add(cmd.GetAttribute("key"), _
                        cmd.GetAttribute("value"))
            Case "clear"
                col.Clear()
        End Select
    Next

    Return col
End Function
```

Given the name of a configuration file, this function simply finds the <appSettings> element and uses its instructions to populate a NameValueCollection. This collection is then returned as the result of the function.

Notice that this method is `Private`. Before it is called, we need to determine if we are running directly from the hard drive or via auto-deployment, so we know which `appSettings` to return. If we're running from the hard drive, then we should just use the normal `.config` file, while if we're running from a URL then we should return the `.remoteconfig` file.

Add this property (which has the same method signature as that in the `System.Configuration.ConfigurationSettings` class):

```
Public Shared ReadOnly Property AppSettings As NameValueCollection
   Get
      Dim URL As String = _
      AppDomain.CurrentDomain.GetData("RemoteEXE")

      If Not (URL Is Nothing Or String.Empty) Then
         ' We are running remote exe and need to load config manually
         If LocalCache Is Nothing Then
            Try
               LocalCache = LoadSettings(URL & ".remoteconfig")
            Catch
               LocalCache = New NameValueCollection()
            End Try
         End If

         Return LocalCache
      Else
         ' We are running normally and can just use regular config
         Return _
         System.Configuration.ConfigurationSettings.AppSettings
      End If
   End Get
End Property
End Class
End Namespace
```

This property retrieves the URL of the application (if any) and uses this value to determine if we're running locally or remotely. Remember that this value won't exist unless the program was run via `Launcher` so it can be used to detect if we are local or remote.

If we are remote, the URL is used to derive the name of the `.remoteconfig` file, which is then loaded and the resulting `NameValueCollection` is returned. If we are local, then `AppSettings` from `System.Configuration` is returned.

This can now be compiled as `AutoDeploy.dll`.

Demonstration

To demonstrate how `AutoDeploy` is used, we need to create two projects – a shell launcher application that we'll call `Launcher`, and a test program (`TestApp`) that is launched remotely.

Any shell program can be as simple as a program to launch a remote EXE or a complete client-side application that dynamically loads DLLs via a URL. This shell program must be installed on the client either via a standard setup program, or via XCOPY, and the client machine must already have the .NET Runtime installed as well.

The test program is a simple Windows Forms application; the only difference is that it needs to use `Wrox.Toolkit.Util.ConfigurationSettings`, instead of `System.Configuration.ConfigurationSettings`, to retrieve its `.config` file. For this example, we'll also create a simple class that uses serialization to establish that deserialization works in the code.

This application should be placed in a virtual directory or web directory that is accessible from the client via a URL. From there, it will be auto-downloaded to the client by the CLR.

Create a new Windows Application and name it `TestApp`, renaming `Form1.vb` to `TestApp.vb`, and the `Form1` form to `TestApp`. Add a reference to the `AutoDeploy` assembly through the Add References dialog. Remove the default namespace in the Property pages.

Add a class to the project that contains the following:

```
<Serializable()> _
Public Class SampleObject
  Implements ICloneable
  Private SomeData As Integer

  Public Function Clone() As Object Implements ICloneable.Clone
    Dim Buffer As New IO.MemoryStream()
    Dim MyFormatter As _
      New Runtime.Serialization.Formatters.Binary.BinaryFormatter()

    MyFormatter.Serialize(Buffer, Me)
    Buffer.Position = 0
    Return MyFormatter.Deserialize(Buffer)
  End Function
End Class
```

This is a simple, but serializable class that contains a `Clone()` method that uses deep serialization to make an exact duplicate of the original object.

Now add two buttons to `TestApp` named `btnClone` and `btnConfig`. At the top of `TestApp`, place an `Imports` statement:

```
Imports Wrox.Toolkit.Util
```

Then put the following code behind the two buttons:

```
Private Sub btnClone_Click(ByVal sender As System.Object, _
                           ByVal e As System.EventArgs) _
                           Handles btnClone.Click
  Dim obj As New SampleObject()
```

```
        obj = CType(obj.Clone(), SampleObject)
        MsgBox("Clone worked OK")
    End Sub

    Private Sub btnConfig_Click(ByVal sender As System.Object, _
                                ByVal e As System.EventArgs) _
                                Handles btnConfig.Click

        MsgBox("Config setting: " & _
            ConfigurationSettings.AppSettings ("MyValue"))
    End Sub
```

The first button simply creates an instance of Class1 and clones it – establishing that deserialization works in the auto-deployed code.

The second button retrieves a value from the application configuration file. When auto-downloaded from a URL, it should retrieve the value from the .remoteconfig file, and when run directly from a hard drive, it should retrieve the value from the .config file.

Add an application configuration file to the project in Visual Studio by using Project | Add New Item. Name it TestApp.exe.config and create the following entries:

```
<?xml version="1.0" encoding="utf-8" ?>
<configuration>
  <appSettings>
    <add key="MyValue" value="Run from hard drive" />
  </appSettings>
</configuration>
```

In the Solution Explorer click the Show All Files button so the bin directory is visible, and then move this .config file into this directory. Now hide those files again. Notice that the bin directory remains visible since it now contains a non-hidden file.

Do the same thing to create a TestApp.exe.remoteconfig file in the bin directory with the following:

```
<?xml version="1.0" encoding="utf-8" ?>
<configuration>
  <appSettings>
    <add key="MyValue" value="Auto-deployed from URL" />
  </appSettings>
</configuration>
```

Note the different value in each file.

Now build the solution. Using the Internet Services Manager found under Administrative Tools, create a virtual root or web directory and copy the TestApp\bin directory's contents into that web directory.

Technically the PDB (debug) files are not required, only the DLLs, .config, and .remoteconfig files are needed.

59

Use the .NET Framework Configuration tool found under Administrative Tools to add a security entry for this web directory (URL) and give it a setting of FullTrust. To do this, right-click on the LocalIntranet_Zone entry and choose New to launch a wizard that walks through the process of defining the URL and the trust level desired. The result is a new node in the security configuration:

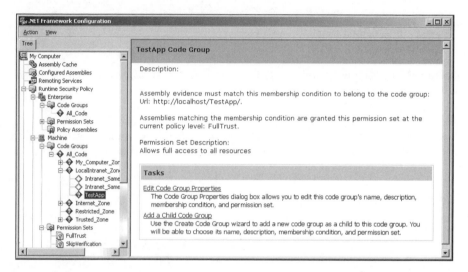

Now we can create a launcher application. Create a new Windows Application project and name it Launcher. Add a reference to the AutoDeploy assembly, and remove the root namespace using the Property pages.

Add a button to Form1 named btnObject and put the following code behind it:

```
Private Sub btnObject_Click(ByVal sender As System.Object, _
                            ByVal e As System.EventArgs) _
                            Handles btnObject.Click

    Wrox.Toolkit.Util.Launcher.RunAppliation( _
    "http://localhost/TestApp/TestApp.exe")

End Sub
```

Change the URL as appropriate to point to the location where your test application resides on the server. Now build and run the program and it will auto-deploy and launch TestApp.exe. Click the buttons on the form to see that serialization and the .remoteconfig file both work as desired.

We can also go to the TestApp\bin directory on the hard drive and run the application by double-clicking on TestApp.exe. In this case, we'll see that the .config file is loaded rather than .remoteconfig.

Limitations

This code requires that security be set up for the URL that contains the remote DLLs or EXE so they run in an appropriate sandbox.

There are obviously some bandwidth considerations here too. When designing an application for auto-deployment, the application should be broken into DLLs, with each one containing related functionality. Remember that DLLs are only downloaded on demand, so with careful design, some users may never have to download DLLs for functionality they don't use.

If an executable is auto-deployed, then that executable needs to use the `Wrox.Toolkit.Util.ConfigurationSettings` class instead of the `System.Configuration.ConfigurationSettings` class to read from its `.config` file. This means that existing applications that use `.config` files will require some change before they will work in an auto-deployment scenario.

Extensions

The benefits of .NET in terms of avoiding "DLL hell" and solving deployment issues are wonderful. However, with just a bit of extra code we can create applications that provide truly zero-touch deployment.

You can use the `GetObject()` method shown here to create a shell application that creates an entirely dynamic menu structure in an MDI window or other UI style. All the code to actually implement the application's functionality can be auto-deployed by calling `GetObject()` to download and create Windows Forms, controls, or business objects as needed.

The `RunApplication()` method shown here can be used to create a simple and generic launcher application that can be used to run any .NET program from a URL. This is a powerful solution, as it allows us to create regular .NET Windows Forms applications and deploy them to clients at essentially no cost.

5

Local/Remote Process Launcher

Windows represents all running applications using a **process** associated with the relevant executable files. Each process is isolated from every other process, so if one program crashes other applications are (usually) unaffected. Therefore, to start another Windows application from within VB.NET we must create a new process.

In the .NET Framework, launching a local process involves using the System.Diagnostics.Process class. If that seems obscure, launching a process on another computer is even more so. Here we develop a pair of classes to programmatically start both local and remote processes.

Scenario

There are many situations where you might want to start another process on the same computer. Microsoft Office applications provide a button in their Help About dialogs that launch the System Information program. A third-party VB.NET text editor needs to launch the VB.NET compiler, vbc.exe. If you're writing a financial application, you may want to provide a menu option to launch Windows Calculator. Finally, if your application contains a web link, you may want to automatically launch a web browser.

Launching programs on another computer is also useful, especially for system administration tasks. Perhaps you need to launch a software installation program on a group of client computers on the network. Rather than going to each computer and starting the process manually, you can remotely start each one over the network.

Technology

The .NET Framework provides the building blocks for starting and controlling processes, but they need to be put together in a useful way. This class uses the `System.Diagnostics.Process` and `ProcessStartInfo` classes to manage local processes, and the `System.Management.ManagementClass` class to manage remote processes.

The `Process` class resides in a slightly unintuitive namespace, `System.Diagnostics`, which sounds like it's for debugging rather than for normal development. Nonetheless, you'll find that it provides lots of support for both controlling and monitoring processes.

Unfortunately, the `Process` class is unable to start a process on a remote computer. For that, we must turn to the Framework's `System.Management` namespace, which provides classes that wrap the **Windows Management Instrumentation** (WMI) API. WMI's `Win32_Process` class, which has methods for starting and terminating processes, is just what we need.

WMI is Microsoft's implementation of the Web-Based Enterprise Management, or WBEM, standard created by the Desktop Management Task Force (DMTF); see http://www.dmtf.org/ for further information. WBEM defines an object-oriented, extensible model for system management known as the Common Information Model, or CIM. The CIM, with Microsoft's WMI extensions, provides access to hardware information, services, performance counters, the file system, registry, and much more. If you need to manage or inspect any area of a Windows system remotely, there's a very good chance you can do it through WMI.

WMI, like .NET, uses the concept of namespaces, and the `Win32_Process` class is located in the "`root\cimv2`" namespace. The namespace can be prefixed with a computer name to access another computer's WMI namespace.

WMI defines dozens of base and derived classes in its object model (which is not related to .NET). Each class can have fields and methods, just like a .NET class. The .NET `ManagementClass` class is used to interact with a WMI class.

Security rights in WMI are also configured per namespace. On Windows NT, 2000, and XP, WMI operates within the contexts of their robust security subsystems, and local and remote access to WMI namespaces uses Windows authentication. On Windows 9x and ME, local access to WMI is not authenticated, but remote access does provide a limited form of security.

WMI is pre-installed with Windows ME, 2000, and XP. For the Win9x and NT 4.0 operating systems, Microsoft offers a free download from its web site.

For another example of using WMI, see the *File System Security* class developed in Chapter 22.

64

Design

Since the underlying code for starting local processes is completely different from that for starting remote processes, it makes sense to split each into its own class: `LocalProcessLauncher` and `RemoteProcessLauncher`.

Since the classes share the common goal of launching a process, they are both derived from an interface called `IProcessLauncher`. The interface defines a method, `Start()`, which must be implemented by each derived class. If you add more functionality that's common to both local and remote processes, you can define additional methods in `IProcessLauncher` or maybe convert it into an abstract class.

Local processes are handled with the `System.Diagnostics.Process` class. The `LocalProcessLauncher` class can start another process and return control immediately, or it can wait for the other process to exit before returning control. To avoid waiting indefinitely, a timeout value can be set, if desired.

For local processes, the class can also capture data that the new process sends to the standard output or standard error streams. The class also defines a delegate that takes a process exit code and output string. Once the class obtains the process's output and exit code, it calls the delegate method, if one has been registered. The caller is free to put any sort of application-specific logic in its implementation of the delegate method.

Remote processes are handled with WMI via `System.Management`. This implementation simply uses the `Win32_Process` WMI class's `Create()` method to launch a process on a specified computer. As discussed previously, the ability to successfully start the remote process depends on the caller's security rights on the remote computer.

Implementation

If you are using Visual Studio .NET, create a new class library and replace `class1.vb` with the code given below, which we'll call `ProcessLauncher.vb`:

```
Imports System
Imports System.IO
Imports System.Diagnostics
Imports System.Management

Namespace Wrox.Toolkit.Util
```

Up front, the code imports the `System.Diagnostics` namespace for `Process` and `ProcessStartInfo`. It also imports `System.Management` for `ManagementClass`; to use this you need to add a reference to the `System.Management.Dll` assembly.

```
Public Interface IProcessLauncher
    Sub Start()
End Interface
```

First, we have the `IProcessLauncher` interface, which defines the `Start()` method that is common to both the local and remote process classes.

```
Public Class LocalProcessLauncher
    Implements IProcessLauncher
```

Next is the `LocalProcessLauncher` class, which implements `IProcessLauncher` and implements its `Start()` method, as you'll see later.

```
Public Enum OutputHandlerTypeEnum
    None
    StandardError
    StandardOutput
End Enum
```

The `OutputHandlerTypeEnum` defines the ways that the class can capture a process's output. The types may not be combined. You can capture standard output, standard error output, or neither.

```
Public Const timedOut As Integer = -1
Public Const waitNone As Integer = -1
Public Const waitInfinite As Integer = 0
```

We define three public constants that are helpful for users of the class. When output is being captured, `timedOut` defines the exit code used if the process doesn't exit before the timeout period expires. If you are not capturing output, `waitNone` causes `Start()` to return immediately after starting the process. Otherwise, `Start()` must wait for the process to exit, so an exception will be thrown if the timeout is `waitNone`. `waitInfinite` indicates that the class should wait indefinitely for the process to exit. Do not directly reference the numeric values of these constants.

```
Private proc As Process = New Process()
Private timeout As Integer = waitNone
Private outHandler As OutputHandler = Nothing
Private outHandlerType As OutputHandlerTypeEnum _
    = OutputHandlerType.None
Public Delegate Sub OutputHandler( _
    ByVal exitCode As Integer, ByVal output As String)
```

Next, we define some private fields; one to maintain an instance of a `Process` object and a timeout that indicates how long, in seconds, to wait for a new process to exit before returning from `Start()`. The class also holds a reference to an output-processing delegate method and an enumeration indicating what, if any, output to capture.

The delegate `OutputHandler()` defines the signature for methods that can work with a process's output data.

```
Public Sub New(ByVal fileName As String)
    Me.New(fileName, Nothing)
End Sub
```

```
Public Sub New(ByVal fileName As String, ByVal args As String)
    Me.New(New ProcessStartInfo(fileName, args))
End Sub
```

Three overloads are defined for the constructor. You may pass New() a filename, a filename and arguments, or a pre-populated ProcessStartInfo object. If the file is not in a directory in the system search path, you must include a complete path and filename. If you are not capturing output, you can specify a document filename instead of an executable filename. Windows will automatically launch the program associated with that file extension.

The New() methods cascade from one to the next, filling in default parameters as necessary. Ultimately, a ProcessStartInfo object is stored in the proc object's StartInfo property.

```
Public Sub New(ByVal startInfo As ProcessStartInfo)
    If startInfo.FileName Is Nothing Then
        Throw New ArgumentNullException("Missing file name.")
    ElseIf startInfo.FileName.Length = 0 Then
        Throw New ArgumentException("Missing file name.")
    End If

    Me.proc.StartInfo = startInfo
End Sub
```

The ProcessStartInfo object must contain, at minimum, a valid filename.

```
Public ReadOnly Property BaseProcess() As Process
    Get
        Return proc
    End Get
End Property
```

The BaseProcess property exposes the internal Process object, which contains properties that expose useful information about a process.

```
Public Property WaitTimeout() As Integer
    Get
        Return timeout
    End Get
    Set(ByVal value As Integer)
        If value < waitNone Then
            Throw New ArgumentOutOfRangeException()
        End If
        timeout = value
    End Set
End Property
```

The WaitTimeout property sets the time, in seconds, that Start() will wait for a process to exit before giving up.

```
Public Sub SetOutputHandler( _
    ByVal type As OutputHandlerTypeEnum, _
    ByVal handler As OutputHandler)
```

```
        If type = OutputHandlerType.None Then
            Me.outHandler = Nothing
        Else
            If handler Is Nothing Then
                Throw New ArgumentNullException("handler")
            End If
            Me.outHandler = handler
        End If
        Me.outHandlerType = type
    End Sub
```

SetOutputHandler() sets the type of output to capture and a handler delegate method. If the type is None, the handler isn't used and it's set to Nothing. Otherwise, the code verifies that the handler is valid, then saves it for later use by the Start() method. In either case, the specified handler type is saved.

```
        Public ReadOnly Property OutputHandlerType() _
            As OutputHandlerTypeEnum
        Get
            Return outHandlerType
        End Get
    End Property
```

The OutputHandlerType property allows read-only access to the current mode of output capture, specified by OutputHandlerTypeEnum.

```
        Public Sub Start() Implements IProcessLauncher.Start
```

The Start() method does all the real work of this class. It starts the process, captures the output, and calls the output handler delegate if necessary.

```
        If outHandlerType = OutputHandlerTypeEnum.None Then
```

First, Start() handles the case where no output capture was requested.

```
        proc.StartInfo.RedirectStandardError = False
        proc.StartInfo.RedirectStandardOutput = False
```

Since the caller may have provided the ProcessStartInfo object, we need to ensure that redirection is disabled.

```
        proc.Start()

        If timeout = waitInfinite Then
            proc.WaitForExit()
        ElseIf timeout <> waitNone Then
            proc.WaitForExit(timeout * 1000)
        End If
```

Next, the new process is started. If an infinite timeout was specified, WaitForExit() will wait indefinitely for the new process to exit. Otherwise, if a valid timeout, in seconds, was specified, the class converts it to milliseconds and passes the value to WaitForExit().

```
Else
        Dim output As String
        Dim outputReader As StreamReader = Nothing
```

In this case, the caller requested that either standard error or standard output be captured. output will hold the captured output, and outputReader will hold a reference to the StreamReader object exposed by the proc object's StandardError or StandardOutput property.

```
If timeout = waitNone Then
    Throw New Exception( _
        "You must specify 'waitInfinite' or a valid timeout " _
        + "when capturing output.")
End If
```

In order to capture output, the class must wait on the process either indefinitely or for a particular length of time. As a result, a timeout of waitNone is invalid, and an exception is thrown if this is the case.

```
If outHandlerType = OutputHandlerTypeEnum.StandardError Then
    proc.StartInfo.UseShellExecute = False
    proc.StartInfo.RedirectStandardError = True
    proc.StartInfo.RedirectStandardOutput = False
Else
    proc.StartInfo.UseShellExecute = False
    proc.StartInfo.RedirectStandardOutput = True
    proc.StartInfo.RedirectStandardError = False
End If
```

In order to capture output, the Process class must receive an executable file path (.exe file extension), not a document file path (.txt, .doc, etc.), and the UseShellExecute property must be set to False. To be safe, the code overrides this property.

```
proc.Start()
```

With the setup done, the new process is started.

```
If outHandlerType = OutputHandlerTypeEnum.StandardError Then
    outputReader = proc.StandardError
Else
    outputReader = proc.StandardOutput
End If
```

To avoid having to repeatedly check the value of outHandlerType, the class saves a reference to StandardError or StandardOutput, both of type StreamReader, in outputReader. This cannot be done until after the new process has been started.

```
If timeout = waitInfinite Then
    output = outputReader.ReadToEnd()
```

69

In the first case, an infinite timeout, the class will wait indefinitely for the process to exit. Before the class begins to wait on the new process, it calls ReadToEnd() on the outputReader object.

If the process writes enough data to the output or error stream to fill a communication buffer, it will block until we read the data. Here, we have already started the new process, and it may have already output lots of data. For that reason, we must call ReadToEnd() before going into a wait state. If we begin to wait and the buffer is already full, the new process will halt until our process clears its output buffer, and our process will halt waiting on the new process. Now, each process is waiting on the other in order to continue, causing a "deadlock".

This is definitely confusing and feels like a workaround, but Microsoft recommends this approach in the documentation. It wouldn't be surprising to see Microsoft address this issue in a future version of the .NET Framework. For more information about this issue, please see the .NET Framework documentation for Process.StandardError or Process.StandardOutput.

```
        proc.WaitForExit()
        outHandler.Invoke(proc.ExitCode, output)
```

The call to WaitForExit() will not return until the process exits. If an output handler was specified, the method must call the delegate method with the process's exit code and output. This is done by calling outHandler.Invoke() with the two required parameters. At that time, the code inside the user-defined handler method will execute.

In the next case, a timeout value was specified, so the class will only wait for the specified number of seconds before giving up and returning control to the caller.

```
        Else
            If proc.WaitForExit(timeout * 1000) Then
                output = proc.StandardOutput.ReadToEnd()
```

First, WaitForExit() is called with the timeout value, converted to milliseconds. The Boolean return value indicates whether the process actually exited before WaitForExit() returned.

As with the code seen earlier, ReadToEnd() is used to read the output data from the outputReader object. In this case, it is not necessary to call ReadToEnd() before WaitForExit() due to the timeout, which makes a deadlock impossible.

```
                outHandler.Invoke(proc.ExitCode, output)
            Else
                output = "Timeout waiting for process to exit."
                outHandler.Invoke(timedOut, output)
            End If
        End If
    End If
    End Sub
End Class
```

Once the process exits or the wait times out, the delegate method is called with the process exit code or the special constant value timedOut.

Next is the second class, RemoteProcessLauncher. This class is quite short, and does its work with WMI via the ManagementClass class. Unlike the preceding class, this one cannot wait for the remote process to exit, nor can it capture the remote process's output.

Please note that security is a factor with this class. As discussed previously, if you do not have permissions to execute a process on the remote computer, the Start() method will fail.

```
Public Class RemoteProcessLauncher
    Implements IProcessLauncher

    Private fileName As String
    Private machineName As String
```

This class must be provided with an executable filename (or full path) and a computer name or IP address. For demonstration purposes, the computer name may be set to "localhost" to use the local computer.

```
Public Sub New( _
    ByVal fileName As String, ByVal machineName As String)
    If fileName Is Nothing Or machineName Is Nothing Then
        Throw New ArgumentNullException()
    ElseIf fileName.Length = 0 Or machineName.Length = 0 Then
        Throw New ArgumentException( _
            "Missing file name or machine name.")
    End If
    Me.fileName = fileName
    Me.machineName = machineName
End Sub
```

The Start() method first creates a new instance of a .NET ManagementClass object. The constructor takes a WMI scope (where to look), a WMI class name, and an ObjectGetOptions object, which can specify settings such as an operation timeout.

```
Public Sub Start() Implements IProcessLauncher.Start
    Dim proc As New ManagementClass( _
        "\\" & machineName & "\root\cimv2", _
        "Win32_Process", New ObjectGetOptions())
```

The standard path for a WMI scope is "\\<computername>\root\cimv2", and the provided computer name is substituted in the scope string. The Win32_Process WMI class allows us to start a process, and, since we have no special options, a default ObjectGetOptions() instance is used.

```
Dim result As Object = _
    proc.InvokeMethod( _
        "Create", New Object() {fileName, Nothing, Nothing, 0})
```

As mentioned earlier, a WMI class can have methods and properties. Since we are accessing the WMI class indirectly through `ManagementClass`, the `InvokeMethod()` method is used to call `Win32_Process.Create()`, which starts a new process.

The second parameter to `InvokeMethod()` is `Create()`'s parameter list, and it's passed as an array of `Objects`. The first parameter is the executable name or path. The remaining parameters, unused here, include a startup directory, process configuration data, and process ID.

```
        If Convert.ToString(result) <> "0" Then
            Throw New Exception( _
                "Remote process start failed. WMI error code is " _
                + Convert.ToString(result) + ".")
        End If
      End Sub
    End Class
End Namespace
```

Unless the return value from `Create()` (via `InvokeMethod()`) equals "0", the remote process failed to start and an exception is thrown.

It is worth remembering that if WMI isn't installed on the remote machine a `System.Management.ManagementException` is thrown, which you should catch in any client code.

Demonstration

To use this example, create a new VB Console Application project and replace the contents of `Module1.vb` with the code below.

First, you must import `System.Diagnostics` for the `ProcessStartInfo` class and `Wrox.Toolkit.Util` for the `LocalProcessLauncher` and `RemoteProcessLauncher` classes.

```
Imports System
Imports System.Diagnostics
Imports Wrox.Toolkit.Util

Module MainModule
```

In order to capture and process the standard output or standard error output of a local process, you must implement a `Sub` with the same method signature as the `LocalProcessLauncher.OutputHandler` delegate. Here, the `PrintOutput()` method simply prints the exit code and output to the console.

```
    Private Sub PrintOutput( _
        ByVal exitCode As Integer, ByVal output As String)
        Console.WriteLine("Output:")
        Console.WriteLine(output)
```

```
Console.WriteLine()
    Console.WriteLine("Exit code: {0}", exitCode)
End Sub
```

This application demonstrates the RemoteProcessLauncher class and four different ways to use the LocalProcessLauncher class. It displays a menu that lets you easily test each case.

```
Sub Main()
    Dim quit As Boolean = False
    Dim choice As String
    Dim wininiPath As String
```

For the purposes of this demonstration, the class builds a path to the WIN.INI file using the Windows directory path in the WINDIR environment variable.

```
winIniPath = _
    System.Environment.GetEnvironmentVariable("WINDIR")
winIniPath += "\win.ini"

Try
    While Not quit
        Console.WriteLine("Menu:")
        Console.WriteLine("1 for Local - Doc filename")
        Console.WriteLine("2 for Local - EXE name")
        Console.WriteLine("3 for Local - ProcessStartInfo")
        Console.WriteLine("4 for Local - Get Standard Output")
        Console.WriteLine("5 for Remote")
        Console.WriteLine("Q to quit")
        Console.WriteLine()
        Console.WriteLine("Type your selection and press Enter:")

        choice = Console.ReadLine()
        Select Case choice
```

The first case uses Windows' file associations to automatically launch the program associated with .INI files. Instead of an executable name, WIN.INI is passed in as the file name.

Using the BaseProcess property to obtain the Process object, and then a ProcessStartInfo object, the UseShellExecute property is set to True. This tells Process to let Windows figure out what program to launch.

```
Case "1"
    Dim localProc _
        As New LocalProcessLauncher(winIniPath)
    localProc.BaseProcess.StartInfo.UseShellExecute = True
    localProc.Start()
```

The second case simply launches Notepad with WIN.INI as an argument.

```
Case "2"
    Dim localProc As New LocalProcessLauncher( _
        "notepad.exe", winIniPath)
    localProc.Start()
```

The third case sets up a new `ProcessStartInfo` object with the same parameters as the previous case. The object is passed directly to `LocalProcessLauncher`'s `New()` method.

```
Case "3"
    Dim startInfo As New ProcessStartInfo()
    startInfo.FileName = "notepad.exe"
    startInfo.Arguments = winIniPath
    Dim localProc As New LocalProcessLauncher(startInfo)
    localProc.Start()
```

The fourth case is a bit more interesting. A new `LocalProcessLauncher` is created to run the DOS command shell, `COMMAND.COM`, with one parameter that causes it to execute the command `"DIR C:\"` and then exit.

```
Case "4"
    Dim localProc _
        As New LocalProcessLauncher( _
        "command.com", "/c dir c:\")
```

The program wants to capture and print the directory listing, so it tells the `localProc` object to capture standard output for the process. It passes a reference to the `PrintOutput()` method discussed earlier by using the `AddressOf` operator.

Next, it tells the object to wait indefinitely for the process to exit. Instead of `waitInfinite`, you could set the number of seconds `LocalProcessLauncher` should wait before giving up and returning from `Start()`. In the case of a timeout, the standard output would be lost.

```
localProc.SetOutputHandler( _
    LocalProcessLauncher. _
        OutputHandlerTypeEnum.StandardOutput, _
    AddressOf PrintOutput)
localProc.WaitTimeout = _
    LocalProcessLauncher.waitInfinite
localProc.Start()
```

Finally, `RemoteProcessLauncher` is used to start a remote process. If you have a second computer, change `"localhost"` to the second computer's name. If you don't have a second computer, using `localhost` to reference your local computer will still allow you to try the demo, but you will incur extra overhead from WMI.

```
Case "5"
    Dim remoteProc As _
        New RemoteProcessLauncher( _
            "c:\windows\notepad.exe", "localhost")
    remoteProc.Start()

    Case "Q", "q"
        quit = True
    End Select
End While
Catch e As Exception
    Console.WriteLine("An exception occurred: " + e.Message)
End Try
End Sub
End Module
```

Limitations

LocalProcessLauncher doesn't contain many significant limitations that aren't present in Process itself as it just builds on and exposes the functionality of Process, without imposing any particular restrictions of its own.

Due to the way that the Process class reads a process's output, it's a bit tricky to handle both standard output and standard error at the same time. That's why, for simplicity, this class only includes one handler. Reading both streams from a single thread may cause the existing and new processes to block on each other. See the .NET Framework documentation for the Process.StandardOutput or StandardError properties for more information.

RemoteProcessLauncher is somewhat limited by its inability to provide the same set of features and information available to local processes. For instance, the current implementation cannot return the output of the remote process. Some of these issues could be addressed with the Win32_Process WMI class's public fields, which include many additional process details.

Extensions

As mentioned previously, the current implementation of LocalProcessLauncher can use only one output handler at a time due to the blocking issues discussed above and in the product documentation. This limitation could be overcome by starting up a new thread for each handler that waits for the output, returns it, and then exits. Also by introducing multiple threads and quite a bit more complexity, the class could be extended to read from multiple output streams at once.

In RemoteProcessLauncher's Start() method, it's possible to provide a few more configuration settings to a remote process with Win32_Process.Create(). The Win32_ProcessStartup WMI class can be created, configured, and passed as an additional parameter to Create().

Command-Line Argument Parser

Before VB.NET, Visual Basic didn't directly support text-based console applications. These applications don't have a GUI, and visibly look like old DOS applications (remember those?). An example of a console application is vbc.exe, the VB.NET compiler.

Unless you were willing to resort to some tricks and hassles, console applications were only available to C/C++ developers. Fortunately, VB.NET comes with built-in support and provides the Console Application project template to get you started.

If you're building a console application, you'll probably need to work with command-line parameters. This class will help you do that with minimal effort.

Scenario

The possible applications for the Argument Parser class are almost limitless. Unless your console application is extremely simple or reads all of its settings from a configuration file, it's going to require command-line argument processing.

Visual Studio .NET and the .NET Framework include dozens of console applications. Some examples include devenv.com, the command-line interface for the Visual Studio .NET IDE, vbc.exe, the VB.NET compiler, and ilasm.exe, the IL Assembler. Many of these console applications are particularly useful for unattended batch processing.

You'll have a specific list of valid **switches**, and some of those switches will require **parameters**. You may need to ensure that parameters are of a certain data type, such as numeric or alphabetic. This class will help you avoid rewriting lots of code every time you build a new application.

The example I'll discuss later will demonstrate the class's flexibility and give you an idea of how you can use it in your own applications.

Technology

It doesn't get much attention these days, but all versions of Windows still have a text-only command-line interface, usually called the **Command Prompt**. In Windows NT, 2000, and XP you can open a command prompt by executing cmd.exe. In Windows 9x, the command prompt is called command.com.

As one example, network administrators often use command-line applications to automate and accelerate common tasks. Microsoft has continued to expand the number of system tasks that can be accomplished without a GUI.

Windows can run many old DOS applications in a command prompt, but a true "console application" is a different animal. A console application is actually a full-blown Windows application, minus all the fancy graphics and windows. Console applications can use all the same (non-graphical) Windows API calls as regular Windows GUI applications.

When you run a console application, you can specify arguments to the program. Windows divides the arguments into an array and then hands them to the application's Main() method. It's up to the application to decipher and act on them.

Finally, it's important to note that Windows GUI applications can also accept command-line parameters, though most don't. One example is ildasm.exe, the IL Disassembler included with the .NET Framework SDK.

Design

This class was designed to provide the following features:

- ❑ A reusable and extensible base class
- ❑ Verification of an argument against a list of valid switches
- ❑ Enforcement of a required parameter on a switch
- ❑ Data type validation of a switch parameter
- ❑ Custom switch and parameter separation characters

First, let's define some terms. A typical command-line parameter list might look like this:

```
CommandLineApp.exe /sw1 /sw2:param1 /sw3
```

sw1, sw2, and sw3 are switches, and param1 is a parameter to a switch, in this case sw2. A switch is a directive to the application to do something, set a flag, etc. A parameter provides additional information that may be needed to process a switch. You'll see these terms used over and over throughout this discussion.

An abstract base class, ArgumentParser, does most of the work, and is marked as MustInherit. An abstract class cannot be instantiated, so your application must implement a class that inherits from ArgumentParser and completes its implementation.

Your derived class will contain application-specific handling of each switch and any error conditions. This keeps virtually all switch processing contained in one class instead of scattered throughout your code. Your class will typically expose a set of read-only properties that provide data derived from the command-line switches and parameters to the rest of the application.

The derived class must override the protected constructor New() and call one of the overloaded Initialize() methods to define valid switches, indicate whether they require parameters, and so on. It must also implement OnValidSwitch(), which has to recognize every valid switch and do some additional processing each time it's called. For example, it might set a flag or save a parameter to a field that's exposed via a public property.

Often you'll want to implement OnInvalidSwitch(), OnInvalidParameter(), and OnUnknownSwitch() to handle error conditions. Don't worry – all of these methods will be explained in detail later.

A class called SwitchDefinition defines all the information about a particular switch. ArgumentParser contains an array of SwitchDefinition objects that it uses to validate switches and parameters, and your override of New() will create these objects. SwitchDefinition also uses two enumerations to define whether parameters are optional or required and their data types.

Figure 1 is a UML class diagram that shows the relationships between the ArgumentParser and SwitchDefinition classes and the enumerations ParamModeEnum and ParamDataTypeEnum.

Figure 1

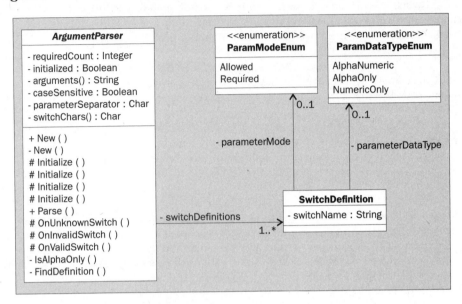

Your application must call the Parse() method of the ArgumentParser class, which does all the hard work. Parse() will call the overridden methods mentioned above during its main loop.

Implementation

Enough discussion – let's have a look at the code. To get started, create a new VB.NET class file named ArgumentParser.vb and replace its contents with the code below:

```
Imports System
Imports Microsoft.VisualBasic

Namespace Wrox.Toolkit.Util
```

As discussed earlier, the SwitchDefinition class defines each individual switch. It doesn't make sense for this class to be reused, so it's marked NotInheritable. The class contains the definitions of two enumerations, ParamDataTypeEnum and ParamModeEnum, which are used to indicate what data type is valid for a parameter and whether a switch requires parameters:

```
Public NotInheritable Class SwitchDefinition

    Public Enum ParamDataTypeEnum
        AlphaOnly
        NumericOnly
        AlphaNumeric
    End Enum
```

```
Public Enum ParamModeEnum
    Required
    Allowed
End Enum
```

Next we declare three private variables to hold the switch name, parameter mode, and parameter data type:

```
Private switchName As String
Private parameterMode As ParamModeEnum
Private parameterDataType As ParamDataTypeEnum
```

The class provides default values for most of its options. It overloads the New() constructor with varying numbers of parameters, calling one method after another until all parameters have been provided. A user of this class can choose to provide all or some of the required parameters, which helps to reduce complexity.

A switch name is always required, but the parameter mode and data type default to allow (not require) a parameter, and to allow data containing any alphanumeric characters:

```
Public Sub New(ByVal name As String)
  Me.New(name, ParamModeEnum.Allowed)
End Sub

Public Sub New(ByVal name As String, _
    ByVal parameterMode As ParamModeEnum)

  Me.New(name, parameterMode, ParamDataTypeEnum.AlphaNumeric)
End Sub

Public Sub New(ByVal name As String, _
    ByVal parameterMode As ParamModeEnum, _
    ByVal parameterDataType As ParamDataTypeEnum)

  If name Is Nothing Then
    Throw New ArgumentNullException("name")
  ElseIf name.Length = 0 Then
    Throw New ArgumentException("Name may not be empty.")
  End If

  Me.switchName = name
  Me.parameterMode = parameterMode
  Me.parameterDataType = parameterDataType
End Sub
```

To complete the class, three properties allow read-only access to the switch name, parameter mode, and parameter data type:

```
Public ReadOnly Property Name() As String
  Get
    Return switchName
  End Get
End Property

Public ReadOnly Property ParamMode() As ParamModeEnum
  Get
    Return parameterMode
```

```
        End Get
    End Property

    Public ReadOnly Property ParamDataType() As ParamDataTypeEnum
        Get
            Return parameterDataType
        End Get
    End Property
End Class
```

The `ArgumentParser` class is the star of this show. It does all the interesting work and serves as the foundation for your application-specific derived class. The class is marked `MustInherit`, and therefore cannot be directly instantiated since it is abstract. It does, however, contain a partial implementation of the code, which is to be completed by the derived class.

The class defines a number of private variables that contain definitions of all valid switches, a list of characters that a switch can begin with, the character used to separate a switch from its parameters, and a flag to indicate whether switches are case-sensitive. In addition, other variables contain the original array of command-line arguments provided to the `Main()` method and indicate whether the class has been initialized:

```
Public MustInherit Class ArgumentParser

    Private switchDefinitions() As SwitchDefinition = Nothing
    Private switchChars() As Char = Nothing
    Private parameterSeparator As Char = ":"
    Private caseSensitive As Boolean = False
    Private arguments() As String = Nothing
    Private initialized As Boolean = False
```

The default constructor is defined as `Private` to prevent its use by anyone outside of this class, including derived classes. The only valid constructor accepts the array of command-line arguments passed into the `Main()` method. Despite the fact that a constructor exists on the class, VB.NET will not allow the class to be created due to the `MustInherit` keyword. Your derived class must override the public constructor in order to define a list of valid switches:

```
    Private Sub New()
    End Sub

    Public Sub New(ByVal arguments() As String)
        If arguments Is Nothing Then
            Throw New ArgumentNullException()
        End If

        Me.arguments = arguments
    End Sub
```

The following code should look similar to the `New()` methods in `SwitchDefinition`. `Initialize()` is overloaded to simplify the list of parameters as much as possible, and the methods cascade until all parameters have been explicitly specified:

```
Public Overloads Sub Initialize( _
    ByVal switchDefinitions() As SwitchDefinition)

    MyClass.Initialize(switchDefinitions, New Char() {"/", "-"})
End Sub

Public Overloads Sub Initialize( _
    ByVal switchDefinitions() As SwitchDefinition, _
    ByVal switchCharArray As Char())

    MyClass.Initialize(switchDefinitions, switchCharArray, False)
End Sub

Public Overloads Sub Initialize( _
    ByVal switchDefinitions() As SwitchDefinition, _
    ByVal switchCharArray As Char(), _
    ByVal caseSensitive As Boolean)

    MyClass.Initialize(switchDefinitions, switchCharArray, _
        caseSensitive, ":")
End Sub

Public Overloads Sub Initialize( _
    ByVal switchDefinitions() As SwitchDefinition, _
    ByVal switchCharArray() As Char, _
    ByVal caseSensitive As Boolean, _
    ByVal parameterSeparator As Char)
```

The final overload of the Initialize() method does some basic validation on its two array parameters to ensure that they are not equal to Nothing. It also uses the Rank property on the arrays to verify that they are one-dimensional:

```
If switchDefinitions Is Nothing _
    Or switchCharArray Is Nothing Then
    Throw New ArgumentNullException( _
        "switchDefinitions and/or switchCharArray")
ElseIf switchDefinitions.Rank <> 1 _
    Or switchCharArray.Rank <> 1 Then
    Throw New ArgumentException( _
        "Arrays must be one-dimensional.")
End If

Me.switchDefinitions = switchDefinitions
Me.switchChars = switchCharArray
Me.caseSensitive = caseSensitive
Me.parameterSeparator = parameterSeparator
```

Now the object is fully initialized and ready to go, so initialized is set to True. The Parse() method will throw an exception if it is called when initialized equals False:

```
Me.initialized = True
End Sub
```

You'll want to override the following methods to provide application-specific handling of each event. When a switch is recognized and passes all validations, OnValidSwitch() is called. When a switch begins with a valid switch character but is not recognized, or if it fails validation, OnInvalidSwitch() is called. When a valid switch is recognized but it has an invalid parameter separator or is missing a required parameter, OnInvalidParameter() is called. Finally, if an argument does not begin with a valid switch character, OnUnknownSwitch() is called.

In your derived class, you can return False in any of these methods to indicate an error condition. The base class will throw an appropriate exception:

```
Protected Overridable Function OnValidSwitch( _
    ByVal switch As String, ByVal parameter As String) As Boolean
  Return False
End Function

Protected Overridable Function OnInvalidSwitch( _
    ByVal argument As String) As Boolean
  Return False
End Function

Protected Overridable Function OnInvalidParameter( _
    ByVal switch As String, ByVal argument As String) As Boolean
  Return False
End Function

Protected Overridable Function OnUnknownSwitch( _
    ByVal argument As String) As Boolean
  Return False
End Function
```

The Parse() method is called by your main application in order to analyze the command-line argument list and compare it with the list of defined switches:

```
Public Sub Parse()
  Dim argument, switch, remainder As String
  Dim switchDef As SwitchDefinition = Nothing
```

An error condition will result in an exception being thrown. If the class has not been initialized by calling Initialize() from an override of the public constructor, Parse() immediately throws an exception:

```
If Not initialized Then
  Throw New Exception("The class has not been initialized. " _
    + "The overload of New() must call Initialize().")
End If
```

First, the method begins a loop through each argument in the argument array:

```
For Each argument In arguments
```

The first validation determines whether the first character of the argument is contained in the list of valid switch characters. If not, it is considered an "unknown" switch.

If the overridden OnUnknownSwitch() method returns False, an exception is thrown. If the method overrides the error by returning True, no exception occurs. This pattern is used to handle errors throughout the code below:

```
If Array.IndexOf(switchChars, argument.Chars(0)) < 0 Then
    If OnUnknownSwitch(argument) = False Then
        Throw New Exception("Unknown switch: " + argument)
    End If
```

If a valid switch character was found, the next step is to search for a switch definition that matches the argument using FindDefinition(). If no match is found, OnInvalidSwitch() is called.

Otherwise, FindDefinition() returns the switch and any text following it into switch and remainder. The remainder will contain any parameters passed with the switch. Finally, ParseParameter() is called to validate the parameter, if present:

```
Else
    switchDef = FindDefinition(argument, switch, remainder)

    If Not switchDef Is Nothing Then
        ParseParameter(argument, switch, remainder, switchDef)
    Else
        If OnInvalidSwitch(argument) = False Then
            Throw New Exception("Invalid switch: " + argument)
        End If
    End If
    End If
Next
End Sub
```

If Parse() finds a valid switch, it calls ParseParameter() to validate any parameter that may have been passed along with the switch:

```
Private Sub ParseParameter(ByVal argument As String, _
    ByVal switch As String, ByVal remainder As String, _
    ByVal switchDef As SwitchDefinition)

    Dim validParam As Boolean = False
```

First, the code determines whether the switch requires a parameter. If it does, and no parameter is present, the switch is in error and OnInvalidParameter() is called:

```
If (remainder Is Nothing OrElse remainder.Length = 0) _
    And switchDef.ParamMode = _
        SwitchDefinition.ParamModeEnum.Required Then
    If OnInvalidParameter(switch, argument) = False Then
        Throw New Exception("Missing required parameter for '" _
            + switch + "': " + argument)
    End If
Else
```

So far so good! If we've reached this point, a parameter is not required. If there isn't one specified, the switch is valid. If a parameter is present and data validation is required, the code needs to validate the parameter:

```
If remainder Is Nothing Then
    If OnValidSwitch(switch, remainder) = False Then
        Throw New Exception("Invalid switch: " + switch)
    End If
Else
```

The code checks to see whether the first character of the parameter matches the parameter separator, and whether there is more text in the parameter other than the separator. If either case fails, OnInvalidParameter() is called in the Else block you'll see later:

```
If remainder.Chars(0) = parameterSeparator _
    And remainder.Length > 1 Then
    remainder = remainder.Substring(1)
```

The last set of validations checks the data type of the parameter, if a specific requirement was defined by the application. The IsNumeric() and IsAlphaOnly() helper methods take care of the data type validation:

```
Select Case switchDef.ParamDataType
    Case SwitchDefinition.ParamDataTypeEnum.NumericOnly
        validParam = IsNumeric(remainder)
    Case SwitchDefinition.ParamDataTypeEnum.AlphaOnly
        validParam = IsAlphaOnly(remainder)
    Case Else
        validParam = True
End Select
```

If the parameter was deemed valid, OnValidSwitch() is called. Otherwise, OnInvalidParameter() is called:

```
If validParam Then
    If OnValidSwitch(switch, remainder) = False Then
        Throw New Exception("Invalid switch: " + switch)
    End If
Else
    If OnInvalidParameter(switch, argument) = False Then
        Throw New Exception("Invalid parameter for '" _
            + switch + "': " + argument)
    End If
End If
    Else
        If OnInvalidSwitch(argument) = False Then
            Throw New Exception("Invalid switch: " + switch)
        End If
    End If
End If
End If
End Sub
```

The `FindDefinition()` method loops through all of the switch definition objects and compares each switch name with the beginning of the argument string, either case-sensitive or not. If it finds a match, it returns the corresponding definition object and the remainder of the argument following the switch, if any. Performance is not a concern since the list of switches is generally small, and the code only executes once as the application starts up:

```
Private Function FindDefinition(ByVal argument As String, _
    ByRef switch As String, ByRef remainder As String) _
    As SwitchDefinition

    Dim tempArgument As String
    Dim tempName As String
    Dim switchDef As switchDefinition = Nothing
```

To avoid having to repeat the string comparison code twice, once for case-sensitive and once for case-insensitive, a temporary variable is used to hold the argument in the correct case. This pattern is also used for the switch name:

```
    If caseSensitive Then
        tempArgument = argument
    Else
        tempArgument = argument.ToLower()
    End If

    For Each switchDef In switchDefinitions
        If caseSensitive Then
            tempName = switchDef.Name.ToLower()
        Else
            tempName = switchDef.Name
        End If
```

`CompareOrdinal()` is used to compare the beginning of the argument, skipping the switch character, with a switch name. If a match is found, any additional text in the argument that follows the switch is copied into `remainder`:

```
        If String.CompareOrdinal( _
            tempArgument, 1, tempName, 0, tempName.Length) = 0 Then
            If tempArgument.Length > tempName.Length + 1 Then
                remainder = argument.Substring(tempName.Length + 1)
            Else
                remainder = Nothing
            End If
```

Finally, `Substring()` is used to separate the switch from the original argument, and the `SwitchDefinition` object is returned to the caller:

```
            switch = argument.Substring(1, tempName.Length)
            Return switchDef
        End If
    Next

    Return Nothing
End Function
```

`IsAlphaOnly()` simply loops through each character in the parameter string. If any character is not a letter, the method returns `False`:

```
Private Function IsAlphaOnly(ByVal parameter As String) As Boolean
    Dim index As Integer

    For index = 0 To parameter.Length - 1
        If Not Char.IsLetter(parameter.Chars(index)) Then
            Return False
        End If
    Next

    Return True
End Function
End Class
End Namespace
```

Demonstration

Now that you've seen the code for `ArgumentParser`, the following class will demonstrate how you can build an application-specific class that derives from it.

The general process is as follows: derive a new class from `ArgumentParser` and override the `New()` method with code to initialize the set of valid switches and parameters. Next, override `OnValidSwitch()`, `OnInvalidSwitch()`, `OnInvalidParameter()`, and `OnUnknownSwitch()`, with code to handle valid, invalid, or unknown switches and to provide usage help. Finally, add fields and properties to the class to expose information based on the switches and parameters to the rest of the application.

To begin, create a new VB.NET Console Application project, rename `Module1.vb` to `ArgumentParserTest.vb`, and replace its contents with the following code:

```
Imports System
Imports Wrox.Toolkit.Util

Module MainModule

    Public Class MyArgumentParser
        Inherits ArgumentParser
```

You should define a set of private fields that will be set based on which switches are present, and what parameters they have, if any. These fields will be exposed as read-only public properties that your application code can use:

```
Private num As String = ""
Private text As String = ""
```

Next, provide an override for the constructor that simply passes the argument list provided to the Main() method to the constructor of the base class. You also need to set up your custom, application-specific switch definitions, and you're free to call any of the base class overloads of Initialize(). In this example, I've defined a few switches using SwitchDefinition's overloaded constructors to simplify the code:

```
Public Sub New(ByVal arguments() As String)
    MyBase.New(arguments)

    Dim switchDefs(2) As SwitchDefinition
```

The following code defines a switch named text that requires a parameter:

```
    switchDefs(0) = New SwitchDefinition("text", _
        SwitchDefinition.ParamModeEnum.Required)
```

This defines a switch named num that allows an optional numeric parameter:

```
    switchDefs(1) = New SwitchDefinition("num", _
        SwitchDefinition.ParamModeEnum.Allowed, _
        SwitchDefinition.ParamDataTypeEnum.NumericOnly)
```

Finally, this defines a switch named ? that uses all of SwitchDefinition's defaults:

```
    switchDefs(2) = New SwitchDefinition("?")

    MyBase.Initialize(switchDefs)
End Sub
```

OnValidSwitch() is where you will process each valid switch and set your private fields as necessary. A Select...Case based on the switch is a good way to implement this method. You may force a switch to be treated as an error by returning False, causing the base class to throw an exception:

```
Protected Overrides Function OnValidSwitch( _
    ByVal switch As String, ByVal parameter As String) As Boolean

    Select Case switch
        Case "num"
            num = "Recognized num switch."
        Case "text"
            text = "Recognized text switch w/ required parameter '" _
                + parameter + "'."
        Case "?"
            ShowUsage()
        Case Else
            ShowUsage()
            Return False
    End Select

    Return True
End Function
```

89

You should override the `OnInvalidSwitch()`, `OnInvalidParameter()`, and/or `OnUnknownSwitch()` methods to handle error conditions:

```
Protected Overrides Function OnInvalidSwitch( _
    ByVal argument As String) As Boolean

    ShowUsage()
    Console.WriteLine()
    Console.WriteLine("Invalid switch: {0}", argument)
    Return False
End Function

Protected Overrides Function OnInvalidParameter( _
    ByVal switch As String, ByVal argument As String) As Boolean

    ShowUsage()
    Console.WriteLine()
    Console.WriteLine("Invalid switch parameter: {0}", argument)
    Return False
End Function

Protected Overrides Function OnUnknownSwitch( _
    ByVal argument As String) As Boolean

    ShowUsage()
    Console.WriteLine()
    Console.WriteLine("Unknown switch: {0}\n", argument)
    Return False
End Function
```

Implement `ShowUsage()` to print out some usage instructions for the user, as shown:

```
Private Sub ShowUsage()
    Console.WriteLine( _
        "ArgumentParserTest.exe [/num] [/text:<param>]")
    Console.WriteLine("Usage: ... etc. etc.")
End Sub
```

The following properties expose information derived from the switches and parameters to the rest of the application:

```
Public ReadOnly Property MyNum()
    Get
        Return num
    End Get
End Property

Public ReadOnly Property MyText()
    Get
        Return text
    End Get
End Property
End Class
```

Finally, to use the class, simply create a new instance of your derived class in the `Main()` method, passing the argument array directly from the `Main()` method's single parameter. Call the `Parse()` method, then use the class's properties to determine which switches were present and their parameter values:

```
Function Main(ByVal CmdArgs() As String) As Integer
    Dim parser As New MyArgumentParser(CmdArgs)

    Try
        parser.Parse()

        If Not parser.MyNum = Nothing Then
            Console.WriteLine(parser.MyNum)
        End If

        If Not parser.MyText = Nothing Then
            Console.WriteLine(parser.MyText)
        End If
    Catch e As Exception
        Console.WriteLine("An exception occurred: " + e.Message)
    End Try
End Function

End Module
```

Here are a couple of sample inputs and outputs executed at a command prompt:

```
> ArgumentParserTest.exe /num /text:abc
Recognized num switch.
Recognized text switch w/ required parameter 'abc'.


> ArgumentParserTest.exe /num /text
ArgumentParserTest.exe [/num] [/text:<param>]
Usage: ... etc. etc.

Invalid switch parameter: /text
An exception occurred: Missing required parameter for 'text': /text
```

Limitations

The nice thing about this class is that it is completely free of worries about scalability and performance. Because the class is only used once during an application's startup, performance is not critical.

The class uses For Each loops instead of optimized searches, which could be considered a limitation. However, the number of switches is often so small that a faster search algorithm would provide no benefit.

There are few limitations, as the class provides only simple numeric or alphabetical parameter validation, and allows only one parameter separator to be specified.

More importantly, the class does not allow you to specify that a particular switch is required.

Extensions

While the class already provides most of the functionality you're likely to need, there are a few ways you might want to extend it.

First, you may want to add support for required switches. The class supports required or optional parameters to switches, but can not enforce the presence of the switches themselves.

The data type validation could be expanded to encompass not just numeric versus alphabetical data, but also structural validation using regular expressions. The .NET Framework provides built-in support for regular expressions in the `System.Text.RegularExpressions` namespace. You could use the regular expression classes to validate the ordering and structure of each parameter.

You might also consider the addition of switch aliases. For instance, you may want to have a long, verbose switch and a short, brief switch that are logically equivalent. For example, `/quiet` and `/q`.

VB.NET

Solutions

Toolkit

GUI and Graphics

Validation Textbox

In almost every modern application, at some point a user has to input some type of information. This is usually done through a textbox of some kind. The information must then be validated by the application before being processed or saved to a data store, in order to maintain data integrity or to prevent any errors. For many standard types of data, the code to perform validation rarely changes The `ValidationTextbox` control that we will be developing in this chapter will use some of Visual Basic .NET's new features to encapsulate all your text validation code in one place, providing you with a flexible and reusable class and the ability to modify the validation requirements with very little impact on already compiled code. This class will provide essentially the same benefits as the new Web Forms Validation controls but will be implemented differently.

Scenario

A better way to prevent the user from entering invalid characters is to provide "instant feedback" on whether the key pressed is a valid one or not. Although this will not prevent your users from entering invalid information in any given field, it will stop them from entering invalid characters. Ensuring that the information typed in by a user is correct can be achieved by either providing them with default values or through the use of prompts.

A common example of text validation is when you want to limit the user to entering numerical values within your input field. If you have done this before, you might have developed a method that you call from the `KeyPress` event of a textbox (or combo box) and that performs the necessary validation. If you have several input fields within a form, adding this functionality to each can be repetitive and time consuming.

Technology

To develop our `ValidationTextbox` class we will be calling upon the following classes:

- ❑ `System.Windows.Forms.TextBox`
- ❑ `System.Globalization.NumberFormatInfo`

Since we want our `ValidationTextbox` control to function in the same basic manner as a normal textbox control to which we have added some functionality, we will inherit our class from the `System.Windows.Forms.TextBox` class.

In different parts of the world, different symbols may be used to represent common informational values. These values, whether numbers, currency, dates, or times can even sometimes use completely different character sets. The .NET Framework provides us with a number of namespaces to enable us to globalize our applications. You can make use these namespaces to make sure that you are using the right symbol or format for any user no matter where they reside in the world. The local preferences of a user can be found in the Regional Settings of the Windows Control Panel. Since we will code our `ValidationTextbox` to test for the correct formatting of numeric information, we will be using the `System.Globalization.NumberFormatInfo` class to check a user's local preferences (for example, for the particular character use as a decimal point or for the negative symbol).

Design

Through the use of inheritance, we are able to extend the base `System.Windows.Forms.TextBox` class. The `ValidationTextbox` will therefore encapsulate all the features of the class from which it inherits, while allowing us to extend its functionality.

The class will be compiled in its own library so that we will be able to reference it from any application without needing to know its inner workings. If, at a later time, you needed to update your code, .NET's side-by-side versioning means that you will not need to update your whole application (as long as the major and minor version numbers do not change).

We will also be using the `System.Globalization` namespace, as we want our class to run under different globalization settings and so want to take into account how this affects the keys being pressed for different characters. When validating numeric values, the symbols used to indicate a negative value or decimal separator can vary from region to region. For example, a comma is used in various European countries instead of a decimal point. Our class will be able to test for decimal and negative symbols according to the particular region of the world the user is in. Note that this version of the class will not test for date, currency, or time formats.

We need to choose when to validate the user's input. We have several alternatives: we could use the KeyPress, Validating, Validated, or the Leave event. Since the KeyPress event is fired every time a single key is pressed within the input area of the ValidationTextbox, we will be creating our own KeyPress event handler that will contain most of the code required to perform the actual validation. This code will execute as and when a user presses a key.

The KeyPress event in .NET passes a KeyPressArgument to a handler method with information about the actual key that was pressed by the user. Each time a user presses a key, our class will evaluate the KeyPressArgument's string value. If this value is outside a specified range, set for the particular input format expected by the textbox, the KeyPressArgument.Handled property will be set to False and used to stop the character from appearing in the textbox.

The KeyPress event is evaluated as follows. First you have to have to read the KeyChar property of the object passed in as a parameter to the event handler. This returns the character value (as a String) of the key that was pressed. The KeyPressEventArgs.Handled property is how you tell the event whether to allow the value to be passed through. If in your code you do not want the value to be passed through, you set the Handled property to True; meaning that the KeyPress event has handled the processing of the value and so nothing more needs to be done; this means that the character is not entered.

This is different from VB6, where the KeyPress event would pass an ASCII value to the handler and you could set the textbox's KeyAscii property to zero to stop the value from being passed to the text area.

The validation code is very similar to what you might have written in the past. We will just make it more flexible, allowing you to reuse it in other applications. In this class, we are restricting the total text entered to one of six different types, so we will have six validation routines for each key pressed (alphabetic, alphanumeric, signed and unsigned whole numbers, and signed and unsigned floats).

The first routine validates whether the key pressed is a Unicode character deemed to be alphabetic (not a digit, punctuation, or other character). This means the 26 letters of the standard Latin alphabet (upper or lower case) in the US. If the key pressed is any of these characters, then we don't handle the KeyPress event, and the character is entered into the textbox. The second routine is very similar to the first but for numeric values. Depending on region, if the key pressed is one of the 10 digits, then don't handle the KeyPress event. The third tests for alphanumeric values (the union of the first and second routines). The fourth routine validates if the negative symbol has been pressed; and is only allowed if the following characters are only digits. The last two routines are similar to the numeric ones, only they also allow one (and no more than one) decimal separator character.

Implementation

Create a new class library project (VTextbox.sln) and rename the class to
VTextbox.vb. Since our VTextbox class inherits from
System.Windows.Forms.TextBox import the System.Windows.Forms namespace.

We are also importing the System.Globalization.NumberFormatInfo class, as we
will be using a couple of its methods to allow us to react to different regional settings.

```
Imports System.Globalization.NumberFormatInfo
Imports System.Windows.Forms

Namespace Wrox.Toolkit.UI
```

Rather than using an enumeration, we're going to implement the required validation as
types, or classes, which implement the following interface:

```
Public Interface IValidationRestriction
    Function Validate(ByVal sender As VTextbox, _
                      ByVal keypress As KeyPressEventArgs) As Boolean
    End Interface
```

This defines a type with a Validate() method, that returns a Boolean value. The
Validate() method will check to see if the character contained within the keypress
parameter, of type System.Windows.Forms.KeyPressEventArgs, is valid. The
specific validation textbox object requiring the validation is also passed to this method.
The first type, Alpha, is shown below:

```
Public Class Alpha
    Implements IValidationRestriction

    Public Function Validate(ByVal sender As VTextbox, _
                             ByVal keypress As KeyPressEventArgs) _
                As Boolean _
                Implements IValidationRestriction.Validate

        Return Char.IsLetter(keypress.KeyChar)

    End Function
End Class
```

The only detail that needs discussion is the Return line. This calls the shared
Char.IsLetter() method on the character pressed to test to see if it is one of the 26
alphabetic characters. If so, then it returns True. The other types will be identical in
every way except for their name, and their implementation of the Validate() method
itself. Here is the Return statement for the AlphaNumeric class:

```
Return Char.IsLetterOrDigit(keypress.KeyChar)
```

This just calls Char.IsLetterOrDigit() on the character and returns True or
False. This tests for alphanumeric characters. For the PositiveNumeric class:

```
Return Char.IsNumber(keypress.KeyChar)
```

This just calls `Char.IsNumber()`, testing for whether the character is one of the ten digits. The `NegativeNumeric` class is a little more interesting:

```
Return (keypress.KeyChar = CurrentInfo.NegativeSign And _
    sender.SelectionStart = 0 Or _
    Char.IsNumber(keypress.KeyChar))
```

This handles both positive and negative numbers. It checks to see if the key pressed is the negative sign (given particular regional settings), and is the first character in the textbox. If not, it checks to see if it is a number. This would allow -123, but not 234-, for instance. Next here is the `UnsignedDecimal` class:

```
Dim separator As String = CurrentInfo.NumberDecimalSeparator
Return (keypress.KeyChar = separator And _
    sender.Text.IndexOfAny(separator.ToCharArray) = -1 Or _
    Char.IsNumber(keypress.KeyChar))
```

This performs a few more tests. It stores the decimal separator (according to the current regional settings) in the `separator` variable, which is likely to be ".", or ",". It then tests to see if the key pressed is this character and, if so, it ensures it is not duplicated elsewhere in the textbox. Otherwise, it just confirms that it is a number. Now for the final type, `SignedDecimal`:

```
Dim separator As String = CurrentInfo.NumberDecimalSeparator
Return (keypress.KeyChar = separator And _
    sender.Text.IndexOfAny(separator.ToCharArray) = -1 Or _
    Char.IsNumber(keypress.KeyChar) Or _
    (keypress.KeyChar = CurrentInfo.NegativeSign And _
    sender.SelectionStart = 0))
```

This is the longest test. Again it checks for the separator and ensures that it doesn't already occur in the textbox. It then tests to see if it is a number. Finally, it will permit a "-" sign at the start of the number.

By specifying these types by using an interface, rather than an enumeration, we can extend the functionality of the textbox by simply defining a new type that implements that interface, and don't need to recompile the code in the Validator. You will see this in action later. So, now on to the component itself:

```
Public Class VTextbox
    Inherits System.Windows.Forms.TextBox

    Private RestrictType As IValidationRestriction
```

This is the class definition for the textbox, which inherits from the `TextBox` class. We also define a private variable, `RestrictType` as an `IValidationRestriction` that will contain the types we wish to allow. This will enable us to validate against almost anything, including a regular expression, if we wish.

```
Public Property Restrict() As IValidationRestriction
  Get
    Return RestrictType
  End Get

  Set(ByVal Value As IValidationRestriction)
    RestrictType = Value
  End Set
End Property
```

This is the public interface for the `RestrictType` variable. When allocating an `IValidationRestriction` type to the `Restrict` property, we need to pass an instance of the type to it, so this code:

```
VTextBox.Restrict = New Alpha()
```

needs to be used. You cannot pass an abstract type to it, nor can our code work with this.

As discussed above, we want to instantly inform the user that they have entered either a valid or invalid character by either displaying or not displaying the input in the text area. We are going to be using the `KeyPress` event to trap each key pressed by the user and validate it against the rules contained in each `IValidationRestriction` set in the `Restrict` property. If the key pressed is between the ranges of valid values then the key-pressed event won't be handled. If the value is outside the valid range then the `KeyPress` event will handle the key press and not let the value proceed through. You will notice that this event handles the base class `KeyPress` event.

```
Private Sub VTextbox_KeyPress(ByVal sender As Object, _
  ByVal e As System.Windows.Forms.KeyPressEventArgs) _
  Handles MyBase.KeyPress

  Try
    If Not RestrictType Is Nothing Then
```

The above code is straightforward for event handling code. We also confirm that `RestrictType` is not `Nothing`, as if it is then we need not perform any more tests and any character would be allowed in the textbox. Look at the rest of the code:

```
      If e.KeyChar = Convert.ToChar( _
                System.Windows.Forms.Keys.Back) Then
        e.Handled = False
Else
        e.Handled = Not RestrictType.Validate(Me, e)
      End If
```

The user will be able to use *Backspace* to remove text from the `ValidationTextbox` text area, so you must not handle the key press when the *Backspace* key is pressed. The *Backspace* must be handled first otherwise the rest of the statement will handle it and evaluate to invalid since it is outside all the restriction rules ranges. The *Delete*, *Home*, *End* and other keys when pressed do not invoke the `KeyPress` event but the `KeyDown` event so they do not have to be trapped or evaluated. The `Else` line does the actual work. This simply calls the `Validate()` method for the specific validation type and passes in the validation textbox instance, and the key press arguments.

```
        Catch ex As Exception
            e.Handled = True
            Throw New System.Exception(ex.ToString)
        End Try
    End Sub
End Class
End Namespace
```

Finally, we catch any exceptions and pass them to the form that contains this control, disallowing whatever input was attempted.

Demonstration

The demonstration of this code is fairly simple. Once you have compiled the above class library you will need to add the control to your toolbox. Right-click on the toolbox and choose the Customize Toolbox... menu item. Click on the .Net Framework Components tab and click Browse..., then add your class library to the list of controls (see below):

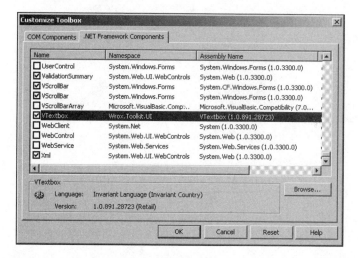

Even though you have not created a user control but a class library, since everything is an object in .NET, .NET knows that the library is a class that is inherited from the Textbox class so it must be a control.

Once the control has been added to your toolbox, all you have to do is create a new Windows Forms application and then drag the control onto the form. Below you will find a small application that will allow you to set a radio button to one of six different restriction types. This will allow you to easily test the control and see how it works for each type.

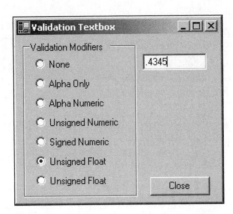

In the demonstration code we have created one method to handle the `Click` event of all the radio buttons; this is the .NET equivalent of a control array. In previous versions of Visual Basic, you would test the `Index` property of the control array to know which radio button initiated the `Click` event; since this property does not exist in .NET, Microsoft suggests you use either the `TabIndex` or `Tag` property.

```
Imports Wrox.Toolkit.UI

Public Class Tester
  Inherits System.Windows.Forms.Form

  Private Sub Button1_Click(ByVal sender As System.Object, _
    ByVal e As System.EventArgs) Handles Button1.Click
    Me.Close()
  End Sub

  Private Sub OptionArray_Click(ByVal sender As System.Object, _
                          ByVal e As System.EventArgs) _
          Handles RadioButton1.Click, _
          RadioButton2.Click, RadioButton3.Click, _
          RadioButton4.Click, RadioButton5.Click, _
          RadioButton6.Click, RadioButton7.Click

    ' The ValidationTextbox does not reevaluate the text when
   ' the Restrict property is changed so you must clear the
     ' current text in order to ensure no old invalid text is
     ' still present

    VTextbox1.Text = ""

    If RadioButton1.Checked Then
       VTextbox1.Restrict = Nothing
    ElseIf RadioButton2.Checked Then
       VTextbox1.Restrict = New Alpha()
    ElseIf RadioButton3.Checked Then
       VTextbox1.Restrict = New AlphaNumeric()
    ElseIf RadioButton4.Checked Then
```

```
        VTextbox1.Restrict = New PositiveNumeric()
     ElseIf RadioButton5.Checked Then
        VTextbox1.Restrict = New NegativeNumeric()
     ElseIf RadioButton6.Checked Then
        VTextbox1.Restrict = New UnsignedDecimal()
     ElseIf RadioButton6.Checked Then
        VTextbox1.Restrict = New SignedDecimal()
     End If
   End Sub
End Class
```

Limitations

The limitations with the code above are related to the regional settings of the machine on which the application is running. We have included code to account for regional differences in the format of the negative and decimal separator symbols but not for the negative number format. The above code does not check the negative number format, which is what dictates the position of the negative symbol itself, and can even indicate if the input contains brackets. By doing a lookup on the System.Globalization.NumberFormatInfo, class you could code for this format to improve the validation textbox.

Extensions

Having learned that inheriting from a control base class is quite easy, there really is no limit on how you can enhance controls to add common code or to enhance functionality.

Once you have created the ValidationTextbox class, you may want to start adding new functionality to create an all-encompassing super textbox class. This class could contain all the common code that a developer may use when using a textbox. This would allow you to just set properties to turn features on or off. In the long run this could ease programming as your requirements change.

Some ideas of how to extend the current design of the ValidationTextbox are listed below:

Since this new ValidationTextbox validates instantly upon a key press but does not display an invalid character, your users may think that they have not pressed the key correctly or that something is wrong. A very simple extension would be to add a beep or some sort of color indicator upon entering an invalid character.

Another extension to create a super textbox class is to add the functionality to automatically select all the text in the text area upon entering the control (this used to be called the GotFocus event). This is implemented to some extent by the standard textbox class; however, .NET will only automatically select from the last position of the cursor. So if you last placed the cursor in the middle of the text and then tabbed back to the control only that half of the text will be selected. Having the text fully selected upon entering the control is a very common function that most developers add to their Windows Forms applications. The following code adds this extension to our class; you can use the SelectAllText property to turn this feature on or off.

```
Private TextSelection As Boolean

Public Property SelectAllText() As Boolean
  Get
    Return TextSelection
  End Get

  Set(ByVal Value As Boolean)
    TextSelection = Value
  End Set
End Property

Private Sub VTextbox_Enter(ByVal sender As Object, _
  ByVal e As System.EventArgs) Handles MyBase.Enter

  If TextSelection Then
    Me.SelectionStart = 0
    Me.SelectionLength = Me.Text.Length
  End If
End Sub
```

Another extension would be to create a similar class but along the lines of the Visual Basic 6 Mask Edit Control. This control currently does not exist for .NET Windows Forms. The control would have properties for the mask, the format, and the prompt of what is to be displayed in the text area. By using the same techniques as VTextbox, this control would be easy to code.

Regular Expression Textbox

Textboxes are an almost ubiquitous feature of both WinForm- and WebForm-based applications, allowing a user to interact with our programs by typing in data. Indeed, the .NET Framework provides us with a `TextBox` control. Its functionality is, however, limited as it does not impose any restrictions on either the nature or the format of the data that can be entered by a user. As this lack of data validation can potentially have some non-trivial security and data integrity consequences, you are left to develop sometimes tedious and lengthy code to ensure the user types in valid data.

Within the .NET Framework, however, Microsoft has included support for regular expressions. Regular expressions were originally developed by UNIX `awk` developers for use within applications that call for extensive text or string manipulation. Using a pattern-matching approach, the regular expression language provides some powerful constructs that allow for the efficient manipulation of large amounts of textual data. They seem, therefore, to be a strong candidate for building a validation mechanism that would extend the basic functionality of .NET's `TextBox` control. The .NET Framework already provides web developers with this type of validating functionality; this chapter will extend this to WinForm controls.

In the previous class, we saw an example of a validating textbox. You could add regular expressions to this textbox by implement regular expressions in the specified type, but this class provides an alternative way of dealing with this capability.

Scenario

The textbox control that we will develop in the following sections will only allow users to enter text that is valid. The validation is done against a particular pattern that may present more complex attributes than simple alphanumeric characters. Assume for example that an application calls for a user to input a ZIP code. The application should be able to handle the different formats of US ZIP codes: not only 5 digits but also say a dash and four digits.

In order to make this class as flexible as possible, the validation mechanism should be able to handle any combination of characters, whether fixed such as a name, where it is safe to assume no numeric characters should be expected, or flexible as in the case of dates, which can be formatted in several ways. Further, some sections of the expressions may be optional, for example phone numbers may have an extension number appended to them.

Technology

As we wish our `TextBox` control to be able to validate the widest possible combination of textual expressions, as we mentioned above we will use **regular expressions** (commonly referred to as regexes). A full treatise of regular expressions is beyond the scope of this chapter; you may find more information on the subject in *Visual Basic .NET Text Manipulation Handbook* (Wrox Press 2002, ISBN 1-86001-730-2) for information on the particular application of regexes within .NET. For a complete overview of regular expression theory, *Mastering Regular Expressions* (O'Reilly 1997, ISBN 1-56592-257-3) is considered the canonical resource, although it does not include specific coverage of .NET. You can also read more on the `RegEx` object in the VB.NET help files.

By using the pattern matching features of the regular expression engine, you validate any pattern of text that you would want the user to enter, including dates, phone numbers, ZIP codes, or any particular sequence of letters.

Design

To make our Regular Expression textbox class easy to implement, we will inherit from the .NET Framework's `TextBox` class. This simplifies our task, as all that is left for us to do is add the regular expression validation mechanism to it. When compiled, this class will be accessible by any WinForm application from any language supported by the .NET Framework.

As mentioned above, the text validation mechanism of our class will be calling upon the built-in .NET regular expression engine (within the `System.Text.RegularExpression` namespace) to implement the required pattern-matching functionality. The class will be able to accept any valid regular expression argument and will validate the user's input against that regular expression.

The `TextBox` control's focus events occur in the following order: `Enter`, `GotFocus`, `Leave`, `Validating`, `Validated`, and `LostFocus`. If the control's `CausesValidation` property is set to `True`, then the `Validating` and `Validated` events will fire once the `Leave` event is raised as the user attempts to leave the control. Note that the `CausesValidation` property is set to `True` by default. We are going to test the user's input against our regular expression within the `TextBox`'s `Validating`. This will guarantee that the textbox does not lose focus, or in other words that the user cannot proceed or leave the textbox, unless the correct text is entered. This is achieved by setting the event parameter's `System.ComponentModel.CancelEventArgs` `Cancel` property to `True`. All events expected after the `Validating` event will not fire. Indeed this will ensure that the user cannot bypass the validation mechanism and leave the textbox.

If on the other hand the user's input matches the regular expression, the event sequence is allowed to resume and eventually the user will be able to move beyond the `textbox`. Just before the textbox looses focus, the `Validated` event is fired. It is within the context of the `Validated` event that we will perform any necessary cleanup.

However, the use of the `Validating` event to perform the necessary text-matching operation might be confusing to the user. The `Validating` event does not fire every time a key is pressed; it fires when a user tries to change focus to another control. We will therefore need to provide the user with some indication as to what is going on and why they are not allowed to continue.

Furthermore, as a user might not be aware of the exact pattern that is expected by the control, any incorrect input needs somehow to be flagged as such and feedback given to the user with some indication of what went wrong and what should be done about it.

To achieve this, we will be using the .NET Framework's `ErrorProvider` control. This control displays an error indicator whenever an error occurs. When the curser hovers over that indicator, a tooltip pops up displaying an error message. By tying the `ErrorProvider` control to our textbox, if an input error occurs (no input or badly formatted input), the error message should indicate to the user the format of the expression that was expected. The `ErrorProvider` control allows us to provide some form of interaction between our control and the user.

Additionally, we should also consider that the objective of a non-password textbox is to make it relatively easy for the user to understand what the expected pattern for the input is. When designing the WinForm's UI, it would be a good idea to use either a `Label` control or a default value within the textbox itself to give the user some indication of what type of input is expected.

Implementation

Create a new Windows Control library project, give the class the name
RegExTextbox.vb, and add a reference to System.Windows.Forms.dll, as a class
library project doesn't have this by default. You must then set your class to inherit from
System.Windows.Forms.TextBox. This is the same as for the VTextBox control
shown in the last chapter, and this will give your class all the features and functionality
of a standard textbox for you to modify as required.

As mentioned above, an ErrorProvider control will be used within this class to feed
back to the user when the text entered does not match what was expected. Double-
click on the RegExTextBox class in Visual Studio .NET's Solution Explorer and drag
and drop an ErrorProvider control onto the design surface of the class library. A
class file does not usually possess a design surface but we have access to a similar
functionality as we are inheriting from a Systems.Window.Forms control (note that
this is not the same as the design surface of a Form). This is by far the easiest and
quickest way to add any type of control to a class library. This operation will add an
ErrorProvider1 control to your class. As the control is added to the design surface,
all declaration and initialization is done for you.

```
Imports System.Text.RegularExpressions
Imports System.Windows.Forms

Namespace Wrox.Toolkit.UI

  Public Class RegExTextbox
    Inherits System.Windows.Forms.TextBox
```

We need to import the System.Text.RegularExpressions namespace, as we will
be using it to provide the regular expression pattern-matching engine for the class.

Next we declare a local variable that will be used to store the regular expression that
will control the format in which text is to be entered by a user. The value of
RegExProperty is set using a RegularExpression property.

```
    Private RegExProperty As String

    Public Property RegularExpression As String
      Get
        Return RegExProperty
      End Get

      Set(ByVal Value As String)
        RegExProperty = Value
      End Set
    End Property
```

As validation will only take place when the user attempts to change the focus of our control, we write a method that will handle the `Validating` event of the base `TextBox` class.

```
Private Sub RegExTextbox_Validating(ByVal sender As Object, _
           ByVal e As System.ComponentModel.CancelEventArgs) _
           Handles MyBase.Validating
```

We then create a local `RegEx` object from the `RegularExpressions` namespace that will be used to store the regular expression pattern against which the user's input will be matched.

```
Dim RegExpression As System.Text.RegularExpressions.Regex
```

If the `RegExProperty` variable is empty, there is no need to set the `RegExpression` object or try to run the match: this will always return `False` and therefore will never release focus from the current control, locking the user into an infinite loop.

```
Try
   If Not RegExProperty Is Nothing Then
```

Next we assign to our `RegExpression` object the regular expression contained in the `RegExProperty` variable and set it be case insensitive by passing the `RegexOptions.IgnoreCase` parameter. If on the other hand you want the pattern-matching mechanism to be case sensitive, set the `RegexOptions` parameter to `None`, or do not pass this argument. The `RegEx` object supports a number of other parameters that provide you with additional functionality; for more information you should consult the .NET Framework's documentation.

```
RegExpression = New Regex(RegExProperty, _
                         RegexOptions.IgnoreCase)
```

Next comes the validation code itself. The `Match` object of the instantiated `RegEx` class, in this case `RegExpression`, performs the pattern matching function. The user's input is passed to the object as a parameter. It then searches the string to match it to the regular expression. We only need to confirm the return value of the `IsMatch()` method to establish whether a match was indeed found. If on the other hand there are no matches, the `ErrorProvider` control's indicator icon will blink next to the textbox and a relevant error message will be displayed. Additionally an exception will be thrown that is caught in the `Catch` error handling mechanism:

```
If Not RegExpression.IsMatch(Me.Text) Then

   'Display the error text in the ErrorProvider control.
   ErrorProvider1.SetError(Me, _
                     "Text does not match expression.")
```

109

As we are evaluating the case where no match was found, we set the `Validating` event's `System.ComponentModel.CancelEventArgs.Cancel` argument to `True`, preventing the user from leaving the textbox. In addition to this, the user's input is selected. Note that if the user types a new set of characters in the textbox, the selected original string will be cleared.

```
    ' Cancel the event and select the text to be
    ' corrected by the user.

        e.Cancel = True
        Me.Select(0, Me.Text.Length)
      End If
    End If

  Catch ex As Exception
    e.Cancel = True
    Console.WriteLine(ex.ToString)
  End Try
End Sub
```

If the `Validating` event is not canceled, the `Validated` event will fire. The `Validated` event sets the `ErrorProvider`'s indicator to `Nothing`. Should the user have made a mistake in their first input, this will remove the indicator; otherwise, nothing happens at all.

```
Private Sub RegExTextbox_Validated(ByVal sender As Object, _
    ByVal e As System.EventArgs) Handles MyBase.Validated

    ErrorProvider1.SetError(Me, "")
  End Sub
 End Class
End Namespace
```

Demonstration

Before compiling your class, close the design window and bring up your project properties. Rename your assembly, and remove the Root namespace.

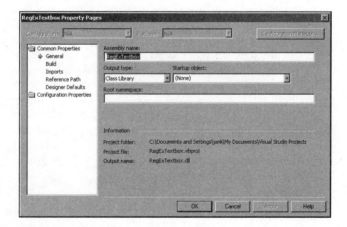

We will now create a small Windows Application that will make use of our newly created Regular Expression textbox. First, create a new Windows Application project. You will need to add your Regular Expression textbox control to Visual Studio .NET's Toolbox. As shown in the previous class, use the Customize Toolbox dialog that is accessible by right-clicking on the Toolbox itself. Then click on the .Net Framework Components tab, click Browse...; and add a reference to your newly created RegExText.dll. Click OK: the new control is now added to your Toolbox.

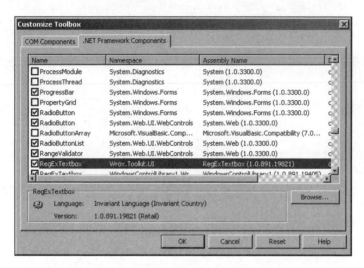

In this sample application, we will use a couple of RegExTextbox controls prompting the user to input a ZIP code and a birth date. Build your form to look something like this:

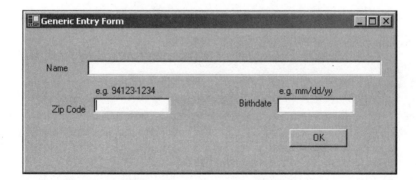

You can set the `RegExTextbox` regular expression against which to test the user's input in the Properties Explorer in Visual Studio, or through code. Add the following code to your Form:

```
Public Class
Form1 Inherits System.Windows.Forms.Form
    Private Sub Form1_Load(ByVal sender As System.Object, _
            ByVal e As System.EventArgs) Handles MyBase.Load
        'Zip code regextextbox
        RegExTextbox1.RegularExpression = "\d{5}(?:-\d{4})?"

        'Birthdate regextextbox
        RegExTextbox2.RegularExpression = _
        "^(?<month>\d{1,2})/(?<day>\d{1,2})/(?<year>\d{2,4})$"
    End Sub

    Private Sub Button1_Click(ByVal sender As Object, ByVal e As _
                        System.EventArgs) Handles Button1.Click
        Me.Close()
    End Sub

End Class
```

Run your application and enter something in the regular expression textbox that does not match one of the regular expressions above. The indicator for the `ErrorProvider` control that is part of the regular expression textbox will be displayed beside the textbox when you try to move off or leave the control. If you try to leave the control when you have entered the text that matches the regular expression property, the indicator for the `ErrorProvider` will disappear. The screenshot below shows what the `ErrorProvider` indicator looks like with its popup message when the cursor is hovering over the indicator.

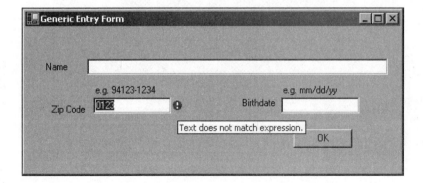

Limitations

The limitations are those of regular expressions themselves, which are not many.

It would be difficult to do interactive validation using this method. As each new character is entered in to the textbox you would have to validate it based on the appropriate part of the regular expression. Figuring out what part of the regular expression is valid for the current text is the tricky part, as expressions don't necessarily match in this way; matching may depend on characters that come after a specific sequence.

Extensions

The class developed in this section only introduces some basic UI design. The error message displayed by the `ErrorProvider` control is quite simple and it could be coded to provide more information to the user, such as the expected format of the text.

Additionally, in this version of the control, the user is not allowed to leave the `RegExTextbox` blank. If a particular bit of information is optional, this could be modified so that the user can leave the control and move on.

Required Form Field Validator

When a user is requested to enter information in a form in an application, the developer may require that at least one of the fields be filled in before the user can continue. This class will look at a technique that will allow any form that has required controls to verify that they are filled in and/or valid before the user can proceed. It will essentially be the WinForms equivalent to the ASP.NET Required Validator control.

Scenario

Many WinForms applications require that a user enter data in different controls before any further processing takes place. An example of this would be when attempting to save a record in a database. If fields in the record are required, and they are not entered by the user, then an error should be generated by the application.

This class will help with automating the task of coding which required controls on a form need to be filled in by the user, and then confirming they are filled in when the user attempts to close the form. This class will provide a visual indicator to the user of what is wrong on the form when any required controls are not filled in.

Technology

The technology issues that must be addressed when creating a class for requiring controls to be valid are:

❑   How to make the code available to any or all forms in an application without any duplication

❏   How to create a validation routine that is extensible without requiring major rewriting or without rewriting the invocation method

❏   How to inform the user of the required fields that are not filled in, without being too intrusive

To solve the issues listed above, we create a base Windows Form class and all forms in our application will inherit from it; this will allow us to have the functionality of required fields available whenever required. With the `System.Reflection` namespace, we can create one invocation method for any control we are trying to validate; dependent on the type of control we will also use objects from the `System.Reflection` namespace to select the correct validation routine for that particular control type. The class will also use the `ErrorProvider` control to inform the user of the failure and suggested resolution of an invalid control entry.

Design

This class is going to use the new .NET feature of inherited forms to allow us to be able to reuse and ease development. Everything in .NET is an object; this will allow us to create a form with all our methods, properties, and events, and use it as base for all the forms in our applications. Since any form inherits from the base `Form` class, any bug fixes or enhancements made to the base form will be automatically incorporated into the inherited form. Once the class is compiled as a component, it will be accessible by any other project you create.

The design for checking all required controls to see if they are valid is in three parts. The class will contain a `Systems.Windows.Forms.Control` array property, where the developer of the form can specify what controls are required to be filled in for the inherited form. This is the only part of the class that the developer must take care of when using this form. If a required control name is not listed, then the control will not be validated upon closing of the form.

The second part of the code should retrieve the required controls from the form's `ControlsCollection` collection. Once the control is found, a reference to it is created and tested to see if it contains valid data. The validation methods will be overloaded to accept different types of component. To determine which validation routine is to be used we will use reflection to determine which validation method is correct for the type of control.

Depending on the control, the value of one property is usually enough to determine if the control contains an entered value. Controls that are very similar to the `TextBox` class (maybe with a few extra properties) will be validated against the control's `Text` property. For all other controls, we will have to use separate validation code for the property. You will see this in the *Implementation* section.

The final part is that the class has to have code that will intercept the closing of the form by the user. There may be some forms where this may not be quite appropriate. An input dialog form where an action occurs when the user clicks an OK button or similar, would want to check the required controls on the click of the OK button instead of on the Form.Closing event.

One further technology technique that this class will have to employ, is to inform the user when a required control needs a value. .NET has a new control in the System.Windows.Forms namespace called ErrorProvider, which can be used to inform users of errors or problems on a form. By setting it to a control and passing it a message string, the ErrorProvider control will place an icon indicator beside the control to visually inform the user of a problem. If the user hovers their mouse pointer over the icon, the message will be displayed in a tool tip.

This design for the class will validate specific controls on a form, and it will inform the user of any issues and so save you time and from developing with repetitive code.

Implementation

To start the implementation of this class, you will need to create a new class library project and give it the name RequiredFieldBaseForm, renaming the code file to RequiredFieldBaseForm.vb. This will be your base form, with the all the required control code that can be used as a base for any inherited forms. The next thing you need to do is add a reference to System.Windows.Forms.

```
Imports System.Windows.Forms
Imports System.Reflection

Namespace Wrox.Toolkit.UI
    Public Class RequiredFieldBaseForm
        Inherits System.Windows.Forms.Form
```

This class should be used instead of the Form class and so we inherit from it here, importing System.Windows.Forms and System.Reflection. We use System.Reflection to inspect the type of the control so that the code can respond appropriately.

```
        Private RequiredCtrls As System.Windows.Forms.Control()
        Private ReqValidatorIndicator As ErrorProvider

        Sub New()
            MyBase.New()
            ReqValidatorIndicator = New ErrorProvider()
        End Sub
```

The `RequiredCtrls` array is for storing the names of the controls that are required to be valid before the form is closed. As an array only contains references to the original objects, this consumes few resources. In addition, because all Windows controls inherit from this object, it can contain any Windows controls. The `ReqValidatorIndicator` is an `ErrorProvider` control, and it is initialized with the current form as its container.

```
Public Property RequiredControls As Control()
   Get
      Return RequiredCtrls
   End Get

   Set
      RequiredCtrls = value
   End Set
End Property
```

To set and access the array listed above, a public property is created. This will be accessible from external code.

```
Public Function AreRequiredFieldsValid() As Boolean
   Dim Result As Boolean = True
   Dim index As Integer
   Dim ValidationMessage As String

   Try
```

This function is called when the form is closed. It will validate all controls contained in the `Control` array. The `ErrorProvider` control can be used to flag any non-filled controls, as you will see. We start by assuming all controls are valid. As we test each control, we will change the `Result` to `False` only if validation fails.

```
If RequiredCtrls Is Nothing Then Return True

For index = 0 To RequiredCtrls.GetUpperBound(0)
   If Not RequiredCtrls(index) Is Nothing Then
```

The code first checks to see if any controls have been added to the `RequiredCtrls` array. If not, then by definition everything is valid, so we return `True` from the function. If it is not empty, we then loop through the array of all the required controls, checking each element to ensure it exists.

```
Dim control As Control = RequiredCtrls(index)
Dim types As Type() = {control.GetType}
```

For each control in the array, we first do a lookup for it in the `Forms` control collection. Then we store the type of the control in an array, as that is what the `GetMethod()` method (shown below) requires.

```
Dim mi As MethodInfo = _
   Me.GetType.GetMethod("Validate", types)
```

Next, we need to store the appropriate overloaded `Validate()` method (shown later) for the type of control we currently have by using the `GetMethod()` method. `GetMethod()` searches a class for a specific public method that matches the argument type passed in. This method will be stored in a `MethodInfo` object. A `MethodInfo` object can parse the metadata of a method to determine its attributes and how to invoke it.

```
Dim args As Object() = {control}
ValidationMessage = mi.Invoke(Me, args)
```

The `Invoke()` method of the `MethodInfo` object is overloaded to accept a number of different possibilities. Since our overloaded `Validate()` method can accept parameters, the `MethodInfo` object needs to know what those parameters are. These are passed to the `MethodInfo` object by saving them to an array of objects. For our method, we only have one parameter argument, which is the control object itself.

This invokes the appropriate `Validate()` method for the type of our control on the actual control being passed in as the argument. The message string indicating if the appropriate `Validate()` method succeeded is then returned and stored in `ValdiationMessage`.

```
If ValidationMessage.Length <> 0 Then
    Result = False
End If
```

If the message returned upon invoking the `Validate()` method is anything other than empty, then we know the conditions specified in the `Validate()` method weren't met and so we need to set the `Result` flag to `False` to inform the calling method that we have an invalid control. We also want to inform the user of the application the validation state of the current control:

```
            ReqValidatorIndicator.SetError(control, ValidationMessage)
        End If
    Next

    Return Result

Catch ex As Exception
    MessageBox.Show(ex.Message)
    Return False
End Try
End Function
```

Here, we set the `ErrorProvider` control with the message returned. The `ErrorProvider` will then indicate to the user with an icon that something is wrong with the control. When the user hovers their mouse pointer over the icon, it will display the validation message in a tooltip. By providing an informative message, we will help the user in understanding why the control is not valid. If the control has been filled correctly, then an empty string is passed, which will do nothing, or remove an existing `ErrorProvider` on that control. After this, we return the contents of the `Result` variable, and catch any exceptions, showing the text of the exception in a message box.

In the next part of this class, we define a number of constant strings that the methods will return if a control is not validated. These are `Protected` constants, so classes that inherit from this one have direct access to them. These are defined as constant for performance reasons, so that if used on a particular form, then the strings become part of the **Intern Pool**, which means that the same `String` object is used, no matter how many identical `Validate()` overloads are called:

```
Protected Const NOCONTROL As String = _
   "Specific Validation not coded for this control."
Protected Const TEXTBOXERROR As String = _
   "The text area cannot be empty."
Protected Const LISTBOXERROR As String = _
   "A Listbox item must be selected."
Protected Const COMBOBOXERROR As String = _
   "A combobox item must be selected."
```

Next we show the various overloaded `Validate()` methods used in this class. There is a different overload for each different type of component passed in. The methods are all defined as `Protected` so that they aren't accessible directly from code outside the class. This is partially to reduce the error checking, as in our code the values being passed have already been checked to ensure they are not `Nothing`:

```
Protected Overloads Function Validate(ByVal value As Control) _
                        As String
   If value Is Nothing Then
      Return String.Empty
   Else
      Return NOCONTROL
   End If
End Function
```

For each type of object that we need to validate, we must know what specific property needs to be checked to say that the object has some valid type of value (in some cases it just may be any text but it we might not know if it is valid text). For every type of control that we want to be a required field in the application, we need a `Validate()` overload for it. Each method will return an empty string if the control or object is valid and an informational message if it is not. This message will be used in the `ErrorProvider` control to inform the user of the potential problem. The first method above is for a generic control object. Note that the Framework will always try to find the most specific overload for the parameter passed in. The above overload should never be called, and if it is, then a new overload will need to be created.

```
Protected Overloads Function Validate(ByVal value As TextBox) _
                        As String
   If value.Text.Trim = String.Empty Then
      Return TEXTBOXERROR
   Else
      Return String.Empty
   End If
End Function
```

This overloaded version of the `Validate()` method accepts a `TextBox` control. If the `Text` property of the textbox control is blank, then we validate it by passing `TEXTBOXERROR` back to the calling method. The last two `Validate()` overloads in this class are shown below:

```
Protected Overloads Function Validate(ByVal value As ListBox) _
                        As String
   If value.SelectedIndex = -1 Then
      Return LISTBOXERROR
   Else
      Return String.Empty
   End If
End Function

Protected Overloads Function Validate(ByVal value As ComboBox) _
                        As String
   If (value.DropDownStyle = ComboBoxStyle.Simple And _
      value.Text.Trim = String.Empty) Or _
      value.SelectedIndex = -1 Then
      Return COMBOBOXERROR
   Else
      Return String.Empty
   End If
End Function
```

These two methods validate the `ListBox` or `ComboBox` controls; since both have unique properties, we must create an individual validation routine for each. If a `ListBox` does not have an item selected, then it is not valid. The same goes for the `ComboBox` if its `DropDownStyle` is not set to `Simple`; if it is set to `Simple`, then the control functions much like a `TextBox`, so we must validate it against its `Text` property.

Finally, all that's left is the method that handles the `Closing` event:

```
Private Sub RequiredFieldBaseForm_Closing( _
            ByVal sender As Object, _
            ByVal e As System.ComponentModel.CancelEventArgs) _
            Handles MyBase.Closing
   If Me.CausesValidation Then
      e.Cancel = Not AreRequiredFieldsValid()
   End If
End Sub
End Class
End Namespace
```

When a user attempts to close the current form, .NET fires the `Closing` event. This event allows the developer to test that the form can be closed. This event is similar to the classic VB6 `QueryUnload` event. If for whatever reason the developer determines that the form should not be closed, the `System.ComponentModel.CancelEventArgs.Cancel` property is set to `False`. This tells .NET to cancel the closing of the form. The user will then have to meet the proper requirements of validation before the form can be closed. If the developer does not want to validate the controls upon closing a form, the `CausesValidation` property needs to be set to `False`.

This class has now been fully described and it can now be compiled into a DLL.

Demonstration

To demonstrate how the Required Form Field Validator code works you don't need much code at all. Just by creating a new test project and completing a couple steps, we can use our new base form.

Once you have compiled your new base form, create a new Windows Form project. The first thing to do is add a reference to the DLL compiled earlier. Next, replace the `Inherits System.Windows.Forms.Form` line underneath the class declaration with `Inherits Wrox.Toolkit.UI.RequiredFieldBaseForm`.

To see the Required Form Field Validator code work, add a textbox and a couple other controls of types for which we have coded. Add a textbox, combo box, and listbox, and then add the following line in the constructor for this form:

```
'Add any initialization after the InitializeComponent() call
Dim vcontrols As Control() = {TextBox1, ComboBox1, ListBox1}
Me.RequiredControls = vcontrols
```

With the application running, click the Close button in the top corner; this will fire the required form's `Closing` event. You should now see an indicator icon beside each control that does not contain text, and if you hover your mouse pointer over this, you will see the error message in a tooltip. Change the value of one of the invalid controls and try to close the form again. The indicator icon should now be gone beside that control. See below for a screenshot of a particular implementation of this form:

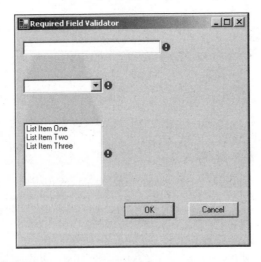

Here is the event handling code that needs to be added to the form shown above. The OK button attempts to close the form and the Cancel button turns off validation and successfully closes the form.

```
Private Sub btnCancel_Click(ByVal sender As System.Object, _
                            ByVal e As System.EventArgs) _
                            Handles btnCancel.Click
    Me.CausesValidation = False
    Me.Close()
End Sub

Private Sub btnOK_Click(ByVal sender As System.Object, _
                        ByVal e As System.EventArgs) _
                        Handles btnOK.Click

    Me.Close()
End Sub
```

Limitations

The current limitations with the above code are that you will have to ensure you add other types of controls that require validation, as this class cannot deal with them all. If there are any errors (for example, a control listed is not found), then the code stops the validation and it will not let the user continue. All controls listed must be in the form's System.Windows.Forms.ControlsCollection collection.

In addition, this particular form does not allow the form to close. In a real world application, you may instead prefer the controls to be checked on the clicking of a Submit button, or similar, and let the users close the form whenever they want. In that case, to use this same code, you would have to write a new class that inherits from this one and code a new Closing event handler that sets CausesValidation to False.

Extensions

This form can be extended to check that a whole host of controls can be validated. You can create a class that inherits from this one, and implements your own Validate() methods, and constants if you wish. The class would work in the same way otherwise. In addition, by using inheritance, you could perform validation that is more detailed, perhaps by using one or both of the previous classes in this section. You would need to override the existing methods with the Overrides keyword if you wished to perform validation that was more specific on these controls.

You could also amend this class so that the collection of components to be validated is specified more easily. You could implement this as a collection of strings that are parsed to retrieve the components themselves. This would allow the controls to be specified using the Properties window in the Visual Studio IDE. Alternatively, you could get the code to automatically retrieve every control from the form's collection, and change the Validate(value As Component) method to do nothing if no specific validation routine has been created for that component.

123

10

Word-Highlighting RichTextBox

WinForms controls are reusable components that provide user-interface functionality to Windows applications (vs. Web applications). Visual Studio .NET includes the tools you need to either build your own controls or extend the controls included with the .NET Framework, as we've seen throughout this section.

The `System.Windows.Forms.RichTextBox` control can already do many great things. It can read and write files, use RTF (Rich Text Format) formatting, automatically detect URLs, and more. One thing it can't do, however, is provide automatic word or syntax highlighting, such as you see in the Visual Studio code editor. It's possible to build this feature right on top of `RichTextBox`'s other bells and whistles by using inheritance.

The `KeywordRichTextBox` control lets you provide a set of keywords and a color and/or font for each one. When the control recognizes a word, it applies your custom formatting. You can drag this control from the Toolbox onto a form, just like any of the built-in controls.

Scenario

It's easy to find uses for a textbox. The `RichTextBox` control is powerful enough to be the main editing interface for a simple text editor. Maybe you need to give your users a very basic XML editor, but you really don't want to build everything from scratch. On the other hand, perhaps you're writing a data-entry application that could help prevent typing errors by coloring important words. Either way, this control could be just what you need.

Technology

It's quite easy to get started with your own control extensions, since Visual Studio .NET provides the Windows Control Library project template to help get you started. You'll still need an understanding of what the base control does and how it works, but the process is straightforward.

Each WinForms control is derived, directly or indirectly, from the `System.Windows.Forms.Control` class. This is critical, because it's what provides consistency to the object model from one control to another. The `Control` class contains dozens of properties, methods, and events that may be customized, if desired, by classes that inherit from `Control`.

The `TextBox` and `RichTextBox` controls derive from the `System.Windows.Forms.TextBoxBase` class, which, in turn, derives from `Control`. Just as `Control` defines properties, methods and events that are common to all controls, `TextBoxBase` adds to that list properties, methods, and events common to all textbox controls.

The WinForms class hierarchy is an excellent example of the power of object-oriented design techniques. Inheritance is what allows us to easily build new controls based on existing controls.

Design

The goal of this control is to demonstrate:

❑ How to extend a WinForms control by handling events and using the control's own properties and methods

❑ How to implement a strongly-typed collection using the `DictionaryBase` class

The `KeywordRichTextBox` control is built on top of the `System.Windows.Forms.RichTextBox` control. A VB.NET Control Library project provides the basis for this control extension.

The particular challenge of this control is to add highlighting to `RichTextBox` without resorting to custom window painting, and without being tripped up by the control's default behavior. The benefit of having `RichTextBox`'s other functionality is what really makes the effort worthwhile.

Avoiding complication naturally leads to tradeoffs, and this is no exception. The control could monitor individual key presses and determine what to do with each one, or simply examine the text around the cursor each time the control's text changed. This control uses the latter approach, which provides less control but is a more straightforward to code.

Every time the control's text changes for any reason, the TextChanged event is fired. In the event handler, the control searches forward and backward from the current cursor position for separators, such as a space or semicolon. This allows the control to identify a set of non-separator characters that could be a keyword.

The keyword collection is searched to find the string in question. If a match is found, the color and/or font are applied to the string. If not, the default color and font are applied to the string instead. Since the control doesn't know where keywords are located in the text, it often ends up re-applying formatting to text that's already in the correct format.

To maintain a programming model consistent with other WinForms controls, the word list is exposed as a collection property called Keywords. You'll find a similar pattern in other controls, such as the ListBox.Items property.

For an efficient way to store up to a few hundred words, the System.Collections.Hashtable collection class was chosen. The .NET Framework provides a base class called DictionaryBase that makes it easy to build a strongly typed collection around the Hashtable class. The collection stores KeywordFormat objects containing a color and font, indexed by keyword.

The ideal implementation of this control would probably monitor key presses, track the location of each keyword in the text and, quite possibly, use custom window painting for complete control. The Visual Studio.NET text editor is an example of an all-custom approach. A complete understanding of this control will enable you to take it to the next level.

Implementation

Let's take a look at the code used to create our custom control.

First, create a new Windows Class Library project called KeywordRichTextBox. Rename the file UserControl1.vb to KeywordRichTextBox.vb and replace its contents with the code below. Finally, open the project's Properties dialog, locate the Common Properties|General|Root Namespace setting, and delete its contents.

The code begins by importing several namespaces. System.Collections contains the collection classes Hashtable and DictionaryBase. System.Drawing includes the formatting classes, Color and Font.

```
Imports System.Drawing
Imports System.Collections
Imports System.Windows.Forms

Namespace Wrox.Toolkit.UI
```

The control allows you to choose a custom color and/or font for each keyword, specified in a KeywordFormat class:

```
Public Class KeywordFormat
```

The `KeywordFormat` class contains two fields: a color and a font. You should be aware that `Color` is a structure, while `Font` is a class:

```
Private keyFont As Font
Private keyColor As Color
```

The class also defines three constructors, and provides default values for unspecified parameters. This makes the interface simpler, since the caller is not forced to specify every parameter when defaults are sufficient.

```
Public Sub New(ByVal keyColor As Color)
    Me.New(keyColor, Nothing)
End Sub

Public Sub New(ByVal keyFont As Font)
    Me.New(Nothing, keyFont)
End Sub

Public Sub New(ByVal keyColor As Color, ByVal keyFont As Font)
    Me.Color = keyColor
    Me.Font = keyFont
End Sub
```

As you can see, the work happens in the third constructor, while the first two just access it using `Nothing` as one of its parameters. The font and color are exposed as read/write properties. As seen above, it's acceptable to pass an empty value or `Nothing` to indicate that the color or font is not used for highlighting.

```
Public Property Font() As Font
    Get
        Return Me.keyFont
    End Get

    Set(ByVal value As Font)
        Me.keyFont = value
    End Set
End Property

Public Property Color() As Color
    Get
        Return Me.keyColor
    End Get

    Set(ByVal value As Color)
        Me.keyColor = value
    End Set
End Property

End Class
```

That's the end of this class definition. The control also needs a way to maintain a collection of keywords and formats. In this case, the `Hashtable` class was chosen, but its public methods, such as `Add()` and `Remove()`, use the generic `System.Object` data type.

It's good practice to strongly type a collection. This allows the compiler to perform type checking, and it also makes it easy for the caller to see what data type is needed.

Usually, to create a strongly typed collection, a new class is created to wrap an existing collection class. The new class simply delegates its methods and properties to the contained collection, while strongly typing them. The .NET Framework provides a base class called `DictionaryBase` that's designed just for this purpose. It provides a wrapper around the `Hashtable` class.

```
Public Class KeywordCollection
    Inherits DictionaryBase
```

The `KeywordCollection` class derives from `DictionaryBase`. The collection's keys are always strings – the keywords themselves. The collection's values are `KeywordFormat` objects.

```
Public Sub Add(ByVal key As String, ByVal value As KeywordFormat)
    If key Is Nothing Or value Is Nothing Then
        Throw New ArgumentNullException()
    ElseIf key.Length = 0 Then
        Throw New ArgumentException("Missing key.")
    End If

    MyBase.Dictionary.Add(key, value)
End Sub

Public Function Contains(ByVal key As String) As Boolean
    Return MyBase.Dictionary.Contains(key)
End Function

Public Sub Remove(ByVal key As String)
    MyBase.Dictionary.Remove(key)
End Sub

Default Public Property Item(ByVal key As String) _
                As KeywordFormat
    Get
        Return MyBase.Dictionary(key)
    End Get

    Set(ByVal value As KeywordFormat)
        If value Is Nothing Then
            Throw New ArgumentNullException()
        Else
            MyBase.Dictionary(key) = value
        End If
    End Set
End Property

End Class
```

The collection provides strongly typed methods for `Add()`, `Contains()`, and `Remove()`, and for the indexed property, `Item()`. The base class contains a protected property called `Dictionary`, of type `IDictionary`, and each method and property simply calls the base methods. Setting `Item` to be a default property (only possible with an indexed property), allows us to access its members by omitting the `Item` property name. This means that to access a value by key in a `KeywordCollection` stored in `MyCollection`, we could set or retrieve it using the following syntax:

```
Console.WriteLine(MyCollection(key))
```

instead of:

```
Console.WriteLine(MyCollection.Item(key))
```

Now, we've reached the main class, `KeywordRichTextBox` itself. The class contains the `NotInheritable` keyword because it is not designed for use as a base class. If you can't guarantee that derived classes won't break the fundamental behavior of your class (in this case keyword highlighting), it's a good idea to make it non-inheritable.

```
Public NotInheritable Class KeywordRichTextBox
    Inherits System.Windows.Forms.RichTextBox
```

This class inherits from `System.Windows.Forms.RichTextBox`, and that one line of code is what lets us add our custom functionality.

```
Private keywordColl As New KeywordCollection()
Private wordSeparators As Char() = _
    {";", " ", ",", ":", "!", "@", "#", "$", "%", "^", "&", "*", _
    "(", ")", "[", "]", "<", ">", "//", """", ControlChars.Lf}
```

The control stores a `KeywordCollection` object as described above, plus a customizable array of word separators.

```
Public Property Separators() As Char()
    Get
        Return wordSeparators
    End Get

    Set(ByVal value As Char())
        If value Is Nothing Then
            Throw New ArgumentNullException()
        ElseIf value.Length = 0 Then
            Throw New ArgumentException( _
                "The array must contain at least one character.")
        Else
            wordSeparators = value
        End If
    End Set
End Property
```

The `Separators` property allows a client to change the separator list. As with any array in .NET, the methods of the `Array` class can be used to manipulate individual elements of the array.

The setter method ensures that at least one word separator is passed.

```
Public Property Keywords() As KeywordCollection
    Get
        Return keywordColl
    End Get
```

```
          Set(ByVal value As KeywordCollection)
            If value Is Nothing Then
              Throw New ArgumentNullException()
            ElseIf
              keywordColl = value
            End If
          End Set
        End Property
```

The Keywords property exposes a collection that allows the caller to configure keywords and their formats.

Unfortunately, a RichTextBox can only apply formatting to text that is selected. The following FormatText() method saves the current selection position and length, selects the target text, applies the specified formatting, and then restores the original selection state:

```
        Private Sub FormatText( _
                  ByVal startPos As Integer, ByVal length As Integer, _
                  ByVal textColor As Color, ByVal textFont As Font)
          Dim saveSelectionStart As Integer = MyBase.SelectionStart
          Dim saveSelectionLength As Integer = MyBase.SelectionLength

          MyBase.Select(startPos, length)
```

Unfortunately, since a RichTextBox always displays a highlight over the current selection, visible flicker can occur when the selection is rapidly moved and then reset.

```
          If Not textColor.IsEmpty Then
            MyBase.SelectionColor = textColor
          Else
            MyBase.SelectionColor = MyBase.ForeColor
          End If

          If Not textFont Is Nothing Then
            MyBase.SelectionFont = textFont
          Else
            MyBase.SelectionFont = MyBase.Font
          End If

          MyBase.Select(saveSelectionStart, saveSelectionLength)
```

Since Color is a structure, it is necessary to use the textColor.IsEmpty() method to determine if it's valid or not. You cannot compare a structure to Nothing.

```
          MyBase.SelectionColor = MyBase.ForeColor
          MyBase.SelectionFont = MyBase.Font
        End Sub
```

The control does not attempt to maintain user-specified formatting information, since it would only interfere with keyword formatting. As a result, the selection color and font are always reset to those used to create the control.

The following `SetWordAttributes()` method tries to locate a separator-delimited string in the keyword collection. If it finds a match, it passes the formatting data in the object to the `FormatText()` method. Otherwise, it passes in the control's default color and font:

```
Private Sub SetWordAttributes(ByVal startPosition As Integer, _
                              ByVal length As Integer)
    Dim keywordFmt As KeywordFormat = _
        keywordColl(MyBase.Text.Substring(startPosition, length))

    If Not keywordFmt Is Nothing Then
        FormatText(startPosition, length, _
                   keywordFmt.Color, keywordFmt.Font)
    Else
        FormatText(startPosition, length, _
                   MyBase.ForeColor, MyBase.Font)
    End If
End Sub
```

The base class property `Text` represents the `RichTextBox` control's complete text.

```
Private Sub FindWord(ByVal searchPosition As Integer, _
                     ByRef position As Integer, _
                     ByRef length As Integer)
    Dim previousPosition As Integer
    Dim nextPosition As Integer
```

`FindWord()` searches forward and backward from the specified position in the control's text to the nearest separator characters, and returns the starting position and length of the delimited text. More detail is provided below:

```
If searchPosition <> 0 Then
    previousPosition = MyBase.Text.LastIndexOfAny( _
                       wordSeparators, searchPosition - 1) + 1
    If previousPosition = -1 Then
        previousPosition = 0
    End If
Else
    previousPosition = 0
End If
```

If the search origin is the beginning of the text, the starting position is zero. Otherwise, the code searches for the first occurrence of a separator to the left of the search origin, searching right to left, using `MyBase.Text.LastIndexOfAny()`. If `LastIndexOfAny()` returns -1, it reached the beginning of the control's text without finding a separator, so the starting position becomes the beginning of the text as well.

```
If searchPosition <> MyBase.Text.Length Then
    nextPosition = _
        MyBase.Text.IndexOfAny(wordSeparators, searchPosition)

    If nextPosition = -1 Then
        nextPosition = MyBase.Text.Length
    End If
Else
    nextPosition = MyBase.Text.Length
End If
```

Next, the code searches for the first separator to the right of the search origin, using the same general logic as shown previously.

```
        position = previousPosition
        length = nextPosition - previousPosition
    End Sub
```

The parameters, position and length, are output parameters marked ByRef, so they are used to return data directly to the caller.

```
Private Sub KeywordRichTextBox_TextChanged( _
            ByVal sender As Object, ByVal e As System.EventArgs) _
            Handles MyBase.TextChanged
    Dim startPosition As Integer
    Dim length As Integer
```

Above is the key method for this class that handles the TextChanged event. Each time this event is fired, the control searches for delimited text and decides whether to highlight it or clear its format.

```
    If MyBase.Text.Length = 0 Then
        Return
    End If
```

If the control's text is empty, there's nothing to do.

```
    FindWord(MyBase.SelectionStart, startPosition, length)

    If length <> 0 Then
        SetWordAttributes(startPosition, length)
    End If
```

The event handler first looks for a "word" between separators to either side of the current cursor position. The RichTextBox exposes the cursor position using SelectionStart, even though the selection may be zero characters long. If a word containing one or more characters is found, SetWordAttributes() is called to apply highlighting or default formatting.

```
    If MyBase.SelectionStart > 0 And _
        Array.IndexOf(wordSeparators, _
        MyBase.Text.Chars(MyBase.SelectionStart - 1)) <> -1 Then
```

If the current cursor position is not the beginning of the text, the code checks to see if the character immediately to the left of the cursor is a separator.

```
        FormatText(MyBase.SelectionStart - 1, 1, _
            MyBase.ForeColor, MyBase.Font)
```

If the character is a separator, its formatting is reset to the defaults. This ensures that highlighting doesn't "bleed" from a keyword into a subsequent separator.

Finally, using logic similar to that described above, the following FindWord() method is used to search for a separator-delimited word to the left of the separator character:

```
      FindWord(MyBase.SelectionStart - 1, startPosition, length)

        If length <> 0 Then
          SetWordAttributes(startPosition, length)
        End If
      End If
    End Sub

  End Class

End Namespace
```

SetWordAttributes() determines whether to apply keyword or default formatting. This handles the case where a user types a separator character between two valid keywords that were not split by a separator. The separator breaks the concatenation into two valid, separate keywords.

Demonstration

The KeywordRichTextBox control is very easy to use. It can reside in the Toolbox with the other WinForms controls, and it too can be placed on a form.

Create a new Windows Application project, and then use the Customize Toolbox option to add KeywordRichTextBox.dll to your Toolbox component list. Drag a KeywordRichTextBox onto your form and name it textbox. Add an Imports statement for the Wrox.Toolkit.UI namespace, which contains KeywordRichTextBox:

```
  Imports Wrox.Toolkit.UI
  ...

    Protected Overrides Sub OnLoad(ByVal e As System.EventArgs)
      textbox.Keywords.Add("info", New KeywordFormat(Color.Red))
      textbox.Keywords.Add("order", New KeywordFormat(Color.Blue))
      textbox.Keywords.Add("customer", New KeywordFormat(Color.Green))
      textbox.Keywords.Add("id", _
        New KeywordFormat(New Font(textbox.Font, FontStyle.Bold)))
```

Finally, override the form's OnLoad() method to set up some keywords and add a new separator.

This simple code will enable highlighting of the words "info", "order", and "customer" in red, blue, and green, respectively. The word "id" will be emboldened. You can use the other methods and properties of the Keywords collection to add, remove, or locate words.

While it's probably rare that you'll need to modify the separators, the following code demonstrates how to add a new separator to the existing list. Add this to the code, so that attribute names can be recognized:

```
Dim separators() As Char = textbox.Separators
ReDim Preserve separators(separators.Length)
separators(separators.Length - 1) = "="
textbox.Separators = separators
End Sub
```

The `ReDim Preserve` statement expands the `separators` array by one element, without destroying the original contents. The new element, located at the end of the array, is set to a question mark, and the new list is saved back to the control.

After typing in some XML, the application might look something like this:

Limitations

This class is primarily limited by redrawing issues. Since it does not know whether any particular character has been highlighted or not, it often repeatedly, and unnecessarily, reapplies default formatting. In addition, since the `RichTextBox` can only apply formatting to the current selection, the selection is frequently moved and reset, often causing visible flicker.

The control is currently keyboard-oriented. It will not find keywords and apply highlights after pasting text into the control or loading text or RTF from a file.

Finally, some features of the base control will cause collisions with the keyword formatting logic. For instance, if you wanted to use the `RichTextBox`'s RTF formatting capabilities, the highlighting will collide with your formatting, rendering both useless.

Extensions

Several ways to extend the control are mentioned here.

Firstly, the word-recognition functionality could be expanded to work on an entire string, rather than just the current cursor position. This would allow you to use the control's file-loading and paste capability while maintaining keyword highlighting.

You could also take the control to the next level by moving from the broad-stroke TextChanged event to a granular event like KeyPress. In that case, you could track and handle each individual key press and decide what to do on a character-by-character basis, which could even lead to an IntelliSense-like word-completion feature.

The control could be more intelligent about formatting if it knew where every keyword was located. You could add another collection to the control to maintain the keyword locations and lengths, and use that knowledge to reapply highlights and default styles only when necessary. To really do this correctly, you'd probably want to leave behind TextChanged, since it doesn't tell you anything more than "something changed somewhere in the control's text".

As all text is stored in the .NET Framework using the UTF-16 Unicode encoding, a Char() array seems an appropriate storage for the separators. However, in the Unicode standard, some characters take up two Char characters, and they are known as surrogate pairs. You may want to support more separators by allowing these characters, which would involve testing to see if a character is part of a surrogate pair.

Finally, keyword matching is currently case sensitive. This default behavior can be overridden by providing a custom IComparer to the Hashtable class.

11

ListView Sorter

The .NET Windows Forms namespace contains a class called `ListView`, which is a .NET class wrapper for the Windows ListView control. ListView controls can be displayed in a `Details` mode, which allows columns of data to be shown in a list. You can see the `Details` mode of a ListView in action from within Windows Explorer. If you place the right pane of Windows Explorer in "Details" mode, you will see that file information is arranged in columns using the Windows ListView in `Details` mode. Data in ListViews can be sorted by calling a method called `Sort()`. The default implementation sorts all data as if it were strings – this may or may not be the ideal situation for certain lists.

Scenario

Consider, for example, a ListView that contains a date column. Dates are formatted using the date formatting options specified in the user's "Date and Time" Control Panel applet. American date formatting, for example, uses the familiar *month/day/year* format (which is the formatting that we'll use in this chapter). Suppose that the list contains a date of November 9 1967, which is displayed in the list as 11/9/1967, and July 1 1914, which is displayed in the list as 7/1/1914. If these two values are to be sorted as date values, then clearly the 1914 date will come before the 1967 date. However, if these two values are sorted as string values, then the 1967 will come first, because the first character in 11/9/1967, which is "1", comes before the first character in 7/1/1914, lexically.

The class developed in this chapter presents a strongly-typed sorter for ListView data. With this class, callers can specify that a list should be sorted using the rules used for sorting a specified type, thereby allowing data to be sorted in accordance with the rules documented for the type. Using this class, with the data in the example above, the `ListViewSorter` class could be used to specify that the list should be sorted using the date column and the rules specified for sorting date types.

The `ListViewSorter` class that we'll develop in this chapter can be used in any WinForms application that makes use of a ListView displaying data in `Details` mode, with each row in the list displaying pieces of data in columns. The form containing the ListView can create a new `ListViewSorter` object and can specify sorting rules when sorting needs to take place.

Technology

This class takes advantage of the `ListView` class' support for writing custom code to perform sorting using the .NET interface `IComparer`. The custom code must be found in a class that implements the .NET `IComparer` interface. The `IComparer` interface supports a single method called `Compare()` that compares two items and returns an integer specifying the relative sort order of the two items.

Once a class is built to implement the .NET `IComparer` interface, an object of the class must be associated with a ListView so that the list will use the object as the implementation of the sort algorithm to use. This association is set using a `ListView` property called `ListViewItemSorter`. The `ListViewItemSorter` property can be assigned to any object that implements the .NET `IComparer` interface. If this property is set to an object before the `ListView Sort()` method is called, then the ListView will call the `IComparer` interface implementation to compare two of the list's items. The `IComparer` implementation may be called many times during a single sort operation, so its implementation needs to be efficient.

We'll also take a look at creating typed variables at run time using the .NET `System` namespace. Implementations of the `IComparer` interface must implement a method called `Compare()`, which compares two items. The `Compare()` method receives the two items to be compared as generic `object` types. However, to perform accurate, type-safe comparisons, we'll need to use the type's sorting logic. If, for example, the `Compare()` method is called with two objects that actually contain integers, then the code will need to convert the objects to integers and use a comparison operator such as < to compare the two integers. Since we won't know what the actual type is at design time, we'll have to create the appropriate type at run time. We'll take a look at an example of this later on in this chapter.

Design

The ListView item sorter implements the `IComparer` interface and its `Compare()` method. Before the ListView is sorted, the caller must specify the ListView column whose data should be used as the sort data and must also specify the data type whose rules are to be used for sorting. For example, consider a ListView with three columns of information about a person:

- ❑ A name column

- ❑ An employee number column

- ❑ A birthdate column

The name column should most likely be sorted using string rules, while the employee number column should be sorted using integer datatype rules. The birthdate column should be interpreted using date datatype rules.

Suppose that the ListView discussed above is placed in a form, and a button on the form sorts the data based on the listed employee numbers. In this case, the button's click handler will use the ListView item sorter's properties to say, "Sort this list based on the data in the second column, and interpret the data as a set of integers". The ListView item sorter object, using its implementation of the IComparer interface, will then sort the data using the data from the specified column and will ensure that the ListView refreshes its display to show the newly sorted data.

Implementation

The implementation of the ListViewSorter class is shown below. Windows Forms projects created within Visual Studio .NET already reference the Windows Forms assembly (System.Windows.Forms.dll), so you won't need to add the reference again to make use of this class. The class implements the IComparer interface, which is a requirement imposed by ListViews for classes that want to control the way the list data is sorted. Create a Class Library project in visual studio called ListViewSorter, rename Class1.vb to ListViewSorter.vb, and replace the template code with following:

```
Imports System
Imports System.Collections
Imports System.Windows.Forms

Namespace Wrox.Toolkit.UI

    Public Class ListViewSorter
        Implements IComparer
```

The ListViewSorter class keeps track of three private values: a reference to the ListView whose data will be sorted by the ListViewSorter, a zero-based integer referencing the column containing the data to be sorted, and a Type object referencing the data type whose sorting rules should be used to sort the data:

```
Private _List As ListView
Private _SortColumn As Integer = 0
Private _SortType As Type = GetType(String)
```

The ListViewSorter class supports a property called List that the caller can use to get or set a reference to the ListView object to be sorted:

```
Public Property List() As ListView
  Get
    Return _List
  End Get
  Set(ByVal Value As ListView)
    _List = Value
    _List.ListViewItemSorter = Me
  End Set
End Property
```

ListViews support a property called `ListViewItemSorter`, which references an object that implements the `IComparer` interface suitable for sorting data using a custom algorithm. This property is set automatically to the `ListViewSorter` object when a new ListView is assigned. Performing this assignment in the property `Set` code frees the user from having to remember to do it and makes for cleaner client code.

The `ListViewSorter` class also supports a property called `SortColumn` that callers use to specify the ListView data column whose contents should be used as the sort data:

```
Public Property SortColumn() As Integer
  Get
    Return _SortColumn
  End Get

  Set(ByVal Value As Integer)
    If Value < 0 Then
      Throw New ArgumentOutOfRangeException()
    End If
    If Value >= _List.Columns.Count Then
      Throw New ArgumentOutOfRangeException()
    End If
    _SortColumn = Value
  End Set
End Property
```

Finally, the `ListViewSorter` class supports a property called `SortType` that callers use to specify the data type of the sort data. The `SortType` property uses a .NET type called `Type`, which describes a specific datatype:

```
Public Property SortType() As Type
  Get
    Return _SortType
  End Get

  Set(ByVal Value As Type)
    _SortType = Value
  End Set
End Property
```

Since the `ListViewSorter` class implements the `IComparer` interface, the class must define a `Compare()` method. The method takes two objects as parameters and returns an integer specifying the relative sort order between those two objects. The `Compare()` method will be called by the ListView when two items need to be compared for sorting purposes. Once the user calls the ListView's `Sort()` method, the implementation of `Sort()` will use the sorter object's implementation of `Compare()` to compare two of the items in the list. If the first object should be sorted ahead of the second object, then the function should return `-1`. If the first object should be sorted after the second object, then the function should return `1`. If the two objects are equal, according to the sorting rules, then the function should return `0`.

```
Public Function Compare(ByVal x As Object, ByVal y As Object) _
    As Integer Implements IComparer.Compare

Dim Item1 As ListViewItem
Dim Item2 As ListViewItem
Dim Object1 As Object
Dim Object2 As Object
```

The `IComparer` interface is used with many .NET classes, so the items to compare are supplied as `Object` references. When the `Compare()` method is used with ListViews, however, the supplied items are actually `ListViewItem` objects. The `ListViewItem` objects represent all of the items in a single row in the list. The `Item1` and `Item2` variables will represent the ListView item objects that are obtained from the original objects supplied in the function's arguments. We'll use the `Object1` and `Object2` variables to hold the actual type-specific value stored in each list item. Remember that, at this point, we don't know what that type will be, so we'll use objects for now and we'll use .NET reflection to create the appropriate type later in the code. Our first task will be to assign the generic object references to `ListViewItem` object references, since we'll need to work with the specifics of a `ListViewItem` object later on:

```
If TypeOf x Is ListViewItem Then
    Item1 = x
Else
    Throw New ArgumentException()
End If

If TypeOf y Is ListViewItem Then
    Item2 = y
Else
    Throw New ArgumentException()
End If
```

Our next job is to create two objects of the requested sort type, assign their values based on the values in the ListView item, and compare the two objects. We'll start by looking at the object creation and assignment code:

```
Try
    Object1 = Activator.CreateInstance(_SortType)
    Object1 = Convert.ChangeType( _
        Item1.SubItems(_SortColumn).Text, _SortType)
    Object2 = Activator.CreateInstance(_SortType)
    Object2 = Convert.ChangeType( _
        Item2.SubItems(_SortColumn).Text, _SortType)
```

The interesting aspect of this code is that we need to create the two objects to be compared, but we won't know what type of object should be created until the code is run. The data type of the object to be created is referenced by the user's setting of the class' SortType property. Since the type is not known at design time, we can't dimension a variable when writing the class. The type will need to be created at run time, and a method called CreateInstance() lets us do just that. This technique makes use of the .NET reflection system, and the System.Activator class allows us to create types at run time.

The CreateInstance() method is found in the Activator class, which is located in the .NET System namespace. The CreateInstance() method has several overloads, but the one we're interested takes a Type object and creates an object of the specified type. For instance, if the user says that ListView data should be sorted using integer rules, then they will set the sorter object's SortType property to GetType(Integer). Using that type in the call to CreateInstance() will create an integer object.

Once the object is created, the next task is to convert the string data from the appropriate list column into data of the appropriate type. We've use the ChangeType() method in the .NET Convert class for this operation. The first parameter to ChangeType() is the data to be converted, which, in our case, is the string ListView column data from the appropriate sort column. The second parameter to ChangeType() is the data type to convert the data to.

Since the CreateInstance() and ChangeType() operations have a chance of failing, we need to wrap the code in a Try...Catch block. The first exception that we'll catch is the MissingMethodException:

```
Catch mme As MissingMethodException
    Object1 = New String(Item1.SubItems(_SortColumn).Text)
    Object2 = New String(Item2.SubItems(_SortColumn).Text)
```

Exceptions of the MissingMethodException class will be thrown if we try to call a method that does not exist. In our case, our use of CreateInstance() assumes that the data types we are creating have constructors with no arguments and can be created without specifying an initial value for the object. Exceptions of this type will be thrown if we try to create an object that does not have a parameterless constructor. In this case, we won't be able to perform any datatype-specific sorting, so we'll just fall back to sorting using string rules. It's not perfect, but it's better than nothing in the case of the exception.

We'll also handle other types of exceptions in another catch clause:

```
Catch e As Exception
    Return -1
End Try
```

In this case, we'll just return -1. We won't have any good information about sorting rules, so we'll fall back to returning a value that is at least known to be valid given the specifications of the Compare() method. If we return -1, then we're telling the caller that the first parameter passed into Compare() should be sorted ahead of the second parameter.

At this point, we have two objects of a valid type and we can compare them, using the type's support for the < and > operators:

```
        If (Object1 < Object2) Then
            Return -1
        ElseIf (Object1 > Object2) Then
            Return 1
        Else
            Return 0
        End If
    End Function
  End Class
End Namespace
```

Demonstration

Consider a VB.NET WinForms form containing a ListView with the three columns we discussed at the beginning of the chapter: a name column, an employee number column, and a birthdate column. Suppose that the form contains three buttons:

❑   A Name Sort button that sorts the name column using string datatype rules

❑   A Number Sort button that sorts the employee number column using integer datatype rules

❑   A Birthdate Sort button that sorts the birthdate column using date rules

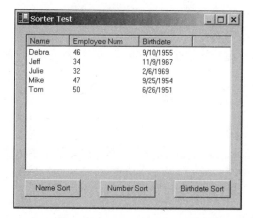

The form code might look like this (WinForms designer code omitted for clarity):

```
Namespace Wrox.Toolkit.UI

  Public Class Form1
    Inherits System.Windows.Forms.Form

    Private SorterObject As New ListViewSorter()

    Private Sub NameSortButton_Click(ByVal sender As Object, _
        ByVal e As System.EventArgs) Handles NameSortButton.Click
```

```
      SorterObject.SortColumn = 0
      SorterObject.SortType = GetType(String)
      ListView1.Sort()
   End Sub

   Private Sub EmployNumSortButton_Click(ByVal sender As Object, _
      ByVal e As System.EventArgs) Handles EmployNumSortButton.Click

      SorterObject.SortColumn = 1
      SorterObject.SortType = GetType(Integer)
      ListView1.Sort()
   End Sub

   Private Sub BirthdateSortButton_Click(ByVal sender As Object, _
      ByVal e As System.EventArgs) Handles BirthdateSortButton.Click

      SorterObject.SortColumn = 2
      SorterObject.SortType = GetType(Date)
      ListView1.Sort()
   End Sub

   Private Sub Form1_Load(ByVal sender As Object, ByVal e As _
      System.EventArgs) Handles MyBase.Load

      SorterObject.List = ListView1
   End Sub

   End Class
End Namespace
```

The form declares a private object of the `ListViewSorter` class and uses the Form's `Load()` event to assign the object's `List` property to the `ListView` object on the form. The button handlers handle button click events, set the `ListViewSorter` object's sort column and sort type properties, and then instruct the ListView to sort itself. The ListView will automatically use the ListView item sorter object to order the data.

Limitations

The `Sort()` method on a ListView object is called in response to a user clicking on a column header. This response sorts on a single column and there is no support for sorting on multiple columns. As a result, the `ListViewSorter` class does not have any support for sorting on multiple columns, either.

The sorting algorithm assumes that the types being sorted support value comparisons using the < and > operators. These operators are supported by most of the types available in the .NET Framework, including virtually all of the primitive types, so you won't have a problem finding this operator support in most of your work. The only obstacle may be with custom objects that you build with VB.NET, since VB.NET does not allow you to specify how the comparison operators behave for a given class. If you're planning on using objects designed in VB.NET as your list row data types, then you might have a problem using the `ListViewSorter` since the < and > operators might not behave in the way that your class would like them to behave.

Extensions

ListViews can have an object associated with each row through the Tag property. The .NET Framework also supports an interface called IComparable that objects can implement to compare themselves with other objects of the same class. It is possible to extend the ListViewSorter class to look for an object in the ListView item's Tag property, and if an object is found, query it to see if the object supports the IComparable interface. If it does, then it can be used for the comparison. This design would allow users to create objects containing data not represented in the list and associate the object with a row in the ListView. Supplying these objects would allow the ListViewSorter class to sort rows using this object data rather than simply the data in the list.

12

Text Image Generator

When designing a web application, developers often end up doing a little bit of graphic design work, even if they do not do the entire design themselves. We usually end up with some text and menus formatted and styled with cascading style sheets or other HTML markup. We also usually have some graphics created in Photoshop, Illustrator, or something similar. One of the tasks that can often take up a significant amount of time is making graphics with a particular style for the text or as a background for the text. While there are multiple ways to achieve this end, this class gives you one more way to get the job done with some particular advantages and suitability to certain scenarios.

Scenario

Creating graphics for text menus, banners, buttons, etc. can sometimes have an advantage over using HTML and CSS. Maybe you have a certain design that is not easy to replicate in CSS or HTML or maybe you want to use a font that most of your users do not have. This class creates images that can be easily updated with new text. The class also can be used to generate images with text dynamically at run time.

There are numerous reasons why you would generate text images at run time; we'll mention two of the most interesting reasons here. The first is related to localization. You can easily place the text that is placed on your images in different languages at run time. The second reason is related to security. You may have seen web sites that require you to type in the text you see in an image during a registration process. The purpose for this is an attempt to stop automated registration scripts from creating numerous bogus accounts. Using the techniques described in this chapter, you could easily replicate a process like that.

Technology

In the `System.Drawing` namespace, we find all the classes we will use to create graphics, primarily `System.Drawing.Graphics` and `System.Drawing.Bitmap`.

`System.Drawing.Graphics` is essentially a library of all the classes that are used to manipulate an image or a drawing. The Graphics library is very powerful, flexible, and easy to use. It supports many different image formats. Examples of the methods it provides are `DrawCurve()`, `DrawLine()`, and `FillPolygon()`.

`System.Drawing.Bitmap` is a straightforward class representation of a bitmap. It has properties to set or get the size of the image and the palette of the image. It also has a number of methods that can be used to initialize the object from different sources, for example, from a file, an icon, a stream, etc. One of the methods we will be using is `Save()`, which can save the bitmap to either a file or a stream. We will be demonstrating both.

In `System.Web`, we find the `HttpResponse` class. This class is used by ASP.NET to send content to a client in response to an `HttpRequest`. We will be using this class to write an image directly to a client web browser in response to a page request. Using the `HttpResponse` class, we can set the response type of an `.aspx` page to `"image/gif"`, for example, and then write the binary contents of an image into the `HttpResponse` buffer. This allows us to use an `.aspx` page as the source for an HTML `<IMG>` tag, for example:

```
<img src="TextImage.aspx">
```

This will also be demonstrated later in the chapter.

Design

The design of this class is simple. The class has three public methods; `DrawImage()`, `DrawTextOnImage()`, and `WriteTo()`, which has three overloads. The class also has one public property called `Image` and one private field called `textImage`. The class has no private methods.

The `DrawImage()` method draws the image that will serve as the background for the text and will likely be implemented with specializations for each particular project that it is used in. On the other hand, perhaps you will overload the drawing methods so that many different visual styles can be used by this single object.

The method `DrawTextOnImage()` draws the text onto the image that is currently held within the class.

The three implementations of `WriteTo()` each output the image, each to their own destination type: a stream, a file, and a web `HttpResponse` output stream.

Implementation

Open Visual Studio .NET, create a **Class Library** project named `TextImageGenerator`, and then remove the default namespace set in the project's properties. Rename `Class1.vb` to `TextImage.vb` and replace the code with the following:

```
Imports System.Drawing
Imports System.Web

Namespace Wrox.Toolkit.UI
  Public Class TextImage
```

We are importing the `System.Drawing` namespace, which will require us to add a reference to `System.Drawing.dll` using the **Add Reference** dialog. This namespace contains the all the classes we will be using to draw our image.

We are also importing `System.Web`, which will require us to add a reference to `System.Web.dll`. The `System.Web` namespace contains the `HttpResponse` class that we will be using to write an image in response to a page request.

Next, add the private field that we will use to store the image and a class constructor that contains no code:

```
Private textImage As Bitmap

Public Sub New()
End Sub
```

Next we'll look at the `DrawImage()` method. The two most significant variables in this method are `bitmap` and `graphics`. The `bitmap` object is the variable that we will use to reference the image for the lifetime of this method. The `graphics` object is the object that we will be using to perform all the drawing on the bitmap.

This method simply draws a box. We outline the shape with lines. To draw the rectangle we use the method `FillRectangle()` and to outline the top and bottom of the rectangle we use `DrawLine()`.

Lastly, we store the `bitmap` object into our private variable `textImage`. Add this code to the class:

```
Public Overridable Sub DrawImage(ByVal imageWidth As Integer, _
      ByVal imageHeight As Integer, _
      ByVal imageForeColor As Color, _
      ByVal imageBackColor As Color)

  Dim bitmap As bitmap
  Dim graphics As Drawing.Graphics
  Dim brush As brush
  Dim pen As pen

  ' Create Bitmap for temporary use
  bitmap = New bitmap(imageWidth, imageHeight)

  ' Get a graphics object to use for all the drawing
  graphics = graphics.FromImage(bitmap)
```

```
        ' Paint the background
        brush = New SolidBrush(imageBackColor)
        graphics.FillRectangle(brush, 0, 0, imageWidth, imageHeight)

        ' Set the pen color
        pen = New pen(imageForeColor, 1)

        ' Paint center portion of the button
        graphics.FillRectangle(brush, 0, 0, imageWidth, imageHeight)

        ' Draw outline (top & bottom) of the button
        graphics.DrawLine(pen, 0, 0, imageWidth, 0)
        graphics.DrawLine(pen, 0, imageHeight - 1, imageWidth, _
            imageHeight - 1)

        ' Draw outline (left & right) of the button
        graphics.DrawLine(pen, 0, 0, 0, imageHeight)
        graphics.DrawLine(pen, imageWidth - 1, 0, imageWidth - 1, _
            imageHeight - 1)

        Image = bitmap
    End Sub
```

Next let's add the `DrawTextOnImage()` method to draw the text on the image. To place the text on the image, we use the `Font` object in conjunction with the `DrawString()` method. To control where we should place the text, we use the margin parameters `imageLeftMargin` and `imageTopMargin`:

```
    Public Sub DrawTextOnImage(ByVal displayText As String, _
        ByVal imageForeColor As Color, _
        ByVal imageLeftMargin As Integer, _
        ByVal imageTopMargin As Integer, _
        ByVal imageFontName As String, _
        ByVal imageFontSize As Integer)

        Dim graphics As Drawing.Graphics
        Dim font As font
        Dim brush As brush

        ' Graphics object to use for writing the text onto the image
        graphics = graphics.FromImage(textImage)

        ' Load Font
        font = New font(imageFontName, imageFontSize, FontStyle.Bold)

        ' Set brush to ForeColor
        brush = New SolidBrush(imageForeColor)

        ' Write the text in the calculated position
        graphics.DrawString(displayText, font, brush, _
            imageLeftMargin, imageTopMargin)
    End Sub
```

Next we need to add the `Image` property's `Get()` and `Set()` methods:

```
    Public Property Image() As Bitmap
        Get
            Return textImage
        End Get
```

```
        Set(ByVal Value As Bitmap)
            textImage = Value
        End Set
    End Property
```

Next we take advantage of the features inside the `Bitmap` class. Our `WriteTo()` method simply calls the `Bitmap.Save()` method. Making this version of `WriteTo()` is really just for convenience since with the next, more versatile version, could accomplish the same result using a file stream.

The method also contains the `Format` parameter, which is of the type `System.Drawing.Imaging.ImageFormat`. This type is used as an enumeration of all the supported image formats (for example: BMP, JPG, GIF, WMF):

```
    Sub WriteTo(ByVal FileName As String, _
        ByVal Format As System.Drawing.Imaging.ImageFormat)

        textImage.Save(FileName, Format)
    End Sub
```

In the second overload, we again take advantage of the methods included in the `Bitmap` class. Rather than taking a `FileName`, this time we use a stream in our call to `Bitmap.Save()` method:

```
    Sub WriteTo(ByVal Stream As System.IO.Stream, _
        ByVal Format As System.Drawing.Imaging.ImageFormat)

        textImage.Save(Stream, Format)
    End Sub
```

This third and final implementation of `WriteTo()` uses the `HttpResponse` object. To send an image as our response, we must first clear out any other HTML and headers that might already be in the response buffer. To accomplish this, we call the `Clear()` method on the `HttpResponse` object.

Next, to ensure the browser understands the rest of the data we are sending to it is an image, we must set the `ContentType`. We use the `Format` parameter to determine what we should set the `ContentType` to (there are other valid image content types, for simplicity's sake, they are omitted).

We use the stream implementation of the `Bitmap.Save()` method to send the actual image.

The last step is to make sure nothing else is sent into the `OutputStream`. We just call the `End()` method of the `Response` object. This also saves unnecessary processing on the web server, since once the `End()` method is called the server stops the processing of the page and flushes the response buffer:

```
    Sub WriteTo(ByVal Response As HttpResponse, _
        ByVal Format As Imaging.ImageFormat)

        Response.Clear()
        If Format.Equals(Imaging.ImageFormat.Gif) Then
            Response.ContentType = "image/gif"
```

```
      ElseIf Format.Equals(Imaging.ImageFormat.Jpeg) Then
         Response.ContentType = "image/jpg"
      Else
         Throw New System.ArgumentOutOfRangeException("Format", _
            Format, _
            "Only Jpeg or Gif allowed by current implementation.")
      End If
      textImage.Save(Response.OutputStream, Format)
      Response.End()
   End Sub

 End Class
 End Namespace
```

That completes the code, so the project is ready to compile.

Demonstration

The following code snippets can be placed behind buttons on a form or in other appropriate places to test the various functions we've implemented. Make sure you import System.Drawing.dll and the TextImage project (or DLL) into any project that uses the TextImage class.

WinForms Example

These code examples assume they are running in a Windows Form, and that the Form has a PictureBox control named PictureBox1.

This code creates and displays a TextImage. This is the simplest test case:

```
Dim textImage As Wrox.Toolkit.Graphics.TextImage

textImage = New Wrox.Toolkit.Graphics.TextImage()
textImage.DrawImage(100, 20, Color.Green, Color.Gainsboro)
textImage.DrawTextOnImage("Hello", Color.Green, 10, 1, "Tahoma", 10)

PictureBox1.Image = textImage.Image
```

This code creates a TextImage and saves it to a file by using the WriteTo() method:

```
Dim textImage As Wrox.Toolkit.Graphics.TextImage

textImage = New Wrox.Toolkit.Graphics.TextImage()
textImage.DrawImage(100, 20, Color.Green, Color.Gainsboro)
textImage.DrawTextOnImage("Hello", Color.Green, 10, 1, "Tahoma", 10)

textImage.WriteTo("c:\textImage.wmf", Imaging.ImageFormat.Wmf)
```

To test this open a recent version of Internet Explorer, go to File | Open, and click the browse button. Browse to the file c:\textImage.wmf. Double-click on the file, then click OK. You are now looking at the image you created.

Class Override Example

To test overriding the drawing functionality of the TextImage class, add a new class to your project, and name it ButtonWithText.

Remember to add an Inherits statement:

```
Imports TextImageGenerator

Public Class ButtonWithText
  Inherits Wrox.Toolkit.Graphics.TextImage

  Public Overrides Sub DrawImage(ByVal imageWidth As Integer, _
      ByVal imageHeight As Integer, _
      ByVal imageForeColor As Color, _
      ByVal imageBackColor As Color)

    Dim bitmap As bitmap
    Dim graphics As Drawing.Graphics
    Dim brush As brush
    Dim blackPen As Pen

    ' Create Bitmap for temporary use
    bitmap = New bitmap(imageWidth, imageHeight)

    ' Get a graphics object to use for all the drawing
    graphics = graphics.FromImage(bitmap)

    ' Paint the background
    brush = New SolidBrush(Color.White)
    graphics.FillRectangle(brush, 0, 0, imageWidth, imageHeight)

    ' Set brush to ForeColor
    brush = New SolidBrush(imageBackColor)
    blackPen = New Pen(Color.Black, 1)

    ' Paint center portion of the button
    graphics.FillRectangle(brush, 10, 0, imageWidth - 20, imageHeight)

    ' Draw outline (top & bottom) of center portion of the button
    graphics.DrawLine(blackPen, 10, 0, imageWidth - 10, 0)
    graphics.DrawLine(blackPen, 10, imageHeight - 1, _
        imageWidth - 10, imageHeight - 1)

    ' Paint left half-circle
    graphics.FillPie(brush, 0, 0, 20, imageHeight - 1, 90, 180)
    ' Draw outline for left half-circle
    graphics.DrawArc(blackPen, 0, 0, 20, imageHeight - 1, 90, 180)

    ' Paint right half-circle
    graphics.FillPie(brush, imageWidth - 21, 0, 20, _
        imageHeight - 1, 270, 180)

    ' Draw outline for right half-circle
    graphics.DrawArc(blackPen, imageWidth - 21, 0, 20, _
        imageHeight - 1, 270, 180)

    MyBase.Image = bitmap

  End Sub
End Class
```

The code above first draws a rectangle and then adds a half circle onto each side. To draw the rectangle we use the `FillRectangle()` method. To outline the top and bottom of the rectangle we simply use `DrawLine()`. For each half circle we use `FillPie()` and then use `DrawArc()` to draw the outline.

To test this, use the WinForms demonstration you built above and change the class that is used from `TextImage` to `ButtonWithText`.

WebForm Example

To test the class in a WebForm, create a VB ASP.NET web application project and add a reference to the `TextImage.dll`. Rename the default WebForm to `WebForm1.aspx` and add another WebForm to the project named `TextImageDemo.aspx`.

`TextImageDemo.aspx` will be the page that hosts an image. No changes are necessary in the code behind. In the `aspx` page, in the HTML view, find the `<Form>` tag. Immediately following the `<Form>` tag, add this HTML code to the `.aspx` page:

```
<img src="TextImage.aspx?text=Hello">
```

In the Solution Explorer window, right-click on `TextImageDemo.aspx` and select Set as Start Page. This will ensure when you run the web application that you will see this page.

`TextImage.aspx` will be the page that generates the image. For this page, no changes are necessary in the `.aspx` code. However, the `Page_Load()` method must be updated in the code behind `TextImage.aspx.vb`. Replace the existing `Page_Load()` method with the one provided here:

```
Private Sub Page_Load(ByVal sender As System.Object, _
        ByVal e As System.EventArgs) Handles MyBase.Load

    Dim textImage As Wrox.Toolkit.Graphics.TextImage

    textImage = New Wrox.Toolkit.Graphics.TextImage()
    textImage.DrawImage(100, 20, Color.Green, Color.Yellow)
    textImage.DrawTextOnImage(Me.Request.QueryString.Item("Text"), _
        Color.Green, 10, 1, "Tahoma", 10)

    textImage.WriteTo(Response, Imaging.ImageFormat.Gif)

End Sub
```

Build the web application, and then run it. Internet Explorer should launch and display `TextImageDemo.aspx`, which should look something like this:

Limitations

There are two general concerns to mention here.

First, regarding colors; customizing this class to meet your specific graphic design needs is a likely requirement. While the .gif format is ideal for this situation for numerous reasons, one thing to watch for is the loss of color. The .gif format can only support 256 colors. Also, if you use the color Color.Transparent, remember that most image formats do not support transparency. However, GIF, WMF, and PNG do support with transparency.

Second, when drawing or imaging is involved, performance and scalability must always be considered. Raw performance isn't much of an issue for any of the demonstrations I've shown here. However, when using this class in a web environment like in the WebForm demo above, scalability is something that should be closely looked at. The problem is that as coded, each request to the server would cause it to generate the images every time. One way to mitigate this scalability problem would be to use ASP.NET's native page caching. When using page caching, ASP.NET only re-renders the page if a dependency changes or a specified amount of time passes.

Extensions

This class could be enhanced with features to use anti-aliasing (a method to make text more readable). The class could also be implemented to make images the proper size based on the size of the text, or the class could be implemented to center the text inside larger images.

Another extension would be to have the class accept multiple text strings, all to be placed on the image at different locations. You could then also generate an HTML image map that could accompany the image on your web page.

13

Stream Helper

Working with streams can often be difficult. The `StreamHelper` class is intended to ease the use of some common operations on streams, and illustrate their basic manipulation.

Scenario

Streams provide a generic way to deal with a sequence of bytes in a .NET application. Streams and streaming IO are prevalent in .NET. Any time you work with files, doing network IO, cryptography, serializing objects using a `BinaryFormatter` or `SoapFormatter`, and more, you are working with streams. While streams are very powerful, they often don't have the features we exactly want. Not all streams can be directly copied to other streams, saved to a file, or converted to a specific type of object, such as an image.

Other applications may have various requirements or functions that could be applied to streams, but which aren't directly supported by the .NET Framework. The `StreamHelper` module will provide some useful methods and a conceptual framework for creating other useful and reusable stream-based functionality.

Technology

In `System.IO` we find the `Stream` class. All other streams are derived from this base, and they each have slightly different behaviors. There are subclasses of the `Stream` class in many of the namespaces throughout the .NET Framework. Some common stream types are:

❑ FileStream

❑ NetworkStream

❑   `MemoryStream`

❑   `BufferedStream`

❑   `CryptoStream`

While all of these have a great deal in common, they are also different and are intended to support different functionality.

A `FileStream` is used to read and write data files on disk. A `NetworkStream` on the other hand, is used to exchange data across the network with another application. A `CryptoStream` doesn't exchange data with anything, it simply encrypts or decrypts any data that is written into the stream. A `MemoryStream` resides entirely in memory – like a RAM disk or arbitrary memory buffer.

Not all of these objects have the same methods or functionality. `MemoryStream`, for instance, has a `WriteTo()` method that allows it to write its contents to another stream. The other streams don't have this.

The `System.Drawing.Image` class has a `Shared` method called `FromStream()`, which allows us to create an image from data in a stream. This works fine with a `MemoryStream`, but doesn't seem to work properly with a `FileStream`.

The problem with streams is that they aren't consistent *enough*. The code to overcome most of these issues is not overly complex, but we could end up writing it in many places in our applications if we frequently use streams. To avoid rewriting or duplicating that code throughout our applications, we can create a `StreamHelper` class.

For the most part, we'll be working with the `Stream` data type and `Byte` arrays. Data from streams can be easily converted into and out of `Byte` arrays. From there, it is up to us to convert the data to or from one of the more useful formats, such as a `String`, an `Image`, or any other type of object.

Design

Since `StreamHelper` contains a set of methods that will operate on a wide variety of different types of object, inheritance is not a workable solution in this case. It would be useful to extend the interface of each type of stream object, adding a `WriteTo()` method to each type of stream for instance. Unfortunately, this would require sub-classing all the different types of stream in the .NET Framework to add the same code to each.

Instead, it is more appropriate to create a shared method library that we can apply to any of the stream classes as needed. The best way to create a function library is to create a `Public Module` that contains `Public` methods. Another option is to place the methods in a class, and declare them all as `Public Shared` methods. The `Module` approach is superior, however, because it allows us to add these methods directly to the namespace, without requiring us to type the name of the class.

It is very likely that you'll have additional requirements beyond those we'll implement here. The intent of the `StreamHelper` class is to provide a few common methods, but more importantly to provide some guidance on how you can add new methods as needed over time. The specific methods we'll add in this implementation are:

Method	Description
Copy(source, target)	Copies one stream into another
SaveToFile(source, fileName)	Saves the contents of a stream into a file
AppendToFile(source, fileName)	Appends the contents of a stream to the end of a file
ConvertToString(source)	Converts the contents of a stream to a string
ConvertToImage(source)	Converts the contents of a stream to an image
WriteLong(data)	Writes a Long (64-bit value) to a stream
ReadLong(source)	Reads a Long (64-bit value) from a stream
WriteObject(object, target)	Writes a <Serializable()> object to a stream in binary format
ReadObject(source)	Reads an object from a stream, assuming that object was written to the stream using WriteObject()

Implementation

The following is the complete code with an explanation for each important section.

Open Visual Studio .NET, create a Visual Basic Class Library project, and call it StreamHelper.

Rename `Class1.vb` to `StreamHelper.vb` and replace the code with the following:

```
Imports System.IO
Imports System.Drawing

Namespace Wrox.Toolkit.Net
  Public Module StreamHelper
```

We are importing `System.IO` because that is the namespace where the `Stream` base class resides, and we'll obviously be working with that a lot. We're also importing `System.Drawing`, which will require us to add a reference to the `System.Drawing.dll` assembly using the Add Reference dialog. This assembly contains the `Image` class, and we'll be using that in one of our methods later.

From here forward, we'll simply add a series of Shared methods to the class. Each method will perform a useful operation on one or more stream objects, regardless of the actual type of the stream object in question. This is a direct application of polymorphism, and to implement it we'll build all of our methods to accept and return Stream objects so they can handle any type of stream object.

The only exception is that *inside* some of our methods we'll be using a MemoryStream for temporary storage or manipulation of data.

Copy a Stream

Let's start with a simple and very common function – copying the contents of one stream into another. While MemoryStream has a WriteTo() method that copies its contents to another stream, most stream objects have no such functionality. Add this method to the class:

```
Public Sub Copy(ByVal source As Stream, _
                ByVal target As Stream)

   Dim Buffer(4095) As Byte
   Dim cnt As Integer

   cnt = source.Read(Buffer, 0, Buffer.Length)
   While cnt > 0
      target.Write(Buffer, 0, cnt)
      cnt = source.Read(Buffer, 0, Buffer.Length)
   End While

End Sub
```

This method takes two streams as parameters and copies the contents of the first into the second. The copy operation is done by reading blocks of data out of the source stream into a Byte array. Each block of data is then written into the target stream. When there's no more data in the source stream the cnt variable will be zero and we exit the loop.

As implemented, this method copies the data in chunks that are 4,096 bytes in length. This is somewhat arbitrary, though the size we select should be a power of 2 so it fits into memory efficiently.

One alternative that might come to mind is to use the Length property of the source stream to create a buffer that would fit the entire set of data. This would work fine assuming our system has enough RAM to support the source stream, the copy that goes into the array and the target stream all at once. Depending on our application, this may or may not be practical, and so this implementation takes the conservative approach by copying blocks of data that are unlikely to exceed any memory constraints on our system.

Write to a File

We started with the copy operation, because it is useful in creating other common functions. For instance, perhaps we want the ability to store a stream into a file:

```
Public Sub SaveToFile(ByVal source As Stream, _
                      ByVal fileName As String)

   Dim MyFile As FileStream = File.Create(fileName)
   Copy(source, MyFile)
   MyFile.Close()

End Sub
```

Since we already have the ability to copy from one stream to another, this is relatively painless. The code creates a new file and retrieves a `FileStream` object in return. At that point, the source stream is copied into the `FileStream` using the `Copy()` method already created. Finally, the `FileStream` is closed.

Append to a File

Similarly, we can append to a file, writing the data from the stream to the end of an existing file, rather than creating a new one:

```
Public Sub AppendToFile(ByVal source As Stream, _
                        ByVal fileName As String)

   Dim MyFile As FileStream = File.Open(fileName, FileMode.Append)
   Copy(source, MyFile)
   MyFile.Close()

End Sub
```

This is basically the same code, but using the `Open()` method of the `File` class to open the output file for an append operation.

Convert to a String

Many times, we'll be using streams to retrieve data. Sometimes that data will be text, other times in binary format such as an image. Let's add a function to return `String` data from a stream:

```
Public Function ConvertToString(ByVal source As Stream) _
                As String

   ' Remember arrays are zero-based, 0 To Length-1 = Length
   Dim Buffer(source.Length - 1) As Byte

   source.Read(Buffer, 0, Buffer.Length)
   Return System.Text.Encoding.ASCII.GetString(Buffer)

End Function
```

This code reads the data from the stream into a `Byte` array. Once it is in a `Byte` array, we can use the `GetString()` method from an `ASCIIEncoding` class to convert the array into a `String`. The 8-bit ASCII character values are converted to 16-bit Unicode character values in our `String`. This assumes that the underlying data was a series of 8-bit ASCII text values to start with – otherwise the resulting text won't be human-readable. This is a reasonable assumption any time we're working with text files or network streams, as they tend to all use 8-bit ASCII.

Convert to an Image

If we know a stream contains an image, we can write a helper method to return that image:

```
Public Function ConvertToImage(ByVal source As Stream) _
                As Image

    Dim Buffer As New MemoryStream()
    Copy(source, Buffer)
    Buffer.Position = 0

    Dim img As Image = Image.FromStream(Buffer)
    Buffer.Close()
    Return img

End Function
```

In this case, we're copying the source stream into a MemoryStream. We then set the cursor, or position, of the MemoryStream back to the beginning and use it to load an Image object.

A possible optimization would be to check if the source stream is a MemoryStream and simply use it directly to create the image. Caution must be used in such a case, however, since the position of the source should not be changed, nor should it be closed when the operation is complete, so there's a fair amount of work involved in trapping the status of the source stream first, then restoring it at the end of the method. In this case, we're avoiding such issues by simply copying the data into our own buffer even if the source is a MemoryStream.

Notice that the Image class has a FromStream() method. We did this with a MemoryStream instead of simply using this method directly against the source stream, because this wouldn't work with all stream types. For instance, a FileStream opened to a file containing an image can't be read into an Image object in this manner.

By copying the source stream into a MemoryStream first, we ensure that the Image class can create an Image object from the data. Of course, this does assume that the source stream really contains image data. If the stream doesn't contain valid image data, an exception will be raised as we attempt to create the image. This exception can be caught by the calling code so the developer gets an indication that the data was invalid.

Reading and Writing Arbitrary Objects

At this point, we've seen how to get String data and an Image object out of a stream. You may want to know how to put arbitrary objects into a stream. Maybe you want to send objects across the network using a NetworkStream, or put them in a file using a FileStream.

The first question is how to convert an arbitrary object into a single chunk of data that can be placed into a stream. Fortunately, the .NET Framework makes this relatively easy through a technology called **serialization**. By marking a class with the <Serializable()> attribute, we can tell .NET that any objects of that type can be converted into a form of raw data. That's all we need to do as .NET handles the rest. In this case, we'll convert them into binary data, which is the most compact form.

The next question is how to put these objects into a stream such that we can get them back out. In particular, when we're reading the objects back out of the stream, we need to know when the first one stops and the next object begins. This is particularly problematic when we need to send objects across a TCP/IP socket using a NetworkStream object.

This process happens automatically when we use .NET Remoting and pass any object marked as <Serializable()> as a parameter, or return it as a method result. However, if we cannot use Remoting and are instead using a TCP/IP socket (NetworkStream) for our network communication, we need an alternative. This can happen when the client workstation needs a long-lived connection to the server due to network address translation or a firewall arrangement that prevents Remoting from operating.

When working with binary data it can be challenging to determine the end of a given chunk of data – such as an object. This is because we can't use any character value as a delimiter since that character could easily end up in our data as well. The solution is to always start by putting the length of the data into the stream. Then when we read the stream, we can read the length first, and then read that many bytes out of the stream to get our object.

Of course, we need to be able to find the length of our data beforehand. When working with serializable objects, we can find the length by first serializing the object into a MemoryStream and then looking at the resulting size of the data in the MemoryStream object. This length value is returned as a 64-bit Long, which is very large, but still finite.

When an object is serialized, the resulting stream will not only include the object's data, but also all the information about the type of the object. This allows .NET to deserialize the object, creating an exact clone of the original object based on the data in the stream.

This implies that we have the ability to write and read numeric values such as a Long. These functions don't exist on stream objects by default, so we need to create them. Since serialized objects can be very large, as mentioned earlier, the data type used for their length is Long – an 8-byte value. Let's create a helper function to write a Long into a stream:

```
Public Sub WriteLong(ByVal data As Long, _
                     ByVal target As Stream)

    Dim Buffer(7) As Byte

    Buffer(0) = (data And &HFFL) / 256L ^ 0L
    Buffer(1) = (data And &HFF00L) / 256L ^ 1L
    Buffer(2) = (data And &HFF0000L) / 256L ^ 2L
    Buffer(3) = (data And &HFF000000L) / 256L ^ 3L
    Buffer(4) = (data And &HFF00000000L) / 256L ^ 4L
    Buffer(5) = (data And &HFF0000000000L) / 256L ^ 5L
    Buffer(6) = (data And &HFF000000000000L) / 256L ^ 6L
    Buffer(7) = (data And &HFF00000000000000L) / 256L ^ 7L
    target.Write(Buffer, 0, 8)

End Sub
```

64 bits is 8 bytes, so we need to create an 8-byte array and then use bit masking to pull each byte's data out of the Long value and place it into the array. Once that's done, we can write the Byte array into the target stream. This is illustrated in Figure 1:

Figure 1

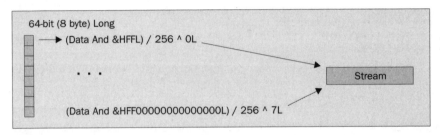

For example, if we have a Long containing the value 721853 then the values of its 8 individual bytes will be 189, 3, 11, and five zeros. Only very large numbers will cause values to exist in the remaining byte slots.

Likewise, we need to be able to read a Long from a stream:

```
Public Function ReadLong(ByVal source As Stream) As Long
  Dim Buffer(7) As Byte
  source.Read(Buffer, 0, 8)

  Dim Data As Long
  Data += Buffer(0) * 256L ^ 0L
  Data += Buffer(1) * 256L ^ 1L
  Data += Buffer(2) * 256L ^ 2L
  Data += Buffer(3) * 256L ^ 3L
  Data += Buffer(4) * 256L ^ 4L
  Data += Buffer(5) * 256L ^ 5L
  Data += Buffer(6) * 256L ^ 6L
  Data += Buffer(7) * 256L ^ 7L
  Return Data
End Function
```

Since a Long is eight bytes, we read the first eight bytes from the stream and put that data into a Byte array. Each byte's data is pulled out of the array and is added to the Long. This is the reverse of the bit-masking process used to decompose the Long in the previous method.

Now we have the tools to write a method that puts an arbitrary <Serializable()> object into a stream:

```
Public Sub WriteObject(ByVal obj As Object, _
                       ByVal target As Stream)

  Dim Buffer As New MemoryStream()
  Dim Formatter As _
    New Runtime.Serialization.Formatters.Binary.BinaryFormatter()

  Formatter.Serialize(Buffer, obj)
  Buffer.Position = 0

  Dim cnt As Long = Buffer.Length
```

```
    WriteLong(cnt, target)

    Buffer.WriteTo(target)
    Buffer.Close()
End Sub
```

The result is a stream containing the length and the start, followed by the object data. There is a lot going on here, so let's break it down a little.

We use a `BinaryFormatter` object to serialize the object into a `MemoryStream`, and reset the `MemoryStream`'s cursor to the start of the stream. With that done, we can get the length of the serialized object's data, which we can then write to the target stream:

```
    WriteLong(cnt, target)
```

Because the length value we're using here is a `Long`, which is the maximum size of a `MemoryStream`, the size of our serialized object can't exceed 9,223,372,036,854,775,807 bytes. This is about 8,796,093,022,208 megabytes, or 8,589,934,592 gigabytes, or 8,388,608 terabytes. Obviously, we'll run out of memory on our machine long before we'll exceed these values.

Next, the serialized object data itself is written to the stream by using the `MemoryStream` object's `WriteTo()` method:

```
    Buffer.WriteTo(target)
```

Finally, the `MemoryStream` is closed to release its underlying data and we're all done.

Reading an object from a stream is essentially the reverse of this process:

```
    Public Function ReadObject(ByVal source As Stream) As Object

    Dim Formatter As _
        New Runtime.Serialization.Formatters.Binary.BinaryFormatter()
    Dim cnt As Long = ReadLong(source)
    Dim Buffer(cnt - 1) As Byte

    source.Read(Buffer, 0, cnt)
    Dim MemStream As New MemoryStream(Buffer)

    Dim out As Object = Formatter.Deserialize(MemStream)
    MemStream.Close()

    Return out

    End Function
```

Here the `Long` value is read from the source stream, so right away we know how many bytes of data should be read from the stream to get the object's serialized data.

We then dimension a `Byte` array to be that size and read that many bytes from the stream:

```
    Dim Buffer(cnt - 1) As Byte
    Source.Read(Buffer, 0, cnt)
```

The result is that the object data is copied to the `Byte` array, which can then be used to create a `MemoryStream` object that can be deserialized using the `BinaryFormatter`:

```
Dim MemStream As New MemoryStream(Buffer)
Dim out As Object = Formatter.Deserialize(MemStream)
```

Note that creating a new `MemoryStream` by passing it a `Byte` array does *not* copy the data out of the `Byte` array. Instead, the array becomes the underlying buffer against which the stream operates. Obviously the deserialization process not only copies the data, but unpacks and decodes it to create an exact clone of the original object.

The `MemoryStream` is then closed to release its underlying data and the object is returned as a result. Notice that it is returned as type `Object`, so this will work with any `<Serializable()>` object that was placed into the stream using the `WriteObject()` method. This does mean that the calling code needs to know the original type of the object so it can use the appropriate type of variable to store the return result. Alternatively, the calling code could use late binding to interact directly with the returned object.

Demonstration

The following code snippets can be placed behind buttons on a form or in other appropriate places to test the various functions we've implemented.

Create a new Windows Application in Visual Studio .NET and name it `StreamTest`. You'll need to add a reference to the assembly or project containing the `StreamHelper` class and import the `Wrox.Toolkit.Net` namespace at the top of the form:

```
Imports Wrox.Toolkit.Net
Imports System.IO
```

Because we implemented our library as a `Module`, by importing `Wrox.Toolkit.Net` here we have just added all the methods from that `Module` directly to the environment. The developer can now call our `Copy()` method without the need for a prefix. If we had used a `Class` with `Shared` methods the developer would be required to use `StreamHelper.Copy()` instead of just `Copy()`.

Rename the form to `StreamTest`, and add five buttons to `Form1` named `btnSaveToFile`, `btnAppendToFile`, `btnConvertToString`, `btnConvertToImage`, and `btnStreamObjects`. Also, add a picture box control called `PictureBox1`. The form should look as follows:

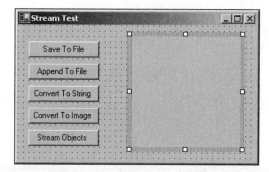

To test saving a stream to a file, add the following code to StreamTest:

```
Private Sub btnSaveToFile_Click(ByVal sender As System.Object, _
    ByVal e As System.EventArgs) Handles btnSaveToFile.Click

    Dim MyFile As FileStream = File.OpenRead("c:\x.txt")

    SaveToFile(MyFile, "c:\y.txt")
    MyFile.Close()

End Sub
```

Use Notepad or another text editor to create a file named c:\x.txt and place some text into the file. Then we can run the application and click the button to copy the contents of x.txt into y.txt. Now use a text editor to read y.txt, where we'll find that the data was in fact copied.

The append operation can be tested as well. Add the following code to the form:

```
Private Sub btnAppendToFile_Click(ByVal sender As System.Object, _
    ByVal e As System.EventArgs) Handles btnAppendToFile.Click

    Dim MyFile As FileStream = File.OpenRead("c:\x.txt")
    Dim Buffer As New MemoryStream()

    Copy(MyFile, Buffer)
    MyFile.Close()

    Buffer.Position = 0
    SaveToFile(Buffer, "c:\y.txt")

    Buffer.Position = 0
    AppendToFile(Buffer, "c:\y.txt")

End Sub
```

This code illustrates a number of things. First, we see how to use the Copy() method to copy the file's data into a MemoryStream object. We can then close the input file because we have its data in memory. From there, we save the data to a new y.txt file using SaveToFile() and then append the data to the file a second time by using AppendToFile(). If we view y.txt in a text editor now we'll see the data in the file twice.

167

Notice that we're setting the `Position` property of the `MemoryStream` back to 0 before we use it each time. This value acts like a cursor within the stream and if we don't reset it we'll attempt to read off the end of the stream and get no data.

To test the `ConvertToString()` method add the following code in the form:

```
Private Sub btnConvertToString_Click( _
          ByVal sender As System.Object, _
          ByVal e As System.EventArgs) _
          Handles btnConvertToString.Click

    Dim MyFile As FileStream = File.OpenRead("c:\x.txt")

    MsgBox(ConvertToString(MyFile))
    MyFile.Close()

End Sub
```

This reads `x.txt` and converts the `FileStream` into a `String` value, which is then displayed in a message box. When this code is run, we'll see the contents of the `x.txt` file displayed on the screen.

To test the `ConvertToImage()` method we use the `PictureBox` control added to the form earlier, and add the following code to the form:

```
Private Sub btnConvertToImage_Click(ByVal sender As System.Object, _
     ByVal e As System.EventArgs) Handles btnConvertToImage.Click

    Dim WinDir As String
    Dim MyFile As FileStream
    Dim img As Image

    WinDir = Environment.GetEnvironmentVariable("windir")
    MyFile = File.OpenRead(windir & "\greenstone.bmp")
    img = ConvertToImage(MyFile)
    MyFile.Close()

    PictureBox1.Image = img

End Sub
```

This code retrieves the path to the Windows directory, where a number of common bitmap images are stored. It then opens `greenstone.bmp` and uses our `ConvertToImage()` method to read its contents and return an `Image` object. The `Image` object is then displayed in the `PictureBox` control on the form.

To test the reading and writing of an object, we first need a serializable class. Add a class named `Person` to the `StreamTest` project with the following code:

```
<Serializable()> _
Public Class Person
    Private mName As String

    Public Property Name() As String
        Get
            Return mName
        End Get
        Set(ByVal Value As String)
            mName = Value
```

```
          End Set
        End Property

  End Class
```

Then we can create code to write instances of this class to a stream and read them back out. In this example we'll use a MemoryStream for simplicity, but where this really shines is in the case where we need to send a series of objects across a TCP/IP socket via a NetworkStream, or perhaps place a series of objects into a FileStream object. Add the following code to StreamTest.vb:

```
Private Sub btnStreamObjects_Click(ByVal sender As System.Object, _
    ByVal e As System.EventArgs) Handles btnStreamObjects.Click

  Dim Buffer As New MemoryStream()

  Dim obj As New Person()

  ' put first object into stream
  obj.Name = "Mary"
  WriteObject(obj, Buffer)

  ' put second object into stream
  obj.Name = "Juan"
  WriteObject(obj, Buffer)

  Buffer.Position = 0

  ' read first object from stream
  obj = CType(ReadObject(Buffer), Person)
  MsgBox(obj.Name)

  ' read second object from stream
  obj = CType(ReadObject(Buffer), Person)
  MsgBox(obj.Name)

End Sub
```

After creating a Person object, we then set its Name property, and serialize the object into the stream. This creates a copy of the object's data in the stream – ignoring all Property values, and just copying the variables, such as mName, directly. Also remember that the serialized data includes the class name, assembly name, and version of the code necessary to decode the data when it is deserialized so we end up with an exact clone of this initial object.

We then change the Name property, which changes the value of mName within the object. The object is again written to the stream, creating another serialized object with different data.

The Position, or cursor, of the stream is reset to the beginning and we then read the first object off the stream. Typically this would be happening on another machine that received the data via the stream or something like that, but for this test it is enough to copy the objects into the MemoryStream and read them back out to demonstrate the concept.

The ReadObject() method reads the length of the first object, then reads the object's data and deserializes that data to create a clone of the original object. That object is then returned as a result of the method. We're using the CType() function to change the data type of the object from the generic System.Object to Person so we can use it to display a message box showing the name of the person – in this case Mary.

We do the same thing again, reading the second object off the stream and displaying its name – in this case Juan.

Limitations

Not all streams are created equally, and some have different quirks when reading and writing to them. In particular, watch out for streams that block your thread on a read attempt or write attempt, as that can get complex. Be cautious in multithreaded environments. When multiple threads operate on the same stream, you need to employ property synchronization to avoid conflicts between threads.

The ConvertToString() assumes the data you are dealing with is ASCII, and the .NET Framework deals with Unicode (UTF-16) as default. Therefore, be careful with this method. A new Unicode-aware method could be created, but as Unicode characters occupy between 2 and 4 bytes, more detail would have been needed here than is really within the scope of this book.

The WriteObject() and ReadObject() methods work in concert. Obviously, an object can be directly serialized into a stream without these methods, but if you are writing *multiple* objects to the same stream then these methods are the way to go.

Extensions

Streaming IO is pervasive within the .NET Framework. There are many opportunities for creating helper functions along the lines of those shown here. You may have other data types you need to read and write from streams, or you may want to have a helper that encrypts or compresses stream data, or any number of operations can be written and added to the StreamHelper.

14

Smart Socket

A Smart Socket will allow you to send serializable objects via a socket without having to manually serialize or deserialize the data on either the client or the server.

Scenario

When working with low-level objects like TCP clients and listeners, much code needs to be written before you can start using the objects and get any results. The Smart Sockets class is a starting point for creating the components for sending objects across a socket including the client, the listener, the server class, and the server collection, which gets you up to speed quickly.

In many cases we can use .NET Remoting to transfer objects across the network. Remoting automatically supports serializable objects, passing them across the network by value. They can be passed as a parameter or returned as the result of a function.

Given this functionality, you might wonder why we might want to send an object over a raw TCP socket. Remoting is a disconnected technology, meaning that each time a server-side method is invoked by the client, a new connection is established to the server. If the server wants to send data to the client, it must open a connection to the client to send the data.

This works great for most applications, as long as both client and server have routable IP addresses and there are no firewalls in the way. This means that simple Remoting typically won't allow bi-directional communication between client and server if there are any NAT routers or firewalls involved. Since most home and corporate networks use NAT routers, and most organizations use firewalls, this can seriously restrict our ability to use Remoting when bi-directional communication is required. To send data through firewalls and NAT routers, you would have to use Remoting over HTTP, which may not be desirable.

Bi-directional communication is required for any scenarios where the server must push data to the client without waiting for the client to poll the server. It is also critical for any peer-to-peer implementations, since both client and server must be able to initiate communication in such a case.

The `SmartSocket` project allows us to easily implement socket-based servers, without directly interacting with any networking or threading code. As the developer, you will be able to extend the class, which provides simple methods for handling communication with a particular client.

Technology

Socket programming can be quite complex. A socket is a very low-level construct that merely allows us to send bytes of data across networks, to different application domains, or elsewhere. It is up to the developer to figure out how to encode and decode the data being sent. Additionally, socket technologies are often multithreaded. This is particularly true on a server, where we will usually use multiple threads to enable maximum performance and scalability.

Socket programming is at its most complex when used to communicate over a network. Web technologies are quite easy to implement, as they don't deal with persistent connections and a socket will only last as long as it takes to send or receive some client-specified item of data.

In our case we want to have a socket that remains connected over a pre-determined period, allowing both clients and servers to send data at will. This allows a server to send data to the client at any time, without waiting for the client to ask for it. However, it also means that we need to develop a protocol to identify when the data has been sent in its entirety.

Detecting the end of a data stream is not trivial. This is arbitrary, binary data, which might contain any mixture of character data. Thus we cannot simply wait for a null, or a close bracket or anything like that, since such values might be embedded *within* our data.

The easiest solution is always to begin a data transfer by sending the data length across the socket. Then the receiving code can simply wait until it has exactly that much data, knowing at that point that it has everything. This is what we'll do in the `SmartSocket` code.

Implementing serialization functionality can be complex, but fortunately the .NET Framework directly supports this concept. When we create a class, we can use the `<Serializable()>` attribute on the class to tell the .NET Framework that it should be able to serialize and deserialze this object. All the hard work happens behind the scenes.

To ensure good performance and scalability, we also need to support multithreading. This can be very complex, leading to code that is very hard to debug, and so we'll try to isolate the threading as much as possible. We'll additionally make use of the built-in thread pool that .NET manages on our behalf. By using the thread pool, we won't have to worry about creating too many or too few threads, although there may be a delay in execution while waiting for a thread to become available.

Finally, in .NET all socket communication occurs through streams. A stream is a way of sending and receiving bytes of data. The previous chapter contained the `StreamHelper` helper functions for working with steams, and we'll use some of these to simplify our use of streams in the `SmartSocket` framework.

Design

When creating a socket-based application we have to worry about creating both client and server components. On the server there are two main components – the listener and our custom server logic.

The listener, named `SmartListener`, runs constantly, waiting for incoming connection requests from clients. When it gets a connection request, it creates an instance of a server object by calling a factory object (based on the **ObjectFactory** design pattern). It then connects the client to this new server object. The server object contains our business logic and handles all interaction with the client.

The factory, by definition, must implement a formal interface – `IServerFactory`. The server class must implement an `IServer` interface. This means that `SmartListener` is totally generic and can be used with any classes we create as long as they implement these interfaces. This is illustrated in Figure 1:

Figure 1

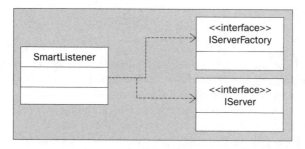

In our design each client connection gets its own server object. This is done to simplify the server-side code. Since each server object is responsible for interacting with just one client, our server code can contain user-specific variables or other data unique to the specific client. The server object contains a connection object for the client, which is responsible for receiving data from the client, sending data to the client, and detecting if the client terminates the connection.

On the client there is just one object – the client connection object. This object is responsible for connecting to the server, receiving data from the server, sending data to the server, and detecting if the server terminates the connection.

Notice the similarity in function between the connection objects on the server and client. Both need to send data, receive data and detect termination of the connection. Because of this commonality, we can build a single SmartConnection class that contains this code such that the same functionality can be used on both client and server.

This has the added benefit of allowing us to write code to support our binary transfer protocol in a single class. For a send operation this code will write the length of the data to be sent, then write the data itself. On the receiving side of things, the code will expect the length of the data to come first, followed by the data itself. By using the same SmartConnection class on both client and server, we ensure that this protocol will be followed for all communications.

As written, this protocol supports the transfer of objects marked with the <Serializable()> attribute. If we needed to send other types of data, we'd need to develop a protocol to support that data and alter our code to implement that protocol.

A more elegant alternative would be to subclass SmartConnection – gaining its core functionality and extending it with business logic. This is illustrated in Figure 2:

Figure 2

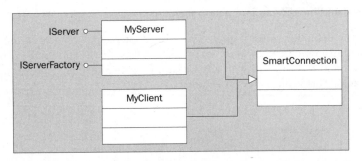

With this framework, we will also have to deal with various threading issues. On the server there may be many threads running concurrently. We will design this so that SmartListener will run in its own thread so it is always available to new clients. Whenever data is received from a client the relevant code will run in a separate thread. We will control this by having each SmartListener running on one thread only, and delegating functions to different threads as needed. This means that our business logic does not have to worry about threading issues at all – they'll be handled internally by the SmartSocket component.

We use the ThreadPool for the connection, but it is only advisable to use the ThreadPool for short-lived connections. In a production environment, it may make more sense to create your own thread pool manager to handle these connections. An implementation of such code can be found in *Visual Basic .NET Threading Handbook*, Wrox Press, ISBN 1-86100-713-2.

Likewise, the client will use a multithreaded approach to receiving data from the server. This will allow the client UI to remain responsive to the user, even when the client application is waiting for server data. Again, the SmartSocket component will handle threading issues internally so the UI developer doesn't have to worry about them and can work with a single thread only.

To make this work on the client, the UI code will need to provide the SmartConnection object with a reference to the main form of the UI. Windows Forms are associated with a specific thread, and we will write code to ensure that our event indicating the reception of data is always raised on the thread for that form.

The .NET Framework provides support for synchronizing with a Windows Form so that we can run code on its thread, and we'll make use of that support.

Implementation

Create a Class Library named SmartSocket.vb, and if coding with Visual Studio .NET, use the Project Properties to clear the root namespace. Add a reference to the SocketHelper assembly, detailed in the previous chapter.

Before you start coding the SmartConnection and SmartListener classes, you must create two interfaces for these classes to implement. Firstly, let's see the Imports statements and namespace declaration.

```
Imports System.IO
Imports System.Threading
Imports System.Net.Sockets

Namespace Wrox.Toolkit.Net
```

The following IServer interface defines the interface for our server object, so SmartListener can interact with the server code. The interface includes a method for connecting to the client (ConnectTo()), and a method for closing the server object (Close()). It is as follows:

```
Public Interface IServer
    Sub ConnectTo(ByVal Client As TcpClient)
    Sub Close()
End Interface
```

IServerFactory defines an interface for objects that can instantiate IServer objects. SmartListener will use this interface any time it needs to create a new server object to service a client connection request. Add a new class to the project named IServerFactory and write the following code:

```
Public Interface IServerFactory
    Function GetServer() As IServer
End Interface
```

SmartConnection

As mentioned above, the object that does the majority of the work is the SmartConnection object. This class is a wrapper around the TCPClient object that understands how to send and receive any serializable class.

Add a new class called SmartConnection. The SmartConnection class will need to raise an event when data has been received and when the TCP connection is closed from the other end:

```
Public Class SmartConnection
  Public Event DataReceived(ByVal Data As Object)
  Public Event ConnectionClosed()

  Private WithEvents ReceivedTimer As System.Timers.Timer
  Private WithEvents ClosedTimer As System.Timers.Timer
```

The last two fields are used later in the code for passing events to the main thread.

Connecting to the Network

Since this class will be a wrapper around the TcpClient class provided by the .NET Framework, we need to declare a TcpClient variable and provide an overloaded method to establish a connection:

```
  Private _Client As TcpClient
  Private _ClientStream As NetworkStream
  Private _ClientBuffer() As Byte
  Private _BufferStream As MemoryStream
  Private _DataLength As Long
  Private _State As Integer
  Private _Sync As Boolean

  Public Overloads Sub ConnectTo(ByVal hostName As String, _
                     ByVal port As Integer)
    ConnectTo(New TcpClient(hostName, port))
  End Sub

  Public Overloads Sub ConnectTo(ByVal client As TcpClient)
    _Client = client
    _ClientStream = _Client.GetStream
    ReDim _ClientBuffer(_Client.ReceiveBufferSize - 1)

    _ClientStream.BeginRead(_ClientBuffer, 0, _
       _Client.ReceiveBufferSize - 1, AddressOf OnReceive, Nothing)
  End Sub
```

The first ConnectTo() overload is merely a friendly front-end to the other. This way we allow the UI developer to either provide us with a host name and port, or a fully initialized TcpClient object as they choose.

We store a reference to the TcpClient object in a private field, as well as a reference to its underlying NetworkStream object. The reference to the stream object is for convenience so that we can use it in our code any time we send data.

When we receive data it will be received into a `Byte` array. This array is sized by using a `ReDim` statement to ensure that it can hold the maximum number of bytes that the `NetworkStream` will accept.

Receiving Data

The real work begins when we call `BeginRead()` on the stream object:

```
_ClientStream.BeginRead(_ClientBuffer, 0, _
    _Client.ReceiveBufferSize - 1, AddressOf OnReceive, Nothing)
```

This method call starts an asynchronous background process that waits for any data to arrive from the socket. When data does arrive, the `OnReceive()` method (which we'll detail shortly) is called on a separate thread. This means that our application code does not wait for data to arrive – the waiting and processing of any received data occurs on background threads.

The `BeginRead()` method states that received data should be placed in the `_ClientBuffer` array starting at position 0 and accepting the maximum number of bytes that will fit. It also provides the address of the `OnReceive()` method to indicate which method will be executed to handle received data.

```
Private Sub OnReceive(ByVal ar As IAsyncResult)
    Dim count As Integer

    Try
        count = _Client.GetStream.EndRead(ar)
    Catch
        count = 0
    End Try

    If count > 0 Then
        Try
            HandleData(count)
        Finally
            _ClientStream.BeginRead(_ClientBuffer, 0, _
                _Client.ReceiveBufferSize, AddressOf OnReceive, Nothing)
        End Try
    Else
        OnConnectionClosed()
    End If
End Sub
```

The parameter must be of type `IAsyncResult`, and it will include any information needed to end the background receive operation. Notice that the first thing we do is call `EndRead()`, passing the `IAsyncResult` object as a parameter (`Nothing` in this case). What we get back from this call is the number of bytes that have been placed into our `Byte` array.

Notice that this is wrapped in a `Try` block. We might get an error at this point – particularly if the other machine closed the connection. In such a case we're simply setting the byte count to zero. The only time we'll end up handling zero bytes of received data is when the connection has been terminated. In this case, it will call `OnConnectionClosed()` (a method added later), which raises the `ConnectionClosed` event to indicate that the connection has been terminated.

177

If we do actually receive some data, it calls the `HandleData()` method (which is shown shortly) where we process the received bytes. Once the data is processed, we again call `BeginRead()` to restart the background read process.

The order of these calls is important. Because we don't call `BeginRead()` until *after* we've finished handling the received data, there is no chance of having multiple threads running `OnReceive()` at the same time. As soon as we call `BeginRead()` we allow another thread to start receiving data. Now, all that remains is to write the `HandleData()` method. This method implements our data transfer protocol. As we discussed earlier, we'll send the length of the data first, followed by the data itself.

Since we've implemented the ability to read and write serializable objects to streams in the `StreamHelper` component, we'll make use of it here. In that implementation, the length data is a `Long`, or 8 bytes. This means that the first 8 bytes we read will contain the `Long` value indicating the number of bytes of data that will follow. Then we'll read the data.

This is complicated by the fact that there is no guarantee that the data will arrive at the same time. We might get a few bytes, then a few more later and so forth. Since the other machine might be sending us a lot of different objects, we might not only get one object, but several – all in a row and all at once. There's no way to predict what might happen. This means that an otherwise simple operation becomes complex.

The `HandleData()` method is implemented as a state machine with three states. State 0 occurs when the application is waiting for the data to be received. State 1 occurs when receiving the first 8 bytes containing the length data. State 2 occurs when the length has been retrieved and so we're retrieving the rest of the data. In any case, the data is written into a `MemoryStream` object, which like a RAM disk is simple in-memory storage of the data:

```
Private Sub HandleData(ByVal count As Integer)
  If _State = 0 Then
    ' This is the start of some new data
    ' Create a new buffer stream
    _BufferStream = New MemoryStream()
    _State = 1
  End If
```

If the code is in State 0 and it receives some data, it creates a new, blank `MemoryStream` buffer to store the data, and then changes the state to 1.

```
  If _State = 1 Then
    ' write the data into the stream
    _BufferStream.Write(_ClientBuffer, 0, count)

    If _BufferStream.Length >= 8 Then
      ' We have at least our header
      ' so get the data length
      _BufferStream.Position = 0
      _DataLength = ReadLong(_BufferStream) + 8
      _BufferStream.Seek(0, SeekOrigin.End)

      ' indicate that we have the length and
      ' now need to read the remainder of the data
      _State = 2
```

In State 1, the data needs to be recorded into the buffer until we have at least 8 bytes. When we have 8 bytes of data we can read the Long value from the MemoryStream buffer to get the length of the data – and then we change the state to 2:

Finally, in State 2 we just keep recording the data into the buffer until we have all the bytes and so can process it:

```
        ElseIf _State = 2 Then
            ' We are reading message data
            _BufferStream.Write(_ClientBuffer, 0, count)
        End If
```

Each time we receive data, after we've gone through the process of finding the length and setting the state, we check to see if we have all the data we need. This can only be the case if we're in State 2 (recording data until we have it all) and the length of our data buffer is at least as large as the number of bytes we're looking for (based on the value we found in State 1):

```
        If _State = 2 AndAlso _BufferStream.Length >= _DataLength Then
            ' Deserialize the data into an object
            _BufferStream.Position = 0
            Dim msg As Object = ReadObject(_BufferStream)

            ' Signal the arrival of an object
            OnMessageReceived(msg)

            ' Reset our state to indicate we're looking for
            ' a new object
            _State = 0
```

If we have all the data for an object, we can deserialize it by using StreamHelper's ReadObject() method. We also call OnMessageReceived() (a method we'll add later) to raise an event to indicate that the data has arrived. Finally, we reset the state to 0 so that the application can start looking for the next object.

Keeping in mind that our buffer might already have the next object, we need a bit more code to see if there's data still to be processed. If there is, we'll simply copy the remaining data from the MemoryStream into the Byte array – just as if it were freshly received from the network. Then we can just call HandleData() to start the process over:

```
            ' Now we need to handle any overflow data
            If _BufferStream.Length > _DataLength Then
                ' We have overflow
                _BufferStream.Read(_ClientBuffer, 0, _
                                _BufferStream.Length - _DataLength)
                HandleData(_BufferStream.Length - _DataLength)
            End If
        End If
    End Sub
```

Other than detailing the methods to raise the events, we're now ready to receive data.

Raising the Events

Raising the events isn't as simple as just calling `RaiseEvent`. This is because our code is running on a background thread. On a server this is often just fine, but on a client with a Windows Forms UI it is very important that the events be raised on the same thread that is running the UI. This means we need to add some code to allow our events to be optionally synchronized with the UI thread.

The technique used relies on the `System.Timers.Timer` class. This timer has some extra abilities, most importantly the ability to synchronize its `Elapsed` event so it always fires on the thread that owns a form.

We'll use this ability to allow code running on a background thread to trigger code to run on the UI thread. Remember that we inserted two `Timer` variables at the start of the class:

```
Private WithEvents ReceivedTimer As System.Timers.Timer
Private WithEvents ClosedTimer As System.Timers.Timer
```

The first is for the `DataReceived` event, and the other for the `ConnectionClosed` event. Now code the default constructor to initialize these `Timer` objects:

```
Public Sub New()
    ReceivedTimer = New System.Timers.Timer()
    ReceivedTimer.AutoReset = False
    ReceivedTimer.Interval = 1

    ClosedTimer = New System.Timers.Timer()
    ClosedTimer.AutoReset = False
    ClosedTimer.Interval = 1
End Sub
```

Note that both are set with an interval of 1 millisecond so they'll fire virtually immediately upon being enabled. Also notice the `AutoReset` event is set as `False`. This means that when the control is enabled, it will automatically disable itself after firing its `Elapsed` event.

Below is the code to handle the `Elapsed` event for `ClosedTimer`:

```
Private Sub ClosedTimer_Elapsed(ByVal sender As Object, _
            ByVal e As System.Timers.ElapsedEventArgs) _
            Handles ClosedTimer.Elapsed
    RaiseEvent ConnectionClosed()
End Sub
```

Here we call `RaiseEvent` and since the `Elapsed` event is raised on the UI thread, our `DataReceived` and `ConnectionClosed` events will also be raised on the UI thread.

We still need to get a reference to the form so we can synchronize with it. Add the following method:

```
Public Sub Synchronize(ByVal synchronizingObject As Object)
    ReceivedTimer.SynchronizingObject = synchronizingObject
    ClosedTimer.SynchronizingObject = synchronizingObject

    If synchronizingObject Is Nothing Then
```

```
            _Sync = False
         Else
            _Sync = True
         End If
      End Sub
```

The _Sync field was declared at the start of the class and it is used to confirm if the form is synchronized. Add a property that provides read-only access to the _Sync field, so the developer can see if the object is synchronized with the form:

```
      Public ReadOnly Property IsSynchronized As Boolean
         Get
            Return _Sync
         End Get
      End Property
```

Now we can implement the OnConnectionClosed() method:

```
      Protected Overridable Sub OnConnectionClosed()
         If _Sync Then
            ' Raise event on main thread
            ClosedTimer.Enabled = True
         Else
            ' Raise event on background thread
            RaiseEvent ConnectionClosed
         End If
      End Sub
```

This method detects whether the form is synchronized. If it is, it enables the timer so the Elapsed event will fire on the UI thread. If it isn't synchronized, it raises the event directly – this will cause the event to be raised on the current (background) thread.

The OnMessageReceived() method is a little more complex. In this case, we are not only raising an event, but we have data to return – one or more received objects must be made available.

There is no way to pass data to a Timer. We have to take data that's on the background thread and allow the Elapsed event to retrieve it and use it to raise the event to the form. Because this application is multithreaded, so could receive multiple objects, we use a Queue object to store the objects so they can be passed to the UI in turn.

Declare the queue as a class-level variable:

```
      Private _Queue As Queue = Queue.Synchronized(New Queue())
```

Note that this is not an ordinary Queue – it is a synchronized Queue object. This means it is safe to use in a multithreaded environment. The synchronization adds some overhead, but it is necessary to prevent multiple threads from attempting to update the queue at the same time, which could corrupt its data.

Now we can write the OnMessageReceived method:

```
Protected Overridable Sub OnMessageReceived(ByVal data As Object)
  If _Sync Then
    _Queue.Enqueue(Data)
    ' Raise event on main thread
    ReceivedTimer.Enabled = True
  Else
    ' Raise event on background thread
    RaiseEvent DataReceived(data)
  End If
End Sub
```

Again, if we are *not* synchronized, the event can be raised directly. It will run on the background thread.

If we are synchronized, however, the object is placed in the queue and the timer is enabled. When its `Elapsed` event fires, we can read the object off the queue and relay it to the UI:

```
Private Sub ReceivedTimer_Elapsed(ByVal sender As System.Object, _
          ByVal e As System.Timers.ElapsedEventArgs) _
          Handles ReceivedTimer.Elapsed
  Dim data As Object
  SyncLock _Queue.SyncRoot
    While _Queue.Count > 0
      data = _Queue.Dequeue
      RaiseEvent DataReceived(data)
    End While
  End SyncLock
End Sub
```

In the period between when this timer is enabled and the event fires, other objects could be placed in the queue. To ensure that the UI gets them all, we'll simply loop until the queue is empty – raising the `DataReceived` event for each object in turn.

The entire loop is contained within a `SyncLock` block. This ensures that this block of code can only be run on one thread at a time, and that the queue can't be altered during emptying. This extra work means we've created a class that can process data on background threads, but can raise its events on the main UI thread of an application. To Windows Forms developers this is essential because they don't need to deal with any special threading code, as long as the `SmartConnection.Synchronize()` method is called on the object instance.

Sending Data

Sending data is much simpler that receiving it. All we need to do is write the data to the `TcpClient` object's stream. Bearing in mind that we may be in a multithreaded environment, we need to perform some synchronization to ensure that two threads don't attempt to write to the socket at the same time:

```
Private Sub DoSend(ByVal state As Object)
  Dim buffer As New MemoryStream()

  WriteObject(state, buffer)
  SyncLock _ClientStream
    buffer.WriteTo(_ClientStream)
  End SyncLock
End Sub
```

We're using the `WriteObject()` method of `StreamHelper`, which first writes the length as 8 bytes, and then the data. Notice that we must first write the data into a `MemoryStream`, and then write that stream to the `NetworkStream`. This is to ensure that both the length and serialized object data are sent at the same time.

Each individual write operation to a `NetworkStream` is typically sent as a separate TCP packet. The `WriteObject()` method from the `StreamHelper` module writes the length, and then writes the object data – which would result in two network packets being sent. Technically that would work, but it is not optimal from a performance perspective.

Note that this method is `Private`. That is because we'll implement a thread-aware `Send()` method to call it. This `Send()` method will allow us to either send data synchronously, or by using a background thread. Using a background thread can be good because serializing an object takes some time and if we are sending much data, performance may be improved by being asynchronous. Keep in mind, however, that the *order* that data is sent is not predictable if it is transmitted asynchronously. If the order in which the objects are sent is important, the method needs to be synchronous.

Add the following code to the class:

```
Public Overloads Sub Send(ByVal data As Object)
   Send(ByVal data As Object, False)
End Sub

Public Overloads Sub Send(ByVal data As Object, _
                          ByVal sync As Boolean)
   If sync Then
      DoSend(data)
   Else
      ThreadPool.QueueUserWorkItem(AddressOf DoSend, data)
   End If
End Sub
```

If we want to send the data synchronously, we just call `DoSend()` directly. However, if we want to send the data asynchronously, we queue the request into the .NET thread pool.

The thread pool is an automatically managed group of threads that are available for use by any application. We're already using the thread pool actually, because all the asynchronous read operations are handled by the thread pool automatically. Here we're simply choosing to use it directly.

The `QueueUserWorkItem` takes the address of the method to be called, and an object to be passed as a parameter to that method. In this case, we want to invoke the `DoSend()` method, passing it the object to be sent over the socket. The request is queued, and as soon as there is a free thread in the pool, it will be executed on it.

There is now only one more method that needs to be added, the `Disconnect()` method:

```
Public Sub Disconnect()
    If Not _Client Is Nothing Then
        _ClientStream.Close()
        _Client.Close()
        _Client = Nothing
    End If
End Sub
```

This disconnects the server from the client, if it isn't already disconnected. It closes the NetworkStream and the TCPClient connection.

That's the end of the SmartConnection class. We now have a thread-aware and thread-safe implementation of a TCP connection object. It can receive serialized objects on background threads and deliver them directly, or marshal them back to the UI thread. It can send serialized objects synchronously or asynchronously.

This class will be used on the server side to handle communication with a client and it will be used on the client side to handle communication with the server. On both sides we need to incorporate business logic as needed – SmartConnection merely handles the data transfer.

SmartListener

The next class we need to add is the listener. This class will be run on the server and it runs on a background thread, listening for client connection requests. When a request comes in, the listener uses the IServerFactory interface to create a new server object to service the request.

Add a class to the project named SmartListener. It needs an object that implements IServerFactory passed to its constructor:

```
Public Class SmartListener
    Private _Factory As IServerFactory
    Private _Port As Integer
    Private _Listener As TcpListener
    Private _ListenThread As Thread

    ' keep a list of active servers
    Private Shared _Servers As ArrayList

    Shared Sub New()    ' Initializes _Servers before its use
        _Servers = New ArrayList()
    End Sub

    Public Sub New(ByVal serverFactory As IServerFactory)
        _Factory = serverFactory
    End Sub
```

We declare private fields to store the port we're listening on, the TcpListener object we'll use to do the actual listening, and the background thread on which our listener will listen. We'll also want to keep a list of the server objects we've created, so we need to declare a class-level variable for this purpose.

First, let's implement the `ListenOn()` method that starts the listening process:

```
Public Sub ListenOn(ByVal port As Integer)
    If Not _ListenThread Is Nothing Then
        ' Called a second time - reset
        Close()
    End If

    _Port = port
    _Listener = New TcpListener(port)
    _ListenThread = New Thread(AddressOf DoListen)
    _ListenThread.Start()
End Sub
```

This method accepts the port number as a parameter and starts the background thread on which we'll run the `DoListen()` method, shown later. In the case that the thread has already been started, we call the objects' `Close()` method. This method not only stops the listening process, but it also runs through the list of open servers and disconnects them from their clients:

```
Public Sub Close()
    Dim svr As IServer

    While _Servers.Count > 0
        svr = _Servers.Item(0)
        svr.Close()
    End While

    If Not _ListenThread Is Nothing Then
        _ListenThread.Abort()
        _Listener.Stop()
    End If
End Sub
```

Now we implement the `DoListen()` method. This method listens for client connection requests:

```
Private Sub DoListen()
    Thread.CurrentThread.Name = "SmartListener:" & _Port

    _Listener.Start()

    While True
        Dim client As TcpClient = _Listener.AcceptTcpClient

        ' We got a new connection - get a server for it
        Dim svr As IServer = _Factory.GetServer
        svr.ConnectTo(client)

        ' Add this server to our list to keep it alive
        _Servers.Add(svr)
    End While
End Sub
```

Because this will be a dedicated background thread, we'll give it a name by concatenating `SmartListener` with the port number on which we'll listen. This can be helpful when debugging, since the Visual Studio .NET IDE will display the thread name when the thread is terminated.

We then start the `TcpListener` object so it begins listening for incoming requests. The `AcceptTcpClient()` call is a blocking call, so our code will stop there and wait until a request comes in. A successful client connection will return a `TcpClient` object representing the client.

Using the `IServerFactory` interface, we call `GetServer()`, which returns an object that implements the `IServer` interface. Using the `IServer` interface, we provide the server object with the `TcpClient` object so it can communicate with the client across the network. Finally, we add the new server object to our list of servers.

The last method in the class is the one that removes a specific server:

```
Public Shared Sub Remove(ByVal svr As IServer)
  _Servers.Remove(svr)
End Sub
```

This method should be called by any server object as it disconnects, so the server object will be removed from the list of active servers. It may also be useful when creating an administrative console, since it allows us to disconnect a select client from the server.

Demonstration

We now have everything needed to create a powerful client or server application. A client application needs only the `SmartConnection` class, which it can use to send and receive any `<Serializable()>` object from a server.

A server application is a little more complex. It needs classes that implement the `IServerFactory` and `IServer` interfaces, it then needs a `SmartListener` to listen for requests. The object implementing `IServer` will use a `SmartConnection` to interact with the client, so it too can send and receive `<Serialiazable()>` objects across the network.

Add a Windows Application project to the solution and call it `SocketTest`. Add a reference to the `SmartSocket` project. Now add five buttons to the form called btnStartListener, btnOpenClient, btnSendMsg, btnDiscClient, and btnShutdownListener and import the `Wrox.Toolkit.Net` namespace.

We'll need a `<Serializable()>` object to send via the socket. Add a new class to the project called `Message` with the following code:

```
<Serializable()> _
Public Class Message
  Public Data As String

  Public Sub New(ByVal text As String)
    Data = text
  End Sub
End Class
```

A class is needed to provide server functionality. Add another new class to the project named `TestServer`. This class needs to do three things. It needs to implement `IServerFactory` so the listener can create instances of the server object as needed. It also needs to implement `IServer`, so the listener can interact with each server object it creates. Finally, it needs to subclass `SmartConnection` so it can interact with the client.

First, subclass `SmartConnection`:

```
Imports System.Net.Sockets
Imports Wrox.Toolkit.Net

Public Class TestServer
  Inherits SmartConnection

  Implements IServer
  Implements IServerFactory
```

We will now implement the `IServer` interface:

```
Private Sub ServerConnect(ByVal client As TcpClient) _
          Implements IServer.ConnectTo
  ConnectTo(client)
  Send(New Message("Hello"))
End Sub

Private Sub Close() Implements IServer.Close
  Disconnect()
  SmartListener.Remove(Me)
End Sub
```

`ConnectTo()` takes a live `TcpClient` object as a parameter, to which we can then connect. As it is a `SmartConnection`, a `ConnectTo()` method accepts a `TcpClient` object as a parameter.

With this done, we can send objects to the client. In this case, we're sending a `Message` object that contains the text `"Hello"`. There's no requirement to send data right away, but this illustrates how to send an object to the client from the server.

We also need to implement a `Close()` method so the listener can close us if it is being shut down. Remember that `SmartConnection` already implements a `Disconnect()` method that closes everything down. We also need to call the listener's `Remove()` method to remove its reference to the server object so we are no longer considered valid.

Now we'll implement `IServerFactory`:

```
Private Function GetServer() As IServer _
              Implements IServerFactory.GetServer
  Return New TestServer()
End Function
```

The code to implement this interface is straightforward – it simply returns a new instance of `TestServer` as a result. Finally, we need to implement our custom business code. This is done by handling the `DataReceived` and `ConnectionClosed` events.

When data is received we need to process it as appropriate. The data we're receiving is an object, so we need to convert it to a specific data type before we can use it with early binding:

```
Private Sub TestServer_DataReceived(ByVal data As Object) _
            Handles MyBase.DataReceived
  Dim msg As Message = CType(data, Message)
  Send(New Message("Got your message: " & msg.Data))
End Sub
```

First we use `CType()` to convert the generic object to type `Message`. At this point, we'd do something business-specific with the object, but for this test, we're merely echoing it back to the client so the client can confirm that the data has been received.

If the client disconnects, the object needs to call the `Close()` method to tidy up and remove itself from the listener's list:

```
Private Sub TestServer_ConnectionClosed() _
            Handles MyBase.ConnectionClosed
  Close()
End Sub
```

The server is now implemented, so add the following code behind the first button on the form:

```
Private MyListener As SmartListener

Private Sub btnStartListener_Click(ByVal sender As System.Object, _
                        ByVal e As System.EventArgs) _
                        Handles btnStartListener.Click
  If MyListener Is Nothing
    MyListener = New SmartListener(New TestServer())
    MyListener.ListenOn(6000)
  End If
End Sub
```

This creates a `SmartListener` object and starts it listening on port 6000 on a background thread. You may need to choose a different port on your machine – different machines may already have this port in use.

To create a client either we can create a new class and subclass `SmartConnection`, or we can simply use a `SmartConnection` object directly. We'll take the latter approach here, since we've already demonstrated how to subclass `SmartConnection` with our `TestServer` class.

Add a class-level variable to the form:

```
Private WithEvents MyConnection As SmartConnection
```

Then add the following code behind the second button to create the connection to the server:

```
Private Sub btnOpenClient_Click(ByVal sender As System.Object, _
                            ByVal e As System.EventArgs) _
                            Handles btnOpenClient.Click
    MyConnection = New SmartConnection()
    MyConnection.Synchronize(Me)
    MyConnection.ConnectTo("localhost", 6000)
End Sub
```

This code creates a new SmartConnection object and it connects to the local machine on port 6000. Notice that it first calls the Synchronize() method, passing the form as a parameter, thus ensuring that all events raised by the object will arrive on the main UI thread.

Now we have the ability to start a server listening, and then create a client, we can start doing some interaction. We know that the server immediately sends the text Hello to us when we connect, so let's add code to receive that data:

```
Private Sub MyConnection_DataReceived(ByVal data As Object) _
            Handles MyConnection.DataReceived
    Dim msg As Message = data
    MsgBox("Client got " & msg.Data)
End Sub
```

This handles the DataReceived event. Since the SmartConnection is synchronized with the form, the event will run on the main thread, so there are no threading issues to deal with. Let's also handle the ConnectionClosed event so the user knows if the server terminated the connection:

```
Private Sub MyConnection_ConnectionClosed() _
            Handles MyConnection.ConnectionClosed
    MsgBox("Client lost connection")
End Sub
```

Now let's write the code behind the third button to send some text to the server:

```
Private Sub btnSendMsg_Click(ByVal sender As System.Object, _
                        ByVal e As System.EventArgs) _
                        Handles btnSendMessage.Click
    MyConnection.Send(New Message(InputBox("Text", "Message")))
End Sub
```

We don't really send text – we send a Message object that happens to contain text. We could just as easily send a Customer, or any <Serializable()> object.

Next, add code to disconnect the client from the server:

```
Private Sub btnDiscClient_Click(ByVal sender As System.Object, _
                        ByVal e As System.EventArgs) _
                        Handles btnDiscClient.Click
    MyConnection.Disconnect()
    MyConnection = Nothing
    MsgBox("Client is disconnected")
End Sub
```

Finally add code to shut down the listener:

```
Private Sub btnShutdownListener_Click( _
        ByVal sender As System.Object, _
        ByVal e As System.EventArgs) _
        Handles btnShutdownListener.Click
  If Not MyListener Is Nothing
    MyListener.Close()
    MyListener = Nothing
  End If
End Sub
```

It is very important to note that if we *don't* shutdown the listener it won't stop running. Remember that it has a background thread running to listen for incoming requests. Even in the IDE, if we don't shut down using this code, the application will continue to run in the background unless we stop it by stopping the debugging process or otherwise end the process.

To that end, we should shut it down in the form's `Closed` event:

```
Private Sub Form1_Closed(ByVal sender As Object, _
        ByVal e As System.EventArgs) _
        Handles MyBase.Closed
  btnShutdownListener_Click(Nothing, Nothing)
End Sub
```

At this point, we should be able to run the application, click on the button to start the listener and then click the button to connect with a client. The result should be a message box:

Likewise, if we send some data to the server, it should echo it back:

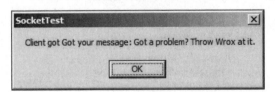

Closing the client should disconnect it from the server. Shutting down the server will cause it to stop listening. If the client is still connected it will be disconnected:

190

We now have a framework for building powerful applications based on sending objects across sockets. While Remoting is still preferable in most cases, this socket-based technique is very useful whenever bi-directional communication is required and the client workstations are behind a NAT router or firewall.

Limitations

Serialized objects carry a lot of metadata with them. Even this simple `Message` object with a little text will run close to 200 bytes when serialized. It is important to keep this overhead in mind when sending small amounts of data, as it may be more efficient to come up with a different protocol that sends the data in a more native format.

Also, this technique only moves the object's *data* across the network. The code (DLL) must already exist on both client and server, and they must be the same version or the deserialization process will fail. The `AutoDeploy` code in this book may be very helpful in ensuring that the appropriate DLL is deployed to both client and server automatically.

Extensions

As implemented this code only handles `<Serializable()>` objects. Sending other types of data would require alterations to `SmartConnection` – specifically the `HandleData()` method. You would need to determine your own protocol for data transfer so both the server and client agree on how the data is sent.

The listener will most likely be run within a Windows Service. There is a project type in Visual Studio .NET for creating a Windows Service. Because the listener is already designed to run itself and its servers on a background thread, it should integrate nicely into a Windows Service.

15

Memory Mapped File Stream

MS Windows allows programs to manage memory in several different ways. Fortunately, you usually don't need to know the details, since Visual Basic and the .NET Framework hide all the complexity. However, one of the most useful memory management techniques, **memory-mapped files** (**MMFs**), is not available in the .NET Framework.

Memory-mapped files are just one of several Win32 memory management techniques. An MMF allows you to access a file on disk the same way you access memory. A file on disk is "mapped" into your process's address space, and it becomes accessible through a simple memory address, or pointer.

While the concept might be new to you, you're actually seeing MMFs in action all the time. Windows uses the same subsystem that's behind memory-mapped files to manage all of your system memory. This subsystem is highly optimized for disk I/O and memory management, and you'll learn more about it later.

The `MemoryMappedFileStream` class takes care of all the gory details and provides you with an easy-to-use class that works just like the familiar `FileStream` class.

Scenario

So, what do memory-mapped files do for you? Well, for one thing, they allow you to easily manage huge files. Remember, the memory-management subsystem excels at both managing memory and performing fast disk I/O.

If you've got a 500 MB data file that you need to search, you certainly aren't going to open it, read it into memory, and then do your work. With a memory-mapped file, you can map all or part of the file into memory, read and write to it just like any other memory buffer, and let the memory manager figure out the details. You don't need to write any code to scan through the file in blocks, perform buffering, and so on.

Memory-mapped files can also be used as an inter-process communication mechanism. As you may know, a process is really just a running application, and is always associated with an executable file on disk. Windows isolates each process from every other; so two processes can't simply pass a variable back and forth in order to communicate. One of the ways that processes can communicate is with shared memory using memory-mapped files.

For example, imagine that you have a Windows service that stores information about its current state in memory. The service creates a memory-mapped file and gives it a name. You're writing a management application that needs to read the data and perhaps write some new configuration information. Your application knows the name that the service used to create the MMF, so it can open the MMF of that same name. The memory manager makes sure that the two processes are sharing the same piece of memory.

The `MemoryMappedFileStream` class is designed to read and write files, as described in the first scenario. It does not allow you to use shared memory, but you could add that functionality with some additional code.

Technology

The concept behind memory-mapped files is relatively simple, but we first need some background. As you know, Windows is responsible for managing the memory in your computer. There's only a finite amount of physical memory, but programs and data often want more.

Windows can pretend that your hard disk is an extension of your physical memory using a concept known as **virtual memory**. Windows divides up your memory into **pages**, which are just small blocks of bytes. Everything in memory, whether it's code, resources, or data, is treated as a set of pages. The **virtual-memory manager**, or **VMM**, figures out when it's safe to copy certain pages from physical memory to the hard disk, thereby freeing that physical memory for other uses.

For instance, say you start Microsoft Word and then minimize its window. You need to do some work with Microsoft PowerPoint and Excel, so you start those programs too. As the memory is divided into pages, the system can move pages of memory used by Microsoft Word to the hard disk, as the application is inactive. With the pages safely copied to disk, it can free them for use by other applications. As soon as you switch back to Word, the VMM will, as necessary, copy some or all of Word's pages back into physical memory again.

This class exposes the fact that Windows treats everything as a page. The MMF API, which is part of the Win32 API, lets you treat a file on disk as if it were actually in memory. The VMM does the work to map a file on disk into pages in memory.

In essence, memory-mapped files let you ignore the difference between a file on disk and a buffer in memory. They look and act exactly the same. You read from and write to memory and the VMM maps it back and forth to a physical file on the hard disk.

For more detailed information about the VMM and memory-mapped files, see the articles *Managing Virtual Memory in Win32* and *Managing Memory-Mapped Files in Win32* by Randy Kath in the Microsoft MSDN Library.

Design

The memory-mapped file API is part of the Win32 API, but is not wrapped by any .NET Framework classes. Fortunately, the .NET Framework includes the platform invoke, or P/Invoke, services to enable managed .NET code to call unmanaged code in DLLs. Unmanaged simply means that it is out of the control of the .NET Common Language Runtime, or CLR.

Just as in previous versions of Visual Basic, Win32 API functions must be declared in .NET code before they can be used. In fact, the `Declare` statement has been carried forward into Visual Basic .NET. However, `Declare` doesn't provide access to all of P/Invoke's options. For more complete control, you can declare the APIs as `Subs` and `Functions` with the `<DllImport>` attribute. This approach is used in the code below.

A common practice is to group all Win32 API declarations into one class called `NativeMethods`. This class should generally have an access modifier of `Friend` so that it's accessible only within its own assembly. The grouping serves to indicate that all methods in this class are going outside the bounds of the .NET Framework's security system.

The .NET Framework recognizes when an application is calling unmanaged code, and an administrator can configure applications to deny such calls. In that case, attempts to call P/Invoke methods will result in a security exception. However, once an application is granted permission to call unmanaged code, the .NET Framework security system cannot control the actions of the API call, such as deleting files or changing system settings.

The Framework includes the `System.IO.Stream` class, which is an abstract base class that defines properties and methods useful for accessing a collection of bytes. A number of .NET Framework classes, including `System.IO.FileStream` and `System.Net.Sockets.NetworkStream`, derive from the `Stream` class. Given this precedent, it makes good sense to implement this class as a stream too, so `MemoryMappedFileStream` is derived from the `Stream` base class.

The class is required to implement all eleven of the `MustOverride` properties and methods of the `Stream` class, including, `Read()`, `Write()`, and `Close()`. It does not implement the asynchronous methods such as `BeginWrite()` and `EndWrite()`, nor the `ReadByte()` and `WriteByte()` methods. These will all be left as exercises for the reader.

To access a file on disk as a memory-mapped file, three things must happen. First, the file is opened with the `CreateFile()` Win32 API. Despite the name, `CreateFile()` opens and creates files. This API returns a file handle, which is passed to the `CreateFileMapping()` API. Finally, `MapViewOfFile()` is called to map all or a portion of the file to a specific address in memory, known as a **view**. All this work happens in the constructor.

Other methods and properties track and update the current position within the stream – in this case, the block of memory containing the view of the file. `Read()` and `Write()` simply copy bytes to and from memory locations. Keep in mind that, behind the scenes, the VMM will actually read from and write to the physical file on disk, as necessary.

To deliberately simplify the implementation, some functionality was left out or defaulted. The class does not support named, shared memory, and it requires you to map an existing, non-empty file. It assumes defaults for other settings, such as the mapping offset into the file. In that particular case, the file will always be mapped starting at the beginning of the file.

Many specific error conditions and exceptions are specified in the `Stream` documentation, and most of these error conditions have been implemented, where appropriate.

Implementation

To get started with the code, create a new VB.NET class file named `MemoryMappedFileStream.vb` and replace its contents with the code below.

The code for this class is quite long, since it includes a number of P/Invoke declarations and must implement all the required properties and methods of the `Stream` class.

First up will be the P/Invoke declarations. They may be defined with `Declare` statements or as empty methods with the `<DllImport>` attribute. The latter gives you more flexibility in specifying the P/Invoke options, so you'll see the attribute used on each method.

If you want to understand what each of the Win32 API functions does and what each parameter means, the MSDN Library or Platform SDK documentation is your best resource. It contains complete documentation for all the APIs used in this class. However, when declaring P/Invoke methods, you'll also sometimes need to refer to the C-language header (`.H`) files included with the Platform SDK. The APIs defined below are found in the file `WINBASE.H`.

The `IntPtr` data type is often used throughout the class. This value type (structure) is a platform-specific type used to represent a pointer or operating-system handle. It is used to manipulate handles and memory addresses passed in and out of the Win32 API functions

```
Imports System.IO
Imports System.Runtime.InteropServices

Namespace Wrox.Toolkit.Filesystem
    Friend Class NativeMethods
```

That was the class declaration; let's look at the first method of this helper class:

```
<DllImport("kernel32.dll", SetLastError:=True, _
CharSet:=CharSet.Auto)> _
Public Shared Function CreateFile( _
                ByVal lpFileName As String, _
                ByVal dwDesiredAccess As Integer, _
                ByVal dwShareMode As Integer, _
                ByVal lpSecurityAttributes As IntPtr, _
                ByVal dwCreationDisposition As Integer, _
                ByVal dwFlagsAndAttributes As Integer, _
                ByVal hTemplateFile As IntPtr) _
                As IntPtr
End Function
```

The DllImport attribute indicates that this is a P/Invoke declaration. The first parameter specifies the DLL in which the Win32 function resides. The next parameter, SetLastError:=True, indicates that we want to have access to the Win32 error code set by the API call.

The final parameter, CharSet:=CharSet.Auto, controls the encoding with which strings are passed from .NET code to the API. Some Win32 APIs have two different versions, one ANSI and one Unicode. CharSet.Auto allows P/Invoke to automatically choose the correct version and encoding. Confusingly, CreateFile() opens an existing file on disk.

The following CreateFileMapping() method is used to create a file-mapping object. A file-mapping object must be created before a file can be mapped into memory:

```
<DllImport("kernel32.dll", SetLastError:=True, _
CharSet:=CharSet.Auto)> _
Public Shared Function CreateFileMapping( _
                ByVal hFile As IntPtr, _
                ByVal lpAttributes As IntPtr, _
                ByVal flProtect As Integer, _
                ByVal dwMaximumSizeHigh As Integer, _
                ByVal dwMaximumSizeLow As Integer, _
                ByVal lpName As String) _
                As IntPtr
End Function
```

MapViewOfFile(), when passed a valid file mapping object, maps all or a portion of a disk file into an address space in memory:

```
<DllImport("kernel32.dll", SetLastError:=True)> _
Public Shared Function MapViewOfFile( _
                ByVal hFileMappingObject As IntPtr, _
                ByVal dwDesiredAccess As Integer, _
                ByVal dwFileOffsetHigh As Integer, _
                ByVal dwFileOffsetLow As Integer, _
                ByVal dwNumberOfBytesToMap As Integer) _
                As IntPtr
End Function
```

UnmapViewOfFile() simply closes a mapping created by MapViewOfFile().

```
<DllImport("kernel32.dll", SetLastError:=True)> _
Public Shared Function UnmapViewOfFile( _
                    ByVal lpBaseAddress As IntPtr) _
                    As Boolean
End Function
```

`FlushViewOfFile()` forces the VMM to flush its buffers and immediately write all changed data to the physical disk file:

```
<DllImport("kernel32.dll", SetLastError:=True)> _
Friend Shared Function FlushViewOfFile( _
                    ByVal lpBaseAddress As IntPtr, _
                    ByVal dwNumberOfBytesToFlush As Integer) _
                    As Boolean
End Function
```

`CloseHandle()` closes an object handle opened by `CreateFile()` or `CreateFileMapping()`:

```
<DllImport("kernel32.dll", SetLastError:=True)> _
Friend Shared Function CloseHandle( _
                    ByVal hObject As IntPtr) _
                    As Boolean
End Function
End Class
```

That's the end of this helper class. The following `MemoryMappedFileStream` class derives from `System.IO.Stream`. The `<ComVisible(False)>` attribute is defined on the class to prevent legacy COM clients from seeing the class. By default, public types are always available to COM clients. Unless the class is designed with backward compatibility in mind, it's a good idea to specify `<ComVisible>`.

```
<ComVisible(False)> _
Public NotInheritable Class MemoryMappedFileStream
    Inherits Stream
```

`ComVisible` is declared `False` here as certain data types used by the class, such as `Long`, a 64-bit integer, are unsupported by VB6 and COM. This class inherits from the `Stream` class.

The following public `AccessType` enumeration allows you to specify whether you want read-only or read/write access to the MMF:

```
Public Enum AccessType
    Read
    ReadWrite
End Enum
```

The public constant `MapEntireFile` can be passed to `New()` to indicate that the entire file should be mapped instead of just a subset:

```
Public Const MAPENTIREFILE As Integer = 0
```

The following three private enumerations are used in calls to `CreateFile()`, `CreateFileMapping()`, and `MapViewOfFile()`. Their values are specifically defined by the Win32 API documentation.

```
    Private Enum MapProtectionType
      PageReadOnly = &H2
      PageReadWrite = &H4
    End Enum

    Private Enum ViewAccessType
      FileMapWrite = &H2
      FileMapRead = &H4
    End Enum

    <Flags()> _
    Private Enum FileAccessType
      FileRead = &H80000000
      FileWrite = &H40000000
    End Enum
```

Win32 defines the constant INVALID_HANDLE_VALUE to indicate a missing or invalid object handle – in this case a file or file-mapping handle. The constant's value is equivalent to -1, but since it's a Win32 handle value, it must be declared as an IntPtr:

```
    Private ReadOnly INVALID_HANDLE_VALUE As IntPtr = New IntPtr(-1)
```

The class needs to retain much information. See the following private members:

```
    Private FileHandle As IntPtr = IntPtr.Zero
    Private MapHandle As IntPtr = IntPtr.Zero
    Private ViewBaseAddress As IntPtr = IntPtr.Zero

    Private IsOpen As Boolean = False
    Private CurrentPosition As Long
    Private ViewLength As Long
    Private AccessLevel As AccessType
```

These private fields hold a filehandle representing the open file on disk, returned by CreateFile(), a map handle representing the open file mapping object, returned by CreateFileMapping(), and a memory address provided by MapViewOfFile().

Other fields include a flag to indicate if the stream is in an open or closed state, the current position within the mapped view, the total view length, and the requested access type (read-only or read/write).

Since the class can manipulate very large files, the position and length are defined as Long, which is (currently) a 64-bit integer type. The handles and address are Win32 objects, so they're defined as IntPtrs.

All of these fields will be initialized by the constructor methods. This class defines two constructors. The first one fills in a default value of MAPENTIREFILE for the bytesToMap parameter and then calls the second overload:

```
    Public Sub New(ByVal path As String, _
                   ByVal access As AccessType)
      Me.New(path, access, MAPENTIREFILE)
    End Sub
```

The constructor requires several parameters. `path` must contain a complete path to an existing file, and the specified file may not be empty. `access` indicates whether you want read-only or read/write access to the MMF. Finally, `bytesToMap` indicates how many bytes you want to map from the file into memory. The special constant value `MAPENTIREFILE` indicates that the entire file is mapped.

```
Public Sub New(ByVal path As String, _
               ByVal access As AccessType, _
               ByVal bytesToMap As Integer)
```

The following two constants defined in this constructor are used in `CreateFile()` to specify that it should open an existing file having no special file attributes (such as hidden or system). These values are defined in the Win32 API documentation and the Platform SDK.

```
Const OPEN_EXISTING As Integer = 3
Const FILE_ATTRIBUTE_NORMAL As Integer = &H80
```

As mentioned in the design discussion, the class requires a non-empty, existing file. The following code verifies that `path` is a valid, non-empty string.

```
If path Is Nothing Then
   Throw New ArgumentNullException()
ElseIf path.Length = 0 Then
   Throw New ArgumentException("The path may not be empty.")
End If
```

Now that we know that `path` contains one or more characters, a new `FileInfo` object is created based on the path. The object is used to determine if the path is valid and points to an existing file, and also to determine the file size in bytes.

```
Dim info As New FileInfo(path)

If Not info.Exists Then
   Throw New ArgumentException( _
      "The specified file does not exist.")
ElseIf info.Length = 0 Then
   Throw New ArgumentException( _
      "The specified file is empty.")
ElseIf bytesToMap < 0 Then
   Throw New ArgumentException( _
      "The number of bytes to map must be zero or greater.")
ElseIf bytesToMap > info.Length Then
   Throw New ArgumentException( _
      "The requested number of bytes to map is larger " & _
      "than the size of the file.")
End If
```

This method also verifies that the requested number of bytes to be mapped is greater than or equal to zero, and less than or equal to the file size. We cannot map more bytes than are contained in the file.

The `CreateFile()`, `CreateFileMapping()`, and `MapViewOfFile()` APIs all require different values for a similar purpose. Each API needs to know whether to grant read-only or read/write access to its respective object.

Based on the access type passed into New(), the method sets the temporary variables mapProtection, viewAccess, and fileAccess to the value appropriate for each API:

```
Dim mapProtection As MapProtectionType
Dim viewAccess As ViewAccessType
Dim fileAccess As FileAccessType

If access = AccessType.Read Then
    mapProtection = MapProtectionType.PageReadOnly
    viewAccess = ViewAccessType.FileMapRead
    fileAccess = FileAccessType.FileRead
Else
    mapProtection = MapProtectionType.PageReadWrite
    viewAccess = ViewAccessType.FileMapWrite
    fileAccess = FileAccessType.FileRead Or _
                 FileAccessType.FileWrite
End If
```

With the preliminary work complete, it's now time to begin creating the file mapping.

First, the method needs to open the file specified by path using CreateFile(). As mentioned earlier, the name may be misleading, but CreateFile() is used here to open an existing file:

```
Dim fileHandleTemp As IntPtr = _
    NativeMethods.CreateFile(path, fileAccess, 0, _
                    IntPtr.Zero, OPEN_EXISTING, _
                    FILE_ATTRIBUTE_NORMAL, IntPtr.Zero)
```

The defaulted parameters specify that file sharing be disallowed, that a default security descriptor should be used, and that no template file is necessary. Refer to the Win32 API documentation for further details. For more information about file system security and security descriptors, see the *File System Security* class in Chapter 22.

CreateFile() returns a file handle to the open file, or INVALID_HANDLE_VALUE upon failure. If the call fails, it also sets the Win32 last-error value, which can be obtained using Marshal.GetLastWin32Error().

```
If fileHandleTemp.Equals(INVALID_HANDLE_VALUE) Then
    Throw New Exception("CreateFile() failed with error " & _
                    Marshal.GetLastWin32Error().ToString() & _
                    ".")
End If
```

IntPtr.Equals() is used to compare the file handle with the read-only IntPtr field INVALID_HANDLE_VALUE defined earlier. If the objects match, then an error occurred and an exception is thrown.

This and subsequent API calls return their handles to temporary local variables instead of to the private fields. In the event of failure, the temporary handles will be cleaned up and the private fields will not be modified. All of the fields are initialized at the end of the constructor.

Now that the file is open, the file handle is passed to CreateFileMapping(), which creates and returns a file-mapping object used with MapViewOfFile():

```
Dim mapHandleTemp As IntPtr = NativeMethods.CreateFileMapping( _
    fileHandleTemp, IntPtr.Zero, mapProtection, 0, 0, Nothing)
```

The default values specify that a default security descriptor should be used, that the maximum size of the file mapping is equal to the size of the file, and that the file mapping is unnamed. Again, see the Win32 API documentation for more information.

`CreateFileMapping()` returns zero in the event of an error and in the event of failure, the method must be sure to close all unmanaged object handles that were successfully opened before the point of failure. The `CloseHandle()` method is used for this purpose:

```
If mapHandleTemp.Equals(IntPtr.Zero) Then
    NativeMethods.CloseHandle(fileHandleTemp)
    Throw New Exception("CreateFileMapping() failed with error " _
                        & Marshal.GetLastWin32Error().ToString() _
                        & ".")
End If
```

The last step is to create a view, which is a range of addresses in memory that are mapped to a file on disk:

```
Dim viewBaseAddressTemp As IntPtr = _
    NativeMethods.MapViewOfFile(mapHandleTemp, viewAccess, _
                                0, 0, bytesToMap)

If viewBaseAddressTemp.Equals(IntPtr.Zero) Then
    NativeMethods.CloseHandle(mapHandleTemp)
    NativeMethods.CloseHandle(fileHandleTemp)

    Throw New Exception("MapViewOfFile() failed with error " & _
                        Marshal.GetLastWin32Error().ToString() & _
                        ".")
End If
```

`MapViewOfFile()` returns a logical, unmanaged memory address that is valid for the current process. The default values specify that the view starts at the beginning of the file.

Now that all API calls and error checks have succeeded, the object handles and view memory address are saved to the class's private fields. The current stream position is initialized to zero and the stream is flagged as open. The view length is equal to either the file size in bytes, or the requested number of bytes:

```
Me.FileHandle = fileHandleTemp
Me.MapHandle  = mapHandleTemp
Me.ViewBaseAddress  = viewBaseAddressTemp

Me.IsOpen  = True

Me.AccessLevel = access
Me.CurrentPosition  = 0

If bytesToMap = MAPENTIREFILE Then
    Me.ViewLength  = info.Length
Else
    Me.ViewLength  = bytesToMap
End If
End Sub
```

The `CanRead` property indicates whether the stream supports reading, which it always does.

```
Public Overrides ReadOnly Property CanRead As Boolean
   Get
      Return True
   End Get
End Property
```

As discussed earlier, the `Stream` base class defines a number of `MustOverride` methods and properties. Each time you see `Overrides` used in a method or property declaration, it indicates that the class is implementing something defined by `Stream`.

`CanWrite` indicates whether the stream supports writing. This is determined simply by checking the value of the private field `AccessLevel`, which was initialized in the constructor:

```
Public Overrides ReadOnly Property CanWrite As Boolean
   Get
      If AccessLevel = AccessType.ReadWrite Then
        Return True
      Else
        Return False
      End If
   End Get
End Property
```

`CanSeek` indicates whether the stream supports random seeks, and it always does:

```
Public Overrides ReadOnly Property CanSeek As Boolean
   Get
      Return True
   End Get
End Property
```

The `Length` property indicates the overall size, in bytes, of the stream, determined by the private field `ViewLength`:

```
Public Overrides ReadOnly Property Length As Long
   Get
      Return ViewLength
   End Get
End Property
```

Next, the `Position` property gets and sets the current zero-based position within the stream. The position is stored in the private field `CurrentPosition`. The setter method validates that the specified position is within the bounds of the stream:

```
Public Overrides Property Position As Long
   Get
      Return CurrentPosition
   End Get

   Set
      If value < 0 Or value > Length Then
         Throw New ArgumentOutOfRangeException("Position is before" _
            & " the start or past the end of the stream.")
      Else
```

```
                CurrentPosition  = value

        End If
     End Set
  End Property
```

The `SetLength()` method provides a direct way to change the length of the stream:

```
     Public Overrides Sub SetLength(ByVal value As Long)
        VerifyStreamIsOpen()

        If value < ViewLength Then
           ViewLength  = value
        ElseIf value > ViewLength Then
           Throw New NotSupportedException("Cannot expand the stream.")
        End If
     End Sub
```

When the MMF is created, the size is fixed at that point in time. In order to change the length, the view and MMF would have to be closed and recreated. In this case, if the requested length is greater than the current length, the method simply throws an exception.

It may seem at first that, to follow the conventions defined by `Stream`, the class should not be able to disallow values of its own choosing. However, not every class that derives from `Stream` is going to perfectly fit the model. Some of the .NET Framework's own `Stream`-based classes define particular restrictions and exceptions.

The private helper method, `VerifyStreamIsOpen()`, simply checks the `IsOpen` field and throws an exception if it's equal to `False`. Many of the following methods call this method to verify that the stream is open and initialized.

```
     Private Sub VerifyStreamIsOpen()
        If Not IsOpen Then
           Throw New ObjectDisposedException("The stream is closed.")
        End If
     End Sub
```

The `ObjectDisposedException` was selected based on the .NET Framework documentation for `Stream`.

The following `ValidateReadWriteParameters()` method is called at the beginning of the `Read()` and `Write()` methods to validate each one's parameters. All of the error checking is mandated by the documentation for `Stream.Read()` and `Stream.Write()`:

```
     Private Sub ValidateReadWriteParameters(ByVal buffer() As Byte, _
                                    ByVal offset As Integer, _
                                    ByVal count As Integer)
        If buffer Is Nothing Then
           Throw New ArgumentNullException("buffer")
        ElseIf offset < 0 Then
           Throw New ArgumentOutOfRangeException("offset", _
              "Offset must be greater than or equal to zero.")
        ElseIf count < 0 Then
           Throw New ArgumentOutOfRangeException("count", _
              "Count must be greater than or equal to zero.")
        ElseIf offset + count > buffer.Length Then
```

```
        Throw New ArgumentException( _
            "Sum of offset and count is greater than buffer length.")
    End If
End Sub
```

We've finally reached the `Read()` method. This method copies data from the unmanaged MMF view, a range of logical addresses in memory, to the managed byte array `buffer`:

```
Public Overrides Function Read(ByVal buffer() As Byte, _
                              ByVal offset As Integer, _
                              ByVal count As Integer) _
                              As Integer
    VerifyStreamIsOpen()
    ValidateReadWriteParameters(buffer, offset, count)
```

If `count` is greater than the number of bytes remaining in the stream, `Read()` copies as much as it can. `copyByteCount` is calculated as the smaller of `count` and the number of bytes between the current position and the end of the stream:

```
    Dim copyByteCount As Integer = _
        Math.Min(count, ViewLength  - CurrentPosition )
```

The `Marshal.Copy()` method overload used below copies a series of bytes from unmanaged memory to a managed byte array. The addition inside the `Copy()` method is actually pointer arithmetic, which means that the values are treated as logical memory addresses in the current process.

```
    If copyByteCount > 0 Then
        Marshal.Copy( _
            New IntPtr(ViewBaseAddress.ToInt64() + CurrentPosition ), _
                      buffer, offset, copyByteCount)
```

With the copy complete, the current position is updated:

```
        CurrentPosition  += copyByteCount
    End If
    GC.KeepAlive(Me)

    Return copyByteCount
End Function
```

`GC.KeepAlive()` is a special instruction to the CLR garbage collector. It prevents the garbage collector from attempting to clean up the object between the point we enter the method and the point at which `GC.KeepAlive()` is called. The GC could attempt to clean up the object if there were no more managed references to the object; however, some unmanaged code might still be interacting with the object.

Microsoft recommends that this method be placed at the end of each method that uses `IntPtrs` to manipulate unmanaged objects.

The code in the following `Write()` method is very similar to `Read()`, except that it writes data from managed memory to the unmanaged memory-mapped file view:

```
Public Overrides Sub Write(ByVal buffer() As Byte, _
                           ByVal offset As Integer, _
                           ByVal count As Integer)
    VerifyStreamIsOpen()
    ValidateReadWriteParameters(buffer, offset, count)
    If ViewLength - CurrentPosition < count Then
        Throw New IOException("Number of bytes from the current " _
                       & "position to the end of the stream " _
                       & "is less than the specified count.")
    ElseIf count > 0 Then
        Marshal.Copy(buffer, offset, _
                     New IntPtr(ViewBaseAddress.ToInt64() _
                                + CurrentPosition ), count)

        CurrentPosition += count
    End If

    GC.KeepAlive(Me)
End Sub
```

If the number of bytes between the current position and the end of the stream is less than the value of count, an exception is thrown because there is not enough room to write all the data. Otherwise, another overload of `Marshal.Copy()` is used to copy a series of bytes from the `buffer` byte array to the calculated unmanaged memory address.

The `Seek()` method allows you to randomly seek anywhere within the stream, given a starting position and a positive or negative byte offset:

```
Public Overrides Function Seek(ByVal offset As Long, _
                              ByVal origin As SeekOrigin) _
                              As Long
    VerifyStreamIsOpen()

    Dim tempPosition As Long
    If origin = SeekOrigin.Begin Then
        tempPosition = offset
    ElseIf origin = SeekOrigin.Current Then
        tempPosition = CurrentPosition + offset
    Else
        tempPosition = ViewLength - offset
    End If
```

The origin parameter can specify the beginning of the stream, the end of the stream, or the current position. The method first calculates the new position and stores it in `tempPosition`. If origin is the beginning of the stream, the new position is equal to the offset. If origin is the current position, the new position may be greater or less than the current position. Finally, if origin is the end of the stream, the new position is the total view length minus offset.

Using the calculated new position, the method verifies that it is within the bounds of the stream, and throws an exception if it isn't:

```
If tempPosition < 0 Or tempPosition > ViewLength Then
    Throw New IOException( _
        "Attempt to seek past the start or end of the stream.")
End If
```

Finally, the `CurrentPosition` field is updated and the new current position is returned:

```
CurrentPosition = tempPosition
Return CurrentPosition
End Function
```

Behind the scenes, the VMM intelligently buffers modified data. However, if you want to ensure that all of the MMF buffers are written to disk immediately, you can call the `Flush()` method:

```
Public Overrides Sub Flush()
    VerifyStreamIsOpen()
    NativeMethods.FlushViewOfFile(ViewBaseAddress, 0)
    GC.KeepAlive(Me)
End Sub
```

You should always call `Close()` when finished with the class. Calling `Close()` ensures that all unmanaged resources are closed and released immediately. If you don't call `Close()`, the garbage collector will eventually call the class's `Finalize()` method. However, in the meantime, the disk file and the memory-mapped file will remain open and locked.

```
Public Overrides Sub Close()
    Dispose()
    GC.SuppressFinalize(Me)
End Sub

Protected Overrides Sub Finalize()
    Dispose()
    MyBase.Finalize()
End Sub
```

`Close()` and `Finalize()` both call `Dispose()`, which is where the real cleanup happens. Once you have explicitly called `Close()`, the object is completely cleaned up and is no longer usable. For that reason, the garbage collector doesn't need to worry about cleaning up the object. The call to `GC.SuppressFinalize()` tells the garbage collector to simply ignore the object.

For more information, see the topic *Programming for Garbage Collection* in the .NET Framework Developer's Guide.

`Dispose()` cleans up all of the unmanaged resources held by the class:

```
Private Sub Dispose()
    If IsOpen Then
        If Not ViewBaseAddress.Equals(IntPtr.Zero) Then
            NativeMethods.UnmapViewOfFile(ViewBaseAddress)
            ViewBaseAddress = IntPtr.Zero
        End If

        If Not MapHandle.Equals(IntPtr.Zero) Then
            NativeMethods.CloseHandle(MapHandle)
            MapHandle = IntPtr.Zero
        End If
```

```
If Not FileHandle.Equals(IntPtr.Zero) _
        And Not FileHandle.Equals(INVALID_HANDLE_VALUE) Then
    NativeMethods.CloseHandle(FileHandle)
    FileHandle = IntPtr.Zero
End If

    IsOpen = False
End If

    GC.KeepAlive(Me)
End Sub

End Class
End Namespace
```

After ensuring that the stream is open, the view is unmapped with a call to
UnmapViewOfFile(), and then the mapping itself is closed with CloseHandle().
Finally, the file handle is closed, the IsOpen flag is set to False, and the object is no
longer usable.

Demonstration

This sample application demonstrates a number of the important methods and
properties of the MemoryMappedFileStream class by reading and writing text to a file
via an MMF.

Create a new VB.NET Console Application project, rename Module1.vb to
MemoryMappedFileTest.vb, and replace its contents with the following code:

```
Imports System.IO
Imports System.Text
Imports Wrox.Toolkit.Filesystem

Module TestFileSystem
    Sub Main()
        Const sampleText As String = _
            "This is a sample file that can be opened by MMF."
```

The contents of sampleText will be written to the stream. The application declares a
number of variables, including a MemoryMappedFileStream object, a FileInfo
object, a byte array, and other variables used to store byte counts and view positions:

```
        Dim mmf As MemoryMappedFileStream
        Dim info As FileInfo
        Dim tempPath As String
        Dim count As Integer
        Dim position As Long
        Dim temp(sampleText.Length - 1) As Byte
```

Whenever you use the MemoryMappedFileStream class (or any Stream-based class),
you must implement a Try...Catch block to trap and handle exceptions:

```
Try
    tempPath = Path.GetTempFileName()
    info = New FileInfo(tempPath)
```

The program first creates a new file containing one line of text. It uses
`Path.GetTempFileName()` to obtain a full path and filename for a unique temporary file.

The `FileInfo` class's `AppendText()` method is used to obtain a `StreamWriter`
object that can write text to the temporary file. One line of text, defined in the
`sampleText` constant, is written to the file before it is closed:

```
Dim writer As StreamWriter = info.AppendText()
writer.WriteLine(sampleText)
writer.Close()
```

Now, a new `MemoryMappedFileStream` object is based on the temporary file, with
read/write access. The application then prints out the initial stream length and position:

```
mmf = New MemoryMappedFileStream(tempPath, _
        MemoryMappedFileStream.AccessType.ReadWrite)

Console.WriteLine("Initial stream length and position:")
Console.WriteLine("  Length: {0}", mmf.Length)
Console.WriteLine("  Position: {0}", mmf.Position)
```

After displaying the initial length and position, `Read()` copies `sampleText.Length`
bytes into the `temp` byte array:

```
count = mmf.Read(temp, 0, sampleText.Length)

Console.WriteLine("After reading sample text from stream:")
Console.WriteLine("  # of bytes read: {0}", count)
Console.WriteLine("  Bytes converted to string: {0}", _
        Encoding.ASCII.GetString(temp))
Console.WriteLine("  Position: {0}", mmf.Position)
```

The number of bytes read, a string representation of the bytes, and the new position,
are then displayed. The original string was in ASCII format, so the
`Encoding.ASCII.GetString()` method is used to convert the array of bytes into a
`String` object.

Next, the application seeks back to the beginning of the word "`sample`" in the stream
and prints the current position. It then clears the `temp` array and reads
"`sample`".`Length` bytes from the stream. Once again, it prints the number of bytes
read, the bytes in string format, and the new position:

```
Console.WriteLine("After seeking to beginning of 'sample':")
position = mmf.Seek("This is a ".Length, SeekOrigin.Begin)
Console.WriteLine("  Position: {0}", position)

Array.Clear(temp, 0, temp.Length)
count = mmf.Read(temp, 0, "sample".Length)

Console.WriteLine("After reading next six bytes:")
```

```
          Console.WriteLine("  # of bytes read: {0}", count)
          Console.WriteLine("  Bytes converted to string: {0}", _
                     Encoding.ASCII.GetString(temp))
          Console.WriteLine("  Position: {0}", mmf.Position)
```

Once again, we return to the beginning of "sample." But this time, the application creates a byte array from the string "abcdef" and writes the byte array to the stream at the current position:

```
          Console.WriteLine( _
             "After seeking back to beginning of 'sample':")
          position = mmf.Seek("This is a ".Length, SeekOrigin.Begin)
          Console.WriteLine("  Position: {0}", position)

          temp = Encoding.ASCII.GetBytes("abcdef")

          Console.WriteLine("After writing 'abcdef' to stream:")
          mmf.Write(temp, 0, temp.Length)
          Console.WriteLine("  Position: {0}", mmf.Position)
```

After writing to the stream, we return for the last time to the (now former) position of "sample":

```
          Console.WriteLine( _
             "After seeking back to former position of 'sample':")
          mmf.Position = "This is a ".Length
          Console.WriteLine("  Position: {0}", mmf.Position)

          count = mmf.Read(temp, 0, "abcdef".Length)

          Console.WriteLine("After reading next six bytes:")
          Console.WriteLine("  # of bytes read: {0}", count)
          Console.WriteLine("  Bytes converted to string: {0}", _
                     Encoding.ASCII.GetString(temp))
          Console.WriteLine("  Position: {0}", mmf.Position)
          Console.ReadLine()
       Catch e As Exception
          Console.WriteLine("Exception: {0}", e.Message)
       Finally
          If Not mmf Is Nothing Then
             mmf.Close()
          End If

          If Not info Is Nothing Then
             info.Delete()
          End If
       End Try
    End Sub
 End Module
```

After reading "abcdef".Length bytes, this time the value is "abcdef" instead of "sample." In fact, the actual file on disk will contain the modified data. You can verify this for yourself by disabling the call to Delete() and locating the temporary file.

Finally, we catch any exceptions and then, before closing this application, dispose of the objects properly. When you run the application, the results should look like this:

```
Initial stream length and position:
   Length: 50
   Position: 0
After reading sample text from stream:
   # of bytes read: 48
   Bytes converted to string: This is a sample file that can be opened
by MMF.
   Position: 48
After seeking to beginning of 'sample':
   Position: 10
After reading next six bytes:
   # of bytes read: 6
   Bytes converted to string: sample
   Position: 16
After seeking back to beginning of 'sample':
   Position: 10
After writing 'abcdef' to stream:
   Position: 16
After seeking back to former position of 'sample':
   Position: 10
After reading next six bytes:
   # of bytes read: 6
   Bytes converted to string: abcdef
   Position: 16
```

Limitations

The class is not thread-safe. For example, if two threads use the same instance of the object and both call `Write()` with the same offset and count, one of the two will have its data overwritten, or, worse, some data from each of the threads will be written, leaving the MMF's data in a meaningless state. You could correct this by adding thread synchronization to the methods.

Also, the class assumes a default offset of zero, the beginning of the file, when creating a new view. For many applications, an adjustable view would be useful.

Finally, the class does not allow you to specify a security descriptor when creating the file mapping, so Windows will provide a default descriptor instead. This would be an issue if the class supported shared memory, since you might want to be specific about who can access the shared memory.

Extensions

You may want to implement the `Stream` class's four asynchronous methods. The asynchronous methods let you start a read or write operation and then continue with other processing. When the operation completes, the asynchronous method calls a delegate that you specified on the original call.

In addition, the default implementations of `ReadByte()` and `WriteByte()` are fairly inefficient, so these methods would benefit from custom overrides. The default implementations create a one-element byte array and then call `Read()` or `Write()`.

For even more flexibility, the class could be extended to support an offset when creating a view, instead of starting only at the beginning of the file. This might be useful if, for instance, you were working with a very large data file and were only interested in a section 200 MB into the file. You could begin the view at that point instead of at the beginning.

16

MP3 ID3v1.1 Tag Editor

As your collection of **MP3**, or **MPEG Layer 3**, audio files grows, it gets harder and harder to manage with filenames alone. You'd probably like to search your collection by artist name, song name, and so on, but the audio-oriented MP3 file format wasn't designed to support that kind of data.

To help solve this problem, the **ID3 tag**, a simple 128-byte data structure appended to an MP3 file, was created to allow an MP3 file to store basic information such as artist, song title, track number, and album. The ID3 tag is not sanctioned or supported by a standards committee. Instead, it was developed by a member of the MP3 user community as the format's popularity exploded.

Today, ID3v1.1, an extension created by Michael Mutschler, has become a defacto standard and is supported by all major MP3 players. The album and artist information you're accustomed to seeing in your MP3s is probably stored in ID3 tags (although some music players also incorporate their own databases). A separate group, organized by Martin Nilsson, has developed a completely new, extensible format called ID3v2. It shares nothing with ID3v1.1 other than the name, and is a much more complex format.

The `ID3Tag` class that we're about to develop will let you easily read and update the ID3 tags embedded in your MP3s.

Scenario

This class would be very useful if you were, for example, building a program to catalog your MP3 music collection. You could write an application to search your hard drives for MP3s, use the class to read the ID3 information, and then update a database, Excel spreadsheet, or text file.

You could build a WinForms application to perform the search or just display the list, and then use the class to allow the user to edit and save the ID3 information for a particular file or files.

Technology

When the MPEG Layer 3 (MP3) format came into existence, no one could have known that it would someday be used in millions of consumer devices and computers around the world. The designers were concerned only with high-quality audio compression, and did not include a general data storage format in the file structure.

Eventually, the ID3 tag was created to give MP3s the ability to hold a song title, artist, album, year, comment, and genre. The ID3v1 format is a simple 128-byte fixed-field data structure that is always placed at the very end of an MP3 file. If any field contains less data than its total capacity, the extra space is filled with zeroed bytes.

A minor tweak to ID3v1 resulted in ID3v1.1. Since the comment field is only 30 characters long, it's not always useful. In v1.1, if the comment is 28 characters or less, the 29th byte of the comment field must be zeroed to indicate the end of the comment, and the last byte holds a track number.

The data structure looks like this:

Offset	Length	Data type	Description
0	3	String (ASCII)	Always "TAG"
3	30	String (ASCII)	Song Title
33	30	String (ASCII)	Artist
63	30	String (ASCII)	Album
93	4	String (ASCII)	Year
97	30	String (ASCII)	Comments
126	1	Byte	Track, if data in Comments is <= 28 chars
127	1	Byte	Genre

For more information about ID3v1.1 and ID3v2, you can visit http://www.id3.org.

Design

Since the ID3v1.1 format is a fixed-field format, the data fields are always in the same place within the overall structure. The class we're going to write defines an enumeration that holds the offset of each field. Determining the length of any field is a simple matter of subtracting the field's offset from that of the field that directly follows it.

For convenience and type safety, another enumeration is used to hold dozens of genre types, such as rock, blues, and techno. The original ID3 tag defined 80 genres, but there is no official source for the complete list. The best source is Michael Mutschler's ID3v1.1 spec, which you can find by searching for "ID3-Tag Specification v1.1 by Michael Mutschler" on the Internet.

Each of the seven data fields is exposed by a read/write property. Each property Set() method ensures that the new data value is valid and will fit into the field.

The public interface consists of several methods: Load(), Save(), and Clear(). The Load() method will initialize the class properties from an MP3's existing ID3 tag, and the Save() method will update an existing ID3 tag. The Clear() method simply resets all the class properties to their default, empty values.

When the class saves an ID3, it always rebuilds each field in the structure from scratch. This is to ensure that the tag follows the correct format, since some ID3 editors incorrectly fill unused space in fields with spaces or other characters instead of zeroed bytes.

All file I/O is done with a .NET FileStream object, and, since an ID3 only contains ASCII characters, not Unicode, the System.Text.ASCIIEncoding.ASCII class is used to convert byte arrays back and forth to Strings.

Implementation

To get started, create a new VB.NET class file named ID3Tag.vb and replace its contents with the code below.

The ID3Tag class starts by defining a public enumeration that contains a list of genre types. There are well over 80 informally-defined types, as mentioned above, but only the first ten are included for brevity. The enumeration is typed as Byte since the ID3 tag uses one byte to store the genre:

```
Imports System
Imports System.IO
Imports System.Text.ASCIIEncoding

Namespace Wrox.Toolkit.FileSystem

    Public NotInheritable Class ID3Tag
```

```
Public Enum GenreType As Byte
  Unknown = 255
  Blues = 0
  ClassicRock = 1
  Country = 2
  Dance = 3
  Disco = 4
  Funk = 5
  Grunge = 6
  HipHop = 7
  Jazz = 8
  Metal = 9
    ' See "ID3-Tag Specification v1.1 by Michael Mutschler" for more
End Enum
```

Since a track number may or may not exist in the tag, the UnknownTrack constant is defined to handle a non-existent track number. As with the genre, the track number is stored as one byte in the tag:

```
Public Const UnknownTrack As Byte = 0      '
```

The private Field enumeration defines the list of fields in the tag:

```
Private Enum Field
  Marker
  Song
  Artist
  Album
  Year
  Comment
  Track
  Genre
End Enum
```

The next few fields define the structure of the tag's individual data fields. The two-dimensional array FieldInfo defines a field offset in the first column and a field length in the second column. The enumeration FieldInfoType defines identifiers for the two columns. There is one row in FieldInfo for each entry in Field, in order:

```
Private ReadOnly FieldInfo(,) As Short = {{0, 3}, {3, 30}, _
  {33, 30}, {63, 30}, {93, 4}, {97, 30}, {126, 1}, {127, 1}}

Private Enum FieldInfoType
  Offset = 0
  Length = 1
End Enum
```

The id3V1Size constant defines the total size of the tag:

```
Private Const id3V1Size As Integer = 128
```

If the tag structure were ever changed, all the relevant structural data is defined in one place, making any amendments an easy task. Since ID3v2 uses a completely new structure, it is highly unlikely that the v1.1 tag will ever be modified.

The path field stores the path and filename of the current MP3 file, and the id3Marker constant defines the standard ID3v1.x identifier that always occurs at the beginning of the tag data:

```
Private path As String = ""
Private Const id3Marker As String = "TAG"
```

Next, the class defines a series of instance fields to hold all the data fields of the ID3 tag:

```
Private id3Song As String = ""
Private id3Artist As String = ""
Private id3Album As String = ""
Private id3Year As String = ""
Private id3Comment As String = ""
Private id3Genre As GenreType = GenreType.Unknown
Private id3Track As Byte = UnknownTrack
```

The class defines one constructor, which accepts a path to an MP3 file and throws an exception if the path is Nothing or an empty string:

```
Public Sub New(ByVal path As String)

    If path Is Nothing Then
      Throw New ArgumentNullException()
    ElseIf path.Length = 0 Then
      Throw New ArgumentException("Invalid path specified.")
    End If

    Me.path = path
End Sub
```

The ValidateField() method is used by many public properties to validate incoming data before it is saved, based on a maximum field length:

```
Private Sub ValidateField(ByVal value As String, _
    ByVal name As String, ByVal maxLength As Integer)

    If value Is Nothing Then
      Throw New ArgumentNullException()
    ElseIf value.Length > maxLength Then
      Throw New ArgumentException(name + " is too long.")
    End If
End Sub
```

A series of read/write properties provide access to the individual data fields. Each property implements data validation as necessary, using `ValidateField()` to ensure that the class will always contain valid data. This is a great benefit that properties provide to your classes.

The offset and length of each field is obtained by using the `Field` and `FieldInfoType` enumerations to locate a row and column in the two-dimensional `FieldInfo` array:

```
Public Property Song() As String
  Get
    Return id3Song
  End Get

  Set(ByVal Value As String)
    ValidateField(value, "Song", _
        FieldInfo(Field.Song, FieldInfoType.Length))
    id3Song = Value
  End Set
End Property

Public Property Artist() As String
  Get
    Return id3Artist
  End Get

  Set(ByVal Value As String)
    ValidateField(value, "Artist", _
        FieldInfo(Field.Artist, FieldInfoType.Length))
    id3Artist = Value
  End Set
End Property

Public Property Album() As String
  Get
    Return id3Album
  End Get

  Set(ByVal Value As String)
    ValidateField(value, "Album", _
        FieldInfo(Field.Album, FieldInfoType.Length))
    id3Album = Value
  End Set
End Property

Public Property Year() As String
  Get
    Return id3Year
  End Get

  Set(ByVal Value As String)
    ValidateField(value, "Year", _
```

```
              FieldInfo(Field.Year, FieldInfoType.Length))
        id3Year = Value
    End Set
End Property

Public Property Comment() As String
    Get
        Return id3Comment
    End Get

    Set(ByVal Value As String)
        ValidateField(value, "Comment", _
            FieldInfo(Field.Comment, FieldInfoType.Length))
        id3Comment = Value
    End Set
End Property

Public Property Genre() As GenreType
    Get
        Return id3Genre
    End Get

    Set(ByVal Value As GenreType)
        id3Genre = Value
    End Set
End Property

Public Property Track() As Byte
    Get
        Return id3Track
    End Get

    Set(ByVal Value As Byte)
        id3Track = Value
    End Set
End Property
```

The Clear() method simply resets all of the tag fields to their default, empty values:

```
Public Sub Clear()
    id3Song = ""
    id3Artist = ""
    id3Album = ""
    id3Year = ""
    id3Comment = ""
    id3Genre = GenreType.Unknown
    id3Track = UnknownTrack
End Sub
```

The ReadBytesAndValidate() method is used by both the Load() and Save() methods. It tries to open the target MP3 file, ensures that the file size is at least as big as an ID3 tag, seeks to 128 bytes from the end of the file (the number specified in the id3V1Size constant), and then reads the tag into the ByRef id3 byte array. Finally, it ensures that the first field equals the string constant id3Marker (TAG).

Rather than a cryptic "invalid file" message, the validation exceptions try to provide some useful detail to the caller. To provide even more detail, you'd need to catch and re-throw any exceptions occurring in the FileStream method calls.

Currently, the code does not verify that the file is actually an MP3 audio file. Of course, this may not be a problem if you're an iPod user – there's at least one app for the iPod that uses ID3 tags to store contacts and appointments, making the iPod an MP3 player/lightweight PDA:

```
Private Sub ReadBytesAndValidate(ByVal file As FileStream, _
    ByRef id3() As Byte)

    If file.Length < id3V1Size Then
        Throw New Exception("The file contains fewer bytes than" _
            + " an ID3 tag and may be corrupt.")
    End If
```

The code seeks backwards id3V1Size bytes from the end of the file. It then reads id3V1Size bytes into the id3 byte array:

```
file.Seek(-id3V1Size, SeekOrigin.End)
file.Read(id3, 0, id3V1Size)
```

Next, the code does a case-sensitive comparison of the contents of the marker field, converted to an ASCII string, with the constant id3Marker. An exact match means that the ID3 tag appears to be valid:

```
    If ASCII.GetString(id3, _
        FieldInfo(Field.Marker, FieldInfoType.Offset), _
        FieldInfo(Field.Marker, FieldInfoType.Length)) _
        <> id3Marker Then

        Throw New Exception("The ID3 tag header is incorrect. " _
            + "The file may not contain an ID3 tag.")
    End If
End Sub
```

The ReadField() method extracts a subset of the ID3 tag byte array and converts it to a string. First, since the actual data may not occupy the total size of the field, the method looks for the first occurrence of a byte with a value of zero (not the ASCII character '0') within the field using Array.IndexOf(). All unused space in the field should be filled with zeroed bytes. If no such byte is found, it is assumed that the entire field contains valid data.

If at least one byte of valid data is found, the valid byte(s) are converted to an ASCII string with ASCII.GetString(), and then any extra spaces are trimmed from the result:

```
    Private Function ReadField(ByVal id3() As Byte, _
        ByVal fieldStart As Integer, _
        ByVal fieldLength As Integer) As String
```

220

```
        Const zero As Byte = 0

        Dim zeroIndex As Integer = _
            Array.IndexOf(id3, zero, fieldStart, fieldLength)
```

If `Array.IndexOf()` didn't find a zeroed byte within the current field, the entire contents of the field are valid:

```
        If zeroIndex = -1 Then
            zeroIndex = fieldStart + fieldLength
        End If

        If zeroIndex > fieldStart Then
            Return ASCII.GetString( _
                id3, fieldStart, zeroIndex - fieldStart).Trim()
        Else
            Return ""
        End If
    End Function
```

The `WriteField()` method reverses the process by taking a string and converting it into a series of bytes in the ID3 byte array:

```
    Private Sub WriteField(ByVal id3() As Byte, _
        ByVal fieldStart As Integer, _
        ByVal value As String)

        ASCII.GetBytes(value, 0, value.Length, id3, fieldStart)
    End Sub
```

By using the helper methods implemented above, the `Load()` and `Save()` methods become quite simple.

The `Load()` method opens the file, reads the ID3 tag into the `id3` byte array using `ReadBytesAndValidate()`, and then reads each of the string fields with `ReadField()`:

```
    Public Sub Load()
        Dim file As FileStream
        Dim id3(id3V1Size - 1) As Byte

        Try
            file = New FileStream(path, FileMode.Open, _
                FileAccess.ReadWrite, FileShare.None, id3V1Size)

            ReadBytesAndValidate(file, id3)

            id3Song = ReadField(id3, _
                FieldInfo(Field.Song, FieldInfoType.Offset), _
                FieldInfo(Field.Song, FieldInfoType.Length))
            id3Artist = ReadField(id3, _
```

```
            FieldInfo(Field.Artist, FieldInfoType.Offset), _
            FieldInfo(Field.Artist, FieldInfoType.Length))
        id3Album = ReadField(id3, _
            FieldInfo(Field.Album, FieldInfoType.Offset), _
            FieldInfo(Field.Album, FieldInfoType.Length))
        id3Year = ReadField(id3, _
            FieldInfo(Field.Year, FieldInfoType.Offset), _
            FieldInfo(Field.Year, FieldInfoType.Length))
        id3Comment = ReadField(id3, _
            FieldInfo(Field.Comment, FieldInfoType.Offset), _
            FieldInfo(Field.Comment, FieldInfoType.Length))
```

If the comment is 28 characters or less, indicated by the second-to-last comment field byte having a value of zero, then the last byte of the comment field is interpreted as a track number. If no track is present and the comment field is not full, the track byte will be zeroed and interpreted as an unknown track. The class defines the UnknownTrack constant for this purpose:

```
        If id3(FieldInfo(Field.Track, FieldInfoType.Offset) - 1) _
            = 0 Then
            id3Track = id3(FieldInfo(Field.Track, FieldInfoType.Offset))
        Else
            id3Track = UnknownTrack
        End If
```

Finally, the genre byte is stored and the load is complete. It's important to note the exception handling logic, which implements a Finally block to ensure that, if an exception occurs, the method always closes the file before returning:

```
        id3Genre = id3(FieldInfo(Field.Genre, FieldInfoType.Offset))

    Finally
        If Not file Is Nothing Then
            file.Close()
        End If
    End Try
End Sub
```

The Save() method first opens the file and attempts to read an existing tag. Since the method can only update an existing tag, this is simply for validation purposes to ensure that a valid tag exists. Next, the id3 byte array is cleared to zeros, except for the first three bytes, which contain the "TAG" header:

```
Public Sub Save()
    Dim file As FileStream
    Dim id3(id3V1Size - 1) As Byte

    Try
        file = New FileStream(path, FileMode.Open, _
            FileAccess.ReadWrite, FileShare.None, id3V1Size)
```

```
ReadBytesAndValidate(file, id3)

    Array.Clear(id3, id3Marker.Length, _
        id3V1Size - id3Marker.Length)
```

Then, each of the data fields is copied into the byte array. Strings are copied using the `WriteField()` method to convert them to byte arrays, and single bytes are copied directly. Since the track number is actually in the last byte of the comment field, the comment is written after the track. If the comment does fill its entire field, the track number is simply overwritten:

```
        WriteField(id3, _
            FieldInfo(Field.Song, FieldInfoType.Offset), id3Song)
        WriteField(id3, _
            FieldInfo(Field.Artist, FieldInfoType.Offset), id3Artist)
        WriteField(id3, _
            FieldInfo(Field.Album, FieldInfoType.Offset), id3Album)
        WriteField(id3, _
            FieldInfo(Field.Year, FieldInfoType.Offset), id3Year)

        id3(FieldInfo(Field.Track, FieldInfoType.Offset)) = id3Track

        WriteField(id3, _
            FieldInfo(Field.Comment, FieldInfoType.Offset), _
            id3Comment)

        id3(FieldInfo(Field.Genre, FieldInfoType.Offset)) = id3Genre
```

Finally, the new tag is saved over the existing tag with the `Seek()` and `Write()` methods:

```
        file.Seek(-id3V1Size, SeekOrigin.End)
        file.Write(id3, 0, id3V1Size)

    Finally
        If Not file Is Nothing Then
            file.Close()
        End If
    End Try
End Sub
End Class

End Namespace
```

Demonstration

The class is very easy to use, as this example demonstrates. Create a new VB.NET Console Application project, rename `Module1.vb` to `ID3TagTest.vb`, and replace its contents with the following code.

This example reads an existing ID3 tag from the MP3 file specified on the command-line, prints the original song, comment, and track, and then updates the comment and track, saves the updated tag, and, finally, prints the new values. Remember to save a copy of your original MP3 before you run the program!

As always, be sure to implement a Try...Catch block to prevent your users from seeing unhandled exceptions:

```
Imports System
Imports Wrox.Toolkit.FileSystem

Module MainModule

    Sub Main(ByVal CmdArgs() As String)
        If CmdArgs.Length <> 1 Then
            Console.WriteLine("Please pass a complete file path to an MP3.")
            Exit Sub
        End If

        Try
            Dim id3 As New ID3Tag(CmdArgs(0))

            id3.Load()

            Console.WriteLine("Song    : {0}", id3.Song)
            Console.WriteLine("Comment: {0}", id3.Comment)
            Console.WriteLine("Track   : {0}", id3.Track)
            Console.WriteLine()

            id3.Comment = "This is a great song!"
            id3.Track = 5

            id3.Save()

            Console.WriteLine("Song    : {0}", id3.Song)
            Console.WriteLine("Comment: {0}", id3.Comment)
            Console.WriteLine("Track   : {0}", id3.Track)

        Catch e As Exception
            Console.WriteLine("An exception occurred: " + e.Message)
        End Try
    End Sub

End Module
```

When you run the demonstration application, you'll see output something like this:

```
Song    : My Favorite Song
Comment: http://www.website.com
Track   : 0

Song    : My Favorite Song
Comment: This is a great song!
Track   : 5
```

Limitations

The main limitation of the class is simply a matter of space in this book! The GenreType enumeration has over 80 different well-known values and a capacity for up to 254. The first ten were included, but you can find the remaining values via your favorite Internet search engine.

Another limitation is the class's inability to add a new ID3 tag to an MP3 that does not already have one. It expects to find an existing tag, and throws an exception if one is not present.

Extensions

The most obvious, and complex, extension to the class is support for the evolving ID3v2 format. This format is quite complicated when compared to the extremely simple ID3v1.1 format. It can store a varying number of fields in a number of data formats. For instance, it can store an image containing album cover art.

Currently, the class can update an existing ID3 tag, but you also may want to be able to add an ID3 tag to an MP3 that doesn't already have one. The class would simply need to verify that a tag doesn't already exist, and then write the new tag starting at the end of the file.

Finally, the class does not verify that the target file is actually an MP3 music file. It concerns itself only with finding a valid ID3 tag.

17

Folder Browser

The Win32 API contains several common dialogs that developers can use in applications to provide a standard look and feel for common tasks. One of these common dialogs is a folder browser. The folder browser dialog is used when applications need to prompt the user for a folder location. An installation application, for example, might prompt the user for the path to a folder in which files should be stored.

The .NET Framework includes support for accessing many of the common dialogs directly. The `System.Windows.Forms` namespace contains classes for displaying several of the common dialogs, such as the **Color**, **Font**, **Print**, **Print Setup** and **Open File** dialogs. However, the folder browser dialog is not one of the supported dialogs. In this chapter, you'll see a class that provides access to the common folder browser dialog from the .NET Framework.

Scenario

The folder browser class that we'll develop in this chapter can be used by any code that needs to display the common folder browser dialog implemented by the Windows shell. Code that uses the class can instruct the folder browser dialog to pop up and can retrieve the path to the folder selected by the user as a string property of the class. An example of the Folder Browser dialog is shown in the following screenshot:

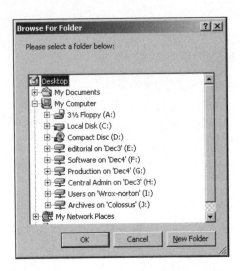

Technology

Since the functionality that we'll need is already built into the Windows operating system, we need to make use of the .NET Framework's ability to invoke platform code (in our case, Win32 API code) from .NET code. This technology is called **Platform Invocation**, and is known as **P/Invoke** for short. The P/Invoke technology allows .NET Framework code to invoke operating system level calls.

Working with P/Invoke from within Visual Basic .NET is straightforward. To call a Win32 API function from VB.NET, you declare a public, shared function with the same name and signature. You then need to annotate your function with an attribute called DLLImport that specifies the name of the DLL containing the Win32 API function that you need to call. The method you write won't have any code in it, as the call will automatically sent to the Win32 API function by the CLR. Code that needs to call the function just calls your .NET stub.

Design

In this chapter, we'll be developing two classes. The first class, called Win32API, will contain all of the P/Invoke code that we'll need to drop down to the operating system level so that we can make the operating system level calls that we'll need. The other class, called FolderBrowser, will contain the code that users can call to invoke the dialog and retrieve the selected folder.

The FolderBrowser class will be the only class with which an end user needs to be concerned. Users create an instance of the FolderBrowser class and call its methods and properties. The Win32API class is an internal helper class and is of no concern to the developer writing code that uses the FolderBrowser class. We'll mark this class as having Friend visibility so that users will not be able to access it from their external code.

The FolderBrowser class will implement the following public overloaded methods:

❑ ShowDialog(), which will display the Folder Browser common dialog using the current window as the dialog's parent window

❑ ShowDialog(IWin32Window), which will display the Folder Browser common dialog using the specified window as the dialog's parent window

The FolderBrowser class will also implement the following public properties:

❑ StartLocationID, which holds a value from an enumeration of folder IDs, which the developer using the FolderBrowser class can use to specify the root of the browsing operation

❑ DirectoryPathName, which holds a string naming the full path to the folder selected by the user at runtime

Implementation

In this section, we will details how the Folder Browser functionality is implemented. We'll start with the Win32API class, as that is necessary for the FolderBrowser class to function. The Win32API class uses P/Invoke to call into the Win32 API.

Implementing the Win32API Class

Below is the class declaration for Win32API. Only System.Text and System.Runtime.InteropServices will be used by this class, the other import statements are for the FolderBrowser class.

```
Imports System.Drawing
Imports System.Text
Imports System.Windows.Forms
Imports System.ComponentModel
Imports System.Security.Permissions
Imports System.Runtime.InteropServices

Namespace Wrox.Toolkit.UI
    Friend Class Win32API
```

The class is marked with Friend visibility because the class only needs to be accessed by the other class in the assembly, FolderBrowser; users do not use this class directly. Remember that classes with Friend visibility can be used by other classes in the same assembly but cannot be accessed by code outside the assembly.

We'll start by defining an import for the Win32 API function SHBrowseForFolder(), which invokes the Folder Browser common dialog:

```
<DllImport("Shell32.DLL", CharSet:=CharSet.Auto)> _
Public Shared Function SHBrowseForFolder( _
            <InAttribute(), Out()> ByRef bi As BROWSEINFO) _
            As IntPtr
End Function
```

No .NET code needs to be added to this method as the attribute in the signature does all the work for us. The next Win32 function that we'll be adding support for is a function called GetActiveWindow(). This function returns a handle to the window with the current application focus. One of the pieces of information that the folder browser needs is a handle to the window that should act as the dialog's owner. We'll design our folder browser class so that the developer can specify a handle. If the developer doesn't specify a handle, then our implementation can just call GetActiveWindow() and use the handle for the active window as the folder browser dialog's owner window. We'll add a DLLImport statement for the Win32 API function GetActiveWindow():

```
<DllImport("User32.DLL")> _
Public Shared Function GetActiveWindow() As IntPtr
End Function
```

The <DllImport> attribute names the system DLL in which the imported function can be found. The code shown above states that we want to use the Win32 API GetActiveWindow() function, which according to the Win32 SDK documentation, is implemented in User32.dll. The DLLImport attribute is followed by an empty function declaration, with a function signature matching the original API call's signature. There is no need to provide an implementation for the function either, as the P/Invoke process will automatically redirect calls to the class function to the appropriate Win32 API call.

Next, we'll define a set of flags that can be used to define the behavior of the folder browser dialog. We'll name the enumeration BffStyles, with Bff standing for "Browse folder flag":

```
<Flags()> _
Public Enum BffStyles
    RestrictToFileSystem = &H1     ' BIF_RETURNONLYFSDIRS
    RestrictToDomain = &H2         ' BIF_DONTGOBELOWDOMAIN
    RestrictToSubfolders = &H8     ' BIF_RETURNFSANCESTORS
    ShowTextBox = &H10             ' BIF_EDITBOX
    ValidateSelection = &H20       ' BIF_VALIDATE
    NewDialogStyle = &H40          ' BIF_NEWDIALOGSTYLE
    BrowseForComputer = &H1000     ' BIF_BROWSEFORCOMPUTER
    BrowseForPrinter = &H2000      ' BIF_BROWSEFORPRINTER
    BrowseForEverything = &H4000   ' BIF_BROWSEINCLUDEFILES
End Enum
```

Each of the values in this enumeration corresponds to a matching flag found in the Win32 SDK for use with the configuration of the browse folder dialog. The original Win32 names for the flags are listed in comments following each value. We'll use these flags to display certain dialog attributes when the Folder Browser dialog is launched through the Win32 API.

The <Flags> attribute provides information to the .NET Framework that the values of the enumerated values should be used as bit flags. Enumerated values described as bit flags can be used in Boolean mathematical operations, such as OR and AND constructs. The values used in the enumeration match the values defined by Win32. We'll look at how these flags are used shortly.

Next, we'll need to define a signature for a folder browser dialog callback function. This is the name of the function in the Win32 API.

```
Public Delegate Function BFFCALLBACK(ByVal hwnd As IntPtr, _
                                     ByVal uMsg As UInt32, _
                                     ByVal lParam As IntPtr, _
                                     ByVal lpData As IntPtr) _
                                     As Integer
```

When code invokes the folder browser dialog, it can define a callback function that receives notifications when events occur in the dialog itself. Events such as dialog initialization and selection changes can be sent to the calling code at the Win32 level using a callback function. The delegate above defines the signature for this callback function.

All of the options that control the display of the Win32 Folder Browser common dialog are specified in a structure called BROWSEINFO. The Visual Basic .NET version of that structure is shown below:

```
<StructLayout(LayoutKind.Sequential)> _
Public Structure BROWSEINFO
    Public hwndOwner As IntPtr
    Public pidlRoot As IntPtr
    Public pszDisplayName As IntPtr
    <MarshalAs(UnmanagedType.LPTStr)> _
      Public lpszTitle As String
    Public ulFlags As Integer
    <MarshalAs(UnmanagedType.FunctionPtr)> _
      Public lpfn As BFFCALLBACK
    Public lParam As IntPtr
    Public iImage As Integer
End Structure
```

The <StructLayout> attribute describes how the data in this structure should be marshaled when the P/Invoke technology sends the data from .NET to the underlying Win32 layer. For this structure, we're noting that the data should be laid out such that the data is sent sequentially, in the same order as the order defined by the structure.

Pay special attention to the <MarshalAs> attribute on the lpszTitle member. This attribute is used to describe that data should be sent using a format other than the default format. Strings in the .NET Framework encoded as 16-bit Unicode, and by default, all .NET strings are marshaled as Unicode strings. However, in this case, the underlying Win32 code expects an ASCII string. We're working around this conversion problem by stating that the lpszTitle string should be marshaled as an unmanaged type called an LPTStr. The LPTStr type describes the string as a Unicode string for P/Invoke calls expecting Unicode strings, and ASCII strings for P/Invoke calls expecting ASCII strings.

We'll finish up by defining two further necessary DLLImports. The imports can be found in the Shell32.Dll system library. We'll start by defining an import for the Win32 API function SHGetSpecialFolderLocation(), which returns information regarding the physical location of a special system folder, such as "My Documents" or "Network Neighborhood", in a descriptor called an **item identifier**:

```
<DllImport("Shell32.DLL")> _
Public Shared Function SHGetSpecialFolderLocation( _
                    ByVal hwndOwner As IntPtr, _
                    ByVal nFolder As Integer, _
                    <Out()> ByRef ppidl As IntPtr) _
                    As Integer
End Function
```

Finally, we define an import for the Win32 API function SHGetPathFromIDList(), which converts an item identifier to a physical path:

```
<DllImport("Shell32.DLL")> _
Public Shared Function SHGetPathFromIDList( _
                    ByVal pidl As IntPtr, _
                    ByVal Path As StringBuilder) _
                    As Integer
End Function
End Class
```

Implementing the FolderBrowser Class

Now that the P/Invoke preliminaries have been taken care of, we can implement the actual FolderBrowser class. We'll start by declaring the class and deriving the class from a .NET Framework class called System.ComponentModel.Component. Classes deriving from this base class can be hosted in container classes, which are classes that can contain references to other objects. Array and list classes are examples of container classes. The benefit of implementing the FolderBrowser class as a component is that it can be inserted as an item into the Visual Studio .NET toolbox. Users can add the class to the toolbox and use it simply by dragging the FolderBrowser tool onto a form.

```
Imports System.Drawing
Imports System.Text
Imports System.Windows.Forms
Imports System.ComponentModel
Imports System.Security.Permissions
Imports System.Runtime.InteropServices
...
Public NotInheritable Class FolderBrowser
    Inherits Component
```

We'll include a definition for the maximum supported size of a Win32 operating system path. We'll use this value later to set a maximum size for the folder path returned from the dialog:

```
Private Shared Const MAX_PATH As Integer = 260
```

The second parameter to the Win32 SHGetSpecialFolderLocation() function is an integer representing the special folder whose physical path should be returned. These values are defined by the operating system, so we'll add an enumeration describing the special folders and the values defined by the Win32 API:

```
Public Enum FolderID
    Desktop = &H0
    Printers = &H4
    MyDocuments = &H5
    Favorites = &H6
    Recent = &H8
    SendTo = &H9
    StartMenu = &HB
    MyComputer = &H11
    NetworkNeighborhood = &H12
    Templates = &H15
    MyPictures = &H27
End Enum
```

This will allow you to help specify where you want the folder browser to open in. Next, we'll define some private variables for the class:

```
Private startLocation As FolderID = FolderID.Desktop
Private publicOptions As Integer = _
    Win32API.BffStyles.RestrictToFileSystem Or _
    Win32API.BffStyles.RestrictToDomain
Private privateOptions As Integer = _
    Win32API.BffStyles.NewDialogStyle
Private descriptionText As String = _
    "Please select a folder below:"
Private directoryPath As String
```

The startLocation variable is used to keep track of the top-level folder to be shown in the folder browser dialog. By default, the Desktop folder should be shown as the root. The user will be able to change this default through a class property called StartLocationID, which we'll define later on.

The publicOptions variable is used to keep track of the browser folder options that can be changed by the end user. Later on, we'll expose a property called OnlyFilesystem that the user can use to change the flags set on the publicOptions variable.

The privateOptions variable is used to keep track of folder browser settings that should not be modified by the developer using the class. These are folder browser bit flags whose settings cannot be controlled by the developer, such as NewDialogStyle, which sets the Folder Browser dialog to display the updated look and feel available on Windows XP systems. In the class implementation, the NewDialogStyle bit is set. This setting cannot be changed by the user.

The descriptionText variable describes a string that is displayed on the dialog just above the folder tree itself. We'll initialize this string to the text "Please select a folder below:".

The directoryPath variable serves as a placeholder for the path selected by the user.

At this point, we can start implementing the class's public functions. The class supports two overloads of a function called ShowDialog(), whose intent is to perform the actual display of the dialog. The first overload of the ShowDialog() method takes no parameters, and the second overload takes a parameter describing the window to serve as the Folder Browser dialog's parent window. Both of these overloads return a standard DialogResult value, which is a standard enumeration in the System.Windows.Forms namespace that describes the return value of a dialog box.

The first overload will implement the no-parameter version of ShowDialog():

```
Public Function ShowDialog() As DialogResult
  Return ShowDialog(Nothing)
End Function
```

This version simply calls the second overload, specifying Nothing as the parent window. The second overload of ShowDialog() is where the real work takes place:

```
Public Function ShowDialog(ByVal owner As IWin32Window) _
                           As DialogResult
  Dim pidlRoot As IntPtr = IntPtr.Zero
  Dim hWndOwner As IntPtr
  Dim mergedOptions As Integer
  Dim pidlRet As IntPtr
```

The owner parameter is a value of a type called IWin32Window. This is an interface defined by the .NET Framework and contains a property that exposes the handle for a window. The Control class in the System.Windows.Forms namespace implements the IWin32Window interface, and objects of the Control class – as well as any classes that derive from Control, such as Form and those that inherit from Control – also implement the IWin32Window interface. You can call this implementation of ShowDialog() by passing in an object that implements IWin32Interface as the parameter to the function call.

After defining a few local variables, we check to find the handle to the window that will act as the parent window for the Folder Browser dialog. This handle will be stored in the local hWndOwner variable:

```
If owner Is Nothing Then
   hWndOwner = Win32API.GetActiveWindow()
Else
   hWndOwner = owner.Handle
End If
```

If the owner supplied as the parameter is Nothing, as will be the case if the caller called the first overload of ShowDialog(), then the currently active window will be used as the parent. We'll use the internal Win32 API GetActiveWindow() method to get this handle.

If the owner supplied as the parameter is not Nothing, then it is assumed to be an implementation of a .NET interface called IWin32Window. This interface is implemented on .NET classes that implement windows, and supports a property called Handle, which supplies the caller with the handle to the actual window.

Next, we'll obtain the path descriptor for the special folder described by the specified special folder:

```
Win32API.SHGetSpecialFolderLocation(hWndOwner, startLocation, _
                                    pidlRoot)
If pidlRoot.Equals(IntPtr.Zero) Then
   Return DialogResult.Cancel
End If
```

If this call fails for some reason, we'll get a null path descriptor back. In this case, we'll just exit the function. Now, we'll collect all of the public and private dialog styles into a single bit flag value called mergedOptions:

```
mergedOptions = publicOptions Or privateOptions
If mergedOptions And Win32API.BffStyles.NewDialogStyle <> 0 Then
   Application.OleRequired()
End If
```

If the NewDialogStyle bit is set in the merged options, then we must make sure that OLE is initialized for the application. The new Folder Browser dialog style uses OLE functionality, and OLE must be initialized in any application that uses this style.

The next task will be to initialize the BROWSEINFO structure used to describe the behavior of the Folder Browser common dialog:

```
pidlRet = IntPtr.Zero
Dim bi As Win32API.BROWSEINFO
Dim buffer As IntPtr
Dim sb As StringBuilder

bi = New Win32API.BROWSEINFO()
buffer = Marshal.AllocHGlobal(MAX_PATH)
bi.pidlRoot = pidlRoot
bi.hwndOwner = hWndOwner
bi.pszDisplayName = buffer
bi.lpszTitle = descriptionText
bi.ulFlags = mergedOptions
```

A variable called bi is used to reference the new BROWSEINFO structure. A buffer is allocated to contain the path selected by the user in the dialog, and the buffer is assigned to the structure's pszDisplayName member. The title and options flags are also assigned into the appropriate structure members.

At this point, everything is ready to go and the Win32 API class's SHBrowseForFolder() method can be called:

```
pidlRet = Win32API.SHBrowseForFolder(bi)
Marshal.FreeHGlobal(buffer)
If pidlRet.Equals(IntPtr.Zero) Then
  Return DialogResult.Cancel
End If
```

Once the call returns, the memory used by the buffer is freed. The function returns a path descriptor referencing the selected folder. Once again, we'll check for a NULL descriptor and return if the descriptor is not available.

Assuming a valid descriptor was returned, we can allocate a new StringBuilder object and obtain the path for the selected descriptor:

```
sb = New StringBuilder(MAX_PATH)
If Win32API.SHGetPathFromIDList(pidlRet, sb) = 0 Then
  Return DialogResult.Cancel
End If
directoryPath = sb.ToString()
```

We'll use the Win32 class' SHGetPathFromIDList() method to obtain the path, and we'll store the path in the directoryPath local variable. Once the variable is set, we can return an "OK" result to the caller:

```
    Return DialogResult.OK
End Function
```

The Boolean property that we'll define in a moment is used to set or unset a bit in the publicOptions bit flag value. We first need to define a private helper method called SetOptionField() that specifies the bit to be set and a Boolean specifying whether the bit should be turned on or off:

```
Private Function SetOptionField(ByVal mask As Integer, _
                                ByVal turnOn As Boolean)
  If turnOn = True Then
    publicOptions = publicOptions Or mask
  Else
    publicOptions = publicOptions And Not mask
  End If
End Function
```

The first parameter specifies a mask to the bit that should be switched. Recall that bit masks are values that contain one bit for the bit to be manipulated and 0 for all other values. For example, working with bit three in an eight-bit value would equate to a bit pattern of 00001000, which equates to a hexadecimal value of 8.

If the second parameter is true, then the value of publicOptions is ORed with the mask, effectively turning on the bit specified by the bit mask. If the second parameter is false, the mask is inverted using the NOT operator. Then the value of publicOptions is ANDed with the inverted mask. This effectively turns off the bit specified in the mask.

The first property that we'll define is a Boolean property called OnlyFilesystem. Setting this property to True will cause only file systems to be shown in the Browser, with other special folders such as "Network Neighborhood" to be hidden. Setting this property to False will cause all special folders to be displayed:

```
<Category("Navigation"), _
  Description("Only return file system directories. " & _
              "If the user selects folders that are not part " & _
              "of the file system, the OK button is " & _
              "unavailable."), DefaultValue(True)> _
Public Property OnlyFilesystem As Boolean
  Get
    Return publicOptions And _
      Win32API.BffStyles.RestrictToFileSystem <> 0
  End Get

  Set
    SetOptionField(Win32API.BffStyles.RestrictToFileSystem, value)
  End Set
End Property
```

The <Category> and <Description> attributes are used to describe how the property should be described in the Visual Studio .NET Properties window. These attributes give the property visibility in the Properties window for the toolbox object, and can allow the property value to be set at design time.

Next, we'll define a property called StartLocationID, which specifies the root folder for the Folder Browser dialog:

```
<Category("Navigation"), _
  Description("Location of the root folder from which " & _
              "to start browsing. Only the specified folder " & _
              "and any folders beneath it in the namespace " & _
              "hierarchy appear in the dialog box."), _
              DefaultValue("0")> _
Public Property StartLocationID As FolderID
  Get
    Return startLocation
  End Get

  Set
    startLocation = Value
  End Set
End Property
```

We'll finish by implementing a read only property called `DirectoryPathName`, which will return the path selected by the user:

```
<Category("Navigation"), _
  Description("Full path to the folder selected by the user.")> _
Public ReadOnly Property DirectoryPathName() As String
  Get
     Return directoryPath
  End Get
End Property

End Class

End Namespace
```

Demonstration

Using the class is simple. Simply create an object of the `FolderBrowser` class and call `ShowDialog()`:

```
Import Wrox.Toolkit.UI

Module TestFolderBrowser
  Sub Main()
    Dim FolderBrowser1 As FolderBrowser
    Dim DialogReturn As DialogResult

    FolderBrowser1 = New FolderBrowser()
    DialogReturn = FolderBrowser1.ShowDialog()
    If DialogReturn = DialogResult.OK Then
       MessageBox.Show(FolderBrowser1.DirectoryPathName)
    End If
  End Sub
End Module
```

If the returned dialog result is "OK", then the user made a selection and the selected path will be available from the `DirectoryPathName` property.

Limitations

The Folder Browser class is implemented using a language supporting the .NET Framework and uses .NET Framework features. This means that the class should work on any platform that supports .NET. Remember, however, that this class is using Win32 specific features as well, and, in fact, is wrapping a Windows specific feature; specifically, the Windows Folder Browser common dialog. Because of this, you won't be able to use the class on non-Windows platforms, even if the non-Windows platform supports the .NET Framework.

Extensions

The FolderBrowser class outlines above exposes a property for just one of the
available folder browser bit flags (RestrictToFileSystem). It would be simple to
add additional properties for the other available bit flags. Another simple property
addition would be a string property to control the dialog's description text, which is
currently set to "Please select a folder below:"

Interface Locator

If you have ever designed a particular application that implements a common interface and then find you wish to locate any other .NET applications or components that implement the same interface, there is no easy way to find those files. The Interface Locator class searches for .NET assemblies that implement a particular interface, in a specific directory (or directories) and passes back information about each file that implements the desired interface.

Scenario

Any occasion where we want to be able to add other assemblies to our application that implement a desired interface. So for example, if we have a special audio application that uses a particular interface for the audio codecs, by having the ability to search for other .NET assemblies that implement that interface, we could locate new codecs to be added to our application.

Technology

There are two basic operations that our class needs:

❏   The ability to search through multiple directories for .NET assembly files

❏   The ability to determine if these files implement a particular interface

A technique that has been used for a long time, with great success, for searching computer directories is **recursion**. Recursion is the technique whereby a method calls itself from within its own code.

Through the use of recursion we can write a directory searching routine that will call itself to search any subdirectories. This technique allows us to write a very small amount of code to search any number of directories without worrying about missing any. However, we do have to be careful when using recursive procedures so that they don't call themselves indefinitely, or run for so long that we run out of memory.

Recursion only provides us with the means to locate each file within a directory though. In order for us to determine whether or not a file is a .NET assembly or not, we will rely on catching an exception when trying to load the file with the `System.Reflection.Assembly.LoadFrom()` method. Only valid assembly files will be successfully loaded by this method, otherwise a `BadImageFormatException` exception will be thrown.

The biggest hurdle with the Interface Locator class is to determine which assemblies contain classes that implement a desired interface. Fortunately, every .NET assembly contains metadata that describes the types, attributes, and other items that it contains. By using reflection through the `System.Reflection` namespace, we can view different parts of an assembly's metadata, which will allow us to find out which interfaces it implements.

Design

The basic design for the class is relatively simple. The Interface Locator class will search a directory and any subdirectories for all files that are .NET assemblies. It will then determine if the located assemblies contain files that implement a particular interface.

As described in the Technology section we will be using recursion to systematically search the directory that is passed in to the class and all of its subdirectories and then their files. If the file is a .NET assembly that implements our source interface, we are going to create an `Enum` of specific information about that assembly:

- ❑ The location of the particular file that is a assembly
- ❑ The internal version of the assembly
- ❑ The classes that the assembly contains

This assembly information is going to be stored in a collection that will contain all the assemblies that are found to implement our source interface during the search. This collection will be passed back to the calling application.

This design provides us with the flexibility to search an unknown number of files and to assemble information on an unknown number of assemblies. In addition, should we wish to collect more information on the assemblies it would be a simple task to extend the `Enum` accordingly.

Our class will therefore contain the following key methods:

❑   Search()
    The only public method takes in all the required operational information
    (the interface to search for, the starting directory, and the file types to
    search), calls the other methods and returns the results as a Collection.

❑   ProcessDirectory()
    This method uses recursion to call itself and the ProcessFile() method
    to loop through all nested directories in the Search() method's starting
    directory and find each directory's files.

❑   ProcessFile()
    This method checks to see if a file is a .NET assembly and if it implements
    the desired interface.

Implementation

We need to create a new VB.NET Class Library project called InterfaceLocator and
rename Class1.vb to InterfaceLocator.vb

The two namespaces that the InterfaceLocator class requires are
System.Reflection.Assembly to view information about a .NET assembly and
System.IO to access the directories and files:

```
Imports System.Reflection.Assembly
Imports System.IO

Namespace Wrox.Toolkit.Filesystem
  Public Class InterfaceLocator
```

We will create a collection to store the information we discover about each file. As
each .NET assembly is found that contains the interface that we are searching for, that
assembly's information is stored in the collection FoundAssemblies. This collection is
ultimately passed back to the calling application so the user can parse the list of
assemblies found implementing the source interface any way they wish.

We also have a couple of class variables for information used in several methods.
FileExtension is used to store a wildcard file extension that is used as the search
criteria for finding files. The SourceInterface type is used for storing which
interface type we are searching for:

```
Private FoundAssemblies As New Collection()
Private FileExtension As String
Private SourceInterface As Type
```

The FoundAssemblyLayout enumerated type holds more detailed information on the
assemblies that meet our search criteria. This Enum will hold .NET assembly
information on the path where the physical file is located, the full name of the class
that implements the interface that is being searched, and the internal version of the
assembly. You can easily allow for other pieces of assembly metadata available by
adding new values to the enumeration:

```
Public Enum FoundAssemblyLayout
   Path = 1
   FullName = 2
   Version = 3
End Enum
```

Search() is the only public method of the class. Its arguments are: the type of the source interface that we are searching for, an optional directory to start searching, and a string for file extensions to limit the search criteria. A collection of information about the located .NET assembly files will be returned. If you do not pass in a file extension to the FileExtensions parameter, only DLLs will be searched and if you pass an empty string all files will be searched:

```
Public Function Search( _
      ByVal SourceType As Type, _
      Optional ByVal StartingDrive As String = "C:\", _
      Optional ByVal FileExtensions As String = "*.DLL") _
      As Collection
```

We will store the interface type that is being searched and the possible file extension in our previously defined class-level variables so we don't have to keep passing them to all the procedures, as they will not change throughout a search:

```
SourceInterface = SourceType
FileExtension = FileExtensions.Trim
```

If an empty string is passed in the StartingDrive parameter, the method will use the current directory of the executing class as its starting point:

```
If StartingDrive.Trim = "" Then
   StartingDrive = Directory.GetCurrentDirectory
End If
```

> *You should be careful of the actual directory that you pass in (or if you don't pass anything and the optional default is used), as there could literally be hundreds of directories to be searched through*

Before we can perform any searches we must make sure that the starting directory is valid; if it isn't, an exception is thrown back to the calling application:

```
If Directory.Exists(StartingDrive) Then
```

Assuming the directory exists, we call the ProcessDirectory() method to begin parsing the files in that directory:

```
ProcessDirectory(StartingDrive)
```

Once the ProcessDirectory() method completes, all relevant assemblies that match our search criteria will have been added to the FoundAssemblies collection, so all we need to do is return the collection:

```
      Return FoundAssemblies
   Else
      Throw New System.Exception(StartingDrive & _
                              " is not a valid directory")
   End If
End Function
```

The `ProcessDirectory()` method takes in the starting location to begin the search:

```
Private Sub ProcessDirectory(ByVal NextDirectory As String)
```

We create two string arrays, one to store the list of files and one to store the list of subdirectories found in a directory:

```
Dim Files As String()
Dim File As String
Dim SubDirectories As String()
Dim SubDirectory As String
```

If the `FileExtension` variable is an empty string (in other words we want to search all file types) then we can simply call the `GetFiles()` method of the `Directory` object, which will return an array of all the files in a particular directory. Otherwise, we will use the overloaded `GetFiles()` method that accepts a string of a wildcard file extension. This of course will only return file names with that file extension. The class defaults the `FileExtension` variable to `*.dll` which will only return all DLL files:

```
Try
   If FileExtension.Trim = "" Then
      Files = Directory.GetFiles(NextDirectory)
   Else
      Files = Directory.GetFiles(NextDirectory, FileExtension)
   End If
```

Then for each file that is in the `Files` array, we pass it to the `ProcessFile()` method to see if it meets our search criteria:

```
For Each File In Files
   ProcessFile(File)
Next File
```

Having checked all the files in the directory, we then need to check if there are any subdirectories to search by calling the `Directory` object's `GetDirectories()` method:

```
SubDirectories = Directory.GetDirectories(NextDirectory)
```

For each subdirectory found in the current directory, we recursively call the
`ProcessDirectory()` method:

```
        For Each SubDirectory In SubDirectories
           ProcessDirectory(SubDirectory)
        Next SubDirectory
     Catch ex As Exception
        Throw new System.Exception(ex.Message)
     End Try
  End Sub
```

The `ProcessFile()` method takes an individual file and checks to see if it is a
.NET assembly:

```
     Private Sub ProcessFile(ByVal path As String)
```

First we create objects for storing individual type object information, an array of `Type`
objects, and the version information of the assembly:

```
        Dim FileType As Type
        Dim FileTypes As Type()
        Dim AssemblyVersion As System.Diagnostics.FileVersionInfo
```

To determine if the file is a valid .NET assembly, we attempt to load it into the
`Assembly` object. If the file is not a .NET assembly, a `BadImageFormatException` is
generated and is caught by the exception handler. We simply ignore the error as it
simply means that we're not interested in parsing this file any further:

```
        Try
           FileTypes = Reflection.Assembly.LoadFrom(path).GetTypes()
        Catch ex As BadImageFormatException
           'The file found is not a .NET assembly so ignore it and simply
           'move to the next file
        End Try
```

Once we know we have a .NET assembly, we can start to pull the relevant information
we want out of it. In order to determine the version of the assembly we can use the
`FileVersionInfo` object from the `System.Diagonostics` namespace. We pass in
the same path information to the `GetVersionInfo()` method of the object and it will
send back the version information:

```
        Try
           FileTypes = Reflection.Assembly.LoadFrom(path).GetTypes()

           AssemblyVersion = FileVersionInfo.GetVersionInfo(path)
        Catch ex As BadImageFormatException
           'The file found is not a .NET assembly so ignore it and simply
           'move to the next file
        End Try
```

Now we need to determine if the assembly we have supports the interface we are
searching for. We can do this by first searching through the types in the assembly for
those that are interfaces, using the `GetInterfaces()` method of the `Type` object:

```
AssemblyVersion = FileVersionInfo.GetVersionInfo(path)

For Each FileType In FileTypes
    Dim index As Integer
    Dim mitypes() As Type = FileType.GetInterfaces()
```

Now that we have all the interfaces for a particular type that is contained in the current assembly, we need to see if any is the same as our source interface. We loop through all the interfaces and use the `AssemblyQualifiedName` property to determine if the type was compiled against our target interface:

```
For index = 0 To mitypes.Length - 1
    Dim implInterface As Type = mitypes(index)
    If implInterface.AssemblyQualifiedName.Equals( _
        SourceInterface.AssemblyQualifiedName) Then
```

If we find a match where an interface of an assembly file is the one we are looking in our application, then we call the `AddToCollection()` method to add the information to the `FoundAssemblies` collection, which is returned to the calling application:

```
                AddToCollection(path, FileType.FullName, _
                    AssemblyVersion.FileVersion)
            End If
        Next
    Next FileType
Catch ex As BadImageFormatException
    'The file found is not a .NET assembly so ignore it and simply
    'move to the next file
End Try
End Sub
```

When we have found a file that is a .NET assembly and that contains the interface we are searching for, we need to save the information to a collection for processing later:

```
Private Sub AddToCollection(ByVal path As String, _
                ByVal FullName As String, _
                ByVal FileVersion As String)

    Dim FoundAssembly As New Collection()

    With FoundAssembly
```

The first piece of information that we need to save is the location and name of the physical file that contains the interface. We already know this as it was passed through to the method:

```
        .Add(path, FoundAssemblyLayout.Path)
```

The interface `Type` object's `FullName` property provides the fully qualified name of the type, which in this case is the full name of the class:

```
        .Add(FullName, FoundAssemblyLayout.FullName)
```

Since one of features of the .NET Framework is to allow multiple different versions of an assembly on a machine, we will want to include the version number of the assembly to help determine the difference if a class and .NET assembly appears more than once:

```
        .Add(FileVersion, FoundAssemblyLayout.Version)
    End With
```

We now add the local collection to our class-level collection, which will be easier to pass back to the calling application:

```
        FoundAssemblies.Add(FoundAssembly)
    End Sub
  End Class
End Namespace
```

Demonstration

To see how this class works we will create a Windows Forms application to display the results of a directory search for a newly created interface.

The first step in demonstrating this class is to create an interface to search for. Open a new solution in VB.NET and create a new Class Library application with the name CodecServer. Change the name of the default class file to ICodec.vb. Now replace the default header code in the class file with the code below:

```
' Defines an interface for a codec object
Public Interface ICodec
    Sub Encode()
    Sub Decode()
    Sub Connect()
    Sub Close()
End Interface
```

Before we can use this interface in another application we must compile it.

Once we have created our interface, we need to create a .NET assembly that will use this interface. For this demonstration we will create another class library. Create another Class Library solution and give it the name of TestDll. Change the name of the default class library to Codec.vb and replace its default code with the code below:

```
Public Class Codec
    Implements CodecServer.ICodec

    Public Sub Close() Implements CodecServer.ICodec.Close
        Console.WriteLine("Close")
    End Sub

    Public Sub Connect() Implements CodecServer.ICodec.Connect
        Console.WriteLine("Connect")
```

```
   End Sub

   Public Sub Decode() Implements CodecServer.ICodec.Decode
      Console.WriteLine("Decode")
   End Sub

   Public Sub Encode() Implements CodecServer.ICodec.Encode
      Console.WriteLine("Encode")
   End Sub

End Class
```

At this point, our new class needs a reference to the new interface we compiled, so right-click on the solution in the Solution Explorer and Add Reference…. Browse for the new .NET assembly that contains our source interface, CodecServer.dll and when located it add it to the solution.

The final step in this demonstration is to create a new Windows Application and either add a reference to our previously created InterfaceLocator class from the Implementation section (if you created a separate class library) or add the class to our new solution. We will need a button control to execute the search, a textbox for entry of the starting directory for the search, a label to display the source interface's full name, a listview control to display the results, and a button control to close the application when finished.

You should have a user interface that looks similar to the one below:

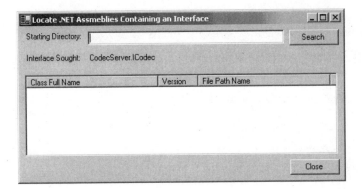

We need to add three columns to the listview control with the indices of 0, 1, and 2. Set the View property of the listview control to Details so we can see all the information for each collection.

Below you will find the rest of the code for the demonstration with a description for each relevant section:

```
Imports CodecServer

Public Class MainForm
  Inherits System.Windows.Forms.Form

  Private Sub Search_Click(ByVal sender As System.Object, _
    ByVal e As System.EventArgs) Handles Search.Click
```

We create an `InterfaceLocator` object, a collection for all the .NET assembly information that has been found, and a local collection to access a particular .NET assembly information collection:

```
Dim LI As New InterfaceLocator.InterfaceLocator()
Dim FoundAssemblies As Collection
Dim FoundAssembly As Collection
```

Each time a search is done we need to clear the listview control so as not to have duplicate or unrelated entries:

```
Try
    FoundItems.Items.Clear()
```

Pass the starting search directory from the textbox to the `InterfaceLocator` object and get the collection of information returned:

```
FoundAssemblies = LI.Search(GetType(CodecServer.ICodec), _
    StartingDirectory.Text)
```

Loop through all the items in the collection to access each individual .NET assembly information collection to view the stored information:

```
For Each FoundAssembly In FoundAssemblies
```

Create a new `ListViewItem` object for each collection of information:

```
Dim listitem = New ListViewItem()

With listitem
```

Since we are using the Details View property of the listview control, the first column contains the `Text` property of a `ListViewItem` object and the rest of the columns will display a `SubItem` object. The first column will display the `FullName` property of the .NET assembly information collection, which is the full name of the class that implements the interface:

```
.Text = FoundAssembly(LI.FoundAssemblyLayout.FullName)
```

The second column is the version of the assembly. This can be helpful to determine any differences if there are two or more copies of a particular .NET assembly on a computer:

```
.SubItems.Add(FoundAssembly(LI.FoundAssemblyLayout.Version))
```

The third column displays the actual path and filename on the computer where the particular interface resides. If you are trying to add a reference to a solution this information will be very important:

```
.SubItems.Add(FoundAssembly(LI.FoundAssemblyLayout.Path))
End With
```

Add the new ListViewItem to the listview control:

```
            FoundItems.Items.Add(listitem)
        Next

        Catch ex As Exception
            MessageBox.Show(ex.Message)

        End Try

    End Sub
```

Once you are finished with the application you can click the other button control to close it down:

```
    Private Sub CloseApp_Click(ByVal sender As System.Object, _
        ByVal e As System.EventArgs) Handles CloseApp.Click
        Me.Close()
    End Sub

    Private Sub MainForm_Load(ByVal sender As System.Object, _
        ByVal e As System.EventArgs) Handles MyBase.Load
        InterfaceName.Text = GetType(CodecServer.ICodec).FullName
    End Sub

End Class
```

When you execute the demonstration application and search for our ICodec interface, you should get something like this:

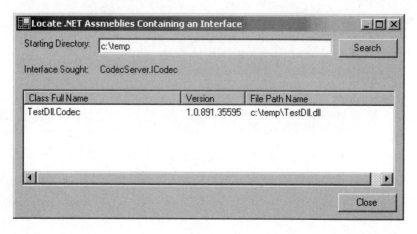

By obtaining the path and class name of a .NET assembly that implements our interface, we can use that information to load the object into our application.

Limitations

If you are constantly executing searches for .NET assemblies on a machine with many directories – which on most machines there tend to be – the search process can take a lot of time. Use as narrow search directory criteria as possible to save time during each search.

Extensions

The design above only allows us to find .NET assemblies that implement a particular interface in a particular directory or nested directories. But we can extend this class to speed up the search operation, as well as supporting more types.

To help with the speeding up of searches, we could persist a collection of .NET assembly information to disk so future searches are quicker. This would require a freshness date on the information, which could be accomplished by creating a service that uses the `FileSystemWatcher` object; so when a directory or file has been updated the service keeps the persisted data up to date.

Another possible way to speed up the search, especially if you are searching many large nested directories, would be to change the class to be multi-threaded and have each thread process a directory.

Another extension would be to change the collection being passed back to contain all information about the types in the found .NET assembly. You could then create a treeview with nodes for different types of information.

This class can also be extended to have it locate types other than interfaces. While looking at new code from a sample on the web or in a book, you may notice a namespace that you are unfamiliar with. If you want to use a feature from that namespace in your solution, the first thing you need to know is the file name of the physical file on your computer that contains that particular namespace. Since many namespaces can reside in one physical .NET assembly and there is no built-in tool in VS.NET to find out which namespaces are in a particular assembly (you could use ILDASM but it can only search one file at a time and it is not automatic).

PeopleSearcher

Although Active Directory is not the only directory service solution, the fact that Microsoft has integrated it so tightly with Windows clients and servers almost guarantees that Active Directory will be a part of most enterprise customer environments. This means that developers should have at least a basic understanding of how to use ADSI (Active Directory Services Interface). This class provides a solid foundation behind the proper way to use ADSI to query Active Directory.

Scenario

Active Directory stores location and configuration information for many different types of objects on the network, such as users, computers, printers, etc, and is designed to make the most up-to-date information readily available to multiple applications. A developer using ADSI for the first time usually finds that the learning curve is tremendous because of the knowledge required just to query for information.

For a complete understanding of this class, you will need at least a basic knowledge of the following:

- ❑ The ADSI API
- ❑ LDAP syntax
- ❑ Server limitations
- ❑ Performance enhancements

Without the proper information to set attributes correctly and execute fast queries, an ADSI-based application will not perform consistently and will be difficult to debug. It would make life for the new ADSI developer a little easier if there was a class that implemented the proper technique for searching Active Directory. With the help of some classes already built in to the .NET Framework, we can build the `PeopleSearcher` class for just that purpose.

Technology

This class needs to be run on a Windows 2000 network with Active Directory Services installed. Before attempting to build this sample, make sure that the user account that you are logged on to the network with has access to query non-sensitive information from Active Directory. A basic user account is usually sufficient. The `PeopleSearcher` will find people information on your network, so your results will be different than the results shown in this sample.

The .NET Framework Class Library contains a class that performs queries against Active Directory. This class, the `DirectorySearcher` class, is generic and can be used to search any type of object in the Active Directory. It is difficult to use and understand without a few hints to speed up the learning process. We can use the `DirectorySearcher` as a base class for our new class, and make the adjustments necessary for our new class to be easier to use.

Design

The `PeopleSearcher` class does not require a lot of code to implement. Its sole purpose is to make querying Active Directory objects easier and more intuitive. The `PeopleSearcher` will not require any LDAP syntax as input and will set all the options required to perform a fast query.

Implementation

To get started, open Visual Studio .NET and create a Console Application. Name it `PeopleSearcher`. We'll create three classes in this project – one to handle the searching, one to use for returned objects, and one to demonstrate the use of the other two classes.

Using the project menu, add a reference to the `System.DirectoryServices.dll`. Doing this will enable us to import the `System.DirectoryServices` namespace.

PeopleSearcher Class

Add a new class file to the project and rename it from `Class1.vb` to `PeopleSearcher.vb` and replace the code with the following (don't use `Module1.vb` as we'll be using that later):

```vb
Imports System.DirectoryServices

Namespace Wrox.Toolkit.Net

  Public Class PeopleSearcher
    Inherits DirectorySearcher

    Private PeopleFound As SearchResultCollection

    Public Sub New()

      Dim root As New DirectoryEntry("LDAP://rootDSE")

      ' serverless binding
      Const RootName As String = "LDAP://" & _
          root.Properties("defaultNamingContext").Value

      SearchRoot = New DirectoryEntry(RootName)
      PageSize = 100
      SearchScope = SearchScope.Subtree

      PropertiesToLoad.Add("displayName")
      PropertiesToLoad.Add("department")
      PropertiesToLoad.Add("sn")
      PropertiesToLoad.Add("givenName")
      PropertiesToLoad.Add("streetAddress")
      PropertiesToLoad.Add("l")
      PropertiesToLoad.Add("st")
      PropertiesToLoad.Add("postalCode")
      PropertiesToLoad.Add("co")
      PropertiesToLoad.Add("telephoneNumber")

    End Sub
```

The code above declares a class that inherits from the `DirectorySearcher` class. The class contains a private member variable and a default constructor. This default constructor creates a `DirectoryEntry` object using `rootDSE` to retrieve the DN (distinguished name) for the domain. The DN can then be used to do *serverless binding*, which means that a server name is not explicitly stated in the path that is supplied. This enables Active Directory to use the default domain without specifying a domain controller. It is important to never hard-code server and domain names so that specific location and namespace dependencies can be eliminated. The `DirectoryEntry` object includes username and password properties to specify the different credentials for binding to the object. It is not good practice to use these properties since it is a security risk to include usernames and passwords in code. Windows authentication should be used whenever possible.

After the binding is done, a `PageSize` should be set. If left unset, the system could attempt to return thousands of items but the result of the search will stop after the server-defined limit (usually 1000) is reached, regardless of how many items should be returned. Setting the `PageSize` to 100 will return a result set in pages with 100 items in each page. Returning 100 items at a time rather than thousands at once puts less strain on the system and will ensure that all results will be returned.

Since we are searching for user objects, which could be scattered anywhere in the Active Directory forest, we set `SearchScope` to `SubTree`. This means that we want the server to search for objects that meet the filter criteria from the base object and all its descendents.

We complete the `New()` method by indicating which object attributes to return. It is important to only return the attributes that are actually needed.

Next, add a method called `FindAll()` to find all people with a specific last name:

```
Public Overloads Sub FindAll(ByVal LastName As String)
    Filter = "(&(sn=" + LastName + ")(objectClass=Person))"
    PeopleFound = FindAll()
End Sub
```

The `FindAll()` method takes the string passed in and creates an LDAP filter (`&(sn=lastname)(objectClass=Person)`). This compound statement indicates we want all the objects in the `Person` class ANDed with the last name provided.

Before you can ensure that a filter will return the proper results, you should make sure that the attributes in the filter are indexed. The `sn` and `objectClass` attributes are usually indexed by default, but if you were to choose other attributes in your search filter, check with your system administrator first.

Next, add a property to return the number of objects found with the previous query and a property to return an object located at a specific index:

```
Public ReadOnly Property Count() As Long
    Get
        Return PeopleFound.Count
    End Get
End Property

Default Public ReadOnly Property Item _
    (ByVal index As Integer) As Person
    Get
        Return New Person(PeopleFound(index))
    End Get
End Property

End Class
```

To use the `Item` property, we'll also need to declare a `Person` class.

Person Class

Add the following code for the `Person` class below the `PeopleSearcher` class:

```
Public Class Person

    Private displayName As String
    Private department As String
    Private sn As String
    Private givenName As String
    Private streetAddress As String
    Private l As String
    Private st As String
    Private postalCode As String
    Private co As String
    Private telephoneNumber As String
    Private adsPath As String

    Public Sub New(ByVal PersonFound As SearchResult)

        On Error Resume Next

        displayName = PersonFound.Properties("displayName")(0)
        department = PersonFound.Properties("department")(0)
        sn = PersonFound.Properties("sn")(0)
        givenName = PersonFound.Properties("givenName")(0)
        streetAddress = PersonFound.Properties("streetAddress")(0)
        l = PersonFound.Properties("l")(0)
        st = PersonFound.Properties("st")(0)
        postalCode = PersonFound.Properties("postalCode")(0)
        co = PersonFound.Properties("co")(0)
        telephoneNumber = PersonFound.Properties("telephoneNumber")(0)
        adsPath = PersonFound.Path

    End Sub

    Public ReadOnly Property FullName() As String
        Get
            Return displayName
        End Get
    End Property

    Public ReadOnly Property DepartmentName() As String
        Get
            Return department
        End Get
    End Property

    Public ReadOnly Property LastName() As String
        Get
            Return sn
        End Get
    End Property


    Public ReadOnly Property FirstName() As String
        Get
            Return givenName
```

```
            End Get
         End Property

         Public ReadOnly Property Address() As String
            Get
               Return streetAddress
            End Get
         End Property

         Public ReadOnly Property City() As String
            Get
               Return l
            End Get
         End Property

         Public ReadOnly Property State() As String
            Get
               Return st
            End Get
         End Property

         Public ReadOnly Property Zip() As String
            Get
               Return postalCode
            End Get
         End Property

         Public ReadOnly Property Country() As String
            Get
               Return co
            End Get
         End Property

         Public ReadOnly Property Phone() As String
            Get
               Return telephoneNumber
            End Get
         End Property

         Public ReadOnly Property Path() As String
            Get
               Return adsPath
            End Get
         End Property

      End Class

   End Namespace
```

Demonstration

Now that we've completed our PeopleSearcher and Person classes, it's time to demonstrate how to use them. Replace the code in module1.vb of the console application that we created with the following:

```
Imports PeopleSearcher
Module Module1

  Sub Main()

    Dim ps As New Wrox.Toolkit.Net.PeopleSearcher()
    Dim person As Wrox.Toolkit.Net.Person
    Dim index As Long

    Console.WriteLine(ps.SearchRoot.Path)
    ps.FindAll("Smith")

    For index = 1 To ps.Count

      person = ps(index - 1)
      Console.WriteLine()
      Console.WriteLine("***** Person #" & CStr(index) & " *****")
      Console.WriteLine(" Full Name: " & person.FullName)
      Console.WriteLine("Department: " & person.DepartmentName)
      Console.WriteLine(" Last Name: " + person.LastName)
      Console.WriteLine("First Name: " + person.FirstName)
      Console.WriteLine("   Address: " + person.Address)
      Console.WriteLine("      City: " + person.City)
      Console.WriteLine("     State: " + person.State)
      Console.WriteLine("       Zip: " + person.Zip)
      Console.WriteLine("   Country: " + person.Country)
      Console.WriteLine("     Phone: " + person.Phone)

    Next

  End Sub

End Module
```

Change the call to `FindAll()` to use a last name that's more suitable to your environment. Try using your own last name for kicks. Some sample output for this would be:

```
LDAP://DC=sf,DC=magenic,DC=net

***** Person #1 *****
 Full Name: Smith, Joe
Department: Accounting
 Last Name: Smith
First Name: Joe
   Address: 555 Center Avenue
      City: San Francisco
     State: CA
       Zip: 94103
   Country:
     Phone: 555-5555


***** Person #2 *****
```

Notice that there are some attributes with no values. This is true of most person objects on any given network and could cause problems if a developer assumes that all attributes have values.

To see all the attributes set for a given object, add the following code to the main subroutine:

```
Dim entry As DirectoryServices.DirectoryEntry
Dim propName As String
Dim value As Object

entry = new DirectoryServices.DirectoryEntry(ps(0).Path)
For Each propName In entry.Properties.PropertyNames
   For Each value in entry.Properties(propName)
      Console.WriteLine("name=" & propName & " value = " & value)
   Next value
Next propName
```

The code above creates a `DirectoryEntry` from the path of the first person found from our previous search. Then it iterates through each property name and associated values.

Limitations

It is worthwhile to mention that the security measures placed in the Active Directory forest are quite robust. If someone were to query for information and did not have the permission required to view certain material, then null values would be returned. Often, these null values are mistaken for nonexistent values.

Extensions

The possibilities for extending this class are seemingly endless. We used the `FindAll()` method to search people with a given last name. With no code changes, we can use the method to search sub-strings of last names. For example, instead of passing "Smith" to find all users with the last name "Smith", you can use "S*" to find all users with a last name beginning with "S".

Other attributes can be returned to exhibit a more detailed company white pages application. The class can also be used in a yellow pages application that lists people by department or area.

Finding people is always important in a large organization. Since Active Directory is accessible to multiple types of applications, it is often the best repository to search for the latest information.

VB.NET

Solutions

Toolkit

Security

20

Encrypted Communicator

The encrypted communicator class encapsulates the code needed to use public and private key cryptography to carry out a secure data conversation between two entities (clients/servers/programs). It has methods for exchanging a symmetric key via asymmetric encryption, and encrypting and decrypting data with the symmetric key.

The combination of using asymmetric and symmetric encryption is the standard method of exchanging large amounts of encrypted data, because asymmetric encryption and decryption is more secure, but much slower than symmetric encryption and decryption. This combined technique takes advantage of the strengths of both.

Scenario

Secure communication between two applications is a requirement that most programmers run up against at some point. The two applications could be a client and server communicating over a LAN, or they could even be two instances of the same application running on the same machine at different times, using files as message stores (ensuring that application data is stored securely). They could even be peer-to-peer applications communicating across the internet. The basic methods and algorithms for encrypting and exchanging data are very similar in all of these scenarios. In this class, we will explore those methods and look at how to employ them in VB.NET.

Technology

We will use two types of cryptography in this class: symmetric and asymmetric. Symmetric cryptography (also called secret-key cryptography) is what most people think of when they think about securing data. It uses an algorithm to hash together source data and a secret key to produce encrypted data. You can use the key and algorithm later on to decrypt the encrypted data. This type of encryption is simple to understand and not too processor intensive. Applications can use it to exchange large amounts of data efficiently, provided both parties know the same secret key. The problem is, how do you securely communicate the key between the parties? If you transmit it in the clear, and some malicious third-party eavesdropper manages to pick it up, then they will be able to decrypt any data you transmit that has been encrypted with that key.

Asymmetric cryptography is better known as public key cryptography. The principle behind asymmetric cryptography is that two keys are needed: one to perform the encryption (the public key) and one to perform the decryption (the private key). This means that anyone that has a copy of the public key can encrypt data and be certain that only the person with the private key can decrypt it – which means that key distribution is not a problem. The private key never has to be sent anywhere, so no information about how to decrypt the encrypted data has to be transferred between the communicating parties. The disadvantage of asymmetric cryptography is that it is very processor intensive – about a thousand times more so than with symmetric cryptography. This makes it a bad choice for encrypting large amounts of data. It is, however, a great method for securely exchanging keys for symmetric encryption, and symmetric encryption does a fine job of encrypting and decrypting large amounts of data. In this class, we will be using the RSA algorithm for our asymmetric cryptography. RSA is the most widely used asymmetric cryptography algorithm, and is used, for example, in the Internet SSL (Secure Sockets Layer) protocol that enables secure communication between browsers and web sites.

The generally accepted scenario for securing communications using asymmetric cryptography involves using asymmetric encryption to establish a shared secret (symmetric) key, and then performing subsequent data exchange by using symmetric encryption based on the secret key. This method has two advantages. The first is that the two parties do not have to have prior agreement on a symmetric key. It can be proposed and agreed upon via asymmetric data exchange. The second advantage is that large amounts of data can be exchanged without taking up too much processor time. We will be making use of this technique in the Encrypted Communication Class. In this class, we will be using the DES (Digital Encryption Standard) algorithm for our symmetric cryptography. DES is a little outdated, but it is widely adopted and very fast. For more security-sensitive applications, you may want to use algorithms such as triple-DES, or the relatively new AES (Advanced Encryption Standard), which use larger keys and provide more security. Both are also supported by .NET.

When we talk about keys and data in this chapter, what we are referring to are actually byte arrays. This enables us to encode any kind of data, not just text. While it is tempting to think of a byte array as being exactly the same as a string, this isn't quite the case in .NET, where characters stored in Unicode take up two bytes each. In addition, .NET's immutable string objects don't make a good place to store sensitive data. The data within a `String` object will hang around in memory until the garbage collector chooses to clear it up, and it is overwritten by another object's state. A byte array's values can be changed in place to overwrite sensitive data, removing it from memory immediately, under the control of our code.

Microsoft has many classes for writing cryptographic code in .NET. Here is a list of the ones we will be using:

❑ `RSACryptoServiceProvider` – used as public and private keys for the asymmetric encryption and decryption

❑ `DESCryptoServiceProvider` – used to create the symmetric key and for creating objects to perform encryption and decryption with that key

❑ `RSAPKCS1KeyExchangeFormatter` – used to exchange the symmetric key between the two entities carrying on the encrypted communication

❑ `RSAPKCS1KeyExchangeDeformatter` – used to exchange the symmetric key between the two entities carrying on the encrypted communication

❑ `CryptoStream` – used to encrypt and decrypt data

In addition to these classes, which you can find in `System.Security.Cryptography`, we will use classes in the `System.IO.MemoryStream` and `System.Text.ASCIIEncoding` namespaces.

Design

The code needed to implement symmetric and asymmetric cryptography in .NET is not overly complicated, but it can be a little daunting the first time. We will design our class so that it hides all of the cryptographic code. The class will provide a simple interface that enables us to use cryptographic key exchange without worrying about the implementation details.

In order to participate in encrypted communication using our class, both parties will need to create a public-private key pair. They will then need to exchange public keys. .NET's RSA keys can easily be written out in an XML format, which makes transferring the public keys simple. We'll see how to generate such keys in .NET in the demonstration code.

From this point forward, when talking about the parties that communicate using this class, we will refer to the communication initiator as the client, and the party at the other end of the communication as the server. Both of these entities must create instances of our class. This does not mean that you can only use the Encrypted Communication class for communication between client and server applications, but that is probably the most common scenario.

So, the client needs to have a public-private key pair, and a copy of the server's public key, and the server needs its own public-private key pair, and a copy of the client's public key.

We'll make our class so that it has a constructor that takes as arguments XML strings representing the public-private key pair of one entity, and the public key of the other entity. So, both client and server applications will be able to obtain an instance of the class for communicating with one another, by providing their own key pair, and the other party's public key.

The client and server need to configure their respective instances of our class so that both instances know the same symmetric key. This is done using a key exchange. First, the client needs to propose a key to the server. Our class will have a method, `GenerateInitialKeyExchangeData()`, which will return a byte array containing a proposed symmetric key, encoded with the other party's public key. So, our client will call this method. It then transmits this key exchange data to the server (the actual transport mechanism is up to the code using the class).

The server then takes this data, and passes it to our class's `GetKeyExchangeResponse()` method. This decrypts the symmetric key, and then re-encrypts it with the client's public key. Again, this is returned as a byte array. The server should then send this package back to the client.

The client completes key exchange by validating the server's response, by passing it in to our class's `CheckKeyExchangeResponse()` method. If the package decrypts using the client's secret key and matches the original symmetric key, then the connection has been validated. Both objects are now configured for symmetric encryption.

To quickly summarize, here's the key exchange process in full:

Client	Server
1. Send random symmetric key encrypted with server's asymmetric public key to Server.	
	2. Decrypt symmetric key from client using Server's asymmetric private key.
	3. Re-encrypt symmetric key with client's asymmetric public key and send back to client.

Client	Server
4. Decrypt response from server using client's asymmetric private key. If the decrypted response matches the symmetric key it sent when it initiated the communication, then the two entities are ready to start communicating using the symmetric key they have exchanged with each other.	

We'll provide two encryption and two decryption methods on our class – one to encrypt a byte array, one to encrypt a string, one that decrypts to a byte array, and one that decrypts to a string. Encrypted data is returned as a byte array, and the decryption methods take a byte array as an argument.

We will perform the symmetric encryption using DES, One thing you may need to be aware with DES is that the DES key consists of two parts, a key and an initialization vector (IV). Understanding how the key and IV relate to each other is not necessary in order to use DES.

Implementation

Create a VB.NET Class Library Project called `EncryptedCommunicator`, clear the default namespace, and rename `Class1.vb` to `EncryptedCommunicator.vb`. Enter the following code:

```
Imports System
Imports System.Security.Cryptography
Imports System.IO
Imports System.Text

Namespace Wrox.Toolkit.Security

   Public Class EncryptedCommunicator

   End Class
End Namespace
```

As stated in the design section of this chapter, we will be requiring calling code to know what the public and private key for this instance of the class are, as well as the public key of whatever entity this class is communicating with. These three pieces of data are essential, so we will require them in order to create the class. By not creating a constructor without parameters, calling code will be forced to use the constructor that takes key parameters.

We need to store the keys somewhere, so add the following variable declarations at the class level.

```
Private localPublicAndPrivateKeyValue As AsymmetricAlgorithm
Private remotePublicKeyValue As AsymmetricAlgorithm
Private desKeyValue() As Byte
Private desIVValue() As Byte
```

The `AsymmetricAlgorithm` class is extended by all asymmetric cryptography provider classes in .NET, so by declaring the member variables as this type, you will not have to change the variable declaration should you decide to use an algorithm other than RSA (such as DSA). We also need two byte arrays to store the DES key and the initialization vector.

Now we can add the constructor:

```
Public Sub New(ByVal LocalPublicAndPrivateKey As String, _
               ByVal RemotePublicKey As String)

    localPublicAndPrivateKeyValue = New RSACryptoServiceProvider()
    localPublicAndPrivateKeyValue.FromXmlString( _
        LocalPublicAndPrivateKey)
    remotePublicKeyValue = New RSACryptoServiceProvider()
    remotePublicKeyValue.FromXmlString(RemotePublicKey)

End Sub
```

Here we create two instances of the `RSACryptoServiceProvider()` class. This class uses unmanaged Windows API calls behind the scenes to work with the underlying Windows cryptographic services. The `RSACryptoServiceProvider` objects act as a pair of public-private or just public key values. When you create them, they are initialized with a randomly generated pair of public and private keys, but we want to use the key data passed in to the constructor, so we use the `FromXMLString()` method to load them up with the proper data. This requires the key parameters passed to the constructor to have valid data for RSA keys in XML format.

There will be three methods involved in the key exchange process if both ends of the communication process are instances of our class:

❑ `GenerateInitialKeyExchangeData()` (called on the Client object)

❑ `GetKeyExchangeResponse()` (called on the Server object)

❑ `CheckKeyExchangeResponse()` (called on the Client object)

`GenerateInitialKeyExchangeData()` returns the encrypted symmetric key and the client application must get it to the other entity by whatever means the application requires.

```
Public Function GenerateInitialKeyExchangeData () As Byte()

    ' Create symmetric key and initialization vector
    Dim des As New DESCryptoServiceProvider()
    desKeyValue = des.Key
    desIVValue = des.IV
```

```
' Package symmetric key and initialization vector
' into a single byte array (DES algorithm specific)
Dim desKeyAndIV() As Byte
ReDim desKeyAndIV(desKeyValue.Length + desIVValue.Length - 1)
desKeyValue.CopyTo(desKeyAndIV, 0)
desIVValue.CopyTo(desKeyAndIV, desKeyValue.Length)

' Encrypt the packaged key and initialization vector
' using the public key from the other entity
Dim keyExchangeFormatter As _
    New RSAPKCS1KeyExchangeFormatter(remotePublicKeyValue)
Dim keyExchangeData() As Byte
keyExchangeData = keyExchangeFormatter.CreateKeyExchange( _
                    desKeyAndIV)

' Return the encrypted key exchange data
Return keyExchangeData

End Function
```

The first thing we do is create our symmetric key, which for DES also includes an initialization vector. The next block of code is specific to the DES algorithm. It takes both parts of the DES key and places them into a single byte array for encryption. After that, we create a key formatter object that uses RSA encryption and the public key of the remote (server) entity to encrypt the symmetric key. CreateKeyExchange() performs the encryption, and then we just return the encrypted data.

The second method used in the key exchange, GetKeyExchangeResponse() should be utilized from the server object, as previously stated. It takes the data encrypted in the first method, decrypts it with its private key, and then re-encrypts it with the public key of the client object and returns the newly encrypted data. If the client object can decrypt the data we return with its private key, and the decrypted data matches the symmetric key it generated originally, then we can expect the client object to start sending us data encrypted with the symmetric key. Here is the code for GetKeyExchangeResponse():

```
Public Function GetKeyExchangeResponse( _
                    ByVal KeyExchangeData() As Byte) _
                As Byte()

    ' Decrypt the secret data into a des key and IV
    Dim keyExchangeDeformatter As New _
            RSAPKCS1KeyExchangeDeformatter( _
            localPublicAndPrivateKeyValue)
    Dim desKeyAndIV() As Byte
    desKeyAndIV = keyExchangeDeformatter.DecryptKeyExchange( _
                    KeyExchangeData)

    ' Store the key and IV values locally
    ' DES keys and initialization vectors
    ' are 8 bytes by default
    ReDim desKeyValue(7)
    ReDim desIVValue(7)
```

271

```
desKeyAndIV.Copy(desKeyAndIV, 0, desKeyValue, 0, 8)
desKeyAndIV.Copy(desKeyAndIV, 8, desIVValue, 0, 8)

' Encrypt the packaged key and initialization vector
' using the public key from the other entity
Dim keyExchangeFormatter As New _
        RSAPKCS1KeyExchangeFormatter( _
        remotePublicKeyValue)

' Return the encrypted key exchange data
Return keyExchangeFormatter.CreateKeyExchange(desKeyAndIV)

End Function
```

Just as we used a key exchange formatter object to originally encrypt the key exchange data, here we use a key exchange deformatter object to decrypt the data. This deformatter uses the RSA algorithm to decrypt the data using the server object's private key, which it obtained in its constructor. After calling `DecryptKeyExchange()` to decrypt the data, we store the symmetric key in a member variable. Again, since we are using DES for our symmetric cryptography, we need to store both a key and IV, so we split up the decrypted data into those values. Next, we use a new key exchange formatter object to encrypt the decrypted data using the public key of the client application and return the newly encrypted data.

The third method, `CheckKeyExchangeResponse()`, is called on the client object once the client application has the key exchange response data from the server. This method attempts to decrypt the data returned from `GetKeyExchangeResponse()` using the local private key. If it is successful, and the values match those created in the `GenerateInitialKeyExchangeData()` method, then we have verified that each side is dealing with the entity they think they are dealing with (or least someone who has the public and private key of the entity they think they are dealing with). If you call `CheckKeyExchangeResponse()` and it does not throw any exceptions, we can consider ourselves ready to hold a proper encrypted conversation. Here is the code for this final verification

```
Public Sub CheckKeyExchangeResponse(ByVal _
                                KeyExchangeDataReply() _
                                As Byte)

' Decrypt the secret data into a des key and IV
Dim keyExchangeDeformatter As New _
        RSAPKCS1KeyExchangeDeformatter( _
        localPublicAndPrivateKeyValue)
Dim desKeyAndIV() As Byte
desKeyAndIV = keyExchangeDeformatter.DecryptKeyExchange( _
                KeyExchangeDataReply)

' Compare the decrypted key and IV to the locally stored values
Dim i As Integer
For i = 0 To 7
    If desKeyAndIV(i) <> desKeyValue(i) Then
        Throw New Exception("Invalid Key Exchange Reply")
    End If
Next
```

```
    For i = 0 To 7
        If desKeyAndIV(i + 8) <> desIVValue(i) Then
            Throw New Exception("Invalid Key Exchange Reply")
        End If
    Next
End Sub
```

Once again, we create a key exchange deformatter object to decrypt the response from the server application using the private key of the client object. Then we simply iterate through the decrypted data, comparing it byte-for-byte with the symmetric key we originally stored in the `GenerateInitialKeyExchangeData` method. If we find that the data does not match exactly, then we throw an error.

The asymmetric handshaking routines are now in place. All we now have to add are methods for the client and server to encrypt and decrypt data using the agreed symmetric key. Either party can encrypt the message or data it wants to send by calling one of the two `EncryptData()` methods we're going to code. The code would then send the data returned from `EncryptData()` to the other party, where it can be decrypted using the symmetric key. One of our `EncryptData()` methods will take a string as its parameter and the other will take a byte array. Both of them will return byte arrays. Let us code the method that takes the byte array first since that is what all cryptographic classes in .NET like to deal with.

```
Public Overloads Function EncryptData(ByVal Data() As Byte) _
    As Byte()

    ' Create a stream for reading from the unencrypted byte array
    Dim reader As New MemoryStream(Data)

    ' Create the crypto stream based on
    ' a DES transformation and the previously
    ' agreed upon key and initialization vector
    Dim des As New DESCryptoServiceProvider()
    Dim encryptor As New CryptoStream( _
            reader, _
            des.CreateEncryptor(desKeyValue, desIVValue), _
            CryptoStreamMode.Read)

    ' Create a byte array for reading from the encryptor
    Dim encryptedData() As Byte

    ' Create a stream for writing encrypted data to
    Dim encryptedStream As New MemoryStream()

    ' Read from the encryptor until there is nothing more
    ' to read, writing everything to the encryptedStream
    Dim bytesRead As Integer
    ReDim encryptedData(des.BlockSize)
    Do
        bytesRead = encryptor.Read(encryptedData, 0, des.BlockSize)
        If bytesRead <> 0 Then
            encryptedStream.Write(encryptedData, 0, bytesRead)
        End If
    Loop While bytesRead > 0
```

```
' Redim the encryptedData array to hold all of the data
' in the encryptedStream
ReDim encryptedData(encryptedStream.Length - 1)

' Read data from the encrypted stream into the byte array
encryptedStream.Position = 0
encryptedStream.Read(encryptedData, 0, encryptedStream.Length)

Return encryptedData

End Function
```

The first thing we do is create a new memory stream based on the data passed in so that the `CryptoStream` can encrypt the data. A `CryptoStream` must be initialized on an existing stream of data. A `DESCryptoServiceProvider` is used to create an encryptor, which is an object that uses the DES algorithm to encrypt data for the `CryptoStream` when in read mode.

Next, we create a byte array to read data from the `CryptoStream`, and a `MemoryStream` to write that data to. Then we loop until we have read all of the data from the crypto stream and into the memory stream. The last thing we do is get the encrypted data out of the memory stream and into a byte array so that we can return it.

The code for encrypting a string into a byte array is very simple as it delegates to the overloaded method we just wrote.

```
Public Overloads Function EncryptData(ByVal Data As String) _
    As Byte()
    Return EncryptData(ASCIIEncoding.ASCII.GetBytes(Data))
End Function
```

Now the client application can send the encrypted data to the other server application. Remember that the server application would call the same method on the server object to get encrypted data to send to the client application.

We need to create our two methods for decrypting the data next. One will be for decrypting into a byte array and one for decrypting into a string. The two methods are `DecryptAsByteArray()` and `DecryptAsString()`. Here is the code for the former:

```
Public Function DecryptAsByteArray(ByVal Data() As Byte) _
    As Byte()

    ' Create a stream for writing encrypted data to
    Dim encryptedStream As New MemoryStream()

    ' Write the encrypted data to the memory stream
    encryptedStream.Write(Data, 0, Data.Length)

    ' Create the crypto stream based on
    ' a DES transformation, the previously
    ' agreed upon key and initialization vector,
    ' and the stream of encrypted data
    Dim des As New DESCryptoServiceProvider()
    Dim decryptor As New CryptoStream( _
```

```
            encryptedStream, _
            des.CreateDecryptor(desKeyValue, desIVValue), _
            CryptoStreamMode.Read)

    ' Create a BinaryReader to get the byte
    ' array of decrypted data from the
    ' crypto stream
    Dim br As New BinaryReader(decryptor)

    ' Get the decrypted bytes
    Dim decryptedData() As Byte
    encryptedStream.Position = 0
    decryptedData = br.ReadBytes(encryptedStream.Length)

    Return decryptedData

End Function
```

The first thing we do is take the byte array that was passed in and write it to a memory stream. This is because we need to use a CryptoStream to perform the decryption, and it needs a stream to read the encrypted data from. Next, we create the CryptoStream exactly as we did in the EncryptData() method, except here we are initializing it with a stream that already has encrypted data, and we are giving it a decryptor created by the DES object instead of an encryptor. Finally, to read decrypted data from the CryptoStream into a byte array, we create a binary reader based on the CryptoStream.

Much as the version of EncryptData() that deals with strings was easy to write, so is the decryption method that deals with strings easy to write. It too delegates to the method that deals with byte arrays. Here is the code.

```
Public Function DecryptAsString(ByVal Data() As Byte) As String
    Return ASCIIEncoding.ASCII.GetString(DecryptAsByteArray(Data))
End Function
End Class
End Namespace
```

That should do it for the code in our class, now let us look at how we can use it.

Demonstration

This demonstration will use two instances of the EncryptedCommunicator class. One will act as a client machine requesting secure communications with a server, and the other will act as the server with which it is trying to talk. This example is not entirely realistic in that there would probably be a network stream or some remoting going on between the two objects, but for demonstration purposes, both objects will be in the same process. Create a new console application that references the project containing the EncryptedCommunicator class and enter the following code:

```
Imports System
Imports Wrox.Toolkit.Security
Imports System.Security.Cryptography
Module Module1
```

```vb
Sub Main()

    ' Create a key set for both client and server
    Dim serverKey As New RSACryptoServiceProvider()
    Dim clientKey As New RSACryptoServiceProvider()

    ' Create the client and server objects
    Dim server As EncryptedCommunicator
    Dim client As EncryptedCommunicator
    server = New EncryptedCommunicator( _
                serverKey.ToXmlString(True), _
                clientKey.ToXmlString(False))
    client = New EncryptedCommunicator( _
                clientKey.ToXmlString(True), _
                serverKey.ToXmlString(False))

    ' Perform the key exchange
    Dim keyExchangeData() As Byte
    keyExchangeData = client.GenerateInitialKeyExchangeData
    keyExchangeData = server.GetKeyExchangeResponse(keyExchangeData)
    client.CheckKeyExchangeResponse(keyExchangeData)

    ' Create the first message from the client to the server
    Dim clientMessage As String = "Hello, Server. This is the client."
    Console.WriteLine("clientMessage = " & clientMessage & vbCrLf)

    ' Get the encrypted client message
    Dim encryptedData() As Byte = client.EncryptData(clientMessage)
    Console.WriteLine("Client's encrypted data: " & _
            System.Text.ASCIIEncoding.ASCII.GetString(encryptedData) _
            & vbCrLf)

    ' Decrypt the client message on the server
    Console.WriteLine("decryptedData = " & _
                    server.DecryptAsString(encryptedData) _
                    & vbCrLf)

    ' Create message from the server to the client
    Dim serverMessage As String = "Hello, Client. This is the server."
    Console.WriteLine("serverMessage = " & serverMessage & vbCrLf)

    ' Get the encrypted server message
    encryptedData = server.EncryptData(serverMessage)
    Console.WriteLine("Server's encrypted data: " & _
            System.Text.ASCIIEncoding.ASCII.GetString(encryptedData) _
            & vbCrLf)

    ' Decrypt the server message on the client
    Console.WriteLine("decryptedData = " & _
                    client.DecryptAsString(encryptedData) _
                    & vbCrLf)

    Console.ReadLine()
End Sub
End Module
```

You should see a screen similar to the following when you run the demo application:

```
C:\SecureComms\CryptoDemo\bin\CryptoDemo.exe                    _ □ ×
clientMessage = Hello, Server. This is the client.
Client's encrypted data: )=!4ZWzhyЛ!!OjQzJ7p.!)%ehЛ="uyS+!xH5zo.8!

decryptedData = Hello, Server. This is the client.

serverMessage = Hello, Client. This is the server.

Server's encrypted data: XN">
    c('Л   a l-!4!)!d;DOI[TKyX♠X!9 ¶ru l! !u

decryptedData = Hello, Client. This is the server.
```

You may not see this exactly though. The precise output will differ from one run to the next, because a new DES key is generated each time. Because we are putting encrypted byte data into a string and displaying it on a console, there is a good chance that an escape code for the console will be found in the encrypted data. Any bytes following the escape code will be interpreted as console commands and could mess up the display of the demo application. Here is a screenshot of this very thing happening:

```
C:\SecureComms\CryptoDemo\bin\CryptoDemo.exe                    _ □ ×
clientMessage = Hello, Server. This is the client.
OnY9B♠:b26◙l◊fD)nrθ ~Øqj'+&`Oq%az—E1g

decryptedData = Hello, Server. This is the client.

serverMessage = Hello, Client. This is the server.

Server's encrypted data: .S=¶ôp]z~.vEEFbvθ▧vSRS<LΤ?oc3♥YjS!i

decryptedData = Hello, Client. This is the server.
```

Notice how the line that should start with "Client's encrypted data: " only shows encrypted data. This is okay, it just means an escape code was found, and the subsequent bytes probably told the console to move back to the beginning of the line.

Limitations

This class is not thread-safe because its member variables are not. You will need to be careful when using it in a multi-threaded application.

As coded, the exact algorithms and key sizes used by the class are hard-coded into it, and changing them would require modification of the source.

Extensions

Even though this class works well just as it is presented in this chapter, it practically begs for extensions. It expects the server object to know the public key of the client object when the class is instantiated. One way of allowing the server to reuse its instance of the class to communicate with multiple clients would be to allow the client's public key to be specified during the key exchange. You could make this an optional parameter on the GetKeyExchangeResponse() method, or overload it to do the same thing.

You could also give the class new constructors that take X.509 certificates instead of XML-formatted RSA keys, or specify certificates from the Windows certificate store. If you are adventurous, you could even redesign the class to be stream based instead of based on byte arrays for data exchange.

21

XML Signing and Verification Class

The XML Signing and Verification class provides the ability to create signed XML documents. Your applications can then consume these documents with full certainty that the entity that created the document is the same as they claim to be and that there has been no tampering with the document in transit.

Scenario

XML is a technology that enables applications running on different platforms and storing data in disparate formats to easily exchange and describe data. XML achieves this compatibility by being very open – both figuratively as a standard and literally as a file or data store. This openness, which underlies the entire concept of XML and easy data exchange, is also something that makes it a rather insecure means of executing these data exchanges.

When you need to be certain that the XML documents you are consuming in your applications have come from the proper source and have not been modified, you currently must rely on code in your application, network safeguards, and other measures external to the data exchange to provide the security you need. Up until recently, there was no standard way of packaging up the security safeguards with the data.

The W3C has recommended a standard for signing XML documents using asymmetric (public and private key) cryptography that allows this packaging of security safeguards with the data. This standard defines rules for signing XML documents in such a way that a signature (which is itself XML) can be checked against the contents of the XML to verify that the XML has not been modified. It is also possible, using an XML signature, to verify that the entity that signed the XML document is who they say they are, since the verification will not work if the wrong entity signed the file.

The ability to secure XML documents in this fashion should give XML yet another boost into mainstream programming and data exchange, as there are many scenarios in which it could be employed.

For example, if your company exchanges data with another company via XML over the internet, there is a good chance that one or both of you will have a secure FTP site or a server listening at a hole in a firewall for data transmission. Your data exchange process in these scenarios relies on server security to keep out unauthorized data. However, with XML signing, you could take a load off your firewall administrators' minds and build a more robust application at the same time. If your data exchange relied on XML signing for security, you could move your data transmission to e-mail instead of FTP or direct socket communication. This would allow your administrators to close up some possible security gaps and put a level of queuing into your data exchange process that is more forgiving during times of network outages. You would not have to worry about IP or e-mail address spoofing because the proof of sender identity would be in the XML attached to or embedded in the e-mail. This approach would also make the entire process more scalable since client applications or data exchange initiators would not have to wait for your server resources to become available before processing their end of the transmission.

Another great scenario for using XML signing involves configuration files. You can use configuration files to change the behavior of applications without having to recompile them. As a developer, you can write code that checks the values in a configuration file and does different things based on these values. There are times, though, when this flexibility can represent a security risk. If a malicious user is able to modify the contents of your configuration file, then they can cause code to run which they may not have been meant to have access to. There is no built-in method for you as a developer to verify that your configuration file has not been tampered with. What we will demonstrate in this section of the book is a method for verifying not only that application configuration files have not been tampered with, but also any other XML document that you need secure.

Technology

As mentioned earlier, the W3C has recommended a standard called XML Signature for signing XML documents. You can read about the standard at http://www.w3c.org/Signature/, but we will go over it briefly here.

An XML signature is an XML element that contains data, which, by itself or along with other data, can be used to verify that a document has not been changed since it was signed, and that a certain entity signed it. The signature is computed by creating a hash of the original XML document using a secret or private key of whatever entity is doing the signing. A corresponding public or not so secret key, which is mathematically related to the private key, can be used along with the hash to check the contents of the signed XML document for any modifications.

There are three types of XML signatures:

❑ Enveloped

❑ Enveloping

❑ Detached

An enveloped signature is created when the signature element becomes part of the of the signed document's DOM hierarchy at a level somewhere below that of the document element. The signature is said to be enveloped by the signed document.

An enveloping signature is created when the signature element becomes the document element and the signed document gets contained within a data object element within the signature element. In this case, the signature is said to be enveloping the signed document.

The third type of signature, a detached signature, is created when the signature is stored in separate document from the signed document. The signature document is detached from the signed document.

Microsoft provides classes in .NET for creating and verifying all three types of XML signatures. In this chapter, we will be concerned only with classes needed to create enveloping and detached signatures.

Design

Microsoft has been good enough to provide us with a set of .NET classes for signing and verifying XML documents. We will create our own class that encapsulates the code needed to use these classes to sign XML and verify signatures. If we do it correctly, then calling code will only have to provide a source document and a private key for us to generate a signature, or a public key, signature document, and sometimes a suspect document for us to check a signature.

The .NET class that is used to create an enveloping signature, `SignedXml`, can also be used to create a detached signature. It works great for detached signatures, so long as the document that you are signing *never changes location*. The reason for this is that the URI of the detached document is hashed, and then the hash is included as part of the signature. This means that you cannot use relative paths when creating detached signatures. It would be extremely handy to be able to use a relative path though, so we will work around this limitation by using an enveloping signature and swapping out the signed content in the enveloping signature with the contents of the suspect document. The only way verification would work in this scenario is if the suspect document's contents are identical to those of the enveloping signature's signed data. This fact is what allows us to get away with the workaround.

Once the class for signing and verifying the documents and signatures is created, we will build a couple of demo apps that show us how to use our class to create console applications for signing and verifying signatures. The file signing application will use a private key to sign the file. The verification application will use a public key to verify that a configuration file has not been modified. When we sign the XML file, we will not actually modify it. We will create a new file with a file name that the user specifies. This 'verify file' will contain the XML signature element.

Implementation

The first thing we want to do is create a class that does the job of signing and verifying XML documents. This is a simple class, so let's jump right in.

Create a new class named XMLSigner. It will have three main methods: CreateDetachedSignature(), CreateEnvelopingSignature(), and VerifySignature(). The CreateDetachedSignature() and overloaded CreateEnvelopingSignature() methods each return an XML document containing the computed signature and VerifySignature() returns a Boolean value indicating success (True) or failure (False). The VerifySignature() method will be overloaded to allow for verifying detached signatures by not passing in a suspect XML document. The signature document will already have the URI embedded in the signature, so it will be able to perform the check based on that URI. VerifySignature() can check enveloping signatures with the same method since the data we will also be verifying is also in the signature document. In order to accomplish our workaround of being able to verify detached signatures with a suspect document that may change locations, we will implement a version of VerifySignature() that also takes a suspect XmlDocument as a parameter.

Let's start our class with the following code:

```
Imports System
Imports System.Xml
Imports System.Security.Cryptography
Imports System.Security.Cryptography.Xml

Namespace Wrox.Toolkit.Security

    Public Class XMLSigner
```

The compiler will not know where to find the System.Security.Cryptography.Xml namespace, so you will need to add a reference in your project to System.Security.dll when compiling.

We'll start by adding the first CreateEnvelopingSignature() method. We will use the SignedXml object and associated objects to create an XML signature that we will return in an XML document. The reason for CreateEnvelopingSignature() being overloaded is that this will allow us to add a version that simply takes a file name for the input document later on.

The .NET SignedXml object will need to know for what data it is creating a signature. We tell it by putting the XML nodes that need signing into a DataObject and adding the DataObject to the SignedXml object. A single XML signature can have multiple data objects that it signs. Each data object needs a corresponding Reference element that contains a hash and hash algorithm for the data object.

After adding a DataObject and corresponding Reference to the SignedXml, we can tell it what the key is that it should use for computing the signature. All that we have left to do is to ask the SignedXml to compute the signature.

Here are the entire contents for CreateEnvelopingSignature():

```
Public Overloads Shared Function CreateEnvelopingSignature( _
    ByVal InputDocument As XmlDocument, _
    ByVal PrivateKey As RSACryptoServiceProvider) _
    As XmlDocument

    If InputDocument Is Nothing Then
      Throw New ArgumentNullException("InputDocument")
    End If
    If PrivateKey Is Nothing Then
      Throw New ArgumentNullException("PrivateKey")
    End If

    Dim signedXml As New SignedXml()

    Dim dataObject As New DataObject()
    dataObject.Data = InputDocument.ChildNodes
    dataObject.Id = "SignedXML"

    signedXml.AddObject(dataObject)

    Dim reference As New Reference()
    reference.Uri = "#SignedXML"
    signedXml.AddReference(reference)

    signedXml.SigningKey = PrivateKey
    signedXml.ComputeSignature()

    Dim returnDocument As New XmlDocument()
    returnDocument.LoadXml(signedXml.GetXml().OuterXml)
    Return returnDocument

End Function
```

The CreateDetachedSignature() method is very similar to the CreateEnvelopingSignature() method. The only difference is that we do not need to create a DataObject, and we need to assign the URI parameter to the Reference object:

```
Public Shared Function CreateDetachedSignature( _
    ByVal InputDocumentURI As Uri, _
    ByVal PrivateKey As RSACryptoServiceProvider) _
    As XmlDocument

  If InputDocumentURI Is Nothing Then
    Throw New ArgumentNullException("InputDocumentURI")
  End If

  If PrivateKey Is Nothing Then
    Throw New ArgumentNullException("PrivateKey")
  End If

  Dim signedXml As New SignedXml()
  Dim reference As New Reference()

  reference.Uri = InputDocumentURI.ToString()

  signedXml.AddReference(reference)

  signedXml.SigningKey = PrivateKey
  signedXml.ComputeSignature()

  Dim returnDocument As New XmlDocument()
  returnDocument.LoadXml(signedXml.GetXml().OuterXml)
  Return returnDocument

End Function
```

Now let's tackle the first VerifySignature() overload. This method has two parameters: SignatureDocument and PublicKey. The SignatureDocument is the XML document that we need to check, and the PublicKey is the key we will use to perform the verification. Here is the code for the first overload of VerifySignature():

```
Public Overloads Shared Function VerifySignature( _
    ByVal SignatureDocument As XmlDocument, _
    ByVal PublicKey As RSACryptoServiceProvider) _
    As Boolean

  If SignatureDocument Is Nothing Then
    Throw New ArgumentNullException("SignatureDocument")
  End If
  If PublicKey Is Nothing Then
    Throw New ArgumentNullException("PublicKey")
  End If

  Dim signatureNode As XmlNode
  Dim nsm As XmlNamespaceManager
  Dim signedXml As New SignedXml()

  nsm = New XmlNamespaceManager(SignatureDocument.NameTable)
  nsm.AddNamespace("xmlsig", "http://www.w3.org/2000/09/xmldsig#")
```

```
        signatureNode = SignatureDocument.SelectSingleNode( _
            "//xmlsig:Signature", nsm)

        signedXml.LoadXml(signatureNode)

        Try
            Return signedXml.CheckSignature(PublicKey)

        Catch ex As Exception

        End Try

        Return False
    End Function
```

Let's look at the XmlNamespaceManager. When you create an XML signature, the elements of the signature are all in the namespace http://www.w3.org/2000/09/xmldsig# This is specified on the elements by the xmlns attribute. If you only pass in an XPath query to the SelectSingleNode() method, it will only search for elements with no namespace. So, in order to get the XPath query to return an element from a different namespace, you need to pass it an XmlNamespaceManager with the appropriate namespaces.

We could have used the GetElementsByTagName() method, because it is namespace insensitive. By using SelectSingleNode() with a namespace manager, we allow signed documents to contain other elements named Signature as long as they are in a different namespace, and we can be sure that we are selecting the correct one when we perform the verification.

The next overload of VerifySignature() is our workaround that will allow us to verify documents that will not always be accessible at a single URI. This method takes another parameter – the suspect document that we will be checking. Our workaround will involve replacing the enveloped data in the signature with the data from the original document.

To replace the enveloped data, our approach will be to create a dummy node on the signature document and set its InnerXml property to the OuterXml property of the document element from the original document. This will ensure that any and all attributes and children of the document element get copied over to this element. Once we have done this, we can call ReplaceChild() on the ObjectNode of the signature and give it the data from the original document. Then we pass the signature to the first overloaded VerifySignature() method and, if the verification is successful, then we know that the original data has not been modified. Here is the code:

```
    Public Overloads Shared Function VerifySignature( _
        ByVal SignatureDocument As XmlDocument, _
        ByVal SuspectDocument As XmlDocument, _
        ByVal PublicKey As RSACryptoServiceProvider) _
        As Boolean
```

```
If SignatureDocument Is Nothing Then
  Throw New ArgumentNullException("SignatureDocument")
End If
If SuspectDocument Is Nothing Then
  Throw New ArgumentNullException("SuspectDocument")
End If
If PublicKey Is Nothing Then
  Throw New ArgumentNullException("PublicKey")
End If

Dim testDocument As New XmlDocument()
testDocument.LoadXml(SignatureDocument.OuterXml)

Dim nsm As XmlNamespaceManager
nsm = New XmlNamespaceManager(SignatureDocument.NameTable)
nsm.AddNamespace("xmlsig", "http://www.w3.org/2000/09/xmldsig#")

Dim objectNode As XmlNode
Dim data As XmlNode
Dim dataToCheck As XmlNode

objectNode = testDocument.SelectSingleNode( _
    "//xmlsig:Object", nsm)
dataToCheck = testDocument.CreateElement("Junk", _
    SuspectDocument.DocumentElement.NamespaceURI)
dataToCheck.InnerXml = SuspectDocument.DocumentElement.OuterXml
data = objectNode.FirstChild
objectNode.ReplaceChild(dataToCheck.FirstChild, data)

Return VerifySignature(testDocument, PublicKey)
End Function
```

The last thing we need to do before we move on to the demonstration code is to create an overloaded function for `CreateEnvelopingSignature()` that accepts a file name instead of `XmlDocument` as input, and overloaded functions for both versions of the `VerifySignature()` method that take file names instead of `XmlDocuments` for input. Here is the code for these three methods:

```
Public Overloads Shared Function CreateEnvelopingSignature( _
    ByVal InputFile As String, _
    ByVal PrivateKey As RSACryptoServiceProvider) _
    As XmlDocument

If InputFile = "" Then
  Throw New ArgumentNullException("InputFile")
End If

Dim inputDoc As New XmlDocument()
inputDoc.Load(InputFile)
inputDoc.LoadXml(inputDoc.DocumentElement.OuterXml)
```

```
        Return CreateEnvelopingSignature(inputDoc, PrivateKey)
    End Function

    Public Overloads Shared Function VerifySignature( _
        ByVal SignatureFile As String, _
        ByVal PublicKey As RSACryptoServiceProvider) _
        As Boolean

        If SignatureFile = "" Then
            Throw New ArgumentNullException("SignatureFile")
        End If

        Dim signatureDoc As New XmlDocument()
        signatureDoc.Load(SignatureFile)

        Return VerifySignature(signatureDoc, PublicKey)
    End Function

    Public Overloads Shared Function VerifySignature( _
        ByVal SignatureFile As String, _
        ByVal SuspectFile As String, _
        ByVal PublicKey As RSACryptoServiceProvider) _
        As Boolean

        If SignatureFile = "" Then
            Throw New ArgumentNullException("SignatureFile")
        End If
        If SuspectFile = "" Then
            Throw New ArgumentNullException("SuspectFile")
        End If

        Dim signatureDoc As New XmlDocument()
        signatureDoc.Load(SignatureFile)

        Dim suspectDoc As New XmlDocument()
        suspectDoc.Load(SuspectFile)

        Return VerifySignature(signatureDoc, suspectDoc, PublicKey)
    End Function

    End Class
End Namespace
```

Now that we've created our XMLSigner class, let's look how to use it.

Demonstrations

The next order of business is to create a couple of applications to demonstrate our XMLSigner class. We'll start with an application that can sign an XML document.

Signing Demonstration

This application will use a private key to sign the file. We will let the person signing the file either specify a file that has the key information in it, or tell us to generate a new key file and use that to sign the configuration file. This will be a console application that will take four parameters. The first parameter will specify the file to be signed. The second parameter will specify the output file. The third parameter tells us whether to create a detached signature or not. The fourth parameter is optional and will specify a key file that will be used to do the signing. If no key file is specified, then we will create a new key pair, use it to do the signing, and then write the key pair out to a file named keyfile.xml.

Create a new console application called SignXML, and replace the code in Module1 with the following code. Do not forget to add a reference to the project that has the XMLSigner class:

```vb
Imports System
Imports System.Xml
Imports Wrox.Toolkit.Security
Imports System.Security.Cryptography

Module SignXML

  Sub Main(ByVal args As String())

    Try
      If args.Length < 3 Or args.Length > 4 Then
        Console.WriteLine("Invalid number of arguments")
        Return
      End If

      Dim xmlSigner As New XMLSigner()
      Dim keypair As New RSACryptoServiceProvider()
      Dim xml As XmlDocument
      Dim signed As XmlDocument

      If args.Length = 4 Then
        ' Keyfile was specified, so load it up
        Console.WriteLine("Loading keypair from file """ & _
          args(3) & """ ...")
        xml = New XmlDocument()
        xml.Load(args(3))
        ' Load the key
        keypair.FromXmlString( _
          xml.SelectSingleNode("RSAKeyValue").OuterXml)
      Else
        ' No keyfile was specified so create new keypair and save it
        Console.WriteLine("Creating new keypair and saving " & _
          "to ""keyfile.xml"" ...")
        xml = New XmlDocument()
        xml.LoadXml(keypair.ToXmlString(True))
        xml.Save("keyfile.xml")
      End If
```

```
        If args(2) = "d" Then
            ' Create detached signature
            Console.WriteLine("Computing signature ...")
            signed = xmlSigner.CreateDetachedSignature( _
                New Uri(args(0)), keypair)
            Console.WriteLine(signed.OuterXml)
        Else
            ' Create enveloping signature
            Console.WriteLine("Computing signature ...")
            signed = xmlSigner.CreateEnvelopingSignature(args(0), keypair)
            Console.WriteLine(signed.OuterXml)
        End If

        ' Write the signature to file
        Console.WriteLine("Writing signature to file ...")
        signed.Save(args(1))
        Console.WriteLine("Done")

    Catch e as Exception
        Console.WriteLine("An error occurred: " + e.Message)

    End Try
  End Sub
End Module
```

The first thing we do is check the number of arguments, which must be at least three and no more than four. If the number of arguments passed is OK we then determine if a key is being supplied by the used by checking the optional fourth parameter. If no key is supplied then we create a new one.

Next we determine which of type of key we wish to create. If the third parameter supplied is d then we use the `CreateDetachedSignature()` method of the `XMLSigner` class, if it anything else then we use the `CreateEnvelopingSignature()` method. In either case, we write the contents of the signed file to the command line and to the file specified in the second parameter.

The `SignXML` console application can be tested with the following at the command line:

```
>SignXML infile.xml outfile.xml e
>SignXML infile.xml outfile.xml e keyfile.xml
>SignXML http://localhost/infile.xml outfile.xml d
>SignXML http://localhost/infile.xml outfile.xml d keyfile.xml
```

Verifying Demonstration

Now let's move on to the verification application. Create another VB.NET console application named `VerifyXML`, add a reference to the `XMLSigner` class, and replace `Module1` code with the following code:

```
Imports System
Imports System.Xml
Imports Wrox.Toolkit.Security
Imports System.Security.Cryptography
Module VerifyXML
```

```
Sub Main(ByVal args As String())

  Try
    ' Check number of arguments
    If args.Length < 2 Or args.Length > 3 Then
      Console.WriteLine("Invalid number of arguments")
      Return
    End If

    ' Does the verification
    Dim xmlSigner As New XMLSigner()
    ' The key to check the XML with
    Dim keypair As New RSACryptoServiceProvider()
    ' Used to load documents
    Dim keyFile As XmlDocument
    Dim original As XmlDocument
    Dim signature As XmlDocument
    ' Used for XPath queries
    Dim nsm As XmlNamespaceManager

    If args.Length = 3 Then
      ' Keyfile was specified, so load it up
      Console.WriteLine("Loading key from file """ & args(2) & _
                        """ ...")
      keyFile = New XmlDocument()
      keyFile.Load(args(2))
      keypair.FromXmlString( _
          keyFile.SelectSingleNode("RSAKeyValue").OuterXml)
    Else
      ' No keyfile was specified so we'll assume the public key
      ' is stored in the signature
      Console.WriteLine("No keyfile specified. " & _
                        "Will use key from signature ...")
    End If

    ' Load the signature document
    signature = New XmlDocument()
    Console.WriteLine("Reading signature file ...")
    signature.Load(args(1))
    nsm = New XmlNamespaceManager(signature.NameTable)
    nsm.AddNamespace("xmlsig", "http://www.w3.org/2000/09/xmldsig#")

    If keypair Is Nothing Then
      ' Get the key from the source file
      Console.WriteLine("Creating key from verification file ...")
      Dim keyNode As XmlNode
      keyNode = signature.SelectSingleNode("//xmlsig:RSAKeyValue")
      If keyNode Is Nothing Then
        Console.WriteLine("No public key specified")
        Exit Sub
      End If
      keypair.FromXmlString(keyNode.OuterXml)
    End If

    ' Load the original file
    original = New XmlDocument()
    Console.WriteLine("Reading original file ...")
    original.Load(args(0))
```

```
' Replace the contents of the Object node with the contents of
' the original file. If we can do this and the verification is
' still successful, then the contents of the original document
' have not been modified
Dim objectNode As XmlNode
Dim data As XmlNode
Dim dataToCheck As XmlNode

' Get the existing content node from the signature
objectNode = signature.SelectSingleNode("//xmlsig:Object", nsm)

' Create a new content node
dataToCheck = signature.CreateElement("Temp", _
    original.DocumentElement.NamespaceURI)
dataToCheck.InnerXml = original.DocumentElement.OuterXml

' Replace the content
data = objectNode.FirstChild
objectNode.ReplaceChild(dataToCheck.FirstChild, data)
Console.WriteLine(signature.OuterXml)

Console.WriteLine("Checking signature ...")
If xmlSigner.VerifySignature(signature, keypair) Then
  Console.WriteLine("Verification successful")
Else
  Console.WriteLine("Verification did not succeed")
End If

Console.WriteLine("Done")

Catch e as Exception
  Console.WriteLine("An error occurred: " + e.Message)

End Try
End Sub
End Module
```

In this application, we are again expecting to get either two or three parameters. The first parameter is the original (we hope!) XML document. The second parameter is the signature file. The third optional parameter is the key file.

The VerifyXML application can be tested at the command line with the following:

```
>VerifyXML infile.xml outfile.xml keyfile.xml
>VerifyXML http://localhost/infile.xml outfile.xml keyfile.xml
```

Limitations

The XMLSigner class always names and expects the data object that it creates to envelop the signed document to be named the same thing: SignedXml. If you need to exchange data with an entity that is expecting some other name, there may be trouble. This implementation also does not allow for multiple data objects in the same signature.

When loading large XML documents into a DOM as we are doing here, there could be resource issues. When you have many large documents loaded into memory, it could adversely affect your application's performance. Not only are RAM resources being gobbled up in this case, but also the processor cycles need to compute a hash based on the RSA algorithm are a scalability nightmare. In other words, XML signature is a great for infrequent use or for smaller or midsize XML documents, depending on your hardware.

The .NET `SignedXml` class creates enveloping and detached signatures, so that is what the code in the section of the book is expecting to work with. If you have signatures created with other tools and they are not enveloping or detached signatures, they may not work with this code.

Extensions

Microsoft has another class in the .NET Framework that you can use to create enveloped (as opposed to enveloping or detached) signatures that is called `XmlDsigEnvelopedSignatureTransform`. It would be handy to extend the `XMLSigner` class to be able to work with all three types of signature.

22

File System Security

Windows NT, 2000, and XP all support an advanced file system called **NTFS**. One of the many benefits that NTFS provides is granular **permissions** on file system objects. Permissions may be set per user or per group, and the available permissions include read, write, execute, and more.

The permissions of a file or directory can be found in Windows Explorer on the Security tab of the object's Property page. Unfortunately, however, programmatic access to these permissions isn't directly available in the .NET Framework.

This class provides an easy way to add or modify NTFS permissions on a file or directory, and also provides some useful permissions-related helper methods. You can use this class as a starting point for building classes to manage other types of permissions.

Scenario

NTFS permissions play a critical role in any security plan. Windows uses NTFS permissions to control access to important system files and directories, such as the Windows and System32 directories.

There are a number of applications where you might want to programmatically work with NTFS permissions. Here's an example to get you started: perhaps you're building an intranet site to host personal employee Web pages. When an employee registers on the site, the ASP.NET application creates a new virtual directory for the user, and then uses this class to restrict access to the directory, to the employee's domain user account, and also to the Administrators group.

Technology

NTFS gives administrators a great deal of control over file system permissions. These permissions may be customized on individual files or directories, or, as in recent versions of NTFS, may be efficiently inherited by child directories from parent directories without having to copy or repeatedly set permissions.

It's worth mentioning that the FAT16 and FAT32 file systems, which are supported in varying degrees by Windows 9x, Windows NT, 2000, and XP, do not support any sort of security. Keep this in mind when choosing a file system!

NTFS permissions are based on a structure called a **security descriptor**. A security descriptor may be obtained from any file or directory. Each security descriptor contains a whole host of data, including who owns the object, who has rights to access the object, what access attempts result in audit log entries (who accessed what, and when they did so), and more.

For this class, we're most interested in the security descriptor's **DACL**, or **Discretionary Access Control List**. A DACL consists of a list of **ACE**s, or **Access Control Entries**. Each ACE defines a set of access rights and a **SID**, or **Security IDentifier**, that indicates the user or group that is allowed or denied those rights.

Unfortunately, Microsoft did not include any direct facilities for working with NTFS permissions in the .NET Framework. That leaves a couple of options: calling the Win32 API with .NET's platform invoke (P/Invoke) services, or using the classes in System.Management to call through **Windows Management Instrumentation (WMI)**. In order to utilize the Framework's classes as much as possible, I've chosen to use WMI.

WMI provides an object-oriented, extensible interface for system management. It's a very powerful model that provides access to hardware information, services, performance counters, the file system and registry, and much more. If you need to manage or inspect any area of a Windows system, there's a very good chance you can do it through WMI.

For lots of additional information about all the concepts just mentioned, the Microsoft MSDN Library is a great source.

Design

This class relies heavily on the system management capabilities provided by WMI. The System.Management namespace, in turn, provides an easy way to use WMI with the .NET Framework.

The class we're about to write is called FileSystemSecurity. When you create a new instance of the FileSystemSecurity class, you must provide a fully qualified path to a file or a directory.

The class currently maintains the path in a private field, but, if you prefer, this could be changed to make the class completely stateless, in which case all methods could be marked Shared. You'll find some examples of the latter approach in the .NET Framework, such as the File class.

The class defines three enumerations to define all possible access rights for an ACE, the inheritance behavior of the ACE, and whether the ACE is allowing or denying control.

It's always good practice to hide a class's implementation details. However, to do so in this case would have made the code much longer and much more complex. Instead, the class exposes exceptions thrown by management objects, and uses management objects in its public methods.

Many of the public methods can serve dual purposes. They are used internally by the class, but can also be used by an application to do basic tasks such as obtaining a security descriptor.

To add a new permission to a file or directory, the code carries out the following general process: obtain the SID of the new user or group, create a new ACE with the desired access rights and SID, obtain the security descriptor, expand the current DACL, insert the new ACE into the DACL, and save the updated security descriptor. You'll find this code in the AddPermission() method.

Implementation

First, create a new VB.NET class file named FileSystemSecurity.vb and replace its contents with the code below. You must import System.Management to access the .NET WMI classes. You'll also need to add a reference for the System.Management.Dll assembly to your project.

```
Imports System
Imports System.Management

Namespace Wrox.Toolkit.Filesystem
   Public Class FileSystemSecurity
```

The class's code begins below with the definition of some hefty enumerations. Note the Flags() attribute on each Enum. This allows the enumerations, which are implicitly based on Integers, to be accessed as bit fields in bitwise operations such as Xor.

The two enumerations are nested inside the FileSystemSecurity class since they are so closely tied to it. They aren't generally useful in any other context, so it is logical to encapsulate them in the class.

The first enumeration, AccessRights, defines all of the possible security rights that a user or group may be allowed or denied on a file or directory.

You can find the definitions of these constants in the MSDN Library and the Platform SDK C-language header (.H) files. In the MSDN Library, the WMI Win32_ACE topic is a good starting point.

```
<Flags()> _
Public Enum AccessRights
  FileListDirectory = &H1
  FileAddFile = &H2
  FileAddSubDirectory = &H4
  FileReadEA = &H8
  FileWriteEA = &H10
  FileTraverse = &H20
  FileDeleteChild = &H40
  FileReadAttributes = &H80
  FileWriteAttributes = &H100
  Delete = &H10000
  ReadControl = &H20000
  WriteDAC = &H40000
  WriteOwner = &H80000
  Synchronize = &H100000
  AllFile = &H1FF
  AllStandard = &H1F0000
  FullControl = AllFile Or AllStandard
End Enum
```

The second enumeration, ACEFlags, defines the inheritance properties of an ACE. For example, it can specify that an ACE on a directory be inherited by subdirectories.

```
<Flags()> _
Public Enum ACEFlags
  ObjectInherit = &H1
  ContainerInherit = &H2
  NoPropagateInherit = &H4
  InheritOnly = &H8
  Inherited = &H10
End Enum
```

The last enumeration, ACEType, simply defines whether an ACE allows or denies permission.

```
<Flags()> _
Public Enum ACEType
  Allow = 0
  Deny = 1
End Enum

Private filePath As String
```

To create a new instance of the class, provide a fully qualified path to a file or directory:

```
Public Sub New(ByVal filePath As String)
  If filePath Is Nothing Then
    Throw New ArgumentNullException("filePath")
  ElseIf filePath.Length = 0 Then
    Throw New ArgumentException("filePath may not be empty.")
  Else
    Me.filePath = filePath
  End If
End Sub
```

At this point you're about to find the first of many uses of the System.Management classes. WMI defines dozens of base and derived classes in its object model (which is not related to .NET). Each class can have fields and methods, just like a .NET class.

The .NET ManagementBaseObject class is the base class of ManagementObject, and ManagementObject is the base class of ManagementClass. These .NET classes are used to manipulate WMI object instances and class definitions. In many cases, the management classes return ManagementBaseObject references.

Before we can do any work with NTFS permissions, we must obtain a security descriptor, since it contains all the security data for a particular file system object.

GetDescriptor() returns a Win32_SecurityDescriptor WMI object through the reference parameter descriptor. It also returns a ManagementStatus enumeration to indicate either NoError or an appropriate WMI error code.

```
Public Function GetDescriptor( _
    ByRef descriptor As ManagementBaseObject) As ManagementStatus
```

The first step is to obtain an instance of the Win32_LogicalFileSecuritySetting WMI class associated with the specified file or directory. The WMI class exposes a method called GetSecurityDescriptor(), which takes no parameters, and returns a Win32_SecurityDescriptor WMI object.

```
Dim logFileSecSetting As ManagementObject = _
    New ManagementObject( _
        "Win32_LogicalFileSecuritySetting.Path='" _
        + filePath + "'")
```

ManagementObject.InvokeMethod() is used to call Win32_LogicalFileSecuritySetting's GetSecurityDescriptor() method, which returns a ManagementBaseObject containing two properties, ReturnValue and Descriptor.

```
Dim result As ManagementBaseObject = _
    logFileSecSetting.InvokeMethod( _
        "GetSecurityDescriptor", Nothing, Nothing)
```

The return value is of type System.UInt32, but ManagementStatus is a VB.NET Integer, or System.Int32. We use Convert.ToInt32() to convert the return value's type to match the enumeration's type.

```
Dim returnValue As ManagementStatus = _
    Convert.ToInt32(result.Properties("ReturnValue").Value)
```

If the value of ReturnValue is ManagementStatus.NoError, the method succeeded and the descriptor is returned to the caller. If it was unsuccessful though, descriptor is set to Nothing and an exception is thrown.

297

```
          If returnValue <> ManagementStatus.NoError Then
              descriptor = Nothing
              Throw New Exception( _
                  "GetSecurityDescriptor() failed with code " _
                  + returnValue.ToString())
          Else
              descriptor = result.Properties("Descriptor").Value
          End If

          Return returnValue
      End Function
```

`SetDescriptor()` should look familiar, as it's very similar to `GetDescriptor()`. In this case, the code uses `GetMethodParameters()` to obtain a `ManagementBaseObject` that contains one property for each parameter of the `SetSecurityDescriptor()` WMI method.

```
      Public Function SetDescriptor( _
          ByVal descriptor As ManagementBaseObject) As ManagementStatus
          Dim logFileSecSetting As ManagementObject = _
              New ManagementObject( _
                  "Win32_LogicalFileSecuritySetting.Path='" _
                  + filePath + "'")

          Dim params As ManagementBaseObject = _
              logFileSecSetting.GetMethodParameters( _
                  "SetSecurityDescriptor")
```

The new descriptor is saved in the `Descriptor` property, and then `InvokeMethod()` calls `SetSecurityDescriptor()` to save it. If the method call fails, an exception is thrown.

```
          params.Properties("Descriptor").Value = descriptor

          Dim result As ManagementBaseObject = _
              logFileSecSetting.InvokeMethod( _
                  "SetSecurityDescriptor", params, Nothing)

          Dim returnValue As ManagementStatus = _
              Convert.ToInt32(result.Properties("ReturnValue").Value)

          If returnValue <> ManagementStatus.NoError Then
              Throw New Exception( _
                  "SetSecurityDescriptor() failed with code " _
                  + returnValue.ToString())
          End If

          Return returnValue
      End Function
```

The next two methods each carry out a three-step process. First, they create a new `ManagementClass` object representing a particular WMI class definition. Next, they create a new WMI object based on the class definition. Finally, they set properties on the WMI object and return it to the caller.

`CreateTrustee()` creates a `Win32_Trustee` WMI object to define a **trustee**. In this case, the trustee defines to whom permissions apply. Each ACE in the security descriptor's DACL contains a set of permissions in addition to a trustee. The SID specifies the user or group, and is obtained with the `GetSID()` method, explained later.

```
Public Function CreateTrustee( _
    ByVal domain As String, ByVal name As String, _
    ByVal sid As String) As ManagementObject
Dim trustee As New ManagementClass("Win32_Trustee")

Dim trusteeObj As ManagementObject = trustee.CreateInstance()
trusteeObj.Properties("Domain").Value = domain
trusteeObj.Properties("Name").Value = name
trusteeObj.Properties("SidString").Value = sid

Return trusteeObj
End Function
```

CreateACE() creates a Win32_ACE WMI object that defines a set of permissions for a user or group specified in a Win32_Trustee object.

```
Public Function CreateACE( _
    ByVal accessRights As AccessRights, _
    ByVal aceFlags As ACEFlags, ByVal aceType As ACEType, _
    ByVal trustee As ManagementObject) _
    As ManagementObject
Dim aceClass As New ManagementClass("Win32_Ace")

Dim aceObj As ManagementObject = aceClass.CreateInstance()
aceObj.Properties("AccessMask").Value = accessRights
aceObj.Properties("ACEFlags").Value = aceFlags
aceObj.Properties("ACEType").Value = aceType
aceObj.Properties("Trustee").Value = trustee

Return aceObj
End Function
```

The GetSID() method searches for the SID of a local or domain user account or group. WMI allows you to run queries with a language called WQL (WMI Query Language), which has a syntax that is very similar to SQL. As an optimization, you can specify whether the account is local, if this information is known.

```
Public Function GetSID( _
    ByVal domain As String, ByVal name As String, _
    ByVal isLocal As Boolean) As String
Dim query, sid As String
Dim sidObj As ManagementObject
Dim searchResults As ManagementObjectCollection
Dim search As New ManagementObjectSearcher()
```

The method constructs a query that searches for a SID in Win32_Account, matching the specified name and domain. Please note the use of LocalAccount in this code, which is a new feature in Windows XP (which is version 5.1).

```
query = "SELECT SID FROM Win32_Account "
query += "WHERE Name='" + name + "'"

If Not domain Is Nothing AndAlso domain.Length <> 0 Then
    query += " AND Domain='" + domain + "'"
End If

If Environment.OSVersion.Major >= 5 _
    And Environment.OSVersion.Minor >= 1 Then
```

```
        If isLocal Then
            query += " AND LocalAccount = TRUE"
        End If
    End If
```

The query is wrapped in an ObjectQuery object, which the
ManagementSearcherObject uses to execute the query.

```
        search.Query = New ObjectQuery(query)
        searchResults = search.Get()
```

Since ManagementObjectCollection doesn't provide a way to access individual
items in the collection, a For Each loop is used to obtain the ManagementObject
results. We really only expect either zero or one item in the collection.

```
        For Each sidObj In searchResults
            sid = sidObj.Properties("sid").Value
        Next
```

If no SID was found, an exception is thrown. Otherwise, the SID is returned to the caller.

```
        If sid Is Nothing Then
            Throw New Exception( _
                "The user account '" + name + "' could not be located.")
        End If

        Return sid
    End Function
```

SetDacl() is a public helper method used to save the specified DACL to the target
object's security descriptor. This is useful if you want to create the DACL yourself.

```
    Public Function SetDacl( _
        ByVal dacl() As ManagementObject)
        Dim sd As ManagementBaseObject

        GetDescriptor(sd)
        sd.Properties("DACL").Value = dacl

        SetDescriptor(sd)
    End Function
```

AddPermission() makes adding a new permission to a file or directory very simple.
It accepts a domain (which can be Nothing or an empty string for a local account), a
user or group name, and a flag indicating whether the account is local or not. The
remaining parameters indicate the desired access rights, ACE inheritance behavior, and
whether the ACE allows or denies permission.

The method locates the SID corresponding to the user or group, creates a new WMI
Win32_Ace object, gets the current security descriptor, expands the current DACL by
one element, inserts the new ACE, and then saves the updated descriptor.

```
Public Function AddPermission( _
    ByVal domain As String, ByVal name As String, _
    ByVal isLocalAccount As Boolean, _
    ByVal accessRights As AccessRights, _
    ByVal aceFlags As ACEFlags, ByVal aceType As ACEType) _
    As ManagementStatus
    Dim sid As String
    Dim sd As ManagementBaseObject
    Dim dacl As ManagementBaseObject()

    sid = GetSID(domain, name, isLocalAccount)
```

A new ACE is created to define the desired permissions and trustee. This ACE will later be inserted into the target object's DACL.

```
    Dim ace As ManagementObject = _
        CreateACE( _
            accessRights, aceFlags, aceType, _
            CreateTrustee(domain, name, sid))

    GetDescriptor(sd)

    dacl = sd.Properties("DACL").Value
```

The current DACL must be expanded by one element to allow the insertion of the new ACE. ReDim Preserve is used to maintain dacl's original contents while expanding its size by one.

```
    ReDim Preserve dacl(dacl.Length)
    dacl(dacl.Length - 1) = ace

    sd.Properties("DACL").Value = dacl

    Return SetDescriptor(sd)
    End Function
    End Class
End Namespace
```

Demonstration

Create a new VB.NET Console Application project, rename Module1.vb to FileSystemSecurityTest.vb, and replace its contents with the code below.

Whenever you use this class, you need to reference the System.Management namespace. First, add a reference to System.Management.DLL to your project. Next, add the statement Imports System.Management to your source file.

The following console application accepts a file or directory path on the command line, and then allows the local Administrators group full control of that file or directory. If the path is a directory, subdirectories and their files will also inherit the new permission.

It is very important to implement exception handling. Be sure to wrap any calls to the `FileSystemSecurity` object in a `Try...Catch` block. Many of the exceptions you might receive will be based in the `System.Management` namespace.

```
Imports System
Imports System.Management
Imports Wrox.Toolkit.Filesystem

Module MainModule

    Sub Main(ByVal CmdArgs() As String)
        Dim name As String = "Administrators"
        Dim target As String

        If CmdArgs.Length < 1 Then
            Console.WriteLine("You must specify a file or directory.")
            Exit Sub
        Else
            target = CmdArgs(0)
        End If

        Try
            Dim fss As FileSystemSecurity = _
                New FileSystemSecurity(target)
```

The following call to `AddPermission()` actually modifies the target's security descriptor. The ACE flags specify that subdirectories and their files will inherit the new permission. Note that two or more flags can be combined with the `Or` operator.

```
            fss.AddPermission( _
                Nothing, name, True, _
                fss.AccessRights.FullControl, _
                fss.ACEFlags.ContainerInherit _
                    Or fss.ACEFlags.ObjectInherit, fss.ACEType.Allow)

            Console.WriteLine( _
                "'" + target + "'" _
                    + "now gives Administrators Full Control.")
        Catch e As Exception
            Console.WriteLine("Exception: {0}", e.Message)
        End Try
    End Sub
End Module
```

This is a sample command-line execution of the program:

```
> FileSystemSecurityTest.exe C:\SecureTest\MyFile.txt
'C:\SecureTest\MyFile.txt' now gives Administrators Full Control.
```

Limitations

In order to keep the code to a reasonable length, and to keep it as easily understandable as possible, there are some limitations to the class's functionality.

It does not provide a simple way to determine whether a certain user or group have permissions to the file or directory, though you can use the class to get the necessary information. You can use the GetDescriptor() method to obtain the descriptor, and then you can search the DACL for the user or group of interest.

In addition, the class does not directly expose some pieces of useful information in the security descriptor, such as the object owner. Again, however, the class can provide an application with the information in raw form.

Finally, some problems may arise when using this class under Windows 2000 due to a small bug in the operating system. The code works correctly under other versions of Windows.

Extensions

This class is a great starting point for your own extensions and security classes. The security descriptor is a common way that many objects in Windows control access permissions. Once you have fully grasped the concepts and code in this class, you'll be ready to take on security configuration of other types of objects.

There are lots of ways to extend the class, but here are just a few examples.

First, file shares can be controlled in almost the same way as NTFS permissions, so the class could be extended to support shares in addition to files and directories. The WMI Win32_Share class and its SetShareInfo() method can be used to modify share permissions.

Another way to enhance the class is to provide methods for examining the existing permissions that a user or group has for a file or directory, and methods for removing or changing existing permissions.

Finally, WMI is capable of managing permissions on remote computers, so the class could be extended to support not just local, but remote configuration of permissions. This could be accomplished by modifying GetDescriptor() and SetDescriptor() to use a fully qualified WMI scope when creating the Win32_LogicalFileSecuritySetting ManagementObject. In addition to a path, the class constructor would also need to accept a computer name.

Principal Logon Class

The Principal Logon Class provides a method of performing a logon within an application that is not tied to any particular data source for authentication or authorization. You can use it with objects that perform authentication against, and get user role membership information from, various data stores such as relational databases, XML files, Active Directory, and Windows itself. If your code uses the Principal Logon class to coordinate the authentication, then the objects that check the logon credentials and retrieve role membership information can easily be changed to allow you to alter the logon data store with minimal change to your existing code.

Scenario

Many applications have a login process to control user access. This process involves authentication and authorization. **Authentication** is the act of logging into an application with a username and password, and verifying the username/password combination against some kind of lookup list. Authentication verifies that the user is who they claim to be, and informs the program of the success or failure. **Authorization** takes place when the application allows access to, or blocks access from, certain functionality or resources based upon either the user's identity or the user's group membership.

An application built on the Windows platform will generally perform *authentication* (as opposed to authorization) in one of two ways. The first method is simply by using the built-in Windows login to verify identity. If users can log into Windows and run the application, then they are authenticated. The second method involves prompting the user for a username and password when the application starts and then checking the username/password combination against a data store. This data store can be most things, including (but not limited to) a relational database, XML file, LDAP store, or another application. No matter how your code performs the authentication, it just needs to know if the logon process was successful or if it failed.

The same is true of *authorization*. In the scenario where built-in Windows authentication is used, an application will employ security privileges associated with the Windows user or group to access resources needed by the application. If the resources are inaccessible, then the user is not an authorized user of the application. The application can also use the identity of the user to determine programmatically if the user should have access to a certain resource or functionality. When performing this type of authorization, your code may need to know the type of authenticated user. This is often done by assigning roles to the user (and roles to groups, of which the user may be a member) and checking the roles at run time. Again, the data store that maps users to roles can vary. Often, the data store will be the same one from which the authentication was performed, but your application need not depend upon this. It just needs to be able to determine if the user has a specific role or not.

The class created in this section is a facilitator for the process of authentication and authorization. It will provide a common method to obtain authentication and authorization objects that your code can use, regardless of how the authentication and role assignment has taken place. It does not provide the implementation of authenticating and determining user roles. Examples of implementation of this class are illustrated in Chapters 24 and 25.

Technology

Microsoft designed .NET so that using authentication and role-based authorization is very straightforward for developers. There are two interfaces in the .NET Framework and they provide a common means of verifying identity (authentication) and checking role membership (authorization). The two interfaces are:

❑ `System.Security.Principal.IIdentity`

❑ `System.Security.Principal.IPrincipal`

Objects that implement `IIdentity` represent a specific user, and these objects need to provide a name, authentication type (a string whose contents have no intrinsic meaning), and Boolean value that indicates whether the user is authenticated or not. Objects that implement `IPrincipal` represent both a user and the roles that the user belongs to, and these objects need to provide a means of checking whether or not the identity associated with them has any given role.

Your code works with identity objects (which implement the `IIdentity` interface) by accessing the `Name`, `AuthenticationType`, and `IsAuthenticated` properties of the interface, which is all `IIdentity` contains. You can consider classes that implement the `IIdentity` interface to be authentication classes.

You use principal objects (which implement the IPrincipal interface) to check the roles or group memberships of an identity. The IPrincipal interface specifies one property (Identity) that returns an identity object and one method (IsInRole()) that returns True if the Identity property is in the role passed to the method, and False if not. Calls to the IsInRole() method apply to the identity object stored in the Identity property. You can consider classes that implement IPrincipal to be authorization classes.

Any logon function that you write for a .NET application would ideally provide you with a principal object (that implements IPrincipal) as the result of a successful logon. Your code can then use that principal and its associated identity (stored in the Identity property) as proof of authentication and as a means of checking roles.

Design

We will provide logon functionality through a shared method in our logon class so that an instance of our logon class does not have to be instantiated in order to perform a logon. We will define a couple of generic authentication and authorization exceptions, and define interfaces for classes that want to provide authentication or authorization services for our logon class. The Logon class merely needs to coordinate the calling of the authentication and authorization classes. Figure 1 shows the design of this and two other essential classes (covered next in this section), WindowsLogon and XMLLogon:

Figure 1

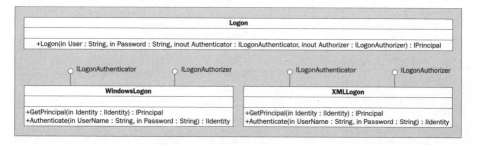

As you can see, it is a fairly simple design. The Logon class contains a Logon() method, which takes a user's evidence of authentication (user name and password), an object that will perform authentication based on the evidence, and an object that will look up role membership (for authorization). The WindowsLogon and XMLLogon classes implement both the ILogonAuthenticator and ILogonAuthorizer interfaces because they provide implementations of code to both authenticate and get role membership for a user from their respective data stores (Windows and an XML file). WindowsLogon and XMLLogon are described in Chapter 24 and 25 and they could have been split into Authenticator and Authorizer classes, but was not necessary.

With this design, the shared `Logon()` method on the `Logon` object can be called, passing in a `WindowsLogon` object for both the `Authenticator` and `Authorizer`, or you can mix and match so that you pass in a `WindowsLogon` object as the `Authenticator`, and an `XMLLogon` object as the `Authorizer`. This allows you to separate the application-specific role memberships (in an XML file) from the authorization store (Windows).

Implementation

We will start by creating a new class, called `Logon`. Open Visual Studio .NET and create a Class Library project named `Logon`, Rename `Class1.vb` to `Logon.vb` and replace the code with the following:

```
Imports System.Security.Principal

Namespace Wrox.Toolkit.Security
```

The `IIdentity` and `IPrincipal` interfaces are found in the `System.Security.Principal` namespace, so we need to import that.

We do not want to provide an implementation of authenticating a user or looking up role mapping in this class, but we will want to work with classes that perform these functions. We will use interfaces to define how we want to interact with those classes. We will call the interface for classes that perform authentication `ILogonAuthenticator`. Classes that perform mapping of roles to authenticated users should implement our second interface called `ILogonAuthorizer`.

Add the following code to the code, outside the `Logon` class definition:

```
Public Interface ILogonAuthenticator
    Function Authenticate( _
            ByVal UserName As String, ByVal Password As String) _
            As IIdentity
End Interface

Public Interface ILogonAuthorizer
    Function GetPrincipal(ByVal Identity As IIdentity) As IPrincipal
End Interface
```

The `ILogonAuthenticator` interface contains one method, `Authenticate()`, which takes a username and password as parameters. Classes that implement this interface should return an `IIdentity` object from the function if authentication is successful. If authentication is unsuccessful, an exception should be thrown.

The `ILogonAuthorizer` interface also contains one method. Its name is `GetPrincipal()` and it takes an `IIdentity` object as its single parameter. Classes that implement this interface should return an `IPrincipal` object containing the `IIdentity` object passed in and the roles mapped to the user specified by the `IIdentity` object. Calling code can then call the `IsInRole()` method on the `IPrincipal` object to check role membership.

We need to provide some exception classes for the Logon class and authentication and authorization classes so that calling code can gracefully handle any exceptions we may raise because of an unsuccessful logon.

We will create three different exceptions, one for each of the three types of object involved in the logon process. The three exceptions classes are:

❑   LogonException

❑   AuthenticationException

❑   AuthorizationException

If an error or invalid state occurs within the Logon class (not the classes that implement ILogonAuthenticator and ILogonAuthorizer) then our code will throw a LogonException. If we cannot authenticate or determine role membership, then classes that implement ILogonAuthenticator or ILogonAuthorizer can throw an AuthenticationException or AuthorizationException, respectively.

Add the following exceptions to the namespace:

```
Public Class LogonException
  Inherits ApplicationException

  Sub New(ByVal message As String)
    MyBase.New(message)
  End Sub
End Class

Public Class AuthenticationException
  Inherits ApplicationException

  Sub New(ByVal message As String)
    MyBase.New(message)
  End Sub
End Class

Public Class AuthorizationException
  Inherits ApplicationException

  Public Sub New(ByVal message As String)
    MyBase.New(message)
  End Sub
End Class
```

Now to the principle method of the Logon class. The name of this method will be the same as the class name. For parameters, it should take a username, a password, an object that will be performing the authentication, and an object that will be getting the roles. We will want the method to return an IPrincipal object for the calling code if everything goes smoothly inside the method, so that calling code can check role memberships via the IsInRole() method. If an error occurs during the logon process, then calling code can expect to catch a LogonException, AuthenticationException, or AuthorizationException. We give the class a private constructor so it cannot be instantiated from external code:

```
Public Class Logon

    Private Sub New()
      'Prevent instantiation
    End Sub
```

Insert the following method in the Logon class:

```
Public Shared Function Logon( _
             ByVal UserName As String, _
             ByVal Password As String, _
             ByVal Authenticator As ILogonAuthenticator, _
             ByVal Authorizer As ILogonAuthorizer) _
             As IPrincipal
```

The first thing to do in the function is verify that the calling code passed existing Authenticator and Authorizer objects:

```
If Authenticator Is Nothing Then
    Throw New LogonException("Invalid Authenticator class")
ElseIf Authorizer Is Nothing Then
    Throw New LogonException("Invalid Authorizer class")
End If
```

Now we call the Authenticate() method on the Authorizer to get an IIdentity object. This IIdentity object will be used to retrieve an IPrincipal object from Authorizer:

```
Dim identity As IIdentity
identity = Authenticator.Authenticate(UserName, Password)
```

Next, we need to get the IPrincipal object we want to return, and we do that by calling GetPrincipal() on the Authorizer object:

```
Dim principal As IPrincipal
principal = Authorizer.GetPrincipal(identity)
```

Finally, we can return the IPrincipal:

```
    Return principal
  End Function

End Class
End Namespace
```

Demonstration

You can find demonstrations of this class in action under the next classes in this section of the book, which will implement the ILogonAuthenticator and ILogonAuthorizer interfaces created with this class.

Limitations

The Principal Logon Class is limited to providing authentication based on usernames and passwords. Biometric security devices and smart cards are becoming more common these days, and unless the data processed by the devices can be converted into a string format of a sensible length, then the Principal Logon class cannot be used with these devices.

Extensions

This class constitutes a very simple framework. You can extend its functionality in many ways. For instance, you could overload the Logon() method to receive just a username and password as parameters. Within the overloaded function, you could then read class and assembly names from an App.config file via a System.Configuration.ConfigurationSettings object to determine what class types the Logon() function should use as authenticator and authorizer. This would allow you to change how your application performs authentication in different operating environments without changing the code in your application.

You can accomplish the dynamic class loading by using a System.Reflection.Assembly object and calling its LoadFrom() method with the assembly name loaded from the App.config file. You can then create an instance of an authenticator or authorizer class in the loaded assembly, by calling the CreateInstance() method on the assembly and passing in the class name loaded from the configuration file. This type of dynamic loading should only be used in secure environments, because a malicious person could change the configuration file to use an authenticator that they have created, and so bypass the usual authentication process.

Alternatively, your application could programmatically determine what type of authenticator or authorizer to use based on options in a logon form. If your application can run on a disconnected mobile device or laptop as well as when connected to a network, then you may have a checkbox in the logon form that specifies if you are logging in locally or over the network. Your code could then provide a different authenticator or authorizer, based on the logon type; for instance, when connected to the Internet, you may choose to logon using an XML Web Service on a remote machine, but if you are not connected to the Internet, then Windows authentication may be all that's required.

Another extension for this class would be to overload the `Logon.Logon()` method and `ILogonAuthenticator.Authenticate()` method to take some arbitrary authentication evidence, instead of a username and password. This could allow the Logon class to be used with biometric and smartcard devices.

24

Windows Logon Class

The Windows Logon Class is meant to provide you with the ability to authenticate a domain/username/password combination to a specific Windows account. This class is designed for use with the Principal Logon Class from the previous chapter, but you can use it by itself. See the design section of the Principal Logon class in Chapter 23 for more information on how this class relates to that one. The demonstration section of this chapter assumes you will be using it in conjunction with the Principal Logon class.

Scenario

There are many scenarios where you may want to authenticate a user to a Windows account. For instance, if you are writing code for a web site that does not use Windows authentication, but you want to restrict access to the site to users in a Windows domain. There are also times when you want your code to impersonate a user other than the one it is running as. To borrow from the previous example, impersonation will allow you access e-mail messages in Exchange for the web site user. In these situations, you need some code that can log into a Windows account and optionally impersonate the authenticated user. This is where the Windows Logon Class can come in handy. It will handle the code needed to perform a Windows logon and create an identity and principal based on that logon. You will be able to use the principal it creates for authorization by checking membership of Windows groups via the principal object's IsInRole() method. After creating the Windows Logon Class, we will look at how to use the objects generated by the class to check role membership and perform impersonation so that subsequent code can run in the security context of the Windows user.

Technology

The authentication and authorization (roles) data store for this class is Windows itself, so we will need to ask Windows to perform the authentication for us. We will do this using P/Invoke (platform invoke) to call a function in an unmanaged library (advapi32.dll) that performs a Windows logon. For a more in-depth coverage of P/Invoke than we'll get into here, you should check out *Professional Visual Basic Interoperability: COM and VB6 to .NET* published by Wrox Press, ISBN 1-86100-565-2. Once we have performed the logon, we will have access to a security token that references a Windows user. At this point, .NET provides us with two classes for working with the security token:

❑　System.Security.Principal.WindowsIdentity

❑　System.Security.Principal.WindowsPrincipal

The WindowsIdentity and WindowsPrincipal have all of the necessary code within them to check roles for the identity and perform impersonation.

Design

Our Windows Logon class will implement the ILogonAuthenticator and ILogonAuthorizer interfaces created in the Principal Logon class. This will allow applications that utilize the Principal Logon class to employ Windows authentication and authorization very easily.

By supporting the ILogonAuthenticator interface, we are saying that this object can perform authentication based on a username-password combination. We will create a WindowsIdentity object to return to calling code if the authentication is successful, and we'll throw an AuthenticationException if the authentication fails. In order to verify the domain/username/password we will need to call out to unmanaged code. If this call is successful, we will have a token handle that can be used to create the WindowsIdentity.

By supporting the ILogonAuthorizer interface, we are saying that this object can retrieve role information for the identity provided by calling code. The identity provided to us will need to be a WindowsIdentity in order to get Windows group/role information. We will create a WindowsPrincipal object to return to the calling code to allow the calling code to check the role membership of the WindowsIdentity.

Implementation

We will start by creating a new class called WindowsLogon. This class will contain all of the code we need to perform Windows authentication and authorization.

Add a class named `WindowsLogon` to your project containing the Logon class, and add the following code to the class definition:

```
Imports System.Runtime.InteropServices
Imports System.Security.Principal

Namespace Wrox.Toolkit.Security

  Public Class WindowsLogon
    Implements ILogonAuthenticator
    Implements ILogonAuthorizer

  End Class
End Namespace
```

This code tells .NET that the class implements the `ILogonAuthenticator` and `ILogonAuthorizer` interfaces. We import `System.Security.Principal` to have easy code access to the `IIdentity` and `IPrincipal` interfaces and the `WindowsIdentity` and `WindowsPrincipal` classes.

We need `System.Runtime.InteropServices` so that we can perform the P/Invoke code needed to call the Windows API function `LogonUser()`. We've also provide the method stubs needs to support the `ILogonAuthenticator` and `ILogonAuthorizer` interfaces; we'll finish those methods of soon, but first we'll look at how we call into Windows' , built-in logon functions.

The `LogonUser()` method takes a user name and password, and performs the Windows logon for us. Here is the `LogonUser()` signature defined in the C header file `Winbase.h`:

```
BOOL LogonUser(
  LPTSTR lpszUsername,      // user name
  LPTSTR lpszDomain,        // domain or server
  LPTSTR lpszPassword,      // password
  DWORD dwLogonType,        // type of logon operation
  DWORD dwLogonProvider,    // logon provider
  PHANDLE phToken           // receive tokens handle
);
```

You can see that some of the parameters for `LogonUser()` are types that do not have direct equivalents in VB.NET. All of the string parameters are 32 bit values that reference a string location in memory, the logon type and logon provider are just numeric constants, and the token handle parameter is another 32 bit number that will be returned from the function as an 'out' or ByRef parameter. VB.NET does not allow us to create variables that are pointers (which are what the `LogonUser()` method expects for the string parameters), but if we declare the function properly, then the .NET P/Invoke marshaller will be able to manage the pointers to the strings for us. The `dwLogonType` and `dwLogonProvider` parameters are of the type DWORD, which maps to `System.UInt32` types in .NET. We will be passing in an enumeration that we define for these parameters, but VB.NET only allows enumerations to be Bytes, Integers, Longs, or Shorts. This is fine because the marshaller will again figure out how to properly convert the data. The last parameter, phToken, is a pointer to a numeric value, and we need to handle it differently from string pointers. .NET provides us with a structure called `IntPtr`, which should be used when dealing with pointers to numbers.

In order to use the `LogonUser()` method that resides in a C DLL, we have to 'declare' it so that the .NET runtime knows where to find it. Before we declare the `LogonUser()` method, we need to create a couple of enumerations that we can use to specify the type of Windows logon to perform and the logon provider to use. Most of the time, the code will just use default settings for this, but it will not hurt to provide code that calls this class with the ability to specify its own values for the parameters.

Add the following enumerations to your class. You can refer to MSDN documentation for explanations of what the various values mean:

```
Public Enum LOGON32_LOGON
    LOGON32_LOGON_INTERACTIVE = 2
    LOGON32_LOGON_NETWORK = 3
    LOGON32_LOGON_BATCH = 4
    LOGON32_LOGON_SERVICE = 5
    LOGON32_LOGON_UNLOCK = 7
    LOGON32_LOGON_NETWORK_CLEARTEXT = 8
    LOGON32_LOGON_NEW_CREDENTIALS = 9
End Enum

Public Enum LOGON32_PROVIDER
    LOGON32_PROVIDER_DEFAULT = 0
    LOGON32_PROVIDER_WINNT35 = 1
    LOGON32_PROVIDER_WINNT40 = 2
    LOGON32_PROVIDER_WINNT50 = 3
End Enum
```

You need to be careful when specifying the logon type that is passed to the `LogonUser()` method. If you are using this class in an environment that needs to be highly scalable, then having the `LOGON32_LOGON_NETWORK_CLEARTEXT` value passed in may not be the best choice. This is because the security token created for the clear text logon type uses more resources so that it can retain security information that will allow impersonation with this logon type to access network resources as the user being impersonated. If no network resources are to be accessed, then you may want to use a logon type other than clear text or interactive (which uses even more resources than clear text).

Now for the `LogonUser()` declaration. This will describe the `LogonUser()` method to the .NET P/Invoke marshaller so that we can call it from our code:

```
<DllImport("advapi32.dll")> _
Private Shared Function LogonUser( _
    ByVal lpszUsername As String, _
    ByVal lpszDomain As String, _
    ByVal lpszPassword As String, _
    ByVal dwLogonType As LOGON32_LOGON, _
    ByVal dwLogonProvider As LOGON32_PROVIDER, _
    ByRef phToken As IntPtr) As Boolean

End Function
```

The `<DllImport("advapi32.dll")>` part of the preceding code is a method attribute. This attribute tells the P/Invoke marshaller where to find the library containing the method that the attribute is used to modify.

We have declared the method as Shared because the marshaller always requires calls to unmanaged methods to be Shared.

In order to provide calling code with the ability to specify the Windows logon type and logon provider, we will need to store the values it specifies somewhere. Let us add the following variables to our class to store them:

```
Private logonTypeValue As LOGON32_LOGON = _
    LOGON32_LOGON.LOGON32_LOGON_NETWORK_CLEARTEXT
Private logonProviderValue As LOGON32_PROVIDER = _
    LOGON32_PROVIDER.LOGON32_PROVIDER_DEFAULT
```

If the calling code does not specify any values to use, then our default values will be those specified in the variable declaration. In order to let calling code access these variables we can add a couple properties and constructors to the class:

```
Public Sub New()
    ' Default constructor
End Sub

Public Sub New(ByVal LogonType As LOGON32_LOGON, _
    ByVal LogonProvider As LOGON32_PROVIDER)

    Me.LogonType = LogonType
    Me.LogonProvider = LogonProvider
End Sub

Public Property LogonType() As LOGON32_LOGON
    Get
        Return logonTypeValue
    End Get

    Set(ByVal Value As LOGON32_LOGON)
        logonTypeValue = Value
    End Set
End Property

Public Property LogonProvider() As LOGON32_PROVIDER
    Get
        Return logonProviderValue
    End Get

    Set(ByVal Value As LOGON32_PROVIDER)
        logonProviderValue = Value
    End Set
End Property
```

By default, VB.NET does not require you to provide a default constructor for a class, but because we have added another constructor, it no longer provides the default constructor for us. In order to allow our class to be instantiated without providing any constructor parameters, we need to go back and add a constructor that takes no parameters.

Now we are ready to begin writing the code for the Authenticate() method. The first order of business is to verify that the UserName string passed in to the method is in the form <domain>\<username>. We will need both a user name and domain in order to call the LogonUser() method, so if they are not both provided in the UserName parameter, then we will not be able to continue:

```
Public Function Authenticate(ByVal UserName As String, _
    ByVal Password As String) _
    As IIdentity Implements ILogonAuthenticator.Authenticate

Dim domainAndUser As String()
If UserName.IndexOf("\") = -1 Then
   Throw New AuthenticationException("Authentication unsuccessful")
End If
domainAndUser = Split(UserName, "\")
Dim domain As String = domainAndUser(0)
Dim user As String = domainAndUser(1)
```

We are throwing an exception here with a rather generic error message. This is fine because we do not want to be giving out too many hints of what is happening under the covers in case the error message makes its way up to an end user.

Now that we have the domain, username, and password, and the logon type and logon provider are stored at the class level with default values or values that the calling code has specified, we can call the LogonUser() method from advapi32.dll. First we'll create the IntPtr structure, which we mentioned earlier, to allow the marshaller to properly handle the phToken output value, and then we call the method:

```
Dim tokenHandle As IntPtr = IntPtr.Zero
If Not LogonUser(user, domain, Password, logonTypeValue, _
             logonProviderValue, tokenHandle) Then
   Throw New AuthenticationException("Authentication unsuccessful")
End If
```

If the return value from the method is False, then the calling code passed in an invalid username and password, and we will throw an exception indicating failure.

Next, we can create the WindowsIdentity object by giving it the tokenHandle. We will want to specify the Windows account type to the WindowsIdentity object, but this should also be overridable by the calling code. Add the following variable declaration at the top of the class:

```
Private windowsAccountTypeValue As WindowsAccountType = _
   WindowsAccountType.Normal
```

Getting back to the Authenticate() method, the code for creating the WindowsIdentity from the tokenHandle and returning it looks like this:

```
Dim identity As IIdentity
identity = New WindowsIdentity(tokenHandle, "Windows", _
   windowsAccountTypeValue, True)

Return identity
End Function
```

The `tokenHandle` parameter tells the `WindowsIdentity` object who it represents. The `"Windows"` parameter is just a string that can later be accessed through the `AuthenticationType` property of the `WindowsIdentity` object's `IIdentity` interface. The value you put in here is not actually that important to get the code to run properly. The same is true for the `windowsAccountTypeValue` parameter. By passing in `True` as the last parameter, we are telling the new `WindowsIdentity` object to set its `IsAuthenticated` property to `True`.

We will also want a public property and another constructor to allow the calling code to specify a `WindowsAccountType` other than the default that we provided with the class level `windowsAccountTypeValue`:

```
Public Sub New(ByVal LogonType As LOGON32_LOGON, _
    ByVal LogonProvider As LOGON32_PROVIDER, _
    ByVal AccountType As WindowsAccountType)

  Me.LogonType = LogonType
  Me.LogonProvider = LogonProvider
  Me.AccountType = AccountType
End Sub

Public Property AccountType() As WindowsAccountType
  Get
    Return windowsAccountTypeValue
  End Get

  Set(ByVal Value As WindowsAccountType)
    windowsAccountTypeValue = Value
  End Set
End Property
```

That covers the code needed for authenticating a Windows user and implementing the `Authenticate()` method of the `ILogonAuthenticator` interface. Now let us look at the code for implementing the `GetPrincipal()` method of the `ILogonAuthorizer` interface. This method will return a `WindowsPrincipal` object that will allow calling code to perform authorization by checking roles via the `IsInRole()` method. It is a significantly easier method to write.

Add the following code to the `GetPrincipal()` method:

```
Public Function GetPrincipal(ByVal Identity As IIdentity) _
    As IPrincipal Implements ILogonAuthorizer.GetPrincipal

  If Identity Is Nothing Then
    Throw New AuthorizationException("Authorization unsuccessful")
  End If

  If Not TypeOf Identity Is WindowsIdentity Then
    Throw New AuthorizationException("Authorization unsuccessful")
  End If

  Return New WindowsPrincipal(Identity)
End Function
```

All that we are doing here is checking to make sure the `Identity` passed in to the function is a `WindowsIdentity` object, and then returning a `WindowsPrincipal` created from the `Identity`. We need to verify that the `Identity` parameter is a `WindowsPrincipal` object, because that is the only type of object from which the `WindowsPrincipal` can create itself. It is not, however, the only type of object that calling code could try to pass in to the method. Because we are supporting the `GetPrincipal()` method of the `ILogonAuthorizer` interface, our parameter is defined as an interface – `IIdentity`. This means that .NET will allow any object implementing `IIdentity` to be passed in. We only want to work with `WindowsIdentity` objects, so we check to make sure that we have one.

The `WindowsPrincipal` object already has all of the code needed to check if a `WindowsIdentity` is in specified Windows groups. It does, however, have some rules you will want to follow when checking roles. We will go over those rules in the demonstration section. Now would be a good time to try compiling your code to make sure everything is in order.

Demonstration

We will demonstrate using this class by making a console application that prompts you for a domain, username, and password, and then uses that information to authenticate against your local machine. Once we have the `WindowsPrincipal` object returned, we will look at the `IsInRole()` overloads that are specific to the `WindowsPrincipal` class.

Let us start by adding a new VB.NET Console Application project to our solution and add a reference to the project containing the `WindowsLogon` class. Next, add the following import statements to the top of `Module1.vb`:

```
Imports Wrox.Toolkit.Security
Imports System.Security.Principal
```

In the `Main()` procedure of `Module1`, place the following code for getting the logon information from the user (which will be you!):

```
Module Module1

    Sub Main()
        Dim domain As String
        Dim userName As String
        Dim password As String

        Console.Write("  Domain: ")
        domain = Console.ReadLine()
        Console.Write("    User: ")
        userName = Console.ReadLine()
        Console.Write("Password: ")
        password = Console.ReadLine()
```

Now that we have the logon information, we can create our `WindowsLogon` class and use it to authenticate:

```
Dim winLogon As New WindowsLogon()
Dim principal As IPrincipal

Try
    principal = Logon.Logon(domain & "\" & userName, password, _
        winLogon, winLogon)

Catch authentEx As AuthenticationException
    Console.WriteLine("Caught an authentication exception! " & _
                      "The error is " & authentEx.Message & "")
    Console.ReadLine()
    Return

Catch authorEx As AuthorizationException
    Console.WriteLine("Caught an authorization exception! " & _
                      "The error is " & authorEx.Message & "")
    Console.ReadLine()
    Return

End Try

Console.WriteLine("--- Logon Successful ---")
Console.ReadLine()
    End Sub
End Module
```

We create the WindowsLogon() class and a variable to hold the principal returned from the Logon() method. Then make a Try...Catch block to wrap the Logon() method call so that we can gracefully handle any error that might occur during the logon process. This sample shows how your code can tell the difference between an error that happens during the authentication process and an error that happens during the authorization process.

When we call the Logon.Logon() shared method, we concatenate the domain and userName values. This is because the format that the WindowsLogon Authenticate() method expects to receive is <domain>\<username>. Then we pass in the password value and WindowsLogon class as both the authenticator and authorizer. Remember though, that we do not have to pass the same object in as both authenticator and authorizer. We could pass some other object as the authorizer, such as a class that looks up roles for an authenticated user from a database, or an instance of the XMLLogon class discussed in the next chapter of this book.

If all goes well in the Logon() method, we will get an IPrincipal returned to us in the principal variable. You can go ahead and run this code to test your WindowsLogon class. Here is what I get when running it on my machine.

Now let us use this object to check for role membership of the user that you logged into our console application as. Add the following code after the last `Console.ReadLine()` call:

```
' Check if the user is an administrator on this machine
Console.WriteLine(Environ("COMPUTERNAME") & " Administrator: " & _
    principal.IsInRole("BUILTIN\Administrators").ToString())
Console.ReadLine()
```

This code uses the `Environ()` method to get the name of the computer for display purposes and then calls `IsInRole()` on the `principal` object to see if the authenticated user is a member of the *built-in* Windows group "Administrators".

Built-in Windows groups – groups that are part of every installation of Windows – are special cases when checking role membership with a `WindowsPrincipal` object. There are two ways to check membership in a built-in role. The first is to pass a string to `IsInRole()` that has the form BUILTIN\<group name>. If you omit the BUILTIN\ part and just pass in "Administrators", `IsInRole()` will return `False` even if the authenticated user really is a local administrator. The other way to check membership of a built-in role is to change your variable type that holds the `WindowsPrincipal` object from `IPrincipal` to `WindowsPrincipal`. This will give you access to the `WindowsPrincipal`'s overloaded `IsInRole()` method that can take a `WindowsBuiltInRole` enumeration as a parameter. The `WindowsBuiltInRole` enumeration has the following values:

- ❑ AccountOperator
- ❑ Administrator
- ❑ BackupOperator
- ❑ Guest
- ❑ PowerUser
- ❑ PrintOperator
- ❑ Replicator
- ❑ SystemOperator
- ❑ User

You can use the following code to test the same role membership using the overloaded `WindowsPrincipal IsInRole()` method by casting the principal object to a `WindowsPrincipal` type:

```
' Check if the user is an administrator on this machine
Console.WriteLine(Environ("COMPUTERNAME") & " Administrator: " & _
    CType(principal, WindowsPrincipal).IsInRole( _
        WindowsBuiltInRole.Administrator).ToString())

Console.ReadLine()
```

To test for membership in a domain account, use the same format for the role string as for a logon: <domain>\<group name>. For a group local to the machine that is *not* a built-in group, you use <computer name>\<group name>. Remember, a built-in group requires the format BUILTIN\<group name>.

You should be able to go ahead and try running your code again to see if you are member of your machine's administrator group.

Now that we know how to authenticate and authorize, let us look at how easily you can use the principal, or rather the identity in the principal, to let your code impersonate the user that we authenticated. Impersonating will give your code all of the same security privileges as the authenticated user would have if they were running the code themselves. To do this, we will call the Impersonate() method on the Identity object, by casting it to a WindowsIdentity type. After this point the code is now running as the impersonated user. We do not need to do anything else:

```
Dim impContext As WindowsImpersonationContext = _
    CType(principal.Identity, WindowsIdentity).Impersonate()
```

The privileges that Windows grants to your code when you use impersonation depend upon the LOGON32_LOGON enumeration passed to the LogonUser() function inside the WindowsLogon class. With some values, you may still not have access to network resources even though the authenticated user would normally have that access if they logged onto Windows themselves. You can check the documentation in MSDN for the LogonUser() function to see what privileges the different logon types grant your code.

The return value of the Impersonate() method is a WindowsImpersonationContext class. We will want to hold onto this object because we need it to stop impersonating.

From this point on, the current thread will be executing as the authenticated user. When we want to revert to whatever identity the thread was executing as before calling Impersonate(), we just call the Undo() method of the WindowsImpersonationContext object:

```
impContext.Undo()
```

As you can see, the WindowsPrincipal and WindowsIdentity objects make programming with Windows accounts and groups rather simple.

Limitations

You need to be careful about the logon type that you specify, depending on your operating environment, so that you do not use up more resources than necessary.

Extensions

If your main goal is performing impersonation, you could give this class an `Impersonate()` method that takes a domain, user name, and password as parameters (or simply a security token or `WindowsIdentity`) and store the impersonation context at the class level. You would then want to add an `Undo()` method to the class to revert the impersonation. These would not be methods to add to the `ILogonAuthenticator` or `ILogonAuthorizer` interfaces, but to the class itself.

If you have an existing COM+ application that handles authorization through COM+ roles, and you would like your .NET application to be in sync with the COM+ application, then you could subclass the Windows Logon class so that it gets its list of roles for the identity from the existing COM+ application. This would be very handy for simplifying administration of your application's security. You could do this by using COM interop to work with objects in the COM+ Admin library. The logic would go something like this:

1. Create a `WindowsPrincipal` based on the identity if you use Windows groups when assigning users to roles in COM+ – see Step 2.

2. Loop through all of the roles in the COM+ application checking the users configured for each role against the domain and username of the identity. If you have assigned Windows groups to the COM+ roles, then you could use the `IsInRole()` method on the `WindowsPrincipal` to check to see if the identity is a member of those groups.

3. Create a `GenericPrincipal` object based on the `WindowsIdentity` passed in to the `GetPrincipal()` method and the list of roles you created in Step 2.

4. Return the `GenericPrincipal` from the `GetPrincipal()` method instead of the `WindowsPrincipal`.

A `GenericPrincipal` is simply an object that implements the `IPrincipal` interface and takes an identity and an array of role names as parameters to its constructor. Calls to the `IsInRole()` method on the `GenericPrincipal` check the role name against the array of role names passed to its constructor, which in this case would be roles you gathered from COM+.

XML Logon

The XML Logon Class provides you with the ability to authenticate a user against information stored in an XML file. It also provides you with a means of determining application roles for a user. This class may be used with the Principal Logon Class found in Chapter 23, but you can use it by itself. As written, it only works with XML files that follow a certain format, but you can easily create a derived class to fit your own XML file format.

Scenario

Sometimes you do not need an overly complex system of storing usernames and passwords for your application. If your application is 'shrink-wrapped' – as with Microsoft's Visual Source Safe – it can be much easier to generate a user file through some administrative section of your application against which you can authenticate and check roles. If you have a web application that uses Forms Authentication, and you do not need to dynamically access data from the application, then storing user names and passwords in an XML file can save you the trouble of creating a data layer in your architecture simply to authenticate users.

Simplicity is not the only reason that an XML user file solution can be desirable. By storing user information in an XML document, you can post the file on a web server so that instances of your application running anywhere on the Internet can access it. This allows you to work through firewalls and other obstacles that connecting directly to a relational database, or some other data store, over the Internet may present. Naturally, you would want to use some form of encryption with these user files to provide some amount of protection against mischievous eyes.

Authentication is not the only use for this class, however. In fact, you do not have to use it for authentication at all. Authorization, or role retrieval, is a great use for XML files. For role retrieval, you do not even have to worry about encryption since you are just checking a name for a list of roles.

If you use the Principal Logon class found earlier, then you can use the XML Logon class in conjunction with the Windows Logon class to do some very interesting things. You can authenticate your application or web site users against their Windows logins, and retrieve application roles for the user from an XML file that pertains only to your application (not that it has to pertain only to your application).

Technology

The authentication and roles data store for this class is an XML file with a very specific schema. If you already have user information in an XML file, you can easily derive from this class and work with your XML schema by changing the XPath queries that we use to authenticate and retrieve roles from the XML. You could alternatively use XSLT to transform it into the format required by this application.

To conform to the `ILogonAuthenticator` and `ILogonAuthorizer` interfaces (talked about in the Principal Logon chapter), we will be creating a **GenericIdentity** object for our authentication method. To return role information about a user, we will be creating and returning a **GenericPrincipal** object. Both of these objects are provided with the .NET Framework in the `System.Security.Principal` namespace. `GenericIdentity` implements the `IIdentity` interface and objects that represent a user should implement this. You use this interface to check the user name and confirm if they have been authenticated. The `GenericPrincipal` object implements `IPrincipal`, and it is used to determine whether a user represented by an `IIdentity` object is a member of any specified role.

To load and read the XML user file, we will be using an `XMLDocument` object. The `XMLDocument` parses through the user file and provides a standard API for us to query the document for information. We will use the `SelectSingleNode()` method of the `XMLDocument` object to check logins and to get roles using an XPath query. This method takes an XPath query as a parameter and returns an `XMLNode` object as a result if it finds a match. An XPath query is a W3C standards-based query you run against an XML document, much as you use SQL queries on a relational database.

In order to provide some measure of password security, we will be using some .NET cryptography objects to encrypt the passwords. You can find these objects in the `System.Security.Cryptography` namespace. They include:

❑ `CryptoStream` – the workhorse for performing encryption

❑ `ToBase64Transform` – an object that the `CryptoStream` object uses to transform encrypted data into text safe for saving in an XML file

❑ DESCryptoServiceProvider – an object that the CryptoStream object uses to encrypt data using the DES algorithm

In addition to the XMLDocument and the cryptography classes, we use a MemoryStream from the System.IO namespace to allow us to perform the cryptographic transformations without writing to disk or some other data store.

Design

You can use this class for authentication, authorization, or both. It will implement the ILogonAuthenticator and ILogonAuthorizer interfaces created in the Principal Logon Class. This will allow applications that utilize the Principal Logon Class to employ XML-file-based authentication and authorization very easily. Please refer to Chapter 23 for answers to questions about the design of these interfaces. They allow authentication and authorization provider objects, such as the XML Logon and Windows Logon classes, to be easily utilized and switched in and out of an application if needs change.

As mentioned earlier, we will need to encrypt passwords in the XML file. There is no need to be able to decrypt, since we can encrypt the password that authentication is being attempted with, and compare that to the value stored in the XML file. We will be storing the encryption key in the XML Logon class. This key, since we will be using the DES encryption algorithm, is actually a two-part key with the two parts called the **Key**, and **IV**, respectively. IV stands for Initialization Vector. It's a little out of the scope here to cover how these are used by the DES algorithm – all you need to know for this class is that both the Key and IV make up the actual encryption key. DES has been chosen for this example but you could use any algorithm.

The flow of the class goes something like this. The first things that the object needs are paths to the files it will use for authentication and authorization. These can be the same file, or they can be different files. The object will get these paths through one of its constructors. It needs these values so it can authenticate or get user roles.

The authentication file for the class we will be writing needs to contain user elements that have name and password attributes on them. The authorization file needs to have user elements that have roles attributes on them. You can use a single file that has all three attributes, name, password, and roles, on the user elements as well. We will be using a file that has all three in the *Demonstration* section of this chapter.

If you need to use an XML file with a different schema, then you will need to inherit from the XML Logon class. There are protected variables that contain XPath query templates that you can replace with your own XPath query templates in a derived class.

To authenticate a user with the XML Logon class, you execute a method called `Authenticate()`. Username and password parameters on this method will tell us what values to search for in the authentication XML file. If we find the user and the encrypted password of the user matches the encrypted version of the password passed in to the `Authenticate()` method, then we will return a `GenericIdentity` object. This `GenericIdentity` object is an object that implements `IIdentity` and has two properties that can return the name of the user that the object represents, and whether the user has been authenticated. We will be setting the `IsAuthenticated` property of the `GenericIdentity` object to `True`, and the `Name` of the `GenericIdentity` to that of the authenticated user before returning it from the `Authenticate()` method.

To get user roles for authorization, you execute a method called `GetPrincipal()`. It takes one parameter of type `IIdentity`. You can pass in the `GenericIdentity` returned from the `Authenticate()` method, or you can pass in some other object that implements `IIdentity`, such as a `WindowsIdentity` object (from the last chapter). Inside the `GetPrincipal()` method, we will take the `Name` of the user from the identity object passed in, and search for a user by that name in the authorization file (which can be the same file as the authentication file). If we find a user by that name, we will get a comma-separated list of roles from the `roles` attribute of the user. Once we have the list of roles, we will want to create a `GenericPrincipal` object to hold both the identity object passed in, and the roles that we have found. We will return this `GenericPrincipal` object from the `GetPrincipal()` method so that calling code can check roles for the identity object it possesses. The `GenericPrincipal` class has one method, called `IsInRole()`, and one property, which is the identity object. Calls to the `IsInRole()` method will check the list of roles we found in the XML file to determine whether the `Identity` is in the specified role, passed as a parameter.

Implementation

We create a new class called `XmlLogon`. This class will contain all of the code we need to perform XML authentication and authorization. Create a new class library project, called `XMLLogon`, and remove the default namespace using the Property pages.

Add a class named `XmlLogon.vb` to your project, and add the following code to the class definition. You will need to reference the Principal Logon assembly, or compile this into the same assembly, for this to work:

```
Imports System.Security.Principal
Imports System.Xml
Imports System.IO
Imports System.Security.Cryptography
Imports System.Text

Namespace Wrox.Toolkit.Security
    Public Class XMLLogon
        Implements ILogonAuthenticator
        Implements ILogonAuthorizer
```

This code tells .NET that the class implements the `ILogonAuthenticator` and `ILogonAuthorizer` interfaces, and then provides the method needed to support those interfaces. We import `System.Security.Principal` to have easy code access to the `IIdentity` and `IPrincipal` interfaces, and the `GenericIdentity` and `GenericPrincipal` classes. We need `System.Xml` to get at the `XmlDocument` object, and we need `System.IO` and `System.Security.Cryptography` to get at the stream objects needed perform the password encryption. `System.Text` is imported for access to the `StringBuilder` class used later.

In order to provide calling code with the ability to specify what XML file to use for authentication and authorization, you will need to store the values it specifies somewhere, so add the following variables to the class:

```
Private AuthenticationURLValue As String
Private AuthorizationURLValue As String
```

You populate these variables with values through a constructor on the class. This class can be used in three ways: you can use it only for authentication; for authorization; or for both authentication and authorization. This class will be given a constructor that takes one parameter containing the URL of the file to use for both authentication and authorization in all three of these scenarios. To support the case where you have different files for authentication and authorization, add a second constructor that takes two strings as parameters containing the URLs of each file:

```
Public Sub New(ByVal userFileURL As String)
    If userFileURL Is Nothing Or userFileURL = String.Empty Then
        Throw New ArgumentNullException()
    End If
    Me.AuthenticationURLValue = userFileUrl
    Me.AuthorizationURLValue = userFileURL
End Sub

Public Sub New(ByVal authenticationURL As String, _
               ByVal authorizationURL As String)
    If authenticationURL Is Nothing Or authorizationURL Is Nothing _
        Or authenticationURL = String.Empty _
        Or authorizationURL = String.Empty Then
        Throw New ArgumentNullException()
    End If
    Me.AuthenticationURLValue = authenticationURL
    Me.AuthorizationURLValue = authorizationURL
End Sub
```

If the values passed to the constructor are empty or `Nothing`, then an `ArgumentNullException` is thrown.

Before you are able to authenticate, you'll need to know what the XML file looks like. Here are the contents of the file used by the author for testing purposes:

```
<?xml version="1.0" encoding="utf-8" ?>
<users>
  <user name="Matt" password="8DzjktgK20A=" roles="admin, user" />
  <user name="Yovaly" password="kk7gE8gKQ94=" roles="user" />
</users>
```

This schema is required for the code in this class to function properly (unless you make a derived class). The password used for the user named Matt in the file shown was mpass, but it has been stored it in its encrypted form above. These passwords were generated using the Encrypt() method, which will be detailed shortly. You will need to do the same for any XML file you use.

You will be using an XPath query to authenticate against this file, so let's look at that next. To authenticate against the file, a user element is searched for that has the same name and password attributes as the values passed by the user who is attempting to authenticate. If you find a matching element, then the user is authenticated, otherwise not. The XPath query for finding the user element for Matt in the XML document shown above looks like this:

```
*/user[@name="Matt" and @password="8DzjktgK20A="]
```

The */user part tells XPath that you want to find all user elements, regardless of where they may be found in the document. When such nodes are found, by using [@name="Matt" and @password="8DzjktgK20A="], you are limiting the result to only those user elements that have a name attribute equal to Matt, and a password attribute equal to 8DzjktgK20A=. The XPath processor steps through each user element attempting to match those further conditions. This query is stored in a Protected class-level variable so that derived classes can supply their own XPath query to support XML files with different layouts. You do not want to store the actual user name and password in the query, as they will be passed as parameters to the Authenticate() method, so put placeholders in the query that can be replaced at run time with the actual user name and password values. Add the following variable declaration to the class:

```
Protected authenticationQuery As String = _
    "*/user[@name=""{USERNAME}"" and @password=""{PASSWORD}""]"
```

You will do similar for the authorization query, which does not need to worry about passwords since it is just looking up roles for a user. The XPath query for authorizing the user, Matt, looks like this:

```
*/user[@name="Matt"]/@roles
```

Again, you are searching for all user elements, regardless of where in the document they are located (*/user) and then limiting the results to those user elements that have a name attribute equal to Matt ([@name="Matt"]). You then retrieve the contents of the roles attribute from this node.

Here is the variable declaration you should put in your class for the authorization query:

```
Protected authorizationQuery As String = _
    "*/user[@name=""{USERNAME}""]/@roles"
```

Next, you create methods for replacing the placeholders in the queries with real values. For this example, the StringBuilder class will be used.

```
    Private Function CreateAuthenticationQuery( _
                ByVal userName As String, _
                ByVal password As String) _
                As String
       Dim query As New StringBuilder(authenticationQuery)
       query.Replace("{USERNAME}", userName)
       query.Replace("{PASSWORD}", password)
       Return query.ToString()
    End Function

    Private Function CreateAuthorizationQuery( _
                ByVal userName As String) _
                As String
       Dim query As New StringBuilder(authorizationQuery)
       query.Replace("{USERNAME}", userName)
       Return query.ToString()
    End Function
```

`StringBuilder` provides an efficient way of manipulating strings. In the first query, it allocates 64 `Chars` for the object, while the original text is 56 `Chars` in length. The second one allocates 32 `Chars` for the text, and the text is 30 `Chars` in length. If during the replace the text becomes larger, then it will automatically create a new `StringBuilder` object of twice the size and copy the characters into that object. Otherwise, it just directly replaces the characters stored in its instance. If you know that your username and password strings are likely to increase the size of the objects, then you can pass an extra integer argument to the constructor that defines the starting size. The capacity used will be the next highest power of 2. `ToString()` is used to output the `String` representation of this object.

If you used the `String.Replace()` or VB.NET `Replace()` methods, then because strings are immutable, a new `String` object would be created with the new values. Using `StringBuilder` is therefore more efficient with memory. You can read much more about the facilities for manipulating strings in *Visual Basic .NET Text Manipulation Handbook*, Wrox Press, ISBN 1-86100-730-2.

The final bit of information that you need to authenticate is the encrypted form of the password that is given by some calling code. An `Encrypt()` method will be written that takes the unencrypted password and encrypts it. You need to be careful though, because this encrypted version of the password needs to be able to be stored in a text file without causing unwanted line breaks or end of file characters. The results from using DES encryption on the password are not guaranteed to be safe for text files, so you will use a Base64 transformation to encode the password. The Base64 transformation ensures that all of the bytes are safe for storing in even an ASCII text file by shifting bits around so that each byte falls within a certain numeric range. This is safe to do because it is reversible. There is no need to reverse the process in this class, though.

Add the following method to your class:

```
    Public Shared Function Encrypt(ByVal data As String) As String
```

The method is publicly shared so it can be used as a utility for encrypting user passwords, without needing an instance of the class.

The first thing that needs to be done in this method is to define a key for the encryption. Remember that for DES encryption you need two parts for the key called a Key and IV. These are both contained in `Byte` arrays. Add the following variable declarations to the method. Random numbers were used to initialize the values – any others could be used:

```
Dim desKeyValue() As Byte = {0, 27, 213, 84, 169, 97, 72, 50}
Dim desIVValue() As Byte = {0, 49, 0, 58, 188, 92, 77, 36}
```

Encryption in .NET is stream based, so in order to encrypt the `data` string passed in to the Encrypt method, you need to put the string into a stream. You can use a `MemoryStream` object for this, but `MemoryStreams` work with byte arrays, not strings; so you need to put the string into a byte array. You therefore use a `System.Text.ASCIIEncoding` object. Add the following code to the `Encrypt()` method:

```
Dim dataBytes() As Byte
dataBytes = ASCIIEncoding.ASCII.GetBytes(data)
Dim reader As New MemoryStream(dataBytes)
```

Now you are ready to encrypt the data using the DES encryption algorithm and the two-part key defined earlier. You will use a `DESCryptoServiceProvider` object to provide the implementation of the algorithm, and a `CryptoStream` object to execute the algorithm on the data in the `MemoryStream`:

```
Dim des As New DESCryptoServiceProvider()
Dim encryptor As New CryptoStream( _
    reader, _
    des.CreateEncryptor(desKeyValue, desIVValue), _
    CryptoStreamMode.Read)
```

At this point, you could use the `encryptor` object to get the encrypted version of the password, but you still need to do the Base64 transformation on the encrypted data. This would necessitate putting the data back into another `MemoryStream` object and using the `encryptor` object with a `ToBase64Transform` object. Another option is to just chain the `encryptor` object to another `CryptoStream` object based on the `ToBase64Transform` object. This way when data is read from the stream, it will go through both algorithms in succession. To set this up, all you need is the following line of code:

```
Dim b64 As New CryptoStream(encryptor, _
                            New ToBase64Transform(), _
                            CryptoStreamMode.Read)
```

Now you need somewhere to store the encrypted data as it is read from the linked `CryptoStreams`. Use another `MemoryStream` to store the encrypted data temporarily before returning it as a string, and use a `Byte` array to read encrypted data from the linked `CryptoStreams`. The code for doing that looks like the following:

```
Dim encryptedData() As Byte

' Create a stream for writing encrypted data to
Dim encryptedStream As New MemoryStream()
```

```
Dim bytesRead As Integer
    ReDim encryptedData(des.BlockSize)
    Do
      bytesRead = b64.Read(encryptedData, 0, des.BlockSize)
      If bytesRead <> 0 Then
        encryptedStream.Write(encryptedData, 0, bytesRead)
      End If
    Loop While bytesRead > 0
```

Now that you know the size of the encrypted data, you can read the data out of the encryptedStream object and back into the Byte array:

```
ReDim encryptedData(encryptedStream.Length - 1)

encryptedStream.Position = 0
encryptedStream.Read(encryptedData, 0, encryptedStream.Length)
```

Finally, put the data from the byte array into a string and return it:

```
    Return ASCIIEncoding.ASCII.GetString(encryptedData)
End Function
```

That does it for the Encrypt() method. You can now finally move on to the Authenticate() method. Place the following code in the XMLLogon class:

```
Public Function Authenticate( _
            ByVal userName As String, _
            ByVal password As String) _
            As IIdentity _
            Implements ILogonAuthenticator.Authenticate
```

The compiler has been informed that this method is implementing the Authenticate() method specified by the ILogonAuthenticator interface by placing Implements ILogonAuthenticator.Authenticate after the method declaration.

The next thing you need to do is encrypt the password passed in to the method so that you can compare it to an encrypted password in the XML file. All you have to do is call the Encrypt() method:

```
password= Encrypt(password)
```

Since strings are immutable, you can change the value without worrying about affecting the calling code. Now you'll want to load the authentication XML file using an XMLDocument object:

```
Dim userFile As New XmlDocument()
Try
    userFile.Load(authenticationURLValue)
Catch ex As Exception
    Throw New AuthenticationException(ex.Message)
End Try
```

The `AuthenticationException` is defined in the Principal Logon chapter. If you are not using the Principal Logon, then you can throw a normal exception. Now create the XPath query to search for a matching `user` element in the XML file. You can use the method we wrote earlier for this purpose:

```
Dim query As String
query = CreateAuthenticationQuery(userName, password)
```

Now run the query by calling `SelectSingleNode()` on the `XMLDocument`. If a valid user name and password was provided, then this method will return an `XMLNode` object. If not, then it will return `Nothing`. If `Nothing` is returned, then throw an `AuthenticationException`. If something is returned, then authentication was successful, and you indicate that by creating a `GenericIdentity` object for the user, and returning it from the function:

```
If (userFile.SelectSingleNode(query) Is Nothing) Then
    Throw New AuthenticationException("Authentication failed")
Else
    Return New GenericIdentity(UserName, "XML")
End If
End Function
```

The second parameter on the `GenericIdentity` object's constructor just tells the identity object what method was used for authentication.

The code for authorization is similar. Add the following method stub for the `GetPrincipal()` method:

```
Public Function GetPrincipal( _
             ByVal identity As IIdentity) _
             As IPrincipal _
             Implements ILogonAuthorizer.GetPrincipal
```

Once again, you are implementing an interface, so the `Implements` keyword is used to inform the compiler what method on the interface is being implemented.

You will need to load up the authorization XML file and create the XPath query the same way as for the `Authenticate()` method, so add the following code to the `GetPrincipal()` method:

```
Dim userFile As New XmlDocument()
Try
    userFile.Load(authenticationURLValue)
Catch ex As Exception
    Throw New AuthorizationException(ex.Messsage)
End Try

Dim query As String
query = CreateAuthorizationQuery(identity.Name)
```

In this method, you need to use the results to create an array of roles. The result of any XPath query on an XMLDocument in .NET is an XMLNode object. This XMLNode object will represent the roles attribute of the user in the XML file. We need to append /@roles to the end of the query to retrieve the roles attributes. Here is the code for getting the roles from XMLNode.

```
Dim rolesNode As XmlNode
rolesNode = userFile.SelectSingleNode(query)
```

If rolesNode is Nothing, then the user could not be found and authorization failed:

```
If (rolesNode Is Nothing) Then
    Throw New AuthorizationException("Authorization Failed")
End If
```

If the rolesNode variable holds an object then the user was found, so you need to create a string array of roles. The roles attribute should have a comma-delimited list of roles in it, which can be accessed through the Value property of the rolesNode object.

```
Dim roles() As String
roles = rolesNode.Value.Split(",")
```

Now trim off any whitespace from the roles:

```
Dim role As Integer
For role = 0 To roles.Length - 1
    roles(role) = Trim(roles(role))
Next
```

Finally, create a GenericPrincipal object to return based on the identity object passed into the GetPrincipal() method and the roles found in the XML file:

```
        Return New GenericPrincipal(identity, roles)
        End Function
    End Class
End Namespace
```

That's about it for the XMLLogon class; you just need to build it. Let's look at it in action.

Demonstration

Before you begin writing code to demonstrate the XMLLogon class, you will want to create a user XML file to work with. You can copy the contents of the file used when testing, or you can create your own. If you create your own, you will also want to create an application to encrypt passwords for you, and we'll show how to do that next.

Create a new console application, called ViewEncryptedPasssword.vb, and create a reference to the XMLLogon assembly. Replace the code in Module1 with the following:

335

```
Imports Wrox.Toolkit.Security

Module ViewEncryptedPassword
   Sub Main()
      Dim password As String
      Do
         Console.Write("Enter password: ")
         password = Console.ReadLine
         If password <> "" Then
            Console.WriteLine("Encrypted password: " & _
                              XMLLogon.Encrypt(password))
         Console.WriteLine()
         End If
      Loop Until password = String.Empty
   End Sub
End Module
```

We import `Wrox.Toolkit.Security` so that we can use the `XMLLogon` class to encrypt the passwords for us, and since we declared the `Encrypt()` method on the `XMLLogon` class as shared, we can call it from the class without needing to create an `XMLLogon` object. You can copy the encrypted passwords you generate into your XML file.

Now we will demonstrate using the `XMLLogon` class by making a console application that prompts you for a username and password, and then uses that information to authenticate against, and gets user role information from your XML file. This demonstration uses the `Logon` class described in the Principal Logon chapter.

Let's start by adding a new VB.NET Console Application project to our solution, called `XMLAuthenticate` and add a reference to the projects containing the `XMLLogon`, and `Logon` classes. Next, add the following `Imports` statements to the module:

```
Imports Wrox.Toolkit.Security
Imports System.Security.Principal
```

In the `Main()` procedure of `Module1`, place the following code for getting the logon information from the user:

```
Dim userName As String
Dim password As String

Console.Write("    User: ")
userName = Console.ReadLine()
Console.Write("    Password: ")
password = Console.ReadLine()
```

Now you can instantiate the `XMLLogon` class to use for authentication and authorization.

```
Dim xmlLogon As XMLLogon
xmlLogon = New XMLLogon(AppDomain.CurrentDomain.BaseDirectory & _
                        "..\users.xml")
```

Because we're running the test application within the IDE, VS.NET runs the application in a directory called `bin` under the directory where the source files for the demo application are. Stick the XML file in the same directory as the source files and use the `AppDomain` object to get the `BaseDirectory` the application was launched from (the bin directory) and then move up one directory to get the users file.

Next, try authenticating by calling the Logon() method of the Logon class:

```
Dim principal As IPrincipal
Try
   principal = Logon.Logon(userName, _
                           password, _
                           xmlLogon, _
                           xmlLogon)
Catch authentEx As AuthenticationException
   Console.WriteLine("Caught an authentication exception! ")
   Console.WriteLine("The error is: " & authentEx.Message)
   Console.ReadLine()
   Return
Catch authorEx As AuthorizationException
   Console.WriteLine("Caught an authorization exception! ")
   Console.WriteLine("The error is: " & authorEx.Message)

   Console.ReadLine()
   Return
End Try

Console.WriteLine("--- Logon Successful ---")
Console.ReadLine()
```

First, create the principal variable to hold the object returned from the Logon() method. Then create a Try...Catch block to wrap the Logon() method call so that we can gracefully handle any error that might occur during the authentication/authorization process. This example shows how your code can tell the difference between an error that happens during the authentication process, and an error that happens during the authorization process. When we call the Logon.Logon() shared method, we give it the user name, password, and the xmlLogon object for both the authenticator as authorizer.

If all goes well in the Logon() method, you will get a principal object returned to you in the principal variable. You can go ahead and run the code now to test your authentication.

Now let us use this object to check for role membership of the user that you logged into our console application as. Add the following code after the last Console.ReadLine() call:

```
Console.WriteLine("user: " & _
                  principal.IsInRole("user").ToString())
Console.ReadLine()
```

If all went well (and you had set up the user you logged in with a user role) then "user: True" should be printed on the screen. Here is some example output using the XML example file shown earlier:

```
User: Matt
Password: mpass
--- Logon Successful ---

user: True
```

337

Limitations

This class can be quite a memory hog if you are using a very large user file. That could adversely affect scalability. If that were the case, you might want to use a SAX parser instead, and the .NET Framework does provide such a parser in the XMLTextReader class.

The class will only work for authorization with comma-delimited lists of roles. If you store your roles as elements in your XML file, then you will need to override the GetPrincipal() method to consider this.

The key for the encryption is hard-coded in the class, which compromises it if someone else can obtain a copy of your code.

Extensions

Some possible extensions for this class include:

❑ Modifying or overriding the Encrypt() method to get its encryption key from a secure source, such as a secure web service

❑ Modifying or overriding the GetPrincipal() method to allow roles to be stored in forms other than comma-delimited lists, such as role elements within a user element

❑ Modifying or overriding the Encrypt() method to use an encryption algorithm other than DES

In addition, you have seen some examples of using the StringBuilder object to efficiently deal with strings. StringBuilder objects could be used much more in this class so that Strings are barely used. This would result in a more efficient use of memory, and using the StringBuilder.Remove() or StringBuilder.Replace() method, you could overwrite the contents of sensitive text, such as the entered password.

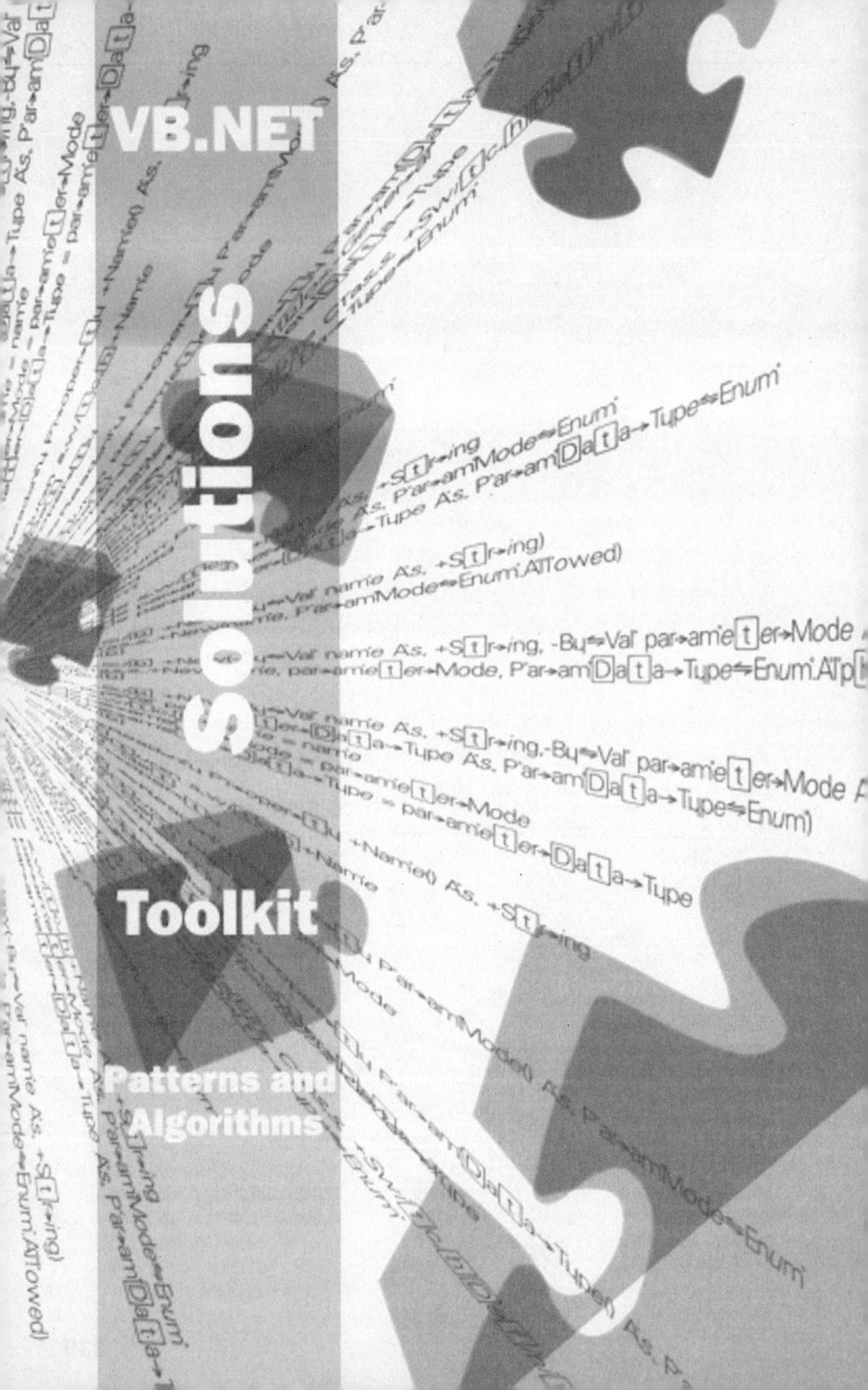
VB.NET
Solutions
Toolkit
Patterns and Algorithms

26

Singleton Template

The most influential book in the field of object-oriented programming is probably *Design Patterns: Elements of Reusable Object-Oriented Software*, by Gamma, Helm, Johnson, and Vlissides (1994, Addison Wesley, ISBN 0-201-63361-2). The book's authors, sometimes referred to as the Gang of Four (GOF), examined a large body of object-oriented code, and found that often, people were solving very similar problems in very similar ways. Borrowing the idea from the world of building architecture of 'pattern languages', they set out to identify and classify the best design patterns that recur in OO programming. The result is a catalogue of coding techniques, which shows how to build combinations of classes that can be used to achieve a particular, commonly desired effect. The patterns typically show how we can use polymorphism and indirection in class design to make classes that can be used in interesting programmatic ways. Written originally to address Smalltalk and C++ programmers, the lessons in this book have proven helpful to developers in all object-oriented environments, from Java to Python, and certainly apply to .NET. The upcoming Wrox book, *VB.NET Design Patterns Applied,* (August 2002, ISBN 0-186100-698-5) demonstrates how to implement many of these design patterns in Visual Basic.

The design patterns the book enumerates are wide ranging and applicable in a vast number of coding scenarios, to do with how objects communicate, how they co-operate, how they can be combined, and how they are created. Design patterns crop up throughout .NET itself; the .NET event model is an implementation of the book's *Observer* pattern; ASP.NET's page/control structure is an example of the *Composite*. Many .NET objects are obtained through an *Abstract Factory*. In this template, we'll be addressing how VB.NET programmers can make use of one of the book's object-creational techniques, a powerful and very widely applicable pattern: the *Singleton*.

Scenario

Normally, when we design a class to represent a type of entity, we expect code elsewhere in our application to create instances of the class to represent particular entities of that type. So, if we're building a reservations program for a hotel, we might have a Room class that represents a guest room in the hotel, and we might then have Guest, representing a hotel customer. We can then create instances of Room and of Guest to represent the different entities that exist in the real world. This is the kind of programming we normally think of when we are coding object-oriented applications.

But occasionally, we want to design classes so that other code can't just create multiple instances of the class. The nature of the class demands that we control the creation process. This is where *Design Patterns*' creational patterns come in. They enable us to restrict when and how objects are created.

The *Singleton* pattern is used when we want to ensure that there is exactly one instance of a particular class available in an entire application. This is often the case if there is only one real world entity we want the class to represent. For example, within our hotel reservations application, we might have a class Hotel, which represents the hotel itself, and provides methods for obtaining things like Room objects, managing booking of guests into rooms, and so on. But it doesn't make sense for code throughout our application to create new instances of Hotel whenever they need one; it might be possible in such a situation for two different parts of the application, using different Hotel instances, to obtain two different objects representing the same room, and book two different guests into it at the same time. We need to create a single instance of Hotel and make it available to the whole application, and prevent further instances being constructed. The *Singleton* pattern addresses how we ensure that it's impossible for client code to create additional instances of a class, and thus make certain that only a single instance is ever in existence in the program. A class coded such that it is impossible for more than one instance to exist is known as a *Singleton*.

Technology

The *Singleton* pattern is used to ensure that only one instance of a class exists in an application, it should also prevent arbitrary code from instantiating that class. We can do this using a private constructor, which prevents code outside the class itself from calling the constructor at all. We then need to include in the class some code that creates a single instance of the class, and stores it in a shared field. A method can then be used to obtain a reference to the sole singleton instance. Any code that needs to access the singleton instance must call this method to obtain a reference to it.

Implementing such a singleton doesn't *appear* too tricky. Here's some code that seems, at first glance, to do just what we need:

```
'Naïve example of a singleton

Imports System

Public Class NaïveSingleton

   Private Shared instance As NaïveSingleton

   Private Sub New()
      ' private constructor to prevent foreign instantiation
   End Sub

   Public Shared Function GetInstance() As NaïveSingleton

      If instance Is Nothing Then
         instance = New NaïveSingleton()    ' only call to constructor
      End If

      Return instance

   End Function

End Class
```

A reference to the singleton can be obtained, from anywhere in our application, by calling the NaiveSingleton.GetInstance() shared method. This creates a new instance if one hasn't been created already, and otherwise, returns the instance that has already been constructed. Since the only call to the constructor in the entire application is in the GetInstance() method, we know that an instance will only be created if GetInstance() is called, and the Shared variable, instance, is empty. So, it should only be called once, ever, right?

In fact, there are a few problems that we may encounter with a singleton coded in this fashion (although in some limited circumstances it would work fine). Most importantly, it isn't thread-safe. It's perfectly possible, if GetInstance() is called from two separate threads at the same time, that both threads will execute the check to see if instance is empty, both find that it indeed is, and then both move on to instantiate the singleton. In spite of all our efforts, we might end up with references to different instances of the singleton in each thread.

In addition, we'll encounter problems if we decide that the singleton needs to be serialized (turned into a string of data representing the instance's state) for any reason. Imagine the singleton class is storing the common, centralized state for our application. We can persist the application's state by serializing the singleton to a file when the application is shut down and restore that application's state next time it is started by desterilizing the singleton from file. This is a perfectly valid, and indeed common, use for a singleton class. The problem is that this makes it possible for other code to deserialize the singleton from the file, leading to multiple instances of the singleton class existing in the application at the same time. Obviously, we don't want to allow that to happen.

What we'll develop here is a template for the infrastructure of a singleton class that overcomes both of these problems: it's thread-safe, and serializable.

Design

As just mentioned, the two design goals of our singleton template are that it should be thread-safe and serializable.

Thread safety is easy: we simply need to ensure that only one thread can be in the GetInstance() method at a time. VB.NET's SyncLock construction will solve this, by allowing only one thread to enter a block of code locked on a particular object at a time.

Making the singleton serializable requires a little understanding of the .NET deserialization mechanism. An instance of a class can be serialized if it is marked with the <Serializable()> attribute. The string of data created by serializing an instance of the class can then be used to instantiate an exact replica of the original object – the process of deserialization. It is important to remember that the singleton class could be deserialized at any time, not just when an application is starting up, and a new instance of the singleton class created whether or not another one already exists. Obviously, this plays havoc with our carefully controlled singleton creation process. Serialize the singleton instance, then deserialize it, and we could have two instances instead of one.

This means we can't simply replace the stored singleton instance with the newly deserialized instance, since any code that has already called GetInstance() will still be holding a reference to the old singleton; both instances will exist in the program at the same time. The desired effect when deserializing a singleton is that the one true singleton's state should be amended to match the state that was serialized. The new instance created in deserialization needs to be disposed of.

This is a tricky process to manage, but it can be done. The approach we'll take is to create a second class, and have that class manage the serialization and deserialization safely.

Implementation

Here is the structure of a thread-safe, serializable singleton class. You'll want to change the class's name to something relevant to your implementation; for instance, if it represents a hotel, change to Singleton to Hotel. Wherever this name needs changing, it is in bold in the code below. To add your desired singleton functionality, you just need to insert code at each of the numbered steps below:

```
Imports System
Imports System.Threading
Imports System.Runtime.Serialization
```

1. Add any imports needed to support the code in your singleton.

```
Public Class Singleton

Private Shared theInstance As Singleton
Private Shared lock as New Object()
```

2. Insert any private instance fields that are needed to store the singleton's state. For example, if the singleton has a name, we'll need declare a private string here to represent that.

```
Private Sub New()
```

3. In the default constructor, add any initialization logic that should run when the singleton is first created. This would include opening any database connections, initializing instance fields, and so on.

```
    ' Enter initialization code here
End Sub
```

4. Add any instance properties and methods that the singleton needs to access and modify its state. In a multithreaded environment, if any of these accessors and methods accesses more than one part of the singleton's state, you should enclose the contents in a SyncLock Me ... End SyncLock block. This ensures state updates are atomic, that is it prevents any other threads seeing the singleton in an intermediate state.

The following instance ReadOnly property is used to obtain a reference to the singleton instance. It uses a SyncLock on the shared lock object to ensure that only one thread at a time can perform the check to see if an instance has already been created. If it hasn't, then the singleton instance is created, before the lock is released.

```
Public Shared ReadOnly Property Instance As Singleton
  Get
     SyncLock lock
        If theInstance Is Nothing Then
           theInstance = New Singleton()
        End If
     End SyncLock
     Return theInstance
  End Get
End Property
```

The following nested class provides our serialization functionality. If you instantiate it, and serialize that instance, it will then serialize the singleton's state. Deserialize it, and it will set the singleton's state to the state that was serialized.

345

```
<Serializable()> Public Class SerializationHelper
        Implements ISerializable

    Public Sub GetObjectData(info As SerializationInfo, _
                        context As StreamingContext) _
            Implements ISerializable.GetObjectData

        Dim theSingleton As Singleton

        theSingleton = Singleton.Instance
        SyncLock theSingleton
```

5. Add code to serialize the current state of the singleton into the provided info object. This is done by calling info.AddValue(), passing in each of the values that represent the singleton's state.

```
        End SyncLock
    End Sub

    Public Sub New(info As SerializationInfo, _
                context As StreamingContext)

        Dim theSingleton As Singleton

        theSingleton = Singleton.Instance
        SyncLock theSingleton
```

6. Add code to read serialized state from the info object, and set the state of the singleton. This is done by calling info.GetValue() for each of the stored items representing the singleton's state, using CType() to convert it to an appropriate type, and setting each of the singleton's properties.

```
        End SyncLock
    End Sub

    End Class

End Class
```

By following this recipe to code a singleton class, the result will be a singleton that can be stored and restored using the serialization mechanisms of .NET, and which is also safe to use in a multithreaded environment.

Demonstration

We'll apply the template above by developing a singleton that represents the user of our application. When the application is first run, it will ask the user to provide a name and age, and set the user singleton's properties accordingly. Then we'll show how other code can access the singleton properties. Finally, when the application has finished executing, we'll serialize the singleton's state to a file.

When the application is run subsequently, we'll restore the singleton's state from the file, rather than asking the user to provide their name and age.

Enter the following code into a file called singleton_demo.vb. Note that all of the code on a gray background is the code we're adding (to fill in each of the steps shown above); the code on a white background is from the template.

```vb
Imports System
Imports System.Threading
Imports System.Runtime.Serialization
Imports System.Runtime.Serialization.Formatters.Binary
Imports System.IO

Public Class User

    Private Shared theInstance As User
    Private Shared lock as New Object()

    Private _name As String
    Private _age As Integer

    Private Sub New()
        _name = ""
        _age = 0
    End Sub

    Public Property Name as String
      Get
         Return _name
      End Get

      Set
         _name = Value
      End Set
    End Property

    Public Property Age as Integer
      Get
         Return _age
      End Get

      Set
         _age = Value
      End Set
    End Property

    Public Overrides Function ToString() As String
       Return "User: " & Name & " (" & Age & ")"
    End Function

    Public Shared ReadOnly Property Instance As User
      Get
         SyncLock lock
           If theInstance Is Nothing Then
             theInstance = New User()
           End If
         End SyncLock

         Return theInstance

      End Get
    End Property
```

```
<Serializable()> Public Class SerializationHelper
        Implements ISerializable

    Const NAME_LABEL As String = "name"
    Const AGE_LABEL As String = "age"

    Public Sub New()
    End Sub

    Public Sub GetObjectData(info As SerializationInfo, _
                context As StreamingContext) _
            Implements ISerializable.GetObjectData

        Dim _user As User

        _user = User.Instance
        SyncLock _user
            ' write the singleton's state to the SerializationInfo object
            info.AddValue(NAME_LABEL, _user.Name)
            info.AddValue(AGE_LABEL, _user.Age)
        End SyncLock
    End Sub

    Public Sub New(info As SerializationInfo, _
                context As StreamingContext)

        Dim _user As User

        _user = User.Instance
        SyncLock _user
            ' read the state from the SerializationInfo object, and
            ' restore the singleton's state
            _user.Name = info.GetString(NAME_LABEL)
            _user.Age = info.GetInt32(AGE_LABEL)
        End SyncLock
    End Sub

    End Class

End Class
```

That's it for our singleton class, and its serializing assistant. For demonstration
purposes, let's go on to code a command-line module that uses the singleton:

```
Public Module TestSingleton

    Public Sub Main()

        Dim formatter As IFormatter
        formatter = New BinaryFormatter

        Dim stream As FileStream
```

In the following code, we first try to deserialize (read in) any state saved from previous
executions. If the file doesn't exist, then an exception will be thrown. We catch the
exception, and then ask the user to enter their name and age, and use them to set the
properties of the user singleton. If the file is found, it will be deserialized, and the
name and age will be set from the saved state.

```
    Try
        stream = New FileStream("userstate.bin", FileMode.Open, _
                                FileAccess.Read)

        formatter.deserialize(stream)

        stream.close()
    Catch e As FileNotFoundException
        Console.WriteLine("No user configuration found.")
        Dim u As User
        u = User.Instance
        Console.Write("Enter your name: ")
        u.Name = Console.ReadLine()
        Console.Write("Enter your age: ")
        u.Age = CInt(Console.ReadLine())
    End Try
```

Next, we call out to a second method that displays the information from the user singleton.

```
        DisplayUserInfo()
```

Finally, before the application finishes, we serialize the singleton to file.

```
        stream = New FileStream("userstate.bin", FileMode.Create, _
                                FileAccess.Write)

        formatter.serialize(stream, new User.SerializationHelper())

        stream.close()

    End Sub
```

This little method demonstrates how to access and use the singleton. We obtain a reference through the Instance property, and then call methods on that reference. As you'll see, we are guaranteed to obtain the same instance of the singleton as was used in the main method.

```
    Public Sub DisplayUserInfo()

        Dim u As User
        u = User.Instance

        Console.WriteLine(u.ToString())

    End Sub

End Module
```

Once we've compiled this, we can run it on a command prompt. The first time, we have to enter our details:

```
> singleton_demo.exe
No user configuration found.
Enter your name: James
Enter your age: 25
User: James (25)
```

The second time we run it, the singleton is restored from our previous preferences and its details are printed out:

```
> singleton_demo.exe
User: James (25)
```

Limitations

This implementation limits object creation so that only one instance of a class that follows the singleton template will exist at any given time, in a given application domain. It is possible, however, in a distributed environment, for more than one instance to exist, in different application domains. This class is not safe for use in a distributed computing environment.

It isn't normally possible, or desirable, to extend a singleton class; for example, we couldn't extend User to create a SuperUser class. It's actually not possible to compile a class that extends User because User doesn't have an accessible constructor that can be chained to from a subclass. In some situations, it might be desirable to allow client code to select (before the singleton is first instantiated) which subclass of User would be used to provide the singleton instance. That way, a simple configuration change could alter the behavior of the entire application, without requiring a recompilation.

Extensions

The most obvious way to extend the singleton is to allow it to be subclassed. The Instance property needs to be changed so that it decides, when first called, whether to instantiate a subclass of the singleton type, and if so which one. You need to be careful if you allow subclassing of your singleton, though, since it is possible for a subclass to be written with a public constructor, which would enable the subclass to be instantiated multiple times, effectively creating multiple singleton instances.

To make a singleton subclass serializable, you need to provide a subclass of the serialization helper class as well.

27

Doubly Linked List

Despite the .NET Framework's inclusion of numerous data collection classes in the System.Collections namespace, such as ArrayList, Hashtable, and SortedList, a fundamental data structure, the **linked list**, is missing from the Framework.

This class is an implementation of an unsorted, doubly linked list. In order to mimic the design of the Framework's existing collection classes, it implements the IList interface defined in System.Collections.

Scenario

Unsorted linked lists are very fast at inserting new elements. A vector drawing program might use a linked list to capture the rapid series of data points generated while drawing a freehand line with a mouse. A scientific data collection program might use a linked list to record a real-time data stream for later analysis.

One implementation of a hash table data structure also makes use of linked lists. A hash function is used to determine the "bucket" that a particular data element belongs in. Each bucket is really a linked list holding the data elements.

The linked list is a common building block for the queue and stack data structures, and can also be used as a base for other custom data structures.

Technology

The linked list is a classic data structure in computer science, and it's quite easy to understand. A linked list is simply a series of interconnected **nodes**, each containing a data element or elements. The **head** of the list is the first node, and the **tail** is the last node in the list.

There are many variations to the basic linked list, including sorted, unsorted, singly linked, doubly linked, and circularly-linked.

In a singly linked list, each node has a reference to the node that follows it in the list. In a doubly linked list, each node has two references, one to the node that follows it in the list, and a second to the preceding node. In a circularly linked list, the next-node reference at the end of the list refers back to the first node in the list.

Figure 1

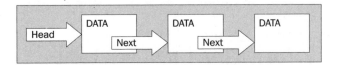

Linked lists are generally slow at searching. Searches are linear; or in other words, nodes are visited one at a time in order until a match is found. In the worst case, where the desired value is at the end of the list, every node is visited.

Inserting and deleting at a known position are fast because a node can be added or removed simply by changing references. Inserting at the head or tail is always fast, since the head and tail are always known. However, inserting or deleting in the middle of the list means a linear traversal to reach the insertion or deletion point.

Whenever you select a data structure, you must consider your particular application. For instance, if search speed is critical, a linked list is a terrible choice. However, because the linked list is relatively simple, it's an excellent choice when you simply need to record a stream of data.

As mentioned previously, the linked list is the building block for other data structures, such as the queue and stack. For instance, a last-in, first-out, or LIFO, queue is simply a linked list in which insertions and deletions always occur at the end of the list.

An alternative linked list design uses an array instead of a series of objects. One tradeoff is that the array is always a fixed size. To prevent frequent reallocation of the array, it is usually sized larger than the current list, which wastes memory. A second, and significant, tradeoff is in insertion and deletion speed. To add or remove an element within an array, all elements from the insertion or deletion point to the end of the array must be shifted by one position.

One benefit to using an array, however, is that if the elements are sorted, faster searching can be achieved with an algorithm such as binary search.

Notably, the list classes in the .NET Framework, such as `ArrayList`, do use an array, with all of its advantages and disadvantages.

You're encouraged to refer to an algorithm reference book for more detailed information. The classic reference for this and many other algorithms is *The Art of Computer Programming*, Donald Knuth, ISBN 0-201-48541-9.

Design

This class is an implementation of an unsorted, doubly linked list that allows duplicate values.

The class defines a private, nested ListNode class that contains a data element of type Object, and references to both the next and previous nodes in the list. The linked list is built entirely with ListNode objects.

To avoid special cases with insertion and deletion at the head or tail of the list, the list always contains a header node containing no data. Since the head and tail always point to a valid node, no special casing is required. If the list is empty, the next and previous references in the header equal Nothing.

The class can be used as a base class for your own extensions, so all fields, methods and properties are public or protected and marked Overridable where necessary. To be consistent with the .NET Framework's collection classes, the class implements the System.Collections.IList interface. As a result, the class includes many public methods and properties, including Add(), Remove(), IndexOf(), Clear(), Contains(), Insert(), CopyTo(), and more.

Many of the methods in IList, such as IndexOf() and RemoveAt(), deal with a zero-based index. When using any of the indexed methods or properties, the class must perform a linear traversal of the list to reach the specified index. As a result, the indexed methods can be quite slow as the list size increases. This is a prerequisite of the linked list, which is not designed for random access. For the fastest possible insertion, the non-indexed Add() method always inserts new nodes at the end of the list, using the known reference to the tail.

You can also use the For...Each statement to traverse the list. IList inherits from IEnumerable, which contains the GetEnumerator() method. VB.NET will use this method to obtain an enumerator for the For...Each loop. A nested enumerator class, LinkedListEnumerator, implements the IEnumerator interface and is returned from GetEnumerator().

Implementation

To get started with the code, create a new VB.NET class file called LinkedList.vb and replace its contents with the code below.

The code begins by importing two namespaces. The System.Collections namespace defines the IList interface used later.

```
Imports System.Collections

Namespace Wrox.Toolkit.Util
  Public Class LinkedList
    Implements IList
```

The protected, nested class ListNode is the heart of the linked list, since the list is built with a series of ListNode objects. The NextNode field refers to the next ListNode object in the list, or Nothing when at the end of the list. The PrevNode field refers to the previous ListNode object. Only the header node's PrevNode field is ever set to Nothing. The Data field contains the data element provided by the caller:

```
Protected Class ListNode
  Public NextNode As ListNode
  Public PrevNode As ListNode
  Public Data As Object
```

The class is only used by the LinkedList class's implementation, so it does not need to use properties to protect its fields. The fields and New() methods are marked Friend to reinforce the fact that they are not publicly available. The fact that ListNode is protected keeps the entire class and its contents hidden from consumers.

ListNode's three constructors allow the class to provide defaults for some or all parameters. They call one after the other until all parameters are specified:

```
    Public Sub New(ByVal data As Object)
      Me.New(data, Nothing, Nothing)
    End Sub

    Public Sub New(ByVal data As Object, _
                            ByVal prevNode As ListNode)
      Me.New(data, prevNode, Nothing)
    End Sub

    Public Sub New(ByVal data As Object, _
                   ByVal prevNode As ListNode, _
                   ByVal nextNode As ListNode)
      Me.Data = data
      Me.PrevNode = prevNode
      Me.NextNode = nextNode
    End Sub
  End Class
```

The class also maintains four protected data fields:

```
    Protected head As ListNode = New ListNode(Nothing)
    Protected tail As ListNode = head
    Protected nodeCount As Integer = 0
    Protected version As Integer = 0
```

First, head contains a reference to the head of the list, which is always the header node, and tail contains a reference to the end of the list, which is equal to head when the list is empty. The class also maintains a count of the number of nodes in the list and a version counter.

While iterating through the list with an enumerator, the enumerator becomes invalid if the list changes. During each insertion in or deletion from the list, `version` is incremented. The enumerator knows the value of `version` at the time enumeration began, so it can verify that the value has not changed.

Three overloaded helper methods, called `Validate()`, are used in several public methods and properties to validate the list index and value parameters passed in by the caller:

```
Protected Overloads Overridable Sub Validate( _
                               ByVal index As Integer)
    If index < 0 Or index >= nodeCount Then
        Throw New ArgumentOutOfRangeException("Invalid index.")
    End If
End Sub

Protected Overloads Overridable Sub Validate( _
                               ByVal value As Object)
    If value Is Nothing Then
        Throw New ArgumentNullException()
    End If
End Sub

Protected Overloads Overridable Sub Validate( _
                               ByVal index As Integer, _
                               ByVal value As Object)
    Validate(index)
    Validate(value)
End Sub
```

The same error checking is used in many methods, so it makes sense to wrap this up in subroutines that do nothing if the values are OK, and throw an exception if not.

Meanwhile, `FindByIndex()` is a helper method used by the class to locate a `ListNode` object by a zero-based index. Since a linked list is not indexed by number, a counter tracks the current index while the list is traversed:

```
Protected Overridable Function FindByIndex( _
                               ByVal index As Integer) As ListNode
```

Recall that a `Protected Overridable` method can be overridden in a derived class, so you're free to build a custom implementation of any such method.

Whenever the list is traversed the same general pattern applies, and you will see it used in other methods later on. First, a `ListNode` variable called `current` is set to the "real" head of the list, the header node's `nextNode`. Recall that the header node is just a placeholder and doesn't contain any data:

```
Dim tempIndex As Integer = 0
Dim current As ListNode = head.nextNode
```

In this case, a temporary index counter also tracks the current index within the list.

```
        Dim returnValue As ListNode = Nothing
        Do
          If index = tempIndex Then
            returnValue = current
          Else
            current = current.nextNode
            tempIndex += 1
          End If
        Loop Until current Is Nothing Or Not returnValue Is Nothing

        Return returnValue
    End Function
```

A Do loop continues until current becomes Nothing, signaling the end of the list, or returnValue is not Nothing, signaling that the node has been found. With each loop iteration, the current variable is updated to current.nextNode. The tail's nextNode will always be Nothing. Here, if the index counter is equal to the requested index, the current node is returned.

Below is the FindByValue() helper method used to search the list for a particular data value:

```
      Protected Overridable Function FindByValue( _
                              ByVal value As Object) _
                              As Integer
        Dim tempIndex As Integer = 0
        Dim current As ListNode = head.nextNode

        Dim returnValue As Integer = -1
        Do
          If value.Equals(current.data) Then
            returnValue = tempIndex
          Else
            current = current.nextNode
            tempIndex += 1
          End If
        Loop Until current Is Nothing Or returnValue > -1
```

The code is almost identical to FindByIndex(), except that the comparison uses value.Equals() to determine the match. Rather than returning a node, this method returns the index at which the object can be found. It sets the return value to -1 at the start, which indicates that no match has been found.

The index, or -1 if the value wasn't found, is then returned:

```
        Return returnValue
    End Function
```

The following IndexOf() method is the first public method from IList:

```
      Public Overridable Function IndexOf(ByVal value As Object) _
                              As Integer _
                              Implements IList.IndexOf
```

```
          Validate(value)
          Return FindByValue(value)
    End Function
```

It returns the index of the specified value in the list, or -1 if the value is not found. After calling `Validate()` to validate the parameter, `FindByValue()` is used to search the list and return the resulting index.

The following public `Add()` method appends the specified data object to the tail of the list:

```
    Public Overridable Function Add(ByVal value As Object) _
                        As Integer _
                        Implements IList.Add
        Validate(value)

        tail.nextNode = New ListNode(value, tail)
        tail = tail.nextNode
```

The `tail` field is always valid; if the list is empty it points to the header node.

The tail's next node is set to a new `ListNode` containing the new data object. The default constructor sets the new node's `prevNode` reference to the current tail. The tail reference is then updated to point to the new node, which becomes the new tail of the list.

```
        version += 1
        nodeCount += 1

        Return nodeCount - 1
    End Function
```

With the addition complete, the version counter is incremented to signal the change to enumerators, and the node count is also increased. Finally, the new node's index is returned.

`Insert()` adds a new value at the specified index:

```
    Public Overridable Sub Insert(ByVal index As Integer, _
                        ByVal value As Object) _
                        Implements IList.Insert
        Validate(index, value)
```

First, `FindByIndex()` is used to locate the node at the specified index:

```
    Dim tempNode As ListNode = FindByIndex(index)
```

`Validate()` already ensured that the index does exist in the list.

Now, a new node must be inserted into the position currently occupied by `tempNode`:

```
        Dim newNode As ListNode = _
            New ListNode(value, tempNode.prevNode, tempNode)
```

First, a new `ListNode` is created. Its previous node equals the current node's previous node, and its `nextNode` becomes the current node.

At this point the new node's references are in place, but the nodes to either side need to be updated:

```
        tempNode.prevNode.nextNode = newNode
        tempNode.prevNode = newNode

        version += 1
        nodeCount += 1
    End Sub
```

The node preceding the current node has its `nextNode` redirected to the new node, and the current node's `prevNode` is redirected to the new node. All of this reference swapping has served to quickly insert a new node into the chain between two existing nodes.

The `RemoveNode()` helper method removes the specified node from the list. It is used in the `Remove()` and `RemoveAt()` methods:

```
    Protected Overridable Sub RemoveNode(ByVal node As ListNode)
```

Removing a node is as simple as bypassing it in the list. The garbage collector will eventually clean up the object.

```
        node.prevNode.nextNode = node.nextNode
```

First, the previous node's `nextNode` is changed to the deleted node's `nextNode`, bypassing it in the forward direction.

Now, the method determines if the deleted node was the tail. If so, there are no backward references to the deleted node, so the tail is simply updated to the deleted node's `prevNode`. Otherwise, the next node's `prevNode`, which points to the deleted node, is updated to point to the deleted node's `prevNode`, bypassing it in the backward direction.

```
        If Not node Is tail Then
            node.nextNode.prevNode = node.prevNode
        Else
            tail = node.prevNode
        End If

        version += 1
        nodeCount -= 1
    End Sub
```

`Remove()` searches for and deletes the specified data object if it exists in the list. The `FindByValue()` and `RemoveNode()` helper methods do the work.

```
Public Overridable Sub Remove(ByVal value As Object) _
                               Implements IList.Remove
   Validate(value)
   RemoveAt(FindByValue(value))
End Sub
```

RemoveAt() deletes the node at the specified index using FindByIndex() and RemoveNode():

```
Public Overridable Sub RemoveAt(ByVal index As Integer) _
                               Implements IList.RemoveAt
   Validate(index)
   Dim node As ListNode = FindByIndex(index)
   RemoveNode(node)
End Sub
```

The following Contains() method simply determines if the specified value exists in the list using the FindByValue() helper method.

```
Public Overridable Function Contains(ByVal value As Object) _
                               As Boolean _
                               Implements IList.Contains
   Validate(value)

   If FindByValue(value) = -1 Then
      Return False
   Else
      Return True
   End If
End Function
```

The list's Clear() method empties the list by removing the references to all the objects.

```
Public Overridable Sub Clear() Implements IList.Clear
```

If the head has a next reference to another node, it means that that node has a reference back to the head. To properly disconnect the list, that back reference must be removed first:

```
If Not head.nextNode Is Nothing Then
   head.nextNode.prevNode = Nothing
End If
```

Now, the head's nextNode reference is safely set to Nothing, the tail is reset to point to the head, and the node count and version are reset to zero. With the former contents of the list now unreferenced, the garbage collector will eventually clean up the unused ListNodes:

```
   head.nextNode = Nothing
   tail = head
   nodeCount = 0
   version = 0
End Sub
```

CopyTo(), part of ICollection, simply walks through the list and copies each data object to the array:

```
Public Overridable Sub CopyTo(ByVal array As System.Array, _
                              ByVal index As Integer) _
                    Implements IList.CopyTo
    If array Is Nothing Then
        Throw New ArgumentNullException()
    ElseIf index < 0 Then
        Throw New ArgumentOutOfRangeException("index")
    ElseIf index >= array.Length _
            Or (array.Length - index - 1) > nodeCount _
            Or array.Rank <> 1 Then
        Throw New ArgumentException()
    End If
```

Most of the error checking code is mandated by the .NET Framework documentation for this method. Since the linked list is not indexed by number, a loop counter is used to step through the array. The current variable is set to the first (non null) value in the list. Remember that the data in the head is always Nothing:

```
    Dim current As ListNode = head.NextNode
    Dim position As Integer = index

    While Not current Is Nothing
        array(position) = current.data
        current = current.nextNode
        position += 1
    End While
End Sub
```

Shown below is the default Item property:

```
Default Public Overridable Property Item( _
                            ByVal index As Integer) As Object _
                    Implements IList.Item
    Get
        Validate(index)
        Return FindByIndex(index).Node
    End Get

    Set
        Validate(index, value)
        FindByIndex(index).data = value
    End Set
End Property
```

This can be used to directly get or set a value by index, using .NET array syntax if desired. For instance, if list were an implementation of this linked list, list(3) would return the object at index 3. The FindByIndex() helper method does most of the work.

GetEnumerator() returns an IEnumerator that can be used to iterate through the list directly, or indirectly with For...Each. The method returns a new instance of the LinkedListEnumerator class, which is discussed later:

```
Public Overridable Function GetEnumerator() As IEnumerator _
                        Implements IList.GetEnumerator
    Return New LinkedListEnumerator(Me)
End Function
```

The next three properties are part of the `ICollection` interface, from which `IList` derives:

```
Public Overridable ReadOnly Property Count As Integer _
                        Implements IList.Count
    Get
        Return nodeCount
    End Get
End Property

Public Overridable ReadOnly Property IsSynchronized As Boolean _
                        Implements IList.IsSynchronized
    Get
        Return False
    End Get
End Property

Public Overridable ReadOnly Property SyncRoot As Object _
                        Implements IList.SyncRoot
    Get
        Return Me
    End Get
End Property
```

`Count` simply returns the node count. `IsSynchronized` always returns `False`, as this class does not provide thread synchronization. `SyncRoot` returns a reference to the class instance, which is a simple but valid implementation of this property. The `SyncRoot` property may be used with the VB.NET `SyncLock` keyword to lock access to the collection.

Meanwhile, the `IsFixedSize` and `IsReadOnly` properties each return `False`:

```
Public Overridable ReadOnly Property IsFixedSize As Boolean _
                        Implements IList.IsFixedSize
    Get
        Return False
    End Get
End Property

Public Overridable ReadOnly Property IsReadOnly As Boolean _
                        Implements IList.IsReadOnly
    Get
        Return False
    End Get
End Property
```

The final part of `LinkedList` is the `LinkedListEnumerator` class, which implements the `IEnumerator` interface. As discussed previously, an instance of the enumerator can be accessed directly with `GetEnumerator()`, or indirectly with `For...Each`:

```
Protected Class LinkedListEnumerator
    Implements IEnumerator
```

361

`LinkedListEnumerator` implements a forward-only traversal of the list. If a node is added or deleted after an enumerator is created, the enumerator becomes invalid.

The enumerator class stores references to the list, the current data element, and the current node. It also stores the list's version counter value at the time the enumerator was created:

```
Protected list As LinkedList
Protected currentElement As Object
Protected currentNode As ListNode
Protected version As Integer
```

The constructor requires a reference to the list associated with this enumerator. Since the enumerator class is nested inside `LinkedList`, it can directly access the list's protected fields to complete its initialization:

```
Public Sub New(ByVal list As LinkedList)
    Me.list = list
    Me.version = list.version
    Me.currentElement = list
    Me.currentNode = list.head
End Sub
```

When the enumerator is first created, or when it is reset with the `Reset()` method, it must be positioned before the first element of the list. Since, like `ArrayList`, you can insert a value of `Nothing` into the list, the enumerator class avoids using `Nothing`. Instead, the initial value of `currentElement` is set to the list itself, and the current node is set to the list's head, the header node.

The helper method `VerifyListIsUnchanged()` simply verifies that the list's current version counter is equal to the counter stored when the object was created:

```
Protected Overridable Sub VerifyListIsUnchanged()
    If Not version = list.version Then
        Throw New InvalidOperationException( _
            "The list has changed since enumeration began.")
    End If
End Sub
```

The read-only `Current` property returns the data value at the current position.

```
Public Overridable ReadOnly Property Current As Object _
                            Implements IEnumerator.Current
    Get
```

First, the code verifies that the list position is valid. If the current element equals the list itself, the current node value can be used to determine the reason for the invalid position.

```
If currentElement Is list Then
    If currentNode Is list.head Then
        Throw New InvalidOperationException( _
            "Current is invalid until MoveNext() is called.")
```

```
            Else
                Throw New InvalidOperationException( _
                    "Current is invalid because the end of the " _
                    & "collection was reached.")
            End If
        End If
```

After ensuring that the position is valid, `Current` returns the current data value:

```
            Return currentElement
        End Get
    End Property
```

`MoveNext()` tries to advance the current position. It returns `True` if it succeeds, or `False` if the end of the list was reached:

```
        Public Overridable Function MoveNext() As Boolean _
                            Implements IEnumerator.MoveNext
            VerifyListIsUnchanged()

            If Not currentNode.nextNode Is Nothing Then
                currentNode = currentNode.nextNode
                currentElement = currentNode.data
                Return True
            Else
                currentElement = list
                currentNode = list.head
                Return False
            End If
        End Function
```

When the current position is the last node in the list, `nextNode` is always `Nothing` and the current data value is set to the list, the current node is reset to the head and `False` is returned. On the other hand, if `nextNode` is valid, the current node is advanced and the data value is updated.

Finally, `Reset()` resets the enumerator to its starting position before the first element of the list, similar to `New()`.

```
        Public Overridable Sub Reset() Implements IEnumerator.Reset
            VerifyListIsUnchanged()
            currentNode = list.head
            currentElement = list
        End Sub
    End Class
End Class
End Namespace
```

Demonstration

This demonstration gives you a sample of how to initialize the linked list and use some of its methods and properties. Many of the methods can throw exceptions, so as always a `Try...Catch` block is used to handle errors.

To use this sample, add a new VB Console Application to the project, named
`LinkedListTest.vb`, reference the linked list assembly, and replace
`LinkedListTest`'s contents with the code below.

```
Imports Wrox.Toolkit.Util

Module LinkedListTest
```

First, you must import `Wrox.Toolkit.Util` for the `LinkedList` class.

```
Sub PrintList(ByVal list As LinkedList)
    Dim data As Object

    Console.WriteLine("  List contains:")

    For Each data In list
        Console.WriteLine("    " & data)
    Next
End Sub
```

This example implements a simple method called `PrintList()` that iterates through
the list with `For...Each` and prints each data value. The remainder of the code
simply adds and removes values to and from the list, walks the list, and so on:

```
Sub Main()
    Try
        Dim list As New LinkedList()
```

The demonstration sets up the initial list with three data values.

```
        Console.WriteLine("Adding 21, 1 and 7 to the list...")
        list.Add(21)
        list.Add(1)
        list.Add(7)
        PrintList(list)

        Console.WriteLine("Count: {0}", list.Count)
        Console.WriteLine("Index of 7: {0}", list.IndexOf(7))
        Console.WriteLine()

        Console.WriteLine("Removing 21...")
        list.Remove(21)
        PrintList(list)

        Console.WriteLine("Count: {0}", list.Count)
        Console.WriteLine()

        Console.WriteLine("Inserting 10 at index 1...")
        list.Insert(1, 10)
        PrintList(list)
        Console.WriteLine()

        Console.WriteLine("Removing value at index 2...")
        list.RemoveAt(2)
        PrintList(list)
        Console.WriteLine()
```

```
        Console.WriteLine("Value at index 0: {0}", list(0))
        Console.WriteLine("List contains 1? {0}", list.Contains(1))
```

The list's CopyTo() method can be used to copy the list contents to an array at a specified offset. Here, the list is copied to the array arr, starting at offset zero.

```
        Dim arr(list.Count - 1) As Integer
        list.CopyTo(arr, 0)

        Console.WriteLine( _
            "Array index of value 1: {0}", Array.IndexOf(arr, 1))
      Catch e As Exception
        Console.WriteLine("Exception: {0}", e.Message)
      End Try
    End Sub

End Module
```

When you run the application from a command prompt, you should see the following output:

```
Adding 21, 1 and 7 to the list...
  List contains:
  21
  1
  7
Count: 3
Index of 7: 2

Removing 21...
  List contains:
  1
  7
Count: 2

Inserting 10 at index 1...
  List contains:
  1
  10
  7

Removing value at index 2...
  List contains:
  1
  10

Value at index 0: 1
List contains 1? True
Array index of value 1: 0
```

Limitations

The class does not include built-in thread synchronization. The SyncRoot property can be used with VB.NET's SyncLock operator, but each lock blocks the entire object. To provide more granular thread safety, a synchronized version of the class would be a better solution.

Extensions

There are many variations to the linked list algorithm, so there are many ways to extend and modify this implementation. You can also use this class as a foundation for your own custom data structures.

You could add a property to allow or disallow duplicate values. If sorting is useful, you could derive a class from `LinkedList` and override the `Add()` and `Insert()` methods to perform sorted inserts. To allow the list to be traversed both forward and backwards, you could implement another enumerator class to perform a reverse enumeration.

28

Binary Search Tree

The .NET Framework includes plenty of useful data-collection classes in the System.Collections namespace, such as Hashtable, ArrayList, and Stack. However, one of the most important data structures, the **binary search tree (BST)**, is missing from the Framework.

A binary search tree is a data structure formed from a collection of linked nodes, each containing data and having up to two children, referred to as the left child and the right child. Every node has one parent, except for a special node at the top of the tree called the root.

Given a particular node, all data values to the left are less than the node's value, and all data values to the right are greater than the node's value. This is the fundamental rule of the binary search tree. Also, be aware that the tree does not allow duplicate values. You'll learn more about the BST structure and algorithm later.

This class is a basic implementation of an unbalanced binary search tree. In order to mimic the design of the Framework's existing collection classes, it also implements the ICollection interface defined in System.Collections.

Scenario

Binary trees are very fast at finding data, even with a large collection of data elements.

Imagine a data importer that reads large inventory files created by a mainframe. The first data field in each line is a manufacturer ID, of which there are thousands. The rest of the line contains pricing, descriptions, and other relevant data. The importer is only interested in data related to 200 of the manufacturers, and must discard all other data.

This is a perfect application of a binary tree. The 200 manufacturer IDs of interest can be loaded into a binary tree when the importer starts, and, as each line is processed the importer can search the tree to determine whether the current line's ID is of interest or not.

Technology

Tree algorithms are a well-worn topic of computer science researchers and scholars. They offer very fast searches, a good insertion and deletion speed, and are excellent at handling large collections of data. Many tree algorithms are very complex, but even a basic tree algorithm can still be highly effective.

The basic units of a simple binary search tree are **nodes**, which can be logically divided into leaf nodes and internal nodes. A leaf node is at the end of a branch and has no children, while an internal node has one or two children. Each leaf node and internal node contains a piece of data.

Every tree has a **root** node with no parent, and every other node has exactly one parent. Each node, including the root, contains a reference to a left node and/or a right node. Given a particular node, the values of every node to the left are less than the node's value, and the values of every node to the right are greater than the node's value. This is the most fundamental rule of the binary search tree. Figure 1 shows an example of a binary search tree.

Figure 1

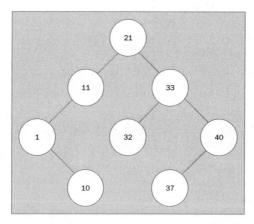

The basic search algorithm works like this: starting at the root node, the node's data is compared to the desired value, or search **key**. If the key matches the data, the search is complete and successful.

If the key does not match, the algorithm determines whether the key is less than or greater than the current node's data value. The left (less than) or right (greater than) node becomes the new current node, and the process repeats. If the algorithm reaches a node where the necessary left or right node doesn't exist, and the node's data doesn't match the key, the tree does not contain the key and the search fails.

The height of a tree is the longest distance from a leaf node to the root. In Figure 1, the height of the tree is three. In this case, since the heights of the root's left and right sub-trees are equal, the tree is balanced. However, as nodes are added and deleted, a tree often becomes unbalanced. In an unbalanced tree, the heights of the root's left and right sub-trees are unequal. As the tree becomes unbalanced, search speed generally decreases.

There are many tree algorithms, such as AVL trees and splay trees, which keep the tree balanced. However, these algorithms are much more complex, so we use the unbalanced implementation in this chapter's class.

You should always be careful to choose an appropriate data structure for your particular situation. Often, a list is a poor choice of structure, unless you have a very small collection of data and/or you don't need to search it. Locating data in lists is usually, depending on the implementation, a linear process, which means it is slow.

For more details, please refer to your favorite algorithm reference book for a discussion of this and many other, more complex, tree algorithms. One of the most well-known and respected reference volumes is *The Art of Computer Programming*, Donald Knuth, ISBN 0-201-48541-9.

Design

This class is intended to be a simple, yet effective, implementation of an unbalanced binary search tree. Once you understand this implementation, you'll be ready to tackle your own implementations of more complex tree algorithms.

The class defines a protected node class, `BstNode`, which contains references to a left and right node and a data value of type `Object`.

The class needs to determine where a value exists in the tree by comparing it with other values in the tree. To determine whether an `Object` value is equal to, less than, or greater than a second `Object` value, the class uses the `IComparer` interface's `Compare()` method. By default, the class uses the `Comparer.Default` implementation of `IComparer`. However, you can provide the class with your own implementation of `IComparer` to customize the comparison.

The default implementation requires at least one of the objects to implement `IComparable`, and uses `IComparable.CompareTo()` to perform the comparison. All of the native VB.NET data types, such as `Integer`, `Long` and `Short`, implement `IComparable`.

The public interface of our binary search tree class consists of the Add(), Remove(), Contains(), and InOrder() methods. In addition, to be consistent with the existing .NET Framework collection classes, the class implements the ICollection interface, which itself inherits from IEnumerable. ICollection contains properties such as Count, for the nu.mber of nodes in the tree, and methods such as CopyTo(), to copy the tree contents to an array.

All of the class's methods navigate the tree using recursion. Recall that recursive methods call back to themselves. Here, most recursive methods begin with a reference to the root node, and call themselves with either the left or right reference of the current node.

IEnumerable.GetEnumerator(), in this implementation, may throw a NotImplementedException. An enumerator is a class that implements the IEnumerator interface, which includes the MoveNext() and Reset() methods and the Current property. MoveNext() is called repeatedly to advance the current position. However, the most straightforward way to navigate the tree is by using recursion, and it is not possible to stop and restart a recursive process.

This class uses recursion and calls a delegate method during traversal. As each value in the tree is visited, the delegate method is called with the current value. Since the caller implements the method, it can be customized for each application.

Implementation

To get started, create a new VB.NET class named BinarySearchTree.vb and replace its contents with the code below.

While this discussion will highlight the main ideas of the binary search tree code, it will not attempt to explain the binary search tree algorithm in detail, and you're encouraged to refer to an algorithm reference book for more information.

```
Imports System.Collections

Namespace Wrox.Toolkit.Util
    Public Class BinarySearchTree
        Implements ICollection
```

The class begins by implementing a protected, nested class called BstNode. The entire tree structure consists of instances of this class. The class stores references to a left child node, a right child node, and a generic Object data value. Every leaf node has its left and right fields equal to Nothing. Every node must be initialized with a data value, and Nothing is considered an acceptable value by the .NET Framework.

The class is only used by the BinarySearchTree class's implementation, so it does not need to use properties to protect its fields from bad data. The fields and the following constructor are marked Friend to reinforce the fact that they are not publicly available. The fact that BstNode is protected keeps the entire class and its contents hidden from consumers.

```
Protected Class BstNode
    Friend Data As Object = Nothing
    Friend Left As BstNode = Nothing
    Friend Right As BstNode = Nothing

    Protected Friend Sub New(ByVal data As Object)
        Me.Data = data
    End Sub
End Class
```

Next, the BinarySearchTree class defines a delegate and three protected fields. The tree may have only one root, and as with all nodes it is of type BstNode. If the tree is empty, root is equal to Nothing. The nodeCount field stores the total number of nodes in the tree. Finally, valueComparer stores the IComparer used to compare two data values, as explained in the design section.

The delegate will be explained later in the context of the InOrder() method.

```
Public Delegate Sub TraverseCallback(ByVal data As Object)

Protected root As BstNode = Nothing
Protected nodeCount As Integer = 0
Protected valueComparer As IComparer
```

The class defines two public constructors that initialize the valueComparer field. The default constructor uses Comparer.Default, and the second version allows the user to specify a custom IComparer.

```
Public Sub New()
    Me.valueComparer = Comparer.Default
End Sub

Public Sub New(ByVal comparer As IComparer)
    If comparer Is Nothing Then
        Throw New ArgumentNullException()
    End If

    Me.valueComparer = comparer
End Sub
```

As discussed in the design section, IComparer.Compare() is used to compare two Object values to determine if they are equal to, greater than, or less than each other. Our Compare() method will call Compare() on the IComparer object stored in the valueComparer field.

```
Protected Overridable Function Compare(ByVal a As Object, _
                                       ByVal b As Object) _
                                       As Integer
```

If the first object (a) is deemed less than the second object (b) then the return value of this method is less than zero. If a is equal to b, the return value is zero; whereas, if b is greater than a, the return value is greater than zero.

IComparer.Compare() will throw an exception if it is unable to compare the two values. In order to provide a consistent exception to our callers, the method catches IComparer.Compare()'s exception and throws a new exception, placing the original exception into the new exception's innerException:

```
    Try
        Return valueComparer.Compare(a, b)
    Catch ex As Exception
        Throw New InvalidOperationException( _
            "IComparer.Compare() failed.", ex)
    End Try
End Function
```

The FindMin() method simply locates the node with the smallest value (the left-most node) in the tree rooted at the specified node. This method is the first example of tree traversal using recursion. This pattern is repeated frequently through the rest of the class. Without a solid understanding of recursion, the algorithm would be very confusing:

```
Protected Overridable Function FindMin(ByVal node As BstNode) _
                                    As BstNode
    If node Is Nothing Then
        Return Nothing
    ElseIf node.Left Is Nothing Then
        Return node
    Else
        Return FindMin(node.Left)
    End If
End Function
```

The method is first called with a particular node, such as the root. If the reference is Nothing, it simply returns. If the node's left reference is Nothing, the current node must contain the minimum value of the tree rooted at node. Refer back to the *Technology* section to confirm that this is always true. Finally, if the node has a valid left, the method calls itself by passing the left reference as the node parameter.

```
Protected Overridable Overloads Sub Add(ByVal value As Object, _
                                    ByRef node _
                                    As BstNode)
    Dim result As Integer
```

The above Add() method is an overloaded method with two versions, one protected and one public. The first method is the protected version, which is recursive and does the actual work. The public version of Add() calls this overload with the new data value and a reference to the root of the tree. The result variable will store the result of the comparison so we can decide where to put the next value.

If Add() is called with node equal to Nothing, it has reached the position in the tree where value should have been located without finding a match. Note that node is ByRef, which means that it contains a writable reference to the original value.

```
If node Is Nothing Then
    node = New BstNode(value)
    nodeCount += 1
    Return
End If
```

If node is Nothing, the method creates a new node and stores it in node, then increases the node count and returns.

Since we are at a valid node, the internal Compare() method is used to determine whether value is equal to, greater than, or less than the current node's data value:

```
result = Compare(value, node.data)

If result < 0 Then
    Add(value, node.Left)
ElseIf result > 0 Then
    Add(value, node.Right)
End If
End Sub
```

If the values are equal, the value already exists in the tree, and the method returns without doing any additional work. If value is less than the node's value, Add() calls itself with the node's Left reference. Otherwise, it calls itself with the node's Right reference.

As mentioned earlier, the following Add() method is the only public version. It simply calls the protected, recursive overload of Add() with a reference to the root of the tree.

```
Public Overridable Overloads Sub Add(ByVal value As Object)
    If value Is Nothing Then
        Throw New ArgumentNullException()
    End If

    Add(value, root)
End Sub
```

The Remove() method searches the tree for the specified value, and deletes the corresponding node if a match is found:

```
Protected Overridable Overloads Sub Remove( _
        ByVal value As Object, ByRef node As BstNode)
    Dim result As Integer
```

A node that is being deleted may be a leaf node (no children), it may have only one child, or it may have two children. A leaf node is simple to delete, as is a node with one child. Some extra work is required when two children are present.

The initial logic is virtually identical to that used in the previous methods:

```
    If node Is Nothing Then
      Return
    End If

    result = Compare(value, node.Data)

    If result < 0 Then
      Remove(value, node.Left)
    ElseIf result > 0 Then
      Remove(value, node.Right)
    Else
```

At this point, some new logic is introduced. If we've reached this point, a node has been found that contains the value to be removed.

```
    If Not node.Left Is Nothing And _
      Not node.Right Is Nothing Then
      node.Data = FindMin(node.Right).data
      Remove(node.Data, node.Right)
    Else
```

The first case determines if the node has two children. If so, the node can be removed by replacing its data value with that of the smallest value in its right sub-tree. The node containing the smallest value must be a leaf node, so its own removal falls into the simpler case.

After the unwanted value is replaced with the minimum value, the original node that contained the minimum is removed by another call to Remove() with the node's right reference as the node parameter and the minimum value as the search key.

In this case, the node contains zero or one child. If the node has no children, the first condition is met, and the node is assigned to node.Right, which must equal Nothing. Otherwise, the node is assigned to the valid left or right reference:

```
    If node.Left Is Nothing Then
      node = node.Right
    Else
      node = node.Left
    End If
```

Here, the original value of node has been changed to a different node or Nothing. Since the original node is no longer referenced, the garbage collector will eventually clean it up. With the removal complete, the node count is decremented:

```
      nodeCount -= 1
    End If
  End If
End Sub
```

As with Add(), the public version of Remove() simply calls the protected overload of Remove() with a reference to the root of the tree.

```
Public Overridable Overloads Sub Remove(ByVal value As Object)
    If value Is Nothing Then
        Throw New ArgumentNullException()
    End If

    Remove(value, root)
End Sub
```

The following protected `Find()` method searches the tree for a node containing the specified value, and returns a reference to the matching `BstNode`, or `Nothing` if no match is found:

```
Protected Overridable Function Find(ByVal value As Object, _
                                    ByVal node As BstNode) _
                                    As BstNode
    Dim result As Integer

    If node Is Nothing Then
        Return Nothing
    End If

    result = Compare(value, node.data)

    If result < 0 Then
        Return Find(value, node.Left)
    ElseIf result > 0 Then
        Return Find(value, node.Right)
    Else
        Return node
    End If
End Function
```

The search algorithm is identical to that described for the `Add()` method.

`Contains()` simply returns `True` or `False` to indicate whether the tree contains the specified value. It calls the protected `Find()` method to carry out the search:

```
Public Overridable Function Contains(ByVal value As Object) _
                                     As Boolean
    If value Is Nothing Then
        Throw New ArgumentNullException()
    End If

    If Not Find(value, root) Is Nothing Then
        Return True
    Else
        Return False
    End If
End Function
```

The `CopyTo()` method, on the other hand, is a member of `ICollection` and copies the collection to an array starting at the specified array index.

Recursive, in-order traversal is used to copy the sorted contents of the tree into the one-dimensional array, starting at the specified index. The `index` parameter, which contains the current index in the output array, is passed by reference so that it can be updated and carried through recursive calls to `CopyToInternal()`.

An in-order traversal means that the left sub-tree of a node is processed, then the node itself is processed, and then the right sub-tree is processed. This will always result in values sorted from least to greatest.

```
Protected Overridable Sub CopyToInternal( _
                    ByVal node As BstNode, _
                    ByVal array As System.Array, _
                    ByRef index As Integer)
    If Not node Is Nothing Then
        CopyToInternal(node.Left, array, index)
        array(index) = node.Data
        index += 1
        CopyToInternal(node.Right, array, index)
    End If
End Sub
```

This pattern is clear in CopyToInternal(), which, assuming a valid node, first calls itself with the node's left reference, then copies the node's value into the array, and then calls itself with the node's right reference.

CopyTo()'s error checking code is mandated by the .NET Framework documentation for this method:

```
Public Overridable Sub CopyTo(ByVal array As System.Array, _
                    ByVal index As Integer) _
                    Implements ICollection.CopyTo
    If array Is Nothing Then
        Throw New ArgumentNullException()
    ElseIf index < 0 Then
        Throw New ArgumentOutOfRangeException("index")
    ElseIf index >= array.Length _
            Or (array.Length - index - 1) > nodeCount _
            Or array.Rank <> 1 Then
        Throw New ArgumentException()
    End If

    CopyToInternal(root, array, index)
End Sub
```

The following InOrder() method performs an in-order traversal of the tree, using the same pattern discussed for CopyTo(). InOrder() simply calls the recursive InOrderInternal() with a reference to the root of the tree:

```
Protected Overridable Sub InOrderInternal( _
            ByVal node As BstNode, _
            ByVal callback As TraverseCallback)
    If Not node Is Nothing Then
        InOrderInternal(node.Left, callback)
        callback(node.Data)
        InOrderInternal(node.Right, callback)
    End If
End Sub

Public Overridable Sub InOrder(ByVal callback As TraverseCallback)
    If callback Is Nothing Then
        Throw New ArgumentNullException()
    End If

    InOrderInternal(root, callback)
End Sub
```

376

The caller must define a delegate method with the same signature as the TraverseCallback delegate, defined above. As InOrderInternal() processes each value, it calls the delegate method and passes it the value. The caller is free to do any sort of application-specific work in the method.

The next three properties are part of the ICollection interface. Count simply returns the node count. Since the class does not provide built-in thread synchronization, IsSynchronized always returns False.

Finally, SyncRoot returns a reference to the class instance, which is a simple but valid implementation of this property. The SyncRoot property may be used with the VB SyncLock keyword to lock access to the collection. For more information, see the .NET Framework documentation for ICollection.SyncRoot:

```
Public Overridable ReadOnly Property Count As Integer _
                         Implements ICollection.Count
   Get
      Return nodeCount
   End Get
End Property

Public Overridable ReadOnly Property IsSynchronized As Boolean _
                         Implements ICollection.IsSynchronized
   Get
      Return False
   End Get
End Property

Public Overridable ReadOnly Property SyncRoot() As Object _
                         Implements ICollection.SyncRoot
   Get
      Return Me
   End Get
End Property
```

The GetEnumerator() method, part of IEnumerable, is not supported and always throws an exception. Refer back to the design discussion for the reasoning behind this decision.

```
Public Overridable Function GetEnumerator() As IEnumerator _
                         Implements ICollection.GetEnumerator
      Throw New NotSupportedException("Enumeration is not supported.")
   End Function
End Class
End Namespace
```

Demonstration

This demonstration gives you a sample of how to initialize a tree and use some of the ICollection methods. Many of the methods can throw exceptions, so as always, a Try...Catch block is used to handle errors.

To use this sample, create a new Console Application project called
BinarySearchTreeTest.vb with the following contents.

First, you must import Wrox.Toolkit.Util and reference the previous project.

```
Imports Wrox.Toolkit.Util

Module TestBinarySearchTree
```

This application begins by implementing a method matching the signature of the
TraverseCallback delegate defined in BinarySearchTree. In this case, it simply
prints the value to the console.

```
Private Sub PrintValue(ByVal value As Object)
   Console.WriteLine("  " & value)
End Sub
```

The remainder of the code adds and removes values to and from the tree, traversing it,
and so on.

Integers are valid elements because the Integer data type is synonymous with
System.Int32, which implements IComparable. IComparable is, in turn, used by
IComparer.Compare().

```
Sub Main()
   Try
      Dim bst As New BinarySearchTree()
```

The program sets up the initial tree with six data values.

```
Console.WriteLine( _
   "Adding 21, 11, 1, 10, 33 and 32 to the tree...")
bst.Add(21)
bst.Add(11)
bst.Add(1)
bst.Add(10)
bst.Add(33)
bst.Add(32)

Console.WriteLine("  Tree contains:")
bst.InOrder(AddressOf PrintValue)
Console.WriteLine("Count: {0}", bst.Count)
Console.WriteLine()

Console.WriteLine("Removing 21...")
bst.Remove(21)

Console.WriteLine("  Tree contains:")
bst.InOrder(AddressOf PrintValue)
Console.WriteLine("Count: {0}", bst.Count)
Console.WriteLine()

Console.WriteLine("Does the tree contain 33? " _
   "(True or False) {0}", bst.Contains(33))
```

The tree's CopyTo() method can be used to copy its contents to an array at a specified offset. Here, the tree is copied to the array arr, starting at offset zero.

```
        Dim arr(bst.Count - 1) As Integer
        bst.CopyTo(arr, 0)

        Console.WriteLine( _
            "Array index of value 10: {0}", Array.IndexOf(arr, 10))
      Catch ex As Exception
        Console.WriteLine("Exception: {0}", ex.Message)
      End Try
    End Sub
End Module
```

After running the program from a command prompt, you should see the following output:

```
Adding 21, 11, 1, 10, 33 and 32 to the tree...
  Tree contains:
  1
  10
  11
  21
  32
  33
Count: 6

Removing 21...
  Tree contains:
  1
  10
  11
  32
  33
Count: 5

Tree contains 33? True
Array index of value 10: 1
```

Limitations

This class implements a very basic binary tree with no balancing logic. As a result, through the course of many insertions and deletions, the tree may become unbalanced and searching performance will likely degrade.

Numerous balanced tree algorithms, such as the AVL and red-black trees, have been developed over the years to address this issue. The tradeoff of keeping the tree balanced is generally an increase in insertion and deletion time.

Extensions

In order to use a `For...Each` statement with this class, the
`IEnumerable.GetEnumerator()` method must be implemented. You would need to
create a new enumerator class that implements `IEnumerator`, and use a restartable,
iterative traversal algorithm to step through an in-order traversal of the tree with
multiple calls to `IEnumerator.MoveNext()`. Each node would need to have an
additional reference to its parent node, which is unnecessary with recursion.

Another simple extension would be the addition of pre-order and post-order traversal
methods. A pre-order traversal processes the node, then its left sub-tree, followed by its
right sub-tree. A post-order traversal processes the left sub-tree, then the right sub-tree,
followed by the node.

29

CRC-32 Calculator

Whenever data is transmitted from one place to another, there is a chance that it can become corrupted. Whether you're sending a file over the network, or just copying a file on your hard drive, errors may occur. Even worse, many errors involve the switching of just the occasional binary bit, and it may not be immediately obvious that anything is wrong.

Most of the data transmission protocols invented over the last several decades have employed the well-known **CRC**, or **Cyclic Redundancy Check** validation algorithm. In addition, many other types of applications, such as data compression utilities, also use CRC for data validation.

In essence, CRC is a mathematical checksum that is calculated over a block of bytes or an entire file. The CRC values identical of set of bytes will always be identical. If they aren't, then the sets of bytes must be different.

As with microprocessor technology, the number of bits employed by the CRC algorithm has steadily increased over the years from 12 to 16 to 32, and now 64, providing greater and greater accuracy. This class implements the most common version of the CRC algorithm today, the 32-bit CRC-32.

Scenario

CRC is present in many applications and technologies that you use almost every day. Ethernet is one of the most common standards to employ CRC-32, but software installation programs, file systems, and virtually every compression algorithm are common applications of CRC.

CRC is intended to warn you if at some point your data gets corrupted. It doesn't prevent corruption, but it gives the computer a tool to indicate when it occurs, so that in networking, for instance, it can request that data packet again.

Imagine a file transfer application, such as FTP, that transfers a file from one computer to another. Before the file is sent, its CRC value is determined. The CRC value is then sent to the other computer along with the file itself. When the remote computer finishes receiving the file, it uses its copy to again determine a CRC value. If the two values match, it is extremely likely (although not guaranteed) that the files are identical.

The demonstration program discussed later will allow you to easily calculate and display the CRC value for a file.

Technology

The CRC algorithm is not designed to provide a full guarantee that one file or block of bytes is identical to another file or block of bytes. The only way to absolutely guarantee a match is by comparing the two sets of data, bit-for-bit. However, with over 4 billion possible values, and a very good checksum algorithm, CRC-32 will provide enough assurance for most practical purposes. The algorithm is simply intended to be a quick, efficient, and repeatable way to validate data.

Over the course of the last few decades, the number of bits used by CRC algorithms has more than doubled, greatly reducing the chances of a false match between two non-identical blocks of data.

The CRC algorithm itself has a complicated mathematical derivation that won't be explained here. If you're interested in the details behind the math, there are hundreds of web sites and books that go into depth on this topic. A classic reference text for this and many other algorithms is *The Art of Computer Programming*, by Donald Knuth, ISBN 0-201-48541-9. Another useful reference is located at the following URL: ftp://ftp.rocksoft.com/papers/crc_v3.txt. It is mirrored at many other locations also.

At a very basic level, the CRC algorithm treats the input bytes like a huge number, which it divides by another fixed number. The remainder of the division is the CRC value.

When dealing with CRC algorithms, you'll hear a lot about polynomials and polynomial arithmetic. In essence, the algorithm treats the divisor, dividend, and remainder as polynomials with binary coefficients. For instance, the number 37 is 100101 in binary, and $x^5+x^2+x^0$ where x=2 in polynomial form. Once again, if you really want to understand the details, you should see one of the algorithm references.

Design

The objective of the class is to provide a simple way to calculate a CRC-32 value for a block of bytes in memory or in a file. Internally, the class uses a common, well-accepted version of the algorithm for calculation, and doesn't add any twists of its own.

Since Zip has become such a widely used, de facto file compression standard, it has become common practice to use the Zip algorithm's polynomial and starting CRC value when calculating CRC-32s for files. You can find the original PKZip format specification at http://www.pkware.com/support/appnote.html. In particular, locate the section entitled *CRC-32*. The default values defined in the class are identical to those for Zip so, for a given file, this class will generate the same CRC-32 value as Zip.

You can verify this by choosing a file on your hard drive and using a Zip utility program such as PKZip or WinZip to compress it. Look at the CRC value reported by the utility, which is the CRC before compression. In WinZip, the CRC value is an optional list column in Classic mode. Use this class's demonstration program to calculate a CRC for the same file, and verify that the values are identical.

The class has a simple public interface specifying the `CalculateBlock()` and `CalculateFile()` methods, and the `Polynomial` property. The `InternalCalculateBlock()` method contains the core functionality of the class. It calculates a CRC based on an array of bytes. `InternalCalculateFile()` takes care of opening and manipulating a file, but it always defers to `InternalCalculateBlock()` for the actual CRC calculation.

There are many ways to implement the CRC algorithm, and computer scientists and mathematicians have spent much time optimizing it. This class implements a common optimization technique that employs a pre-calculated lookup table in the main calculation loop. The lookup table will return a different value depending on the data you pass to it.

The general process, without the mathematical details, is this: first the lookup table is generated and the CRC value is initialized with a starting value. Next, the algorithm loops through each byte in the input.

For each byte, the CRC value is shifted right eight bits and exclusive-ORed with a value from the lookup table. ORing the rightmost byte of the CRC value with the current byte being inspected determines the index in the lookup table.

The resulting CRC value is then passed back into the loop for the next iteration, so the CRC value accumulates as each byte is processed. When the loop is complete, the logical Not of the value becomes the final CRC, as required by the Zip specification.

Several overloaded methods are provided to allow defaults to be provided for the initial CRC value and the polynomial.

Implementation

Create a new Visual Basic .NET class file named `Crc32.vb`:

```
Imports System.IO

Namespace Wrox.Toolkit.Util
  Public Class Crc32
```

The class's implementation begins with three constants and a couple of private fields.

```
Private Const TABLESIZE As Integer = 256
Private Const DEFAULTPOLYNOMIAL As Integer = &HEDB88320
Private Const DEFAULTINITIALVALUE As Integer = &HFFFFFFFF
```

The `TABLESIZE` constant defines the standard lookup table dimension of 256 values. `DEFAULTPOLYNOMIAL` and `DEFAULTINITIALVALUE` specify the polynomial and initial CRC value, respectively, as defined by the Zip format.

Next, instance fields are defined for the lookup table and the polynomial:

```
Private lookup(TABLESIZE - 1) As Integer
Private crcPolynomial As Integer = 0
```

`lookup` is an array of integers as large as the size of the table, the use of which we will see later.

The overloaded constructors give the caller two choices, one simple and one more complex, when creating an instance of the class:

```
Public Sub New()
  Me.New(DEFAULTPOLYNOMIAL)
End Sub

Public Sub New(ByVal crcPolynomial As Integer)
  Me.crcPolynomial = crcPolynomial
  InitLookupTable()
End Sub
```

The implementation provides a default polynomial (which, as mentioned before, is that used by Zip) if an alternative polynomial is not specified. The object is not usable until the lookup table is created, so the constructor initializes the table with the private `InitLookupTable()` method, which you'll see later.

The class's single property, `Polynomial`, allows the caller to get and set the CRC-32 polynomial.

```
Public Property Polynomial() As Integer
  Get
    Return crcPolynomial
  End Get

  Set
    Me.crcPolynomial = value
    InitLookupTable()
```

```
        End Set
    End Property
```

Whenever the value is changed, the lookup table must be regenerated.

The CalculateBlock() method determines the CRC-32 value of the specified array of bytes. It has several overloads that process an entire array or a subset and that allow you to specify an initial CRC value. As mentioned before, the CRC value accumulates as each byte is processed, so the initial value has a direct impact on the final value. The overloaded methods call each other in series until all parameter values have been specified.

```
Public Overloads Function CalculateBlock(ByVal bytes() As Byte) _
                                     As Integer
    Return CalculateBlock(bytes, 0, bytes.Length)
End Function

Public Overloads Function CalculateBlock(ByVal bytes() As Byte, _
                          ByVal index As Integer, _
                          ByVal length As Integer _
                          ) As Integer
    Return CalculateBlock(bytes, index, length, DEFAULTINITIALVALUE)
End Function
```

The above two overloads just provide a more accessible entry point to the overload shown below:

```
Public Overloads Function CalculateBlock( _
                    ByVal bytes() As Byte, _
                    ByVal index As Integer, _
                    ByVal length As Integer, _
                    ByVal initialValue As Integer) _
                    As Integer
    If bytes Is Nothing Then
        Throw New ArgumentNullException("CalculateBlock(): bytes")
    ElseIf index < 0 Or length <= 0 _
           Or index + length > bytes.Length Then
        Throw New ArgumentOutOfRangeException()
    End If

    Return Not InternalCalculateBlock(bytes, index, _
                              length, initialValue)
End Function
```

This calls a private method, called InternalCalculateBlock() to obtain a CRC value, and it then performs a Not operation on the result, as required by Zip:

```
Private Function InternalCalculateBlock( _
                ByVal bytes() As Byte, _
                ByVal index As Integer, _
                ByVal length As Integer, _
                ByVal initialValue As Integer) _
                As Integer
    Dim crc As Integer = initialValue
    Dim shiftedCrc As Integer

    Dim position As Integer
    For position = index To length - 1
```

385

This method is the mathematical heart of the class. `InternalCalculateBlock()` sets `crc` to the specified starting value, and then loops through the array `bytes`, carrying out the CRC calculation one byte at a time. Each CRC value found at the end of the loop iteration is reused in the next iteration, so the value accumulates throughout the process.

To overcome Visual Basic's lack of bit-shifting operators, an 8-bit right shift of the 4-byte integer is done in stages:

```
shiftedCrc = crc And &HFFFFFF00
shiftedCrc = shiftedCrc / &H100
shiftedCrc = shiftedCrc And &HFFFFFF
```

First, the rightmost byte is forced to zero; this occurs because each pair of hexadecimal values represents a byte, and so the binary representation is ANDed with a stream of 1s, followed by eight 0s. This keeps the first 3 bytes the same, and sets the last one to 0. Next, the result is divided by 256 (2^8), effectively shifting the bits eight bits to the right. Just as dividing by an exponent of ten shifts the digits in a decimal number exponent places to the right, maybe past the decimal point, the same happens with the binary number, only there is no decimal point and so any fractional components disappear. Finally, the now-unused leftmost byte is forced to zero. Since `Integer` is signed, and as you may or may not know the leftmost (significant) bit represents the sign, the sign bit is forced to zero at the same time, leaving the value unsigned.

Exclusive-ORing the shifted CRC with a value from the lookup table determines a new CRC value:

```
      crc = shiftedCrc Xor lookup(bytes(position) Xor _
                                        (crc And &HFF))
    Next

    Return crc
End Function
```

The lookup table index is determined by an exclusive-OR of the current byte with the rightmost byte of the current value of `crc`.

The `CalculateFile()` method determines the CRC-32 value of the specified file. An initial value may be provided for the CRC, if desired:

```
Public Overloads Function CalculateFile(ByVal path As String) _
                                    As Integer
    Return CalculateFile(path, DEFAULTINITIALVALUE)
End Function

Public Overloads Function CalculateFile( _
                        ByVal path As String, _
                        ByVal initialValue As Integer) _
                        As Integer
    If path Is Nothing Then
        Throw New ArgumentNullException("path")
    ElseIf path.Length = 0 Then
        Throw New ArgumentException("Invalid path")
    End If

    Return Not InternalCalculateFile(path, initialValue)
End Function
```

After some parameter validation code, the method returns the logical Not of the CRC, as calculated by InternalCalculateFile().

A CRC-32 value can be computed over a large number of bytes by processing a block at a time. InternalCalculateFile() uses that fact to break CRC calculation of a file into blocks of blockSize bytes:

```
Private Function InternalCalculateFile( _
            ByVal path As String, _
            ByVal initialValue As Integer) _
        As Integer
    Const blockSize As Integer = 4096
    Dim count As Integer
    Dim inStream As FileStream
    Dim bytes(blockSize - 1) As Byte
    Dim crc As Integer = initialValue

    Try
        inStream = File.Open(path, FileMode.Open, FileAccess.Read)
```

We first declare the variables used and we'll divide the file into blocks of 4,096 (2^{12}) bytes. An array of this size is created, and the file stream is opened, inside a Try...Finally block.

The method then loops through until the end of the stream is reached:

```
        While inStream.Position < inStream.Length
            count = inStream.Read(bytes, 0, blockSize)
            crc = InternalCalculateBlock(bytes, 0, count, crc)
        End While
    Finally
        If Not inStream Is Nothing Then
            inStream.Close()
        End If
    End Try

    Return crc
End Function
```

On each iteration, it reads up to blockSize bytes from the file, and then passes the crc accumulator to InternalCalculateBlock(). A Try...Finally block is used to ensure that the FileStream object is always closed properly.

The following InitLookupTable() method generates the lookup table, which serves as input to the InternalCalculateBlock() method's CRC calculation. The method generates one value for each entry in the lookup array:

```
Private Sub InitLookupTable()
    Dim byteCount, bitCount As Integer
    Dim crc, shiftedCrc As Integer

    For byteCount = 0 To TABLESIZE - 1
        crc = byteCount

        For bitCount = 0 To 7
```

To overcome Visual Basic's lack of bit-shifting operators, once again, a 1-bit right shift is done in stages. The rightmost bit is forced to zero, the resulting value is divided by two, and the sign bit is forced to zero.

```
            shiftedCrc = crc And &HFFFFFFFE
            shiftedCrc = shiftedCrc \ &H2
            shiftedCrc = shiftedCrc And &H7FFFFFFF

            If (crc And &H1) Then
                crc = shiftedCrc Xor crcPolynomial
            Else
                crc = shiftedCrc
            End If
        Next

        lookup(byteCount) = crc
      Next
    End Sub
  End Class
End Namespace
```

Demonstration

To use this sample, create a new VB Console Application project, rename `Module1.vb` to `Crc32Test.vb` and replace its contents with the code below.

This demonstration is a simple application that calculates and displays the CRC-32 value of a specified file. It accepts a file path on the command line, uses the `Crc32` class's `CalculateFile()` method to determine the CRC-32 value, and then prints the result in hexadecimal format. Reference the `CRC32.dll` assembly.

```
Imports Wrox.Toolkit.Util

Module CRC32Test
  Sub Main(ByVal CmdArgs() As String)
    If CmdArgs.Length <> 1 Then
      Console.WriteLine("Usage: CRC32Test <path>")
      Exit Sub
    End If

    Try
      Dim crc32Val As Integer
      Dim crc As New Crc32()

      crc32Val = crc.CalculateFile(CmdArgs(0))

      Console.WriteLine("CRC32 is {0:x}", crc32Val)
    Catch e As Exception
      Console.WriteLine("An exception occurred: {0}", e.Message)
    End Try
  End Sub
End Module
```

As an exercise, choose a file on your hard drive that you can modify, or create a new file with some dummy data. Use the program to calculate the CRC-32 value of the file. Now, make a small change to the file and save it. Use the program to generate a new CRC-32 value, and notice that the values are very different.

Limitations

There aren't any critical limitations to this class, mostly since the CRC-32 algorithm is so well known and widely implemented. As mentioned already, CRC is simply a tool to detect errors, so it can't help to repair existing errors. Also, if you need an absolute 100% guarantee (instead of CRC-32's roughly 99.9997% guarantee) that two files are identical, you must resort to comparing them bit-for-bit.

Performance may be less than optimal for very large files, due to the relatively small (32k) buffer employed in `CalculateFile()`. A larger buffer size may result in improved performance on very large files, and the buffer size can easily be modified in `InternalCalculateFile()`. However, for very large files, it might make more sense to access the file with Windows' memory-mapped file capabilities (see Chapter 15).

Extensions

While CRC-32 is the most common CRC variant today, it may be useful to support other variants such as CRC-16 or CRC-64. CRC-64 seems like overkill today, but undoubtedly it will become the standard as processor and overall system speeds continue to increase, negating the increased complexity of the calculation. It provides a virtual guarantee that two sets of bytes are identical. CRC-16 may be necessary if you need to interoperate with older systems or file formats.

Also, as a convenience, the class could be extended to perform calculations directly on a `Stream` object, such as `System.IO.MemoryStream`. That way, you wouldn't need to have a physical file or a byte array. You could write data to the `MemoryStream` and then calculate a CRC on it, all without ever writing to disk.

Finally, you may want to calculate CRC values for a particular set of files instead of one at a time, or perhaps calculate a CRC for the combined contents of several files. You could build this functionality on top of the class's existing `InternalCalculateFile()` and `InternalCalculateBlock()` methods.

30

Huffman Encoding

The Huffman Coding algorithm was named after its inventor, the late David A. Huffman. Huffman created the algorithm as a solution to a class assignment while he was a graduate student at the Massachusetts Institute of Technology in 1952.

This method is used by most commercial compression utilities like PKZIP. Compressed file formats such as .mp3 and .jpg can be less than 10% of their uncompressed equivalent formats, .wav and .bmp respectively.

Scenario

This class could be used as a means to add compression functionality to any application that could benefit from it. Compression can be essential when issues such as network bandwidth or disk space are important (which is almost always).

Technology

For the sake of brevity, we will not be able to fully explain the Huffman Coding algorithm here. However, a visit to http://www.huffmancoding.com, a site maintained by Huffman's nephew, is an excellent choice for anyone who needs to know the history and procedure of the algorithm.

Design

The design of our application will be fairly straight forward. We'll create a console application to which we will add two class files that will contain a total of five classes. We will then demonstrate the application from the application's `Main()` method.

Implementation

To start the project, create a console application and call it `HuffmanEncoding`. Add a new class file to the project and call it `HuffmanEncoding.vb`. This file will contain four classes: `HuffmanEngine`, `SymbolTable`, `HuffmanNode`, and `CodeArray`. Start by adding the following `Imports` statements and `Namespace` declaration:

```
Imports System
Imports System.IO
Imports System.Collections

Namespace Wrox.Toolkit.Util
```

Now we'll look at each of the four classes in turn.

HuffmanEngine Class

The `HuffmanEngine` class is the encoding/decoding machine. It needs to be initialized with a symbol table in order to work. We store an instance of `SymbolTable` to map characters to codes and back:

```
Public Class HuffmanEngine
    Private symbols As SymbolTable
```

Next we need a class constructor, which takes a `SymbolTable` as its only argument:

```
Public Sub New(ByVal Syms As SymbolTable)
    symbols = Syms
End Sub
```

The `Encode()` method takes a byte array, encodes it using the previously initialized `SymbolTable`, and returns the resulting, hopefully shorter, byte array:

```
Public Function Encode(ByVal data() As Byte) As Byte()
```

We need to read the code for any given symbol one bit at a time, so need a pointer to the bit we're currently looking at. We also write the data one bit at a time, so we need a pointer to the bit we wrote last:

```
Dim codePointer As Integer
Dim bitPointer As Integer
```

A `System.Collections.BitArray` will hold all the bits we write. It starts off empty:

```
Dim encodedData As New BitArray(0)
```

Next we declare the temporary variables that we'll need in the following loop:

```
Dim i As Integer
Dim symbol As Byte
Dim code As BitArray
```

The `For` loop goes through every byte in the data. We start by reading each byte and looking up its code in the `SymbolTable`. We increase size of the bit array by enough to allow us to write the code and then write the code one bit at a time:

```
For i = 0 To data.Length - 1
  symbol = data(i)
  code = symbols.Code(symbol)
  encodedData.Length += code.Length

  For codePointer = 0 To code.Length - 1
    encodedData(bitPointer) = code(codePointer)
    bitPointer += 1
  Next
Next
```

Now we have to turn the array of bits into an array of bytes that we can return. We create a big enough byte array to hold two pieces of info: the number of bytes in the original array, and the code array. We then stick both of these into the array and return it:

```
Dim byteCount As Integer = bitPointer / 8
Dim countBytes() As Byte = BitConverter.GetBytes(data.Length)

Dim outBytes(byteCount + countBytes.Length) As Byte

countBytes.CopyTo(outBytes, 0)
encodedData.CopyTo(outBytes, countBytes.Length)

Return outBytes
End Function
```

The `Decode()` function takes an array of bytes representing coded data, and returns the array of bytes represented by this code sequence:

```
Public Function Decode(ByVal data() As Byte) As Byte()
```

First we need to read the number of bytes that we can expect to extract from this data and then make an array big enough to hold the result:

```
Dim totalBytes As Integer = BitConverter.ToInt32(data, 0)
Dim decodedData(totalBytes - 1) As Byte
```

Next we turn the input data into an array of bits, and set up a pointer to index into the bit array. It starts at 32 so that it's after the end of the integer we just read out of the array:

```
Dim bits As BitArray = New BitArray(data)
Dim bitPointer As Integer = 32
```

Now, for every byte that we expect to decode from the bit array, we call the `ReadSymbol()` method on the `SymbolTable`. This advances the pointer to the end of the next code, and returns the appropriate symbol:

```
Dim bytePointer As Integer
For bytePointer = 0 To totalBytes - 1
    decodedData(bytePointer) = symbols.ReadSymbol(bits, _
        bitPointer)
Next

    Return decodedData
End Function
End Class
```

That completes the `HuffmanEngine` class

SymbolTable Class

The `SymbolTable` class does most of the real Huffman coding work. It provides a two-way mapping between codes and symbols. There are two ways of constructing a symbol table. If we pass in a byte array, a frequency analysis is performed, which leads to a symbol table that is optimal for that particular set of data. If we pass in a `Stream` containing a particular set of data representing a symbol table, we will obtain that same symbol table.

This allows us to build, for example, a generic symbol table optimized for VB.NET source files, and use it to compress and decompress multiple files. Alternatively, we can create a custom symbol table for a particular file and then include the symbol table data in the file with it. We can then decompress it by recreating the original symbol table, and decoding the data:

```
Public Class SymbolTable
```

The `SymbolTable` class uses a lookup array to translate each possible byte value (0-255) into a second byte value. This value, called the symbol ID, means that if we are compressing data which has only a small vocabulary of symbols, we only need to have arrays large enough to store data about the symbols we're actually using, rather than all 256 possible symbols.

The codes are stored in a special class called a `CodeArray` that we'll explain later. This is an array specially designed to hold variable-length codes efficiently. We also store the root node of our Huffman encoding tree. This is used to decode codes:

```
Private codes As CodeArray
Private symbolLookup(255) As Byte
Private rootNode As HuffmanNode
```

Our first method is the constructor that takes a byte array. This method does a full Huffman frequency analysis and generates a set of Huffman codes accordingly:

```
Public Sub New(ByVal data() As Byte)
```

We'll be iterating through the byte array, so let's store some info about it:

```
Dim byteCount As Integer = data.Length
Dim i As Integer
```

We create a temporary table that will hold a node for every possible symbol. We'll dispose of those we don't use later on, and put the nodes we do need into a smaller array:

```
Dim symbols(255) As HuffmanNode
Dim symbolCount As Integer
Dim symbol As Byte
```

First we need to iterate through our temporary table, initializing every cell with a node:

```
For i = 0 To 255
    symbols(i) = New HuffmanNode(CByte(i), 0)
    symbolLookup(i) = 255
Next
```

Next, we iterate through the entire data set, counting up occurrences of bytes. Each time we read a byte, we look up the appropriate node in our array. If it's the first time we've encountered a particular symbol, we make a note. In any case, we increment the node's frequency count:

```
For i = 0 To byteCount - 1
    symbol = data(i)
    If symbols(symbol).Weight = 0 Then symbolCount += 1
    symbols(symbol).Increment()
Next
```

Now we have an array containing 256 nodes, some of which map to symbols we saw in the data. We also know (because we kept count) how many of those nodes map to real symbols. We need to pick out the nodes that match data symbols, and drop them into a binary tree. Don't get too confused about the use of a binary tree here, just because we're using it to help us construct a tree of our own. From our perspective, the binary tree isn't really a tree at all. It's just a magic box that, when we drop something in the top, automatically sorts it into order with all the things already in the box. This particular box has an opening at one end, so we can always pull out the lowest-ranked item in the box. We also create a shorter array of nodes that will be our final list:

```
Dim NodeSorter As New StackBinaryTree()
Dim HuffmanNodes(symbolCount - 1) As HuffmanNode

symbol = 0

Dim node As HuffmanNode
```

We iterate through our collected nodes, looking for those that actually occur in the data set. Those that do are added to both the collections we just created. An entry is placed in the symbolLookup table, pointing to the location of the node in the shorter array:

```
For i = 0 To symbols.Length - 1
    node = symbols(i)
    If node.Weight > 0 Then
```

```
            NodeSorter.Add(node)
            HuffmanNodes(symbol) = node
            symbolLookup(i) = symbol
            symbol += 1
        End If
        symbols(i) = Nothing
    Next
```

Since we've finished with the larger array of nodes, we get rid of it:

```
    symbols = Nothing
```

Now we have a sorted list of disconnected nodes in the binary tree. Here's where the magic Huffman algorithm happens: We take the two nodes with the lowest weightings (frequencies), and attach them as children of a new node. This new node gets a weighting equal to the sum of the weightings of these nodes. We put this new node back into the binary tree. By the magic of binary trees, it filters down and finds its place in the natural order of nodes. We repeat these steps until there is only one node in the binary tree. This node has all the other nodes hanging off it, so represents the root node of our Huffman tree. Before we start, we need to grab a hold of a reference to the lightest node. This node will have the longest Huffman code, which will be important later on. We pop it out of the tree, store a reference, and then put it back into the tree, so that it can settle back down to where it started:

```
    Dim FirstNode As HuffmanNode = _
        CType(NodeSorter.PopFirstItem(), HuffmanNode)
    NodeSorter.Add(FirstNode)
```

Now we iterate through performing the Huffman algorithm:

```
    While NodeSorter.Count > 1
        Dim LightestNode As HuffmanNode = _
            CType(NodeSorter.PopFirstItem(), HuffmanNode)
        Dim SecondLightestNode As HuffmanNode = _
            CType(NodeSorter.PopFirstItem(), HuffmanNode)

        Dim NewNode As New HuffmanNode()
        NewNode.Attach(LightestNode, SecondLightestNode)
        NodeSorter.Add(NewNode)
    End While
```

Now we can pull out the root node, and store it:

```
    rootNode = CType(NodeSorter.PopFirstItem(), HuffmanNode)
```

Next we need to populate the lookup tables that will be used for encoding. First, we need to know the longest Huffman code we've generated. It'll be the code on the first node we looked at earlier:

```
    Dim maxCodesize As Integer = FirstNode.CodePath.Length
```

Now that we know this, we can construct the `CodeArray` object that will hold our Huffman codes:

```
codes = New CodeArray(symbolCount, maxCodesize)
```

At this point, we iterate through all our symbols, obtaining their Huffman code from the tree, and populate the lookup tables:

```
Dim bits As BitArray

For i = 0 To symbolCount - 1
    node = HuffmanNodes(i)
    bits = node.CodePath()
    codes(symbolLookup(node.Symbol)) = bits
Next
End Sub
```

Now let's look at the second constructor, which takes a `Stream` as an argument. It uses this to reconstruct a lookup table and Huffman tree without performing any frequency analysis:

```
Public Sub New(ByVal stream As Stream)
```

The first 256 bytes are the `symbolLookup` table, so we read those. The rest represent the code array, which has its own `Stream` constructor. We defer to that to finish the job of reading the `Stream`:

```
Dim reader As New BinaryReader(stream)
symbolLookup = reader.ReadBytes(256)
codes = New CodeArray(stream)
```

Now we just have to reconstruct the tree, so we can perform fast decoding with this symbol table:

```
Dim root As New HuffmanNode()
Dim node As HuffmanNode
Dim bit As Byte
Dim code As BitArray
Dim codeLength As Integer

Dim symbol As Byte
Dim i As Integer
```

We iterate through the `symbolLookup` table, looking for symbols that map to nodes, and reconstruct the tree path that represents that node's Huffman code:

```
For i = 0 To 255
    symbol = symbolLookup(i)
    If symbol < 255 Then
        node = root
        code = codes(symbol)
        bit = 0
```

Now we have one of the codes, we can construct the part of the tree that maps that code to a symbol:

```
            For Each bit In code
               If node.IsLeaf Then
                  node.Attach(New HuffmanNode(), New HuffmanNode())
               End If
               If bit Then
                  node = node.RightChild
               Else
                  node = node.LeftChild
               End If
            Next
            node.Symbol = i
         End If
      Next
```

Having built the tree, we store it:

```
         rootNode = root
      End Sub
```

The WriteData() method is the counterpart to the Stream constructor. It effectively serializes the symbol table's state to the Stream:

```
      Public Sub WriteData(ByVal stream As Stream)
         Dim writer As New BinaryWriter(stream)
         writer.Write(symbolLookup)
         codes.WriteData(stream)
      End Sub
```

Our next method is called ReadSymbol() and takes an encoded BitArray, and a reference to a pointer into that array. It reads the next Huffman code from the array, advancing the pointer to the end of the code, and returns the byte symbol that matches the code:

```
      Public Function ReadSymbol(ByVal ba As BitArray, _
            ByRef pointer As Integer) As Byte
```

We basically move the pointer along the bit array, navigating down our tree, until we reach a leaf node. This corresponds to a symbol, so we return it:

```
         Dim n As HuffmanNode = rootNode
         For pointer = pointer To ba.Length - 1
            If n.IsLeaf Then Return CType(n, HuffmanNode).Symbol
            If ba(pointer) Then
               n = n.RightChild
            Else
               n = n.LeftChild
            End If
         Next
         Return CByte(255)
      End Function
```

The opposite method looks up the code for a particular symbol. We use a BitArray to represent the variable length code.

```
      Public ReadOnly Property Code(ByVal symbol As Byte) As BitArray
         Get
            Return codes.Code(symbolLookup(symbol))
         End Get
```

```
        End Property
    End Class
```

That completes the SymbolTable class

HuffmanNode Class

The HuffmanNode class is the core of our Huffman tree. It stores a reference to two
children, and a parent node. The class implements IComparable so that instances can be
compared and sorted by the binary tree. The natural ordering is by weight. The weight of a
node is either the frequency of the node itself, or the combined weights of its children. If a
node has no children, it is a leaf node. If a node has no parent, it is a root node:

```
    Public Class HuffmanNode
        Implements IComparable

        Private _symbol As Byte
        Private _frequency As Integer

        Private _leftChild As HuffmanNode
        Private _rightChild As HuffmanNode
        Private _parent As HuffmanNode

        Public Function CompareTo(ByVal obj As Object) As Integer _
            Implements IComparable.CompareTo

            Dim other As HuffmanNode
            If TypeOf obj Is HuffmanNode Then
                other = CType(obj, HuffmanNode)
                Return Me.Weight - other.Weight
            Else
                Throw New ArgumentException()
            End If
        End Function

        Public Function IsLeaf() As Boolean
            Return ((_leftChild Is Nothing) And (_rightChild Is Nothing))
        End Function

        Public Function IsRoot() As Boolean
            Return _parent Is Nothing
        End Function

        Public Function IsLeftChild() As Boolean
            Return Me._parent._leftChild Is Me
        End Function

        Public Function IsRightChild() As Boolean
            Return Me._parent._rightChild Is Me
        End Function

        Public Sub Attach(ByVal NewLeftChild As HuffmanNode, _
            ByVal NewRightChild As HuffmanNode)

            If Not (NewLeftChild Is Nothing) Then
                NewLeftChild._parent = Me
            End If

            If Not (NewRightChild Is Nothing) Then
                NewRightChild._parent = Me
            End If
```

```
      Me._rightChild = NewRightChild
      Me._leftChild = NewLeftChild
   End Sub

   Public ReadOnly Property LeftChild() As HuffmanNode
      Get
         Return _leftChild
      End Get
   End Property

   Public ReadOnly Property RightChild() As HuffmanNode
      Get
         Return _rightChild
      End Get
   End Property

   Public ReadOnly Property Parent() As HuffmanNode
      Get
         Return _parent
      End Get
   End Property
```

The CodePath() method is neat – it returns the sequence of Boolean trues and falses that you need to follow to reach this node from the root, as a BitArray. It does so by adding on to its parent's CodePath. Call this on a leaf node representing a symbol, and you get the code for that symbol:

```
   Public Function CodePath() As BitArray
      If Me.IsRoot() Then
         Return New BitArray(0)
      Else
         Dim code As BitArray = Me._parent.CodePath()
         code.Length += 1
         code(code.Length - 1) = Me.IsRightChild()
         Return code
      End If
   End Function

   Public Sub New(ByVal symbol As Byte, ByVal frequency As Integer)
      _symbol = symbol
      _frequency = frequency
   End Sub

   Public Sub New()
      Me.New(255, 0)
   End Sub

   Public Sub Increment()
      _frequency += 1
   End Sub

   Public ReadOnly Property Weight() As Integer
      Get
         If Me.IsLeaf() Then
            Return _frequency
         Else
            Return LeftChild.Weight + RightChild.Weight
         End If
      End Get
   End Property

   Public Property Symbol() As Byte
      Get
         Return _symbol
```

```
        End Get
        Set(ByVal Value As Byte)
            _symbol = Value
        End Set
    End Property

End Class
```

That completes the HuffmanNode class

CodeArray Class

The CodeArray class wraps up some of the functionality needed to efficiently store lots of codes, each consisting of a small, but variable number of bits. The solution is to store all of the symbols at regular intervals in a single large bit array. This is why we need to know the size of the largest Huffman code – it dictates the size of the window used to store each code in this class. A second array stores the size of each of the codes.

Like the SymbolTable class, CodeArray can be written out to a Stream, and created from one:

```
Public Class CodeArray
    Private bits As BitArray
    Private _codeCount As Byte
    Private _maxSize As Integer
    Private codeSizes() As Byte

    Public Sub New(ByVal codeCount As Byte, ByVal maxSize As Integer)

        _codeCount = codeCount
        _maxSize = maxSize

        bits = New BitArray(codeCount * maxSize)
        ReDim codeSizes(codeCount - 1)
    End Sub
```

Here's the Stream constructor. We use a reader to read in the data:

```
Public Sub New(ByVal stream As Stream)
    Dim reader As New BinaryReader(stream)
    _maxSize = reader.ReadInt32()
    _codeCount = reader.ReadByte()
    codeSizes = reader.ReadBytes(_codeCount)
    Dim codeBytesLength As Integer = (_codeCount * _maxSize) / 8
    Dim codeBytes() As Byte = reader.ReadBytes(codeBytesLength)
    bits = New BitArray(codeBytes)
End Sub
```

WriteData() is the opposite method, which writes out the data from a CodeArray to a Stream:

```
Public Sub WriteData(ByVal stream As Stream)
    Dim codeBytes(bits.Length / 8) As Byte
    bits.CopyTo(codeBytes, 0)
    Dim writer As New BinaryWriter(stream)
    writer.Write(_maxSize)
    writer.Write(_codeCount)
```

```
         writer.Write(codeSizes)
         writer.Write(codeBytes)
         writer.Flush()
      End Sub

      Public ReadOnly Property Count() As Integer
         Get
            Return _codeCount
         End Get
      End Property

      Public ReadOnly Property CodeLength(ByVal c As Byte)
         Get
            If c >= _codeCount Or c < 0 Then
               Throw New ArgumentOutOfRangeException()
            End If
            Return codeSizes(c)
         End Get
      End Property
```

Next we need a property that accesses the code at a particular index:

```
      Default Public Property Code(ByVal c As Byte) As BitArray
         Set(ByVal Value As BitArray)
            If c >= _codeCount Or c < 0 Or Value.Length > _maxSize Then
               Throw New ArgumentOutOfRangeException()
            End If
            Dim i As Integer
            For i = 0 To Value.Length - 1
               bits(c * _maxSize + i) = Value(i)
            Next
            codeSizes(c) = Value.Length
         End Set

         Get
            If c >= _codeCount Or c < 0 Then
               Throw New ArgumentOutOfRangeException()
            End If
            Dim i As Integer
            Dim codeBits As New BitArray(codeSizes(c))
            For i = 0 To codeBits.Length - 1
               codeBits(i) = bits(c * _maxSize + i)
            Next
            Return codeBits
         End Get
      End Property

   End Class
End Namespace
```

That completes the CodeArray class and HuffmanEncoding.vb.

StackBinaryTree Class

Create a new class file called bst.vb to hold our StackBinaryTree class. This class is a slightly modified version of the Binary Tree. It has a stack-like 'pop' function to pull the first member out of the tree. It also allows multiple items to have comparison-equality, and resolves 'remove' and 'find' queries by testing for reference equality. Add the following code to bst.vb:

```vbnet
Imports System
Imports System.Collections
Namespace Wrox.Toolkit.Util
  Public Class StackBinaryTree
    Implements ICollection

    Protected Class BstNode
      Friend Data As Object = Nothing
      Friend Left As BstNode = Nothing
      Friend Right As BstNode = Nothing

      Protected Friend Sub New(ByVal data As Object)
        Me.Data = data
      End Sub
    End Class

    Public Delegate Sub TraverseCallback(ByVal data As Object)

    Protected root As BstNode = Nothing
    Protected nodeCount As Integer = 0
    Protected valueComparer As IComparer

    Public Sub New()
      Me.valueComparer = Comparer.Default
    End Sub

    Public Sub New(ByVal comparer As IComparer)
      If comparer Is Nothing Then
        Throw New ArgumentNullException()
      End If

      Me.valueComparer = comparer
    End Sub

    Protected Overridable Function Compare(ByVal a As Object, _
        ByVal b As Object) As Integer

      Try
        Return valueComparer.Compare(a, b)
      Catch ex As Exception
        Throw New InvalidOperationException( _
            "IComparer.Compare() failed.", ex)
      End Try
    End Function

    Protected Overridable Function FindMin(ByVal node As BstNode) _
        As BstNode

      If node Is Nothing Then
        Return Nothing
      ElseIf node.Left Is Nothing Then
        Return node
      Else
        Return FindMin(node.Left)
      End If
    End Function

    Protected Overridable Overloads Sub Add(ByVal value As Object, _
        ByRef node As BstNode)

      Dim result As Integer

      If node Is Nothing Then
        node = New BstNode(value)
        nodeCount += 1
```

```
          Return
      End If

      result = Compare(value, node.Data)

      If result <= 0 Then
        Add(value, node.Left)
      ElseIf result > 0 Then
        Add(value, node.Right)
      End If
    End Sub

    Public Overridable Overloads Sub Add(ByVal value As Object)
      If value Is Nothing Then
        Throw New ArgumentNullException()
      End If

      Add(value, root)
    End Sub

    Protected Overridable Overloads Sub Remove( _
        ByVal value As Object, ByRef node As BstNode)

      Dim result As Integer

      If node Is Nothing Then
        Return
      End If

      result = Compare(value, node.Data)
  If result < 0 Then
        Remove(value, node.Left)
      ElseIf result > 0 Then
        Remove(value, node.Right)
      Else
        If value Is node.Data Then
          If Not node.Left Is Nothing And _
            Not node.Right Is Nothing Then
            node.Data = FindMin(node.Right).Data
            Remove(node.Data, node.Right)
          Else
            If node.Left Is Nothing Then
              node = node.Right
            Else
              node = node.Left
            End If
            nodeCount -= 1
          End If
        Else
          Remove(value, node.Left)
        End If
      End If
    End Sub

    Public Overridable Overloads Sub Remove(ByVal value As Object)
      If value Is Nothing Then
        Throw New ArgumentNullException()
      End If

      Remove(value, root)
    End Sub

    Protected Overridable Function Find(ByVal value As Object, _
        ByVal node As BstNode) As BstNode
```

```
      Dim result As Integer

      If node Is Nothing Then
        Return Nothing
      End If

      result = Compare(value, node.Data)

      If result < 0 Then
        Return Find(value, node.Left)
      ElseIf result > 0 Then
        Return Find(value, node.Right)
      Else
        If value Is node.Data Then
          Return node
        Else
          Return Find(value, node.Left)
        End If
      End If
    End Function

    Public Overridable Function Contains(ByVal value As Object) _
        As Boolean

      If value Is Nothing Then
        Throw New ArgumentNullException()
      End If

      If Not Find(value, root) Is Nothing Then
        Return True
      Else
        Return False
      End If
    End Function

    Protected Overridable Sub CopyToInternal(ByVal node As BstNode, _
        ByVal array As System.Array, ByRef index As Integer)

      If Not node Is Nothing Then
        CopyToInternal(node.Left, array, index)
        array(index) = node.Data
        index += 1
        CopyToInternal(node.Right, array, index)
      End If
    End Sub

    Public Overridable Sub CopyTo(ByVal array As System.Array, _
        ByVal index As Integer) Implements ICollection.CopyTo

      If array Is Nothing Then
        Throw New ArgumentNullException()
      ElseIf index < 0 Then
        Throw New ArgumentOutOfRangeException("index")
      ElseIf index >= array.Length _
          Or (array.Length - index - 1) > nodeCount _
          Or array.Rank <> 1 Then
        Throw New ArgumentException()
      End If

      CopyToInternal(root, array, index)
    End Sub

    Protected Overridable Sub InOrderInternal(ByVal node As BstNode, _
        ByVal callback As TraverseCallback)

      If Not node Is Nothing Then
```

405

```
            InOrderInternal(node.Left, callback)
            callback(node.Data)
            InOrderInternal(node.Right, callback)
         End If
      End Sub

      Public Overridable Sub InOrder(ByVal callback As TraverseCallback)
         If callback Is Nothing Then
            Throw New ArgumentNullException()
         End If

         InOrderInternal(root, callback)
      End Sub

      Public Overridable ReadOnly Property Count() As Integer _
            Implements ICollection.Count
         Get
            Return nodeCount
         End Get
      End Property

      Public Overridable ReadOnly Property IsSynchronized() As Boolean _
            Implements ICollection.IsSynchronized
         Get
            Return False
         End Get
      End Property

      Public Overridable ReadOnly Property SyncRoot() As Object _
            Implements ICollection.SyncRoot
         Get
            Return Me
         End Get
      End Property

      Public Overridable Function GetEnumerator() As IEnumerator _
            Implements ICollection.GetEnumerator

         Throw New NotSupportedException("Enumeration is not supported.")
      End Function

      Public Function PopFirstItem() As Object
         Dim o As BstNode = Me.FindMin(root)
         Dim data As Object = o.Data
         Me.Remove(data, root)
         Return data
      End Function
   End Class
End Namespace
```

That completes our StackBinaryTree class.

Demonstration

To demonstrate our Huffman coding classes, start by renaming Module1.vb to
MainModule.vb. Then add the following code to the Main() method:

```
Imports HuffmanEncoding.Wrox.Toolkit.Util
Imports System
Imports System.IO
Imports System.Text
```

```
Module MainModule

  Sub Main()
```

We start by declaring the local variables that we'll be using:

```
Dim Symbols As SymbolTable
Dim HE As HuffmanEngine
Dim Codes() As Byte
Dim Text As String
```

Next, we open a sample file with a `StreamReader` and pass it to our `String` variable. Then we write the length of the file to the console for reference:

```
Dim file As New StreamReader(New FileStream("Sample.txt", _
    FileMode.Open))
Text = file.ReadToEnd()
Console.WriteLine("Characters of raw data: " & Text.Length)
```

Next, we encode our sample. We start by creating a `Byte` array from the `String` we just created. Then we create a `SymbolTable` from that array and a new `HuffmanEngine` from that `SymbolTable`. Finally, we encode our `Byte` array and pass it to a new `Byte` array:

```
Dim Bytes() As Byte = Encoding.ASCII.GetBytes(Text)
Symbols = New SymbolTable(Bytes)
HE = New HuffmanEngine(Symbols)
Codes = (HE.Encode(Bytes))
```

Now we create a `MemoryStream` and pass to it the `Symbols` object we created above. So that we can see how big the symbols table is, we write it to the console along with the length of the encoded `Codes` array:

```
Dim ms As New MemoryStream()
Symbols.WriteData(ms)

Dim tableStore() As Byte = ms.ToArray()
Console.WriteLine("Bytes of symbol table data: " & _
    tableStore.Length)
Console.WriteLine("Bytes of encoded data: " & Codes.Length)
```

Next, we save the encoded array to file for reference:

```
Dim encodedFile As New StreamWriter(New _
    FileStream("EncodedSample.txt", FileMode.Create))
Text = Encoding.ASCII.GetString(Codes)
Console.WriteLine("Writing encoded file to: EncodedSample.txt")
encodedFile.Write(Text)
```

Now we reverse the process and decode the `Codes` array:

```
ms = New MemoryStream(tableStore)
Symbols = New SymbolTable(ms)
HE = New HuffmanEngine(Symbols)
Bytes = HE.Decode(Codes)
Text = Encoding.ASCII.GetString(Bytes)
```

To demonstrate that we have decoded correctly, we write the decoded `String` to file:

```
Dim decodedFile As New StreamWriter(New _
    FileStream("DecodedSample.txt", FileMode.Create))
Console.WriteLine("Writing decoded file to: DecodedSample.txt")
decodedFile.Write(Text)

Console.ReadLine()
  End Sub
End Module
```

Limitations

The engine tends to slow down with larger files.

Extensions

We may be able to achieve greater compression if the distribution of characters varies in different parts of the source file. For instance, if we divided the file into two, we may find that the most common characters in the first half are nowhere near as common in the second half. As such, we may achieve greater compression if we calculate a new distribution pattern. This concept is known as Adaptive Huffman Coding.

With minor changes to the output methods, this class could easily be converted into an encryption utility. Since Huffman encoding relies on variable-bit-length character representations, it's almost impossibly to decrypt a file compressed with this algorithm without the header lookup table. This header could be stripped out and kept as a private key to be shared with only a few privileged people.

Appendix
Support, Errata, and Code Download

We always value hearing from our readers, and we want to know what you think about this book: what you liked, what you didn't like, and what you think we can do better next time. You can send us your comments, either by returning the reply card in the back of the book, or by emailing us at feedback@wrox.com. Please be sure to mention the book title in your message.

How to Download the Sample Code for the Book

When you log on to the Wrox site, http://www.wrox.com/, simply locate the title through our Search facility or by using one of the title lists. Click on Download Code on the book's detail page.

The files that are available for download from our site have been archived using WinZip. When you have saved the attachments to a folder on your hard-drive, you will need to extract the files using WinZip, or a compatible tool. Inside the Zip file will be a folder structure and an HTML file that explains the structure and gives you further information, including links to email support, and suggested further reading.

Errata

We've made every effort to ensure that there are no errors in the text or in the code. However, no one is perfect and mistakes can occur. If you find an error in this book, like a spelling mistake or a faulty piece of code, we would be very grateful for feedback. By sending in errata, you may save another reader hours of frustration, and of course, you will be helping us to provide even higher quality information. Simply email the information to support@wrox.com, your information will be checked and if correct, posted to the Errata page for that title.

To find errata, locate this book on the Wrox web site
(http://www.wrox.com/ACON1.asp?ISBN=1861007396), and click on the **Book Errata** link on
the book's detail page:

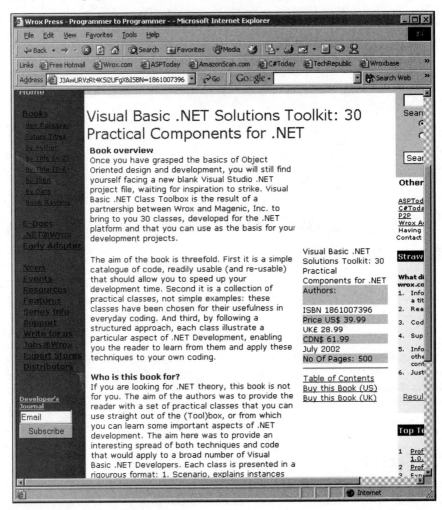

Email Support

If you wish to query a problem in the book with an expert who knows the book in detail
then email support@wrox.com, with the title of the book, and the last four numbers of the
ISBN in the subject field of the email. A typical email should include the following:

❑ The name, last four digits of the ISBN (in this case 7396), and page number
of the problem, in the Subject field

❑ Your name, contact information, and the problem, in the body of the message

We won't send you junk mail. We need the details to save your time and ours. When you send an email message, it will go through the following chain of support:

❑ **Customer Support**

Your message is delivered to our customer support staff. They have files on most frequently asked questions and will answer anything general about the book or the web site immediately.

❑ **Editorial**

More in-depth queries are forwarded to the technical editor responsible for that book. They have experience with the programming language or particular product, and are able to answer detailed technical questions on the subject. Once an issue has been resolved, the editor can post the errata to the web site.

❑ **The Authors**

Finally, in the unlikely event that the editor cannot answer your problem, they will forward the request to the author. We do try to protect the author from any distractions to their writing (or programming); but we are quite happy to forward specific requests to them. All Wrox authors help with the support on their books. They will email the customer and the editor with their response, and again all readers should benefit

The Wrox support process can only offer support for issues that are directly pertinent to the content of our published title. Support for questions that fall outside the scope of normal book support, is provided via our P2P community lists – http://p2p.wrox.com/forum.

p2p.wrox.com

For author and peer discussion, join the P2P mailing lists. Our unique system provides Programmer to Programmer™ contact on mailing lists, forums, and newsgroups, all in addition to our one-to-one email support system. Be confident that the many Wrox authors and other industry experts who are present on our mailing lists are examining any queries posted. At http://p2p.wrox.com/, you will find a number of different lists that will help you, not only while you read this book, but also as you develop your own applications.

To subscribe to a mailing list follow this these steps:

❑ Go to http://p2p.wrox.com/

❑ Choose the appropriate category from the left menu bar

❑ Click on the mailing list you wish to join

❏   Follow the instructions to subscribe and fill in your email address and password

❏   Reply to the confirmation email you receive

❏   Use the subscription manager to join more lists and set your mail preferences

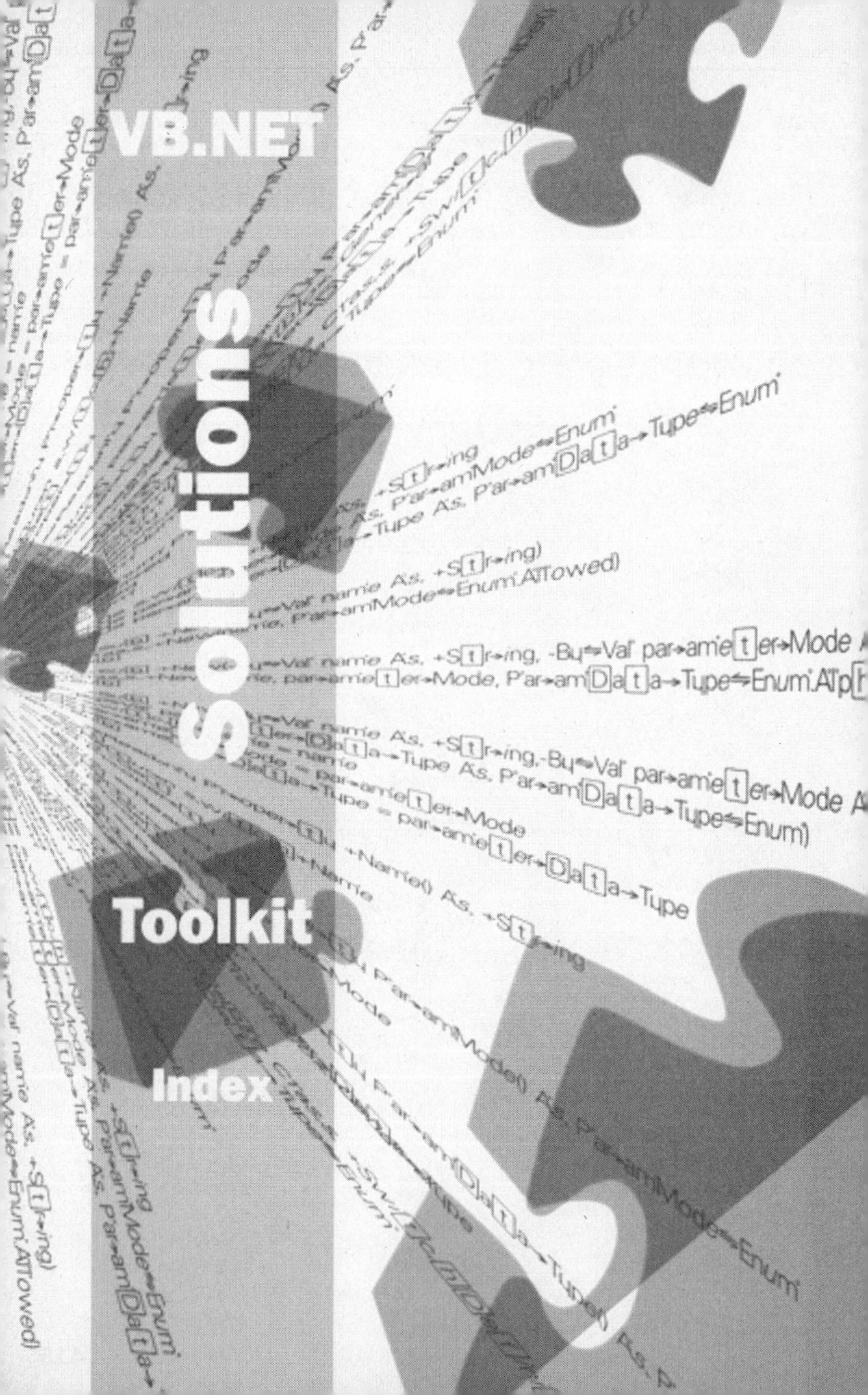
VB.NET
Solutions
Toolkit
Index

Index

A Guide to the Index

The index is arranged hierarchically, in alphabetical order, with symbols preceding the letter A. Most second-level entries and many third-level entries also occur as first-level entries. This is to ensure that users will find the information they require however they choose to search for it.

T

X

Visual Basic .NET Threading Handbook:

Author(s): K. Ardestani, F. C. Ferracchiati, S. Gopikrishna, T. Redkar, S. Sivakumar, T. Titus
ISBN: 1-861007-13-2
US$ 29.99
Can$ 46.99

All .NET languages now have access to the Free Threading Model that many Visual Basic Developers have been waiting for. Compared to the earlier apartment threading model, this gives you much finer control over where to implement threading and what you are given access to. It does also provide several new ways for your application to spin out of control.

This handbook explains how to avoid some common pitfalls when designing multi-threaded applications by presenting some guidelines for good design practice. By investigating .NET's threading model's architecture, you will be able to make sure that your applications take full advantage of it.

What you will learn from this book
- Thread creation
- Using timers to schedule threads to execute at specified intervals
- Synchronizing thread execution - avoiding deadlocks and race conditions
- Spinning threads from within threads, and synchronizing them
- Modelling your applications to a specific thread design model
- Scaling threaded applications by using the ThreadPool class
- Tracing your threaded application's execution in order to debug it

Visual Basic .NET Text Manipulation Handbook:
String Handling and Regular Expressions

Author(s): François Liger, Craig McQueen, Paul Wilton
ISBN: 1-861007-30-2
US$ 29.99
Can$ 46.99

Text forms an integral part of many applications. Earlier version's of Visual Basic would hide from you the intricacies of how text was being handled, limiting your ability to control your program's execution or performance. The .NET Framework gives you much finer control.

This handbook takes an in depth look at the text manipulation classes that are included within the .NET Framework, in all cases providing you with invaluable information as to their relative performance merits. The String and Stringbuilder classes are investigated and the newly acquired support for regular expressions is illustrated in detail.

What you will learn from this book
- String representation and management within the .NET Framework
- Using the StringBuilder object to improve application performance
- Choosing between the different object's methods when manipulating text
- How to safely convert between String and other data types
- How to take advantage of .NET's Unicode representation of text for Internationalization
- The use of regular expressions including syntax and pattern matching to optimize your text manipulation operations

Visual Basic .NET Class Design Handbook:
Coding Effective Classes

Visual Basic .NET Class Design Handbook: Coding Effective Classes

Author(s): Andy Olsen, Damon Allison, James Speer
ISBN: 1-861007-08-6
US$ 29.99
Can$ 46.99

Designing effective classes that you do not need to revisit and revise over and over again is an art. Within the .NET Framework, whatever code you write in Visual Basic .NET is encapsulated within the class hierarchy of the .NET Framework.

By investigating in depth the various members a class can contain, this handbook aims to give you a deep understanding of the implications of all the decisions you can make at design time. This book will equip you with the necessary knowledge to build classes that are robust, flexible, and reusable.

What you will learn from this book
- The role of types in .NET
- The different kinds of type we can create in VB.NET
- How VB.NET defines type members
- The fundamental role of methods as containers of program logic
- The role of constructors and their effective use
- Object cleanup and disposal
- When and how to use properties and indexers to encapsulate data
- How .NET's event system works
- How to control and exploit inheritance in our types
- The logical and physical code organisation through namespaces and assemblies